NAPOLEON'S
OTHER WIFE

NAPOLEON'S OTHER WIFE

The story of Marie-Louise,
Duchess of Parma, the lesser known
wife of Napoleon Bonaparte

DEBORAH JAY

[signature: Deborah Jay]

ROSA'S PRESS

"Freedom is always the freedom of those who
think differently." Rosa Luxemburg

First published by Rosa's Press 2015

ISBN: 978-0-9934-0302-6 (HB)
ISBN: 978-0-9934-0300-2 (PB)
Ebook: 978-0-9934-0301-9

Copyright © Deborah Jay 2015

Illustrations and images courtesy of the Museo Glauco-Lombardi, Parma

The right of Deborah Jay to be identified as the author
of this work has been asserted by her in accordance with
the Copyright, Designs and Patent Act 1988.

All rights reserved. No part of this publication may be
reproduced, stored in a retrieval system or transmitted,
in any form, or by any means, electronic mechanical,
photocopying, recording or otherwise, without the
prior permission of the copyright owner.

Typeset by Ellipsis Digital Limited, Glasgow
Printed by Clays Ltd, St Ives plc

In loving memory of
my father
Desmond Joseph Trenner

"Love is an occupation for the idle, a distraction for the soldier – and a peril for the monarch."
Napoleon I

"Love is a chapter in a man's life, the whole story for a woman."
Entry in Marie-Louise's notebook of reflections

CONTENTS

Author's Note — xi

Foreword by Dott.ssa Francesca Sandrini, Curator of the Museo Glauco-Lombardi, Parma — xiii

Acknowledgements — xvii

Short chronology — xxi

Maps:
    Europe in 1810: Napoleon dominant — xxiv
    The Italian peninsula from settlement after the Vienna Congress 1815 to the unification of Italy 1860-1870 — xxv

Marie-Louise's family tree — xxvi

ONE	The wedding of the century, April 1810	1
TWO	The birth of an heir, March 1811	14
THREE	The firm alliance, May 1812	30
FOUR	Napoleon indomitable, December 1812	41
FIVE	Marie-Louise, Regent of France 1813	52
SIX	Invasion and flight, Spring 1814	78
SEVEN	The mountains of Savoy, Summer 1814	102
EIGHT	The untimely visit, September 1814	116
NINE	Hopes pinned on Blücher and Wellington, June 1815	145
TEN	Parma, 1816	165

ELEVEN	Absent motherhood, 1818	194
TWELVE	Napoleon's heart, 1821	202
THIRTEEN	Resisting the witchhunt, 1822	212
FOURTEEN	Bereavement and revelation, 1829	227
FIFTEEN	The beings, 1829	248
SIXTEEN	The charade revealed	263
SEVENTEEN	Feeling widowhood	267
EIGHTEEN	Repercussions of the July Revolution, 1830	284
NINETEEN	Challenge to sovereignty in the Central Italian States, 1831	295
TWENTY	Impotent against Metternich's vengeance, 1831	315
TWENTY-ONE	The tragedy of competing loyalties, 1832	326
TWENTY-TWO	Manuscripts and pariahs	343
TWENTY-THREE	Realising a daughter's happiness, 1833	355
TWENTY-FOUR	The world destabilised at a change of emperors, 1835	368
TWENTY-FIVE	Cholera, 1836 and its aftermath	381
TWENTY-SIX	Railways and derailment, 1838	397
TWENTY-SEVEN	Verdi and the power of opera, 1846	412
TWENTY-EIGHT	Death of a duchess and expiry of the moratorium, 1847	423
	Afterword	446
	Selected Bibliography	457
	Endnotes	477
	Index	489

AUTHOR'S NOTE

Marie-Louise's correspondence was voluminous, but often silent as to her feelings. Some letters have been destroyed at Marie-Louise's request by recipients, their responses to Marie-Louise revealing her innermost thoughts and state of mind. I have researched Marie-Louise's life and times extensively, scouring archives in France, Austria and Italy; diaries and memoirs of her contemporaries; and innumerable books, catalogues, pamphlets and newspapers which together provide the pieces of the jigsaw puzzle with which to reconstruct Marie-Louise's life. Around the facts of her life, I have woven the web of contemporary memory, interests and intrigues which provide the essential backdrop to understanding Marie-Louise's situation. Wherever possible, I have used the words, honed from letters, speeches or other records of her contemporaries, adapting them to suit the story's flow. Through these, I have sought to convey her inner reality. I have filled some lacunae with authentic details by reference to texts treating of the same or analogous experiences of contemporaries whose perspectives Marie-Louise was more than likely to have shared. Other gaps I have left unfilled, and in contradiction with the current trend, I have refrained from extrapolation, leaving the reader to make his or her own judgement. My aim was to keep to the expedient minimum the explanation of historical events, which provide the context by which to appreciate fully the precarious nature of Marie-Louise's existence. I hope to have avoided the biographer's trap of over-idealising his or her subject, and have not selectively omitted unflattering details. I have not set out to prove any hypothesis or to show her life refracted by an angled prism. My desire only is that this valiant woman be given a fair hearing, that she be understood and explained and that her heroism no longer be consigned to obscurity.

FOREWORD

by Dott.sa Francesca Sandrini Curator of the Museo Glauco Lombardi, Parma

To embark upon the reconstruction of the "puzzle of the life of Maria Luigia", as Deborah Jay has defined the direction of her biography, is no easy task. Italy knows the protagonist by this name, which she herself chose to use in 1816 in anticipation of her taking possession of the Parman territories accorded her by the Congress of Vienna. To carry out this reconstruction, Deborah has had to follow the trail of an historical figure who, for four years, shared her private and public life with one of the giants of modern history. The stature of Napoleon Bonaparte inevitably eclipses those who surrounded him. In particular, his consort is reduced to mere appendage to *"l'empereur"*.

And yet, it is her role as Napoleon's First Lady which has secured a place for Maria Luigia in the great sweep of European history following her entry as a naïve and unworldly eighteen year-old into this glittering Napoleonic world.

This was a status which she never sought, which was brought about by the political and military opportunism of others who flattered themselves that they might be achieving a lasting alliance and a pan-European peace.

By the exertions and determination of the author, the profile and reputation of her subject, whose position, according to French biographers, has been wholly secondary, if not deleterious to the great Napoleonic project, has been rehabilitated.

Ultimately, the character of this young Habsburg deserves to be considered in the round – both in the several political roles which she held in the various phases of her life and in her private role as woman, daughter and wife of emperors, as mother of a male heir to the throne and of two children born outside contemporary social convention, and as lover and wife of men beneath her in rank.

To bring together the resources required to achieve Deborah's objective has been no modest task – and not one which could have been done hastily. Her book, the fruit of years of meticulous, painstaking creative thinking and dogged perseverance is the proof of this. To adopt a perspective, and to create one's own account, notwithstanding everything that has been written about Maria Luigia, involves not only reviewing and sifting through the boundless canon of Napoleonic bibliography, (itself containing no end of references of varying degrees of reliability,) but also involves plunging into archives, libraries and museums of many European countries and in them retracing the copious mass of documentary material relating to this woman. Maria Luigia lived to leave a trail of herself, of her thoughts, of her actions, of her daily existence, in her letters, in her diaries, in her memoirs which are full of fascinating impressions and vignettes. It is from these yellowing papers (many of which are held at the Museo Glauco Lombardi of Parma) in the minutest handwriting, often barely legible and with her own corrections and strikings-out, that a modern woman emerges, a woman who dared to flout convention and expectation in order to assert her own individuality and the right to her own private happiness, freed from the public role allotted her.

One of the most eloquent pieces of evidence is her creation of a wider family in Parma, extending to the children of her consorts the love and affection she showered upon her own kin. In this, Maria Luigia was ahead of her time.

A woman of so many passions, of such diverse interests, who abhorred inactivity and the "total idleness" which she considered a woman's worst enemy, Maria Luigia applied herself with constancy and conviction to a variety of activities, from painting to embroidery, from writing to music, from literature to botany, demonstrating in several of these a degree of skill far from amateur.

PREFACE

In these pages, the author's scope goes far wider than any local context and encompasses the Italian panorama of those years. This enables the reader to appreciate Maria Luigia's deftness in managing the balancing of her private and public personae and the strict political line imposed by the Austrian government during her long thirty years in Parma.

One's thoughts go to her natal country when one thinks of the King of Rome, the other protagonist in this affair, whose story lacks a happy ending. If any accusation can be levelled against this woman, it relates to her relationship with this son, who reminded her perhaps too much of her Napoleonic past and who lived confined for his entire existence in Vienna, subject to his grandfather's rigorous, icy control. In a kind of cruel, and one likes to hope, involuntary continuity, just as Maria Luigia was deprived of a true affectionate relationship with her mother, Marie-Thérèse, she ultimately distanced from her own heart the boy starved of love and personal identity, deprived even of that which makes each one of us unique – his name. The distance between Parma and Vienna, both physically, psychologically and politically, and the lack of true empathy weakened what might otherwise have been a very strong bond. But perhaps this is another story...

Two hundred years exactly have passed since this Austrian duchess first set foot in the city of Parma. And the name of Maria Luigia of Habsburg resounds in her former duchies even today in her portraits, in the places dedicated to her, in the infrastructure, in the theatres and in the many urban projects instigated by her in a city which finally reacquired its ancient prestige thanks to the presence of a court which increasingly became the real economic motor of the capital. Almost in an excess of memory, the same Parmans attribute to her those things which in truth are the results of the enlightened initiatives of former rulers and of other duchies which shaped the face of this city both before and after her.

That which remains incontestably linked to her is a small purple flower, the violet, in origin a symbol of the Napoleonic party during the One Hundred Days, which has emerged to become a lasting emblem of her city and of her as duchess.

Before embarking upon this wonderful adventure of discovery of a personality unjustly consigned to oblivion, let us introduce this woman to the reader through the lens of one of her ladies-in-waiting, Sophie Henriette Cohendet, who described the young girl when she was introduced to the French as their new Empress:

> Marie-Louise, then eighteen-and-a-half years old, had a majestic height, a noble stature, much freshness and éclat, blond hair which had nothing dull about it, blue eyes, but animated, hands and feet which could have served as models. She was possibly slightly overweight, a defect which she did not preserve for long in France. These were the exterior endowments which we first noticed in her. Nothing was more gracious, more loveable than her face, when she was at her ease, whether in her interior or among people with whom she was particularly connected; but in wider society and above all in the first moments after her arrival in France, her shyness gave her an air of embarrassment which many mistakenly took for haughtiness ... .No woman could have suited Napoleon better.

June 2015

ACKNOWLEDGEMENTS

From the moment I first encountered Marie-Louise, the subject of my biography, I was fascinated, driven by the force of an inspirational woman. My journey to completing this book has brought me into contact with many such extraordinary women, and it is to them that I wish first to pay tribute.

Above all, thanks go to Dott.ssa Francesca Sandrini, Curator of the Museo Glauco-Lombardi. In addition to drawing my attention to invaluable sources of which I might never have known, she has given me constant encouragement and kept up my morale when the task I had set myself seemed insurmountable. I am indebted to her and to Mariachiara Bianchi, her assistant for their perseverance, kindness and endless patience. I am also indebted to Eliana Orsi who researched tirelessly, showing a commitment to my project beyond anything I could have expected. Gaia Servadio, formidable author and journalist, introduced me to the movers and shakers of Parma, so that every door was open to me. Picci Tirelli and Luisa Bertogalli Bormioli, two extraordinary sisters, Paola Cirani and the Marchesa Zaira dalla Rosa Prati also provided access to important resources. My thanks also to Lauretta Campanini of the Biblioteca Palatina. Eva Burke provided me with German eyes, ears and tongue, and introduced me into the Habsburg family. Marion Godfrey saved me much labour by translating letters from German. Monika von Habsburg assisted me with Habsburg family matters. The virologist Dr. I van der Velde, provided expertise in relation to Marie-Louise's medical symptoms. Stephanie Kronson-Teeger, Donna Schogger, Linda Langton, Jessica Graham of Primrose Hill

Books, and Jean Kwok believed in me at critical junctures and gave me invaluable feedback and advice. My thanks in this regard also to Kathryn Hughes, Rebecca Stott and Midge Gillis.

Emily Sweet has been heroic in editing my work. Her and my efforts would be of limited value without expert negotiation of the marketing and media worlds by Marie Oldham. Eilis Tobin, Rachel Rogers and Zippy Woolfson have also assisted.

I also owe gratitude to a cohort of men. Perhaps one of the greatest honours was to be able to hear from Dr. Otto von Habsburg who, shortly before his death at the age of 98 in 2011, remembered sitting on his grandfather Franz-Josef's knee, listening to tales of Marie-Louise. Roger Roussel has also been instrumental in facilitating my contact with the Habsburg family descendants. Far more conversant with the life of Napoleon and his general impact than I are Professor Tim Blanning of Gonville & Caius College, Cambridge, Dr. Michael Rowe of King's College University, London and Professor Munro Price of Bradford University. Professor Price very generously read my manuscript for historical accuracy. At the Vienna State Archives, Joachim Tepperberg answered my endless questions. Also in Vienna, Michael von Habsburg-Löthringen told me about Habsburg family life. In Parma, Elvio Ubaldi, Pierluigi Donati, Giulio Sandrini, and Vittorio dalla Rosa Prati for hospitality, doors opened and infinite kindness. Many others have helped me along the way: Professor Barrie Jay, my late father-in-law and Dennis van der Velde who assisted me with postal history, the seemingly indefatigable staff in the British Library, particularly in the Rare Books and Manuscripts Room, and the staff at Christie's and Sotheby's in London who scoured previous auction sales to trace valuable information, and Francis Marx, who also assisted me with translation. I am also indebted to Christopher Sinclair-Stevenson, William Fiennes and Marek Laskowski, Jamie Sandall and Louis Seigal.

My book would never have come to fruition without the love, support and endurance of my husband Robert and daughter Hannah, my

ACKNOWLEDGEMENTS

mother Rosalynde and my generous step-father, Robert Lewis, cousins Norma Coulter and Marion Meltzer, aunt Raymonde Jay and the incomparable Bébé, the Lady Foley, and my infinitely patient friends, Pamela Klaber, Inga and Michael Rose, Gillian and Jeremy Seigal, Dr. Leslie and Juliet Sheinman, Jacqui and Dr. Mike Rubens, Bill and Rachel Schultz, Monica Bard, Professor Emma Tarlo, Judith Farbey, Dr. Clare Gerada, Maggie Wylie, Barbara Latham, Teresa Norman, Geneviève de Lacaze, Georgia Kauffman-Wolfe, Marie Oldham, Monika Kelly, Tina di Carlo, Patti Masri, Dr. Alberto Gabriele, Christine Sandall, David Cooper, Redmond Szell, Phyllida Scrivens, Wilmo Teggi, Dr. Tamara Tolley and Narjes El Hermi, and the wonderful staff at Lemonia Restaurant, Primrose Hill, London.

This is just a small selection of the many people who have helped me over the past decade, to whom I remain ever grateful.

A SHORT CHRONOLOGY FOR THE LIFE OF MARIE-LOUISE

5 December 1791	Mozart dies
12 December 1791	Marie-Louise is born
16 October 1793	Guillotine of Queen Marie-Antoinette
March 1805	Napoleon creates the Kingdom of Italy
2 December 1805	Austria's first defeat by Napoleon at the battle of Austerlitz
5-6 July 1809	Austria's second defeat by Napoleon at the battle of Wagram
10 January 1810	Napoleon divorces Josephine
7 February 1810	Marie-Louise's betrothal to Napoleon
20 March 1811	The King of Rome is born
15-28 May 1812	Marie-Louise and Napoleon entertain sovereigns at Dresden
14 September 1812	Napoleon enters Moscow
26 June 1813	Napoleon's nine hour interview with Metternich in Dresden on the eve of the Battle of the Nations at Leipzig
29 March 1814	Marie-Louise and the King of Rome flee Paris preceding the entry of the allies

7 April 1814	Napoleon abdicates the French throne
18 July 1814	Marie-Louise arrives at Aix-en-Savoie
18 September 1814	Scheduled start of the Vienna Congress
26 February 1815	Napoleon escapes Elba
18 June 1815	Battle of Waterloo at which the allies defeat Napoleon
17 October 1815	Napoleon arrives on St Helena
20 April 1815	Marie-Louise enters Parma
1 May 1817	Albertina is born
8 August 1819	Wilhelm is born
9 March 1820	Bourbon king Ferdinand of Spain is forced to accept a constitution prompting uprisings throughout the Italian Peninsula
5 May 1821	Napoleon dies on St Helena
20 October 1822	Verona Congress
22 February 1829	Neipperg dies
July 1830	Revolution in Paris placing Louis-Philippe on the French throne
February 1831	Uprisings in Parma
November 1831	Cholera outbreak in Vienna
22 July 1832	Duke of Reichstadt dies
November 1832	Publication of Silvio Pellico's Le Mie Prigioni
17 February 1834	Marie-Louise marries Bombelles
Summer 1836	Cholera outbreak in Parma

A SHORT CHRONOLOGY FOR THE LIFE OF MARIE-LOUISE

13 December 1840	The return of Napoleon's ashes to Paris
9 March 1842	Nabucco first performed, an instant success making Verdi famous
23 July 1844	Execution of foiled nationalists the Bandiera brothers as major works promoting Italian nationalism consistent with Catholicism are published
June 1846	Pope Pius IX becomes Pope
17 December 1847	Marie-Louise dies
March 1848	Parma evicts Marie-Louise's successor following revolution which starts in Palermo and erupts throughout the Italian Peninsula and Europe
1860	Parma accedes to the Kingdom of Piedmont which becomes the Kingdom of a united Italy

Europe in 1810: Napoleon dominant

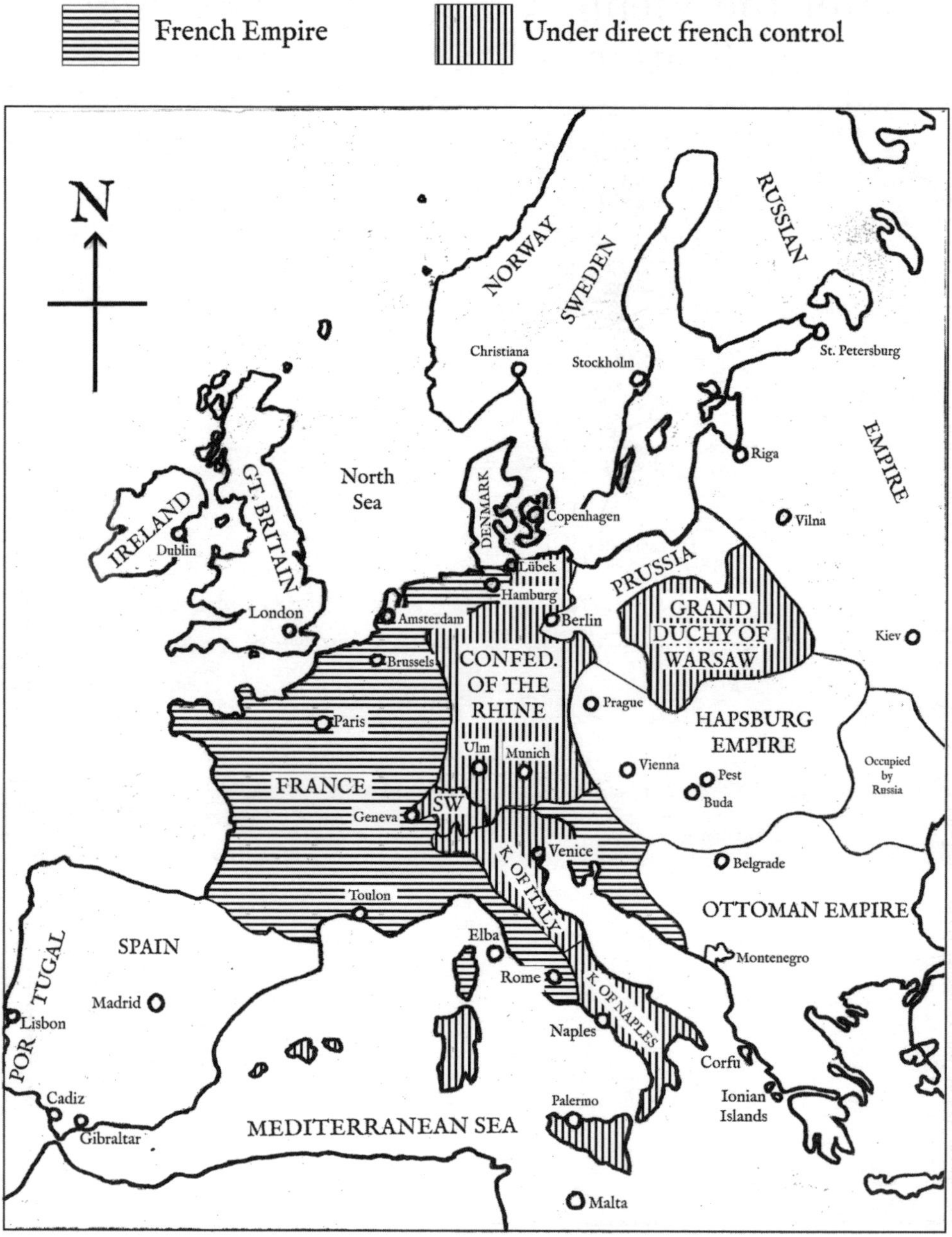

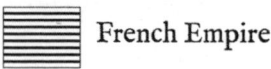 French Empire   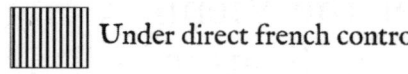 Under direct french control

The Italian peninsula from settlement after the Vienna Congress 1815 to the unification of Italy 1860-1870

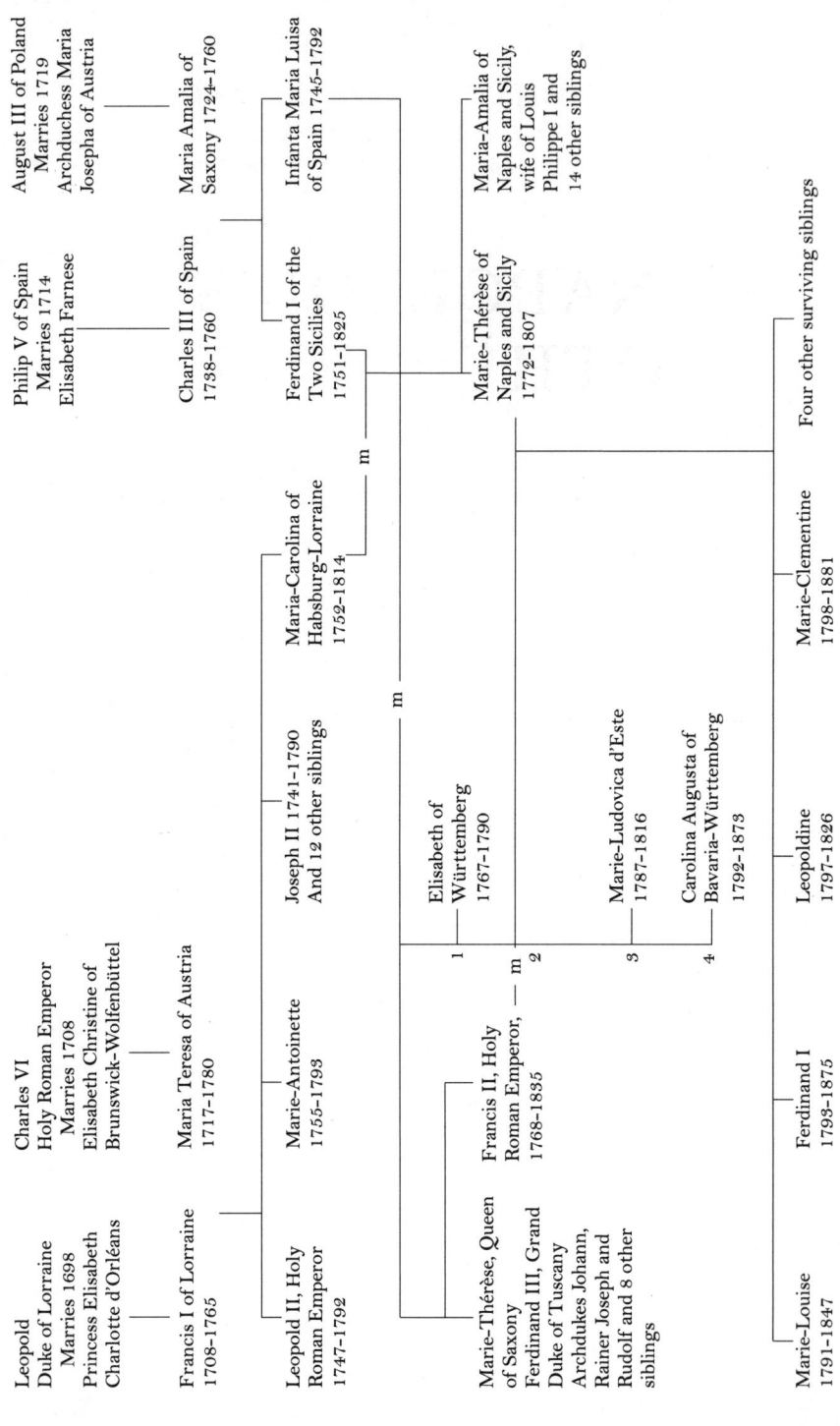

NAPOLEON'S OTHER WIFE

ONE

The wedding of the century, April 1810

Marie-Louise perspired under the heavy ermine cloak and iron crown brought from the Treasury of the Cathedral of Notre Dame which barely five years earlier had graced her predecessor Josephine. A loud gasp reverberated around the vast Galérie de Diane as a triumphal fanfare announced the entrance of the new empress with faltering step. The eighteen-year-old Austrian archduchess could not possibly have anticipated the hard road which lay before her. Marriage to the throne of France would lead her not to the guillotine to which it had led her Great-Aunt Marie-Antoinette, but to the desolate plains of marginalisation. To the end of her days, of indeterminate marital, maternal and political status, she would be rootless, a fugitive and exile, isolated physically, mentally and emotionally. Undeserved scorn would soon be compounded by humiliation and tragedy. And yet, she would become a woman of consequence, shaping an enduring near utopian enclave in a Europe dominated by turmoil and oppression. Her determination, intelligence and profound overriding love for humanity would be a beacon of light for centuries to come to women forced to live with betrayal and deceit. Her heroism would be both unconventional and extraordinary. For now, flush with the hope of youth, she stood in awe of the responsibilities which lay ahead and of her husband by her side.

Barely seven weeks had passed since the early February day when Marie-Louise had been told by her father's foreign minister Count Metternich in his usual dispassionate tone that the French Emperor had asked for her hand in marriage. Her father, Emperor Francis of Austria and his government considered that the interests of State would be served by her acceptance of the proposal but her father would not force her to marry against her will. She could speak her mind freely, he said. Metternich's approach was not unexpected. Her father had already spoken to her in general terms of the prospect of a Bonaparte marriage. It was irrelevant that she had been and remained ignorant of the fact that the contract surrendering her was already signed and sealed. Metternich left his own record of his exchange with the archduchess. She was well prepared for the moment and answered without hesitation:

> I wish only to do that which duty dictates. When the interests of the empire and of my father are in issue, it is those and not my interests, which I must address. Tell my father to take into consideration only his duty as sovereign and not to subordinate this duty to my personal wishes.

This was the only response expected of an eligible Habsburg bargaining counter.

The protocol for Marie-Louise's journey to Paris provided that her first meeting with her husband would take place at a forest clearing not far from Soissons. There, Marie-Louise was to prostrate herself before her husband in total submission to him, and the couple were to sleep under separate roofs before the religious wedding in Paris. But Napoleon lost patience and decided to do things his way. Those who had waited for hours in pouring rain to bear witness to the first imperial encounter were sorely disappointed. Marie-Louise was startled as her carriage door suddenly burst open at the last staging-post of her journey and a small man in grey doublet and riding boots, drenched through, mounted the steps in haste. From the moment he saw her he was entranced, oblivious to her physical shortcomings. Jean Baptiste Isabey's description of the young archduchess whom he painted when she first arrived in Paris, and many times subsequently, is in equivocal terms:

> Marie-Louise dresses without affectation and without style. Her soul is revealed in her smile. She is straightforward,

slightly distracted, slightly shy, but courteous and open. She is not beautiful. Neither her will nor her desires are expressed in her eyes, which are a very bright blue framed by fine blond hair. She has a curvaceous figure and is slightly taller than average. She has tiny little feet, childlike hands and arms. Her nose is broad at its base and set apart from her eyes, reminiscent of Mongolian women. There is a gap between each of her white teeth, which protrude slightly. Her complexion is rosy around her cheekbones. Her upper lip is full, fleshy, droopy, an unmistakeable Habsburg characteristic. On her face, here and there, smallpox and measles have left a visible mark. Though not beautiful, she has the freshness of youth and a natural still childlike grace. She has a very white, supple neck like that of a swan and the tiny waist of an adolescent. She is gay and cheerful, and for her age she has a delightful disposition. She is full of the spice of life.[1]

Throwing off his hood, Napoleon lurched towards his bride and flung his arms around her neck, drawing her to him and showering her with compliments and kisses. "Ah, those full Habsburg lips, oh Louise, Louise, Louise!"[2] Marie-Louise would soon hear from her former lady-in-waiting, Countess Lazansky, that she had been assured that "the Emperor was agreeably surprised finding You very much more good looking than the portrait which had been made for him."[3] The feeling was mutual. "Sire, your portrait did not flatter you," Marie-Louise told him. Ordered to forget the forest clearing, the coachman pressed on to Compiègne at breakneck speed, as Napoleon bombarded her with questions without waiting for an answer. A more romantic start to married life was hard to imagine.

By 2nd April, Marie-Louise had already celebrated two wedding ceremonies. The first, by proxy, had taken place three weeks earlier in the Augustinienkirche, the church attached to Vienna's Hofburg Palace. It had been a sombre occasion in the absence of the groom whom she had not yet met. The second had been a civil marriage two days earlier in the Palace of Saint Cloud in the countryside outside Paris. Modest by comparison to the third ceremony, a small congregation of four hundred privileged guests had been invited to witness the imperial exchange of vows at close quarters.

The day of what was to be the wedding of the century began early. Thirty-eight imperial carriages, accompanied by cavalry forming endless lines of mounted horses caparisoned in plumes and gold, had rolled out of the Palace of Saint Cloud in the first light of day. The Polish Countess Potocka, whom Marie-Louise had known in Vienna, watched the royal cortège from her window. She described the *beau monde* and horses decked out in finery at unconscionable expense, and the golden carriage which conveyed Napoleon and Marie-Louise, surrounded by pubescent pages who walked along the pavement at symmetric intervals, like butterflies ready to take flight at the first opportunity. She thought Napoleon far more preoccupied by the public reaction to the spectacle than Marie-Louise's impressions. Officers, dignitaries and imperial household staff were all conveyed in shining carriages escorted by pages, equerries, colonels and police. Fifty-one mayors and prefects representing all the departmental authorities throughout France augmented the party. Other observers thought the throngs attracted by curiosity rather than any enthusiasm for the event. But Savary, Napoleon's Minister of General Police, concluded that the metropolitan population could not account for the inconceivable density of crowds gathered and that many must have made their way to Paris from the countryside. "France seemed to be enraptured."[4]

Eighteen thousand men and women had gathered in three adjoining rooms of Napoleon's Louvre, the Salon de la Paix, the Galérie au Bord de l'Eau and the Galérie de Diane to watch the wedding party process to the Salon Carré. They had been ushered to their places at six in the morning by one of twenty guardsmen. To

THE WEDDING OF THE CENTURY, APRIL 1810

alleviate the long wait, a hundred junior officers served the women canapés and drinks from niches specially excavated for the occasion at intervals in the thick walls. Four orchestras relieved the boredom. Smelling salts resuscitated several guests who had fainted. Preceded by vast armies of dignitaries and imperial household members, Marie-Louise's entrance immediately revived her audience.

The majority of the guests were crammed into the largest of the three rooms, the Galérie du Bord de l'Eau. Long benches on either side of the vast hall accommodated Parisian high society in order of rank. The men, who represented the bulk of French civil and military administration, stood in ceremonial uniform, black jacket and short trouser, for which the cost of trimmings alone amounted to one thousand, eight hundred francs.* Plumed hats, gold-handled swords, engraved steel diamond-cut buttons and golden buckles gleamed in the sun as it broke through the skylights. The ladies sat in front of their standing consorts in opulent ball-gowns all with décolleté down to the centre of the back, cut at the front to expose shoulders, arms and cleavage. Fresh flowers and dazzling jewellery embellished hair, arms and neck. The elderly inhaled sporadically from saltcellars.

Marie-Louise shimmered in her silver toile gown heavily embroidered with precious gems, and diamonds supplied by the fashionable jewellers Gioconde. She advanced hesitantly, her blond curls peeping out from under the crown Napoleon had carefully set upon her head. Every now and again she attempted to look over her shoulder to ensure that her train, held at intervals by her Bonaparte sisters-in-law (whose own trains were carried by their knights of honour), was following her. Austrian diplomat Count Clary-de-Aldringen noted that the mechanism was like a tortoise with silver claws. The bride moved slowly along the imperial carpet, flanked by walls over a thousand feet high, hung with immense *tableaux* celebrating the triumphs of France over the evil of its aggressors. Exulting in

---

* Well in excess of £20,000 in today's money.

the public exposure, the Queens of Spain, Holland and Westphalia, Julie, Hortense and Catherine, and Princesses Elisa and Pauline, matched Marie-Louise's small steps. Marie-Louise did not know that only that morning there had been shocking temper tantrums, vain entreaties, tears, even feigned falling unconscious, and absolute refusals to try and avoid being bearer of the bride's train. Napoleon had finally settled matters by a decisive, "I desire". Count Clary-de-Aldringen had witnessed the scene, the comical pouting, threats of imminent illness, the persistent dropping of the train to persuade Napoleon of incompetence so that everyone had to rush forward to catch it. The haughty Westphalian Catherine, was the worst culprit. Only Hortense behaved with dignity. Napoleon's sister, Caroline, had been excused in recognition of her role in escorting Marie-Louise to Paris from Branau, the border town where Marie-Louise had been transferred from Austrian to French hands.

Like the bearers of the bridal train, the groom, smiling engagingly, was considerably shorter than his bride. He had chosen a Spanish costume of white satin short coat, pants and silk stockings, all embroidered and edged in gold, starched English collar and cuffs, cloak sewn with the imperial insignia of gold bees. The great necklace of the Légion d'Honneur, his gift to the world, was emblazoned across his chest, sword at his side. The sun broke through as the couple took their vows in the Salon Carré. It seemed an excellent omen. War in Europe would be a thing of the past. As he processed in, he saluted as many as possible to his left and right, while Marie-Louise kept her large cornflower blue eyes fixed ahead.

Finally, the couple made their entrance into the Salon Carré, now transformed into a chapel. Drapes of white taffeta striped in gold and velvet concealed the religious paintings which Napoleon could not abide. The bride and groom knelt at the makeshift altar under a crimson canopy. Having received a sprinkling of Holy Water, Napoleon's uncle, Cardinal Fesch, intoned the wedding benediction. The clergy blessed Marie-Louise's wedding ring and the thirteen pieces of gold symbolically representing her dowry.

THE WEDDING OF THE CENTURY, APRIL 1810

The main focus of one of the most sumptuous ceremonies France had ever seen, Napoleon was in his element. But as the ceremony neared its conclusion, French minister Pasquier noted that Napoleon's triumphal radiance had completely vanished. His usual pallor gave way to the ruddiness of suffused anger. His eyes, which had constantly darted around the room, intermittently settling upon his new bride, were transfixed by vacant seats in the rows which the Cardinals had been invited to occupy. Cardinal Fesch finished his incantation, closed the Gospel in his hand and kissed it, offering it to the bride and bridegroom to do the same. Clouds of grey smoke billowed out from large brass balls, swung from side to side by the prelates, in mystical consecration of the marriage. The couple and their immense retinue processed back accompanied by the triumphant peels of the organ.

A short while later, Marie-Louise and Napoleon stood outside to salute their subjects on the oleander and myrtle clad balcony overlooking the Tuileries Gardens. The newly-weds watched the colourful pageantry, public acclamation soaring for the Corps du Garde who paraded before them against the backdrop of the gilded peristyle built by Napoleon in emulation of Vienna's Schönbrunn Palace, dividing the Tuileries from the Place de la Concorde and the Champs Elysées.

After a festive banquet, and a concert audible far beyond the Tuileries Palace by members of the public, the Emperor and Empress emerged again on to the Tuileries balcony, this time accompanied by Count Metternich. The Austrian minister planned to exploit his matchmaking success to maximum personal advantage.

A vast array of entertainments had been organised for general public consumption. Jugglers, conjurers, physicists, clowns, singers and puppeteers had been engaged to amuse the people of Paris throughout the city for the day and for much of the night. The squares of the metropolis rang with dancing and spectacle. Having organised the distribution of food to the homes of the indigent, Napoleon arranged distribution to the rest of the urban population of a lottery ticket entitling the holder to pâtés, hams, bread and other items. The lottery ticket also entitled them to a litre of wine from the Emperor's new invention, the wine fountain. This avoided the unseemly, violent scramble and subsequent inebriation, often accompanying the availability of free alcohol on festive occasions. The high aristocracy were invited to attend a party at the Hôtel de Ville, where Emperor and Empress dropped in to open the ball. After dancing a quadrille, the couple circulated among the guests, who pressed forward to win the imperial word. From the square before the Hôtel de Ville, Marie-Louise set alight the first illumination of many to celebrate her wedding. Fireworks and torches set the skyline ablaze with colour, bringing the city's public architecture to life, the buildings more visible and magnificent than in daylight. Churches, domes, palaces, hotels and private houses shone with fire. Arcades of flame had been created over bridges, and a Temple of Hymen shone over the towers of Notre Dame. The Place de la Concorde shimmered in the reflected magnificence of the surrounding buildings. At what would normally be the dark dead of night, an ocean of light mirrored the waters of the Seine.

The crowds converging on the Tuileries gardens continued to cheer enthusiastically. Together, Napoleon, Marie-Louise and Metternich looked up in wonder at the illuminated landscape running the full length of the Champs Elysées as far as the facsimile of the planned triumphal arch. Chancellor Metternich raised his glass of champagne.

"Long live the Emperor and Empress of France! To the health of the King of Rome!" Marie-Louise was reminded that her marriage would be worth little if she were unable to produce the golden egg. A son, she must produce a son.

Returning to the Tuileries Palace after a taxing day, Napoleon led Marie-Louise along a warren of dark corridors to one of the many rooms with which she was not yet acquainted. There before her were the objects she most treasured: furniture she had left behind in Vienna and which Napoleon, without her knowledge, had arranged to have transported to Paris. He had also arranged for the piano manufacturer, Erard, to supply a piano and a harp to all the imperial palaces.

Marie-Louise fired off letters reassuring relatives of her delight in her husband, with whom she was fast becoming besotted.

At Napoleon's unscheduled first appearance at Courcelles, she had tried several times to embark upon the speech she had painstakingly memorised in which she was supposed to tell him how good fortune had favoured her, how she was honoured to have been selected as his consort, and other flatteries in similar vein. According to his own report to his household, Napoleon had just kept laughing, telling her not to bother continuing and kissing her, repeating her name again and again, "Louise, Louise, Louise . . . ". Through the carriage window, torches had flickered as they drew into the Château de Compiègne, revealing crowds huddled together under wide-brimmed hats and umbrellas against the sheeting rain. Assembled around the lower steps of the Grand Staircase were Napoleon's family, the famous Bonaparte celebrities whose antics provided a steady stream of print for foreign newspapers. All were anxious to survey the new addition. Napoleon presented Marie-Louise first to his mother, Madame Mère as she was known. Marie-Louise was to make her formal acquaintance and that of Napoleon's siblings and their spouses the following day at a reception, the first of many in her honour.

It was well known that there had been no love lost between the Bonaparte family and Napoleon's first wife, Josephine. They had never liked her blatantly manipulative emotional outbursts, her inconstancy and above all, her past. Marie-Louise warmed immediately to Napoleon's mother, a strict observer of family traditions, and to Josephine's daughter, Hortense. The family was so welcoming that Marie-Louise was convinced that the allegations against them must be untrue. Fresh-faced local children approached the new empress with baskets of daffodils and bluebells. A painting by Pauline Auzou records the blond, statuesque Austrian Archduchess in crimson velvet dress and lace ruff towering over both the children and her mesmerised husband. Napoleon announced that his bride was hungry and tired and withdrew with her and Caroline to the newly decorated Empress's Apartments.

A light meal awaited the three travellers in the Galerie de la Bal. Having dismissed the footmen, Napoleon took up cutlery at the serving table and offered his bride and then his sister chicken breast, potatoes, carrots and cabbage. Having plated the food, he poured the wine and assisted Marie-Louise with her napkin.

After they had eaten, Napoleon took Marie-Louise on her first tour of her apartments. He considered this small former hunting lodge, hidden away in the depths of the forest of Compiègne, a rather humble dwelling. "Our ancestor Louis XVI used to say: "I am housed at Versailles like a King, at Fontainebleau like a Prince, and at Compiègne like a peasant." No-one besides Napoleon would have regarded the late king as a Bonaparte ancestor. And the dwelling was far from humble. Throughout her apartments proliferated the symbols of Abundance and Fecundity, Lightness and Purity in the motifs of the heavy brocade, rich scarlet upholstery and gold leaf woodwork. Marie-Louise's monogram gleamed from every surface. The ornamentation was exquisite. Over the gilt sleigh bed was an enormous crown forming a canopy from which fell festoons of fine shining white curtains held apart by winged seraphs in Greek classical style. White bed-linen beckoned in the candlelight.

Napoleon asked if Marie-Louise's father had given her any instructions. Mme Lazanksy had given her basic directions as to sexual pleasure. "Let the Emperor Napoleon guide you." Marie-Louise stated simply: "My father and Mme Lazansky have both told me that once I am alone with Your Majesty, the Emperor Napoleon, I must do exactly as He asks. I must obey Your Majesty in whatever demands He makes of me."

The following midday, husband and wife were still languishing in bed when Napoleon's uncle, Cardinal Fesch, was announced. Marie-Louise, propped up on pillows, sipped her hot chocolate. Napoleon urged the celibate to marry a German. They were the best women in the world, good natured, innocent – and as fresh as roses.

Cardinal Fesch had reassured Napoleon that he could sleep with his new wife on the day of her arrival, even though the religious marriage in France had yet to take place. Unlike her great-aunt's dauphin, Napoleon knew what to do with his erection. Napoleon recalled later on St Helena that Marie-Louise had enjoyed sexual intercourse so much that she had begged Napoleon to repeat the performance. There is no record of Marie-Louise's assessment of her husband's prowess. Her thoughts seemed to have been elsewhere. "I find that he improves a lot on closer acquaintance. There is something attractive and polite about him which is impossible to resist. I am convinced that I will be able to live with him quite happily. My good fortune would be complete save for not being able to see you, which thought my husband shares most sincerely," she wrote to her father.[5]

Faces familiar to Marie-Louise had been invited to the reception held in the Corinthian-columned ballroom at Compiègne. Among them were Count and Countess Metternich and Prince Schwarzenberg from Vienna, and Marie-Louise's uncle Ferdinand, the witty, urbane Grand Duke of Würzburg. Napoleon seemed as fond as his wife of the Grand Duke, and insisted that he join them on their forthcoming honeymoon, an event in which a substantial party was to participate. Marie-Louise again met the clan, Napoleon's mother, brothers Joseph, King of Spain and wife Julie, Jérôme, King of Westphalia and wife Catherine, Louis, King of Holland, Napoleon's sisters Pauline Princess Borghese and husband Camillo, and Caroline, Queen of Naples and husband Joachim Murat. Only Elisa, Grand Duchess of Tuscany, and Lucien, Prince of Canino, were absent. Progressing with difficulty through a series of tiny rooms in which over fifty people were crammed, Napoleon introduced Marie-Louise to his Italian household, to the top brass of his military, and to his ministers. Count Clary-et-Aldringen complained that one could barely move without knocking over a duchess.

This was Marie-Louise's first taste of French court life. From now on, her existence was to be a succession of receptions, parties, and balls, a whirlwind punctuated by cannon report, artillery salvoes, fireworks and illuminations, at which she was the main attraction. Imperial family members, courtiers, court officials, ambassadors, cardinals and ministers passed before her day after day as if in a carnival parade. Each one she must acknowledge, to each one she must say something to put him or her at ease and to make them feel special. She was baffled at how she would ever remember anyone's name, let alone speak to him or her meaningfully. Habsburg credo dictated that to keep a nation happy, one must appear approachable and affable, never haughty or disdainful. Marie-Louise was bashful before her new countrymen. She watched Napoleon, hoping to learn by his example. He spoke directly and with economy, and then moved swiftly on.

As the balance of her trousseau arrived in the Palace of Saint Cloud, Marie-Louise saw the lengths to which Napoleon had gone to try and win her heart. Napoleon had delegated to Caroline, his sister, the selection of his new wife's personal wardrobe and toilette. In approximately three weeks, the finest tailors and seamstresses in Paris had burned the midnight oil to meet Caroline's exacting requirements, which exceeded the budget three times over. In Vienna, Marie-Louise had led a simple life with relatively few possessions and had been used to wearing the same outerwear for days at a time. Sartorial demands were to be very different in Paris. Leroy, the leading dressmaker of the day, had been commissioned to design day and evening wardrobes for Marie-Louise's life in France. His creations were more fantastical than anything even he had ever produced. Correspondingly, his bill was the most astronomical he had ever issued. Napoleon immediately demanded an audit. He had crossed swords on a number of occasions with Leroy in relation to purchases by his first wife, the profligate Josephine, and had managed to negotiate reductions. This time, there was nothing he could do. The treasury forked out a staggering 411,736 francs 24 centimes.* There were eight dresses intended for formal occasions, the most expensive of which was the white satin wedding dress, dripping with gold leaf and encrusted with gems. Four long dresses in pink tulle and satin with satin under-dress, six ballgowns sewn with gold, others with silver, twelve evening dresses, twelve riding habits, eight hunting habits, morning dresses with matching neckties, all bespoke supreme luxury. Gloves, fans, hats, hair and other accessories were strewn over cashmere shawls, Mexican voiles and Castilian mantillas in every conceivable colour and design. Janssen, shoemakers to the Académie Impériale de Musique in Paris, had employed the artistry honed in their output for the Paris theatre in their production of forty-eight pairs of slippers. Twelve dresses were supplied specifically for her transit to France, five in embroidered muslin, six in embroidered cambric cotton, one in needlepoint. Bath linen, dinner services, flatware and glass, every imaginable accessory for writing, sewing, embroidery, personal comfort and hygiene, dental care and manicure represented the zenith of artistic and technical achievement. Marie-Louise's father, Emperor Francis had been right. All his prophecies as to her future happiness had come true. Her father asked her to thank Napoleon on his behalf for making him a very happy man. Applying herself to the task of conceiving an heir to cement the union between France and Austria was not to be the challenge she had feared.

* Today, the equivalent would be, on a broad estimate, somewhere in the order of £6,000,000.

TWO

The birth of an heir, March 1811

Marie-Louise had vomited frequently from four weeks after her arrival in Paris. She wanted to believe that she was pregnant, but knew it was too early to be sure. One particular night, one of many overnight stops on honeymoon in the Low Countries, she had immersed herself in the bath to wash away the charcoal which had coated her on the road from Cambrai to Mons. Queasiness had developed into a severe headache on the gondola conveying her and Napoleon along the Cambrai Canal, unbearable in all its twenty-two leagues and twenty-three locks. At her call, Napoleon came running in. Seeing her in great discomfort, he immediately summoned Dr. Jouan, surgeon-major attached to the Ambulance of the Imperial Household of the Grande Armée. Both Marie-Louise and Napoleon soon became exasperated by the physician's pompous florid language. Napoleon asked what could be done to make the Empress more comfortable. Jouan said there was no question of her continuing on her honeymoon schedule. She must be bled and then enjoy a period of complete rest for the next six weeks.

As sick as she felt, Marie-Louise had never heard anything so ridiculous. "Doctors are real ignoramuses," she committed to her diary. She was not ill. She was healthy, and pregnant. That was all. "Save for the pains of early pregnancy, I feel quite well," she insisted.[1] Marie-Louise's arrival in Paris had been timed to coincide with the second third of her menstrual cycle, so as to ensure her sexual availability and her optimum fertility. It had been a long three months' waiting as far as Napoleon and his father-in-law were concerned. Emperor Francis had taken the opportunity of reminding his daughter of her overriding duty: "Look after yourself and avoid anything which might get in the way of your most important objective of begetting children."²

Napoleon continued to shower her with further gifts including the balance of her trousseau. A diadem and crown of diamonds was so heavy Marie-Louise could barely wear them.

The days following the marriage at the Palace of Saint Cloud were blissful. Not only was Napoleon charming, he constantly teased her, which she adored, and pulled her nose playfully when she said she had not understood. Paying little heed to his father-in-law's advice, he taught her to ride, exhorting her to dare-devilry, and encouraged her to draw and paint his portrait. She loved every minute with him. She could not believe that the vicious rumours circulating about him in Vienna could have any foundation. She needed nothing more to be happy save to see her family soon, which Napoleon promised her she would. She wrote to her father: "I think every day of you, and tell him that he could not have a truer friend – he agrees with me, knowing that there is no gentler, sweeter father than you."

Notwithstanding her happiness, Marie-Louise had embarked upon the honeymoon with trepidation. She had expressed her anxiety about extensive travel to her stepmother, Empress Marie-Ludovica. Her only previous long journeys had been undertaken in sadness, in flight or into the unknown. The rigours of the journey from Vienna to Paris had left her without appetite for more travel. Marie-Ludovica urged her in her letters to be brave and to travel if Napoleon so desired it. Marie-Louise was surprised to find that she was beginning to enjoy herself. Marie-Ludovica said that, far from surprising, it was natural that she should want to accompany Napoleon, "for a woman is never happier than when she is together with her husband."³ From this advice designed to foster loyalty, Marie-Louise could have wrongly imagined that her stepmother had decided to set aside her hatred for her stepson-in-law.

The entourage accompanying her on her honeymoon was a

mixed blessing. She was glad to be rid of Count Metternich and Queen Caroline, but not of her dear uncle, the Grand Duke of Würzburg, who left the party at Cambrai. She found Eugène de Beauharnais, Napoleon's stepson by Josephine, and Marshall Bessières equally entertaining, loving and gentle. She liked Eugène's wife, a German kindred spirit. She also liked Napoleon's brother Jérôme, whom she found eminently sensible, and his alert wife Catherine, "the prettiest but not the most regular head I have ever seen, and far too fat," who, notwithstanding her looks, soon became Marie-Louise's dearest friend.

A few days after confirming Marie-Louise's pregnancy, Dr. Jouan humbly recommended that she refrain from accompanying her husband to the Island of Walcheren. Marie-Louise could bear neither his manner nor his advice and pressed on. She took vine for her headaches, and ignored nausea, faintness, pain from her right foot caused by a sprain and lumbago from the uncomfortable beds and the uneven roads along which the imperial carriage rumbled. She tried taking short naps to alleviate the overwhelming exhaustion of hours of inactivity in transit, desperate to keep awake for the engagements scheduled by her husband. On several nights, she was exasperated to find herself lodged separately from Napoleon. It was pure joy to be woken by him at four in the morning to go out together on horseback without escort to see her surroundings.

The world seemed to Marie-Louise a fairy-tale, the great fertile plains covered in fruit trees in full bud along country roads, streams bordered by timeless willows and tall windmills promising a life of abundance and prosperity to her well-trained Enlightenment eyes. She was awed by the innovations in industry that Napoleon had shown her, foremost of which were the cotton mills dotted over the landscape. To the cotton mills and soap factories he brought substantial custom from other regions of France and the empire he had conquered. Everywhere, she saw the poverty of the peasantry and the goodwill of landed gentry who muddled along together to promote the common good. Along the route, Napoleon ordered the imperial carriage to stop and invited Marie-Louise to dismount with him to distribute coins brought from the treasury. Devotion could be read in every face. Marie-Louise's heart went out to all, young and old, and to those forced by the misery of their station to resort to begging or even crime. At Vilvoorde, she visited a house of correction, an immense building accommodating beggars from the nearby large towns. She thought such an institution should be established in every region in every country in Europe.

The English Channel provided Marie-Louise's first sight of the sea, her first inhalation of salty air, and an introduction to the world of the sea, of ships, of frigates, of sailors. It was a gusty, overcast day, gulls circling overhead. Napoleon stood next to her on the shingle, pointing out towards England. Napoleon was already contemplating his invasion across the Channel. Protection was necessary from the English, who took their fish and refused to pay for it, he told her. Marie-Louise was mesmerised by the vast expanse of ocean, by all that sailed and floated upon it, the masts of trading and other sea-going vessels destined for the Indies seemed to her like steeple spires. At the port of Boulogne she watched a parade of the French navy. At Scheldt, she felt rather ungainly exposing her legs, clambering aboard the battleship *Charlemagne*. She swore she would only ever board a ship again wearing trousers. No sooner had she regained her balance than she was startled by a deafening report of a thousand guns.

At Antwerp, Napoleon took Marie-Louise on a tour of inspection of the dockyards. Frigates, gunboats and men-of-war lay in the harbour. Determined to strengthen the French fleet for the mother of all battles against the English, he had ordered relentless shipbuilding. Great hulls proliferated, held aloft by scaffolding. When a new vessel was lowered into the water in honour of the imperial couple, Marie-Louise shut her eyes for fear of the impact. "When peace is made with England, Antwerp will be one of the richest and most important commercial towns of the Empire." Napoleon predicted[4].

Jouan tried to dissuade Marie-Louise from continuing her journey for good reason. The island of Walcheren was a malarial swamp, a malodourous pit. Marie-Louise found the stench positively pestilential. Almost three quarters of the inhabitants suffered from fever every year. She wrote in her diary: "There are the most frightful epidemics of malarial fever. Consequently inhabitants seldom live to the age of fifty. Their complexions are yellow and livid. Napoleon relieves the garrison every three months, but soldiers are always ill upon their return. It is best that they only drink wine while on the island." At Middleburg, thirty thousand English soldiers had perished during the epidemic. She shuddered when told that such Englishmen had died in the bed in which she slept. Several of the party, including Napoleon, became violently sick. Peasant traps were hired to leave the island in haste, one of which disintegrated, the horses dragging the Duchess of Montebello's companion along after them.

The convoy advanced at military pace to Holland. The Dutch farms and farmland were remarkably clean and well-tended, Marie-Louise thought. The punishing schedule devised by Napoleon tested Marie-Louise's patience. She found the long stretches without refreshment dire and envied the cattle who could graze without interference. He refused to take in any local sights or break the journey or to allow her to eat in the carriage: "A woman ought never to want to eat." He ignored her pleas that she was carrying his child, burying himself in despatches. On one occasion, Napoleon expedited departure, leaving luggage behind. He refused to allow time for change of outfits for four hot days running. Defiant, Marie-Louise remonstrated with him, saying he was treating his new wife like a grenadier. He told her to get used to it.

On Marie-Louise's arrival in France, her entourage complained that many of the fine goods to which the rich were used, plentiful in Vienna, were much missed in France. The effect of Napoleon's blockade, designed to stifle English commerce and limit the circulation of English goods in France, made them much more desirable.

THE BIRTH OF AN HEIR, MARCH 1811

Her retinue were eagerly looking forward to taking advantage of the black markets flourishing along the Dutch coast. Many gentlemen had stocked up at a warehouse filled with contraband goods at Bois-le-Duc. The Duchess of Montebello accompanied them on their second visit, only to find to her horror that the warehouse had been converted to a house of ill-repute! Marie-Louise found the whole incident extremely funny.

While her entourage were finding ways to circumvent their Emperor's blockade, Marie-Louise was taking her first steps on the beach. She noted in her diary:

> Once we had found passable dunes, which took two hours, we got out of the carriages. My legs sank into the sand. I was astonished! Each step was equally troublesome, but the ascent was nothing to travellers as intrepid as ourselves and we were rewarded with a fine view when we reached the summit. We saw the ocean as an immense surface of water bounded only by the horizon. The sun was setting, and coloured the sea like a rainbow. Far off we could make out some fishing boats returning from their labour protected by a sloop.

By the time the happy couple returned from honeymoon at the beginning of June, Marie-Louise was no longer pregnant, having miscarried. She was free now to enjoy the whirl of social events scheduled for the coming month to celebrate her marriage. Ignoring her father's proscription, she was regularly on horseback during the day, spurred on by her husband until she almost fell off in full gallop. She loved every minute.

Marie-Louise was thrilled to hear that Napoleon intended to confer military honours, usually reserved for those mutilated or distinguished in battle, upon her uncle Archduke Karl, his former formidable adversary and the man he had chosen to act as his proxy at his first marriage to Marie-Louise at the Augustinian Church in

Vienna. Marie-Louise could legitimately interpret the conferral of this honour as both a mark of Napoleon's admiration for her uncle, and of his setting aside of past animosities.

Further evidence of Napoleon's intention to turn a new page in diplomatic relations was his sending of gifts in profusion to his new Austrian family. By night or in the early morning, when Paris was asleep, Napoleon and Marie-Louise set out on horseback to visit the workshops of Savonnerie, Gobelins and Sèvres. There, they selected porcelain and silverware to be sent to Vienna. Napoleon also took her to the Musée du Louvre and the Bibliothèque Impériale. The Louvre was a wonderland. It was hard to imagine that the bulk of its treasures had yet to be put on display. The many Renaissance treasures collected by previous French monarchs and those which Napoleon's victories had brought to the French capital arranged in the converted wings of the Tuileries Palace were extraordinary. Marie-Louise found Paris so large and so full of monuments and public works that one could never be short of amusement.

Exuberant parties thrown by the Emperor's sisters, closest friends and diplomats were scheduled for June and July. Fabulous pavilions, stages, follies and marquees provided the backdrop to lavish entertainments. Napoleon's sister Pauline, the doyenne of Paris high society, made a party to eclipse all others. Marie-Louise was flattered by simulated reconstructions of her Viennese palaces and responded warmly but, considering imperial ostentation distasteful, found excessive the groaning tables of food, *tableaux vivants* and the general array of bacchanalian entertainments for which Princess Pauline was famed. A ball at the Ecole Maritime held in Napoleon and Marie-Louise's honour was attended by over six thousand people falling over themselves to speak or, at the very least, to catch a glimpse of the new Empress. The hall was so overcrowded that the doors had to be closed on several grandees, including members of the Cabinet. Marie-Louise danced, her cheeks red with embarrassment, conscious that all eyes were upon her. Welcomed with wild ovations, the newly-weds graced the Comédie

Française and the Opéra Comique. Evenings without public engagements were spent at intimate soirées in the company of the Bonaparte family in the Tuileries Palace, when musicians, conjurers and animals transformed by the light of magic lanterns into fantastical monsters performed for them.

The last party held to celebrate Marie-Louise was hosted by the Austrian Ambassador, Prince Schwarzenberg. The family were close friends of the Austrian Imperial family, and Princess Marianne, the Ambassador's wife, and particularly Princess Pauline, his sister-in-law, were very good friends of Marie-Louise. In them, she found kindred spirits who mitigated the pain of separation from her own family. The young Empress had received Marianne for a private audience in advance of the party to finalise details. Adored by everyone and a fashion icon in Vienna, Princess Pauline was full of fun, wit and talent.

Marie-Louise and Napoleon were greeted by musicians upon their arrival in the courtyard of the Hotel Montesson in the Rue Chaussée d'Antin. A large wooden ballroom, connected to the house by a gallery, had been constructed over part of the vast gardens beyond. Enormous chandeliers and sconces hung from ceilings of tarpaulin radiating light between magnificent wall-hangings. A full orchestra played a selection of French and German songs, and a choir performed arias accompanied by the harmonica, a new instrument fast gaining in popularity. A spectacle of ballet and musical had been devised on a stage to replicate the gardens of the Laxenburg Palace, known to be dear to Marie-Louise.

Mme Durand recalled in her memoirs seeing Napoleon, seated at the centre of the balcony overlooking the stage, rise abruptly and take Marie-Louise by the arm. Napoleon's brother Jérôme, in a state of agitation, had just whispered in the emperor's ear that one of the draperies in the ballroom had caught fire. The guests of honour slipped out of the nearest door, concealed in one of the wall panels. Bundled into a carriage by Napoleon as screams of panic echoed behind her, Marie-Louise returned, terrified and anxious for her loved ones, to the palace of Saint Cloud. Staying to direct the rescue operation, Napoleon promised her he would be loyal to the ambassador and do everything to limit the spread of inevitable rumours of sabotage.

In the following days, Marie-Louise heard of the terror and panic as people had fought to get out. There were many victims, their bodies so badly burnt that they could later be identified only by their jewels. Survivors were dragged away, shawls, swords, epaulettes, snuff boxes, diamond combs and garters lost in the unsightly wreckage. Outside, street bandits grabbed jewellery from lady guests with such savagery that pieces of flesh and hair came off with the items seized. Firemen arrived but some were drunk, behaved negligently, or disappeared from the scene. Others, along with the musicians, pillaged. In the following weeks, there were arrests and convictions for the most deplorable theft.

Marie-Louise embraced Napoleon at four o'clock in the morning. As they tried to sleep, the death toll mounted. The following morning, she awoke to hear that the lustrous chandelier that she had been admiring moments earlier had collapsed onto the crowd beneath, crushing her dear friend, Princess Pauline. She shed many tears. Napoleon's sister Queen Caroline, who had collapsed with the fumes and been carried out by Marie-Louise's uncle, Grand Duke of Würzburg, had miscarried the baby she was expecting. The Schwarzenberg catastrophe killed the party atmosphere.

As summer wore on, the heat became intolerable, inescapable. Marie-Louise lamented that even the nights were burning hot. Nonetheless, ardour prevailed. "I am twice as happy because the doctor (Dr. Corvisart, Napoleon's private physician,) assures me I am pregnant," Marie-Louise wrote to her family. This time, she was taking no chances. "I have given up riding and dancing." Napoleon doted on her, unable to contain his joy. Breaking from previous marital habit, he lunched and took tea and walks with her, interrogating the doctors on a daily basis. He had her sit for her portrait by court painters Isabey and Prud'hon, miniatures to be sent to Vienna, and for sculptors Chaudet and Bosio. Emperor Francis asked his daughter to thank his new son-in-law. "Take good care of yourself and give me a healthy, strong grandchild."[5]

After a brief sojourn in July in the Palace of Rambouillet, a small turreted, Gothic style hunting lodge to the south of Paris, Emperor and Empress decamped to the grounds of the Palace of Versailles. The Palace itself was still in an uninhabitable condition following the ravages of the French Revolution, all furniture and ornament of the Ancien Régime having been sold off at auction. Napoleon had elaborate plans for its restoration, a mammoth and incalculably expensive undertaking given the interminable number of rooms. The French emperor postponed this project, but decided to restore the Grand and Petit Trianons, half a mile from the main palace.

Marie-Louise had visited the Petit Trianon for lunch once in June with Napoleon and Caroline. Napoleon decided to restore the hamlet, the Little Vienna conceived by and built for Marie-Antoinette scheduled for demolition, for her great-niece. The Petit Trianon comprised a charming country cottage with parkland, artificial mountains, streams, lake, grotto and small waterfall, adjacent miniature farm and dairy, dovecot and water-mill, with its own forest and ponds, pretty English garden and well-stocked greenhouses. Marie-Louise wrote, enclosing plant-cuttings, to tell her father how much she loved the little hunting lodge, reminiscent of her childhood at the Laxenburg Palace.

The layout of the rooms remained exactly as it had been during the late queen's time, save that the oak billiard room was now relocated to the ground floor from the small dining room on the first floor now given over to Marie-Louise's drawing room. Locals remarked that the Petit Trianon seemed to come back to life with Marie-Louise's occupation. However, many speculated as to the thoughts which entered the new Empress's head as she reclined on her gondola-shaped bed under a sky of horticultural motifs in the exact spot as had Marie-Antoinette before her, with the same gold embroidered blue and white silk curtains which her forbear had chosen at the two large north-facing windows. Many considered Marie-Louise's occupation as evidence of indifference to her memory, but they ignored the fact that Marie-Antoinette's spectre hovered in all Marie-Louise's palaces, and that her explicit task was to mend Austro-French diplomatic relations.

The refurbishment of the Grand Trianon, a classical recreation on one floor only, had only just been completed, sculpture and other *objets d'art* brought from the Musée du Louvre. Napoleon had allocated to Marie-Louise the apartments previously destined for his mother and had them redecorated as the only formal state rooms and hence the grandest in all Versailles. It was said that even the Orient could not rival the bronzes, embroidered velvets, porcelain, painting, parquets floors, fireplaces, so exquisite was the taste. Josephine had selected the furniture, mostly crafted out of light-coloured and therefore more feminine ash, elm and other indigenous woods – mahogany, darker and in any event more masculine according to the rules of Antiquity, made scarce by Napoleon's continental blockade. The Emperor's own quarters were much more modestly appointed. Count Clary-de-Aldringen, visiting the Trianons while in Paris for the imperial wedding, described them as something out of a fairy-tale. He noted that Napoleon had tactfully removed a large painting of the surrender of his father-in-law's armies at Ulm that had previously been the centrepiece of the Grand Trianon. The imperial couple spent summer days hunting and fishing, playing rounders in the late afternoon, and music and games in the evenings. Marie-Louise loved to play practical jokes on her new family, sending her brother-in-law Camillo bouquets of stinging nettles for his saint's day and having a bust placed under his bed-linen. It seemed she and Napoleon shared the same sense of humour.

*

THE BIRTH OF AN HEIR, MARCH 1811

Marie-Louise's pregnancy was only officially announced in the first week of November, by which time she was regurgitating everything she had eaten. Marie-Louise had enjoyed her sojourn in the palaces surrounding Paris and had no wish to return to her prison accommodation, as she called the Tuileries. Napoleon tried to humour her with gifts, giving her his portrait, Gobelins and Savonnerie tapestries, and a service in Sèvres porcelain painted with views of the palaces of Schönbrunn and the Laxenburg. Marie-Louise was reluctant to yield to confinement, announced by Napoleon's broadsheet, *Le Moniteur*. She still went out for short trips in her carriage and continued to attend balls and shows. She loved the active life, but, feeling ever more "monstrous", even she had to admit that it was becoming impracticable. Napoleon had for the whole of the period of gestation assumed that the child he had so long desired would be a boy. As the moment of truth approached, he feared the Habsburg trend of producing girl firstborns. He had never known such tension.

Marie-Louise's labour pains began on 19th March, shortly after dinner. The ladies of the court ran for towels. The Duchess of Montebello made a short announcement that Marie-Louise would be unable to attend the evening entertainment and gave orders to summon Napoleon's mother, siblings and their spouses. Marie-Louise was installed on the chaise-longue in her bedroom, her dress unbuttoned and replaced with a nightshirt to enable her to breathe more easily in preparation for the birth. Fussing about her were her Lady of Honour, the Duchess de Montebello, her Lady of the Wardrobe, Madame de Luçay, two ladies who had been appointed under-governesses to the child now struggling in the womb, her battalion of maids and all the ladies of the court. Save for the midwives who were laying out their equipment, everyone had changed out of evening dress into ceremonial costumes in anticipation of the birth ceremony. In the adjoining rooms, wine and hot chocolate and other light refreshments were served while courtiers and courtesans gossiped or fell asleep and ministers idled, portfolios flung haphazardly on chairs or tables. Other ministers made small talk in the billiard room. Bonaparte family members and Marie-Louise's uncle, the Grand Duke of Würzburg, representing Marie-Louise's father for the birth, waited in another adjacent room. Unable to bear the tension, Hortense excused herself, accepting the offer of a bed by one of Marie-Louise's attendants.

Napoleon spent most of the night with his wife, sporadically walking up and down the room with her on his arm. He escaped briefly to his family to vent his anxieties and to courtiers gathered in other rooms of the Empress's apartments to give brief progress reports, and to ease his exhaustion, decided to take a bath in the early morning.

Told that delivery was close at hand, Napoleon leapt out of the bath, hastily threw on a dressing gown and dashed down to be with his beloved. Perspiring profusely as contractions vibrated through her, Marie-Louise clung to him in desperation, trying as hard as she could to obey his instruction to breathe deeply. He also inhaled deeply so as to keep his nerve, too overcome by emotion to offer words of comfort. "Be brave, be brave . . ." exhorted the Duchess of Montebello, who sat the other side of her, holding her other hand. As the hours passed, she regaled Marie-Louise with the details of her own four deliveries. "It is always the same, it is always like this . . . soon you will have a healthy baby and then you will see – it is all worth it in the end!"

Dubois, who had delivered most of the Bonaparte babies born in Paris, called for forceps. The baby was presenting itself in the wrong position. The anxious voices of a team of leading doctors, nurses and midwives quivered inauspiciously. "We may have to surrender one life in order to save the other . . . " Dubois whispered anxiously to Napoleon, who was sitting by Marie-Louise's bedside, leaning across her, holding her left hand in his, her knuckles white with the tightness of her grip. Petrified, Marie-Louise screamed in horror: "Must I die for the sake of the child?" A thirteenth delivery had claimed her mother's life. "God spare me!" she pleaded.

THE BIRTH OF AN HEIR, MARCH 1811

"Save the mother! Think only of her and devote all your efforts to her! For God's sake, treat her like a common townswoman of the Rue Saint Denis!" Napoleon ordered Dubois.

After five of the twenty-six minutes of digging and cajoling with the irons, Soon, Napoleon beat a hasty retreat to his washroom. He could not bear the sight of his wife in such agony. He sent a messenger every minute to obtain a commentary. He had felt more at ease in the heat of battle, he later confessed to Marie-Louise. Napoleon was by her side again caressing her, wiping her temples with a soft linen cloth. A minute lifeless form was receiving vigorous slaps from the midwife. One of the nurses dipped his little finger into a small glass of eau-de-vie and inserted his finger into the baby's mouth. The baby, swaddled in warm towels, gave out a little, but unmistakeable, reassuring cry. Napoleon scooped Marie-Louise into his arms and hugged her, his face awash with tears. Exhausted, Marie-Louise collapsed back into her bed and fell asleep.

Hortense later told Marie-Louise that she had bumped into Napoleon as he left Marie-Louise to give orders for the firing of the cannon, twenty-one times for a girl, one hundred and one for a boy, to announce the birth. Hortense regretted that she had not been present. A tearful attendant had woken her to tell her that he feared the worst, that Marie-Louise had been emitting the most atrocious screams. Napoleon could barely breathe, all colour gone from his face. "It's finished. She is spared."

By the time Marie-Louise revived a quarter of an hour later, Napoleon was back standing by the golden cradle presented by the City of Paris. Good wishes and congratulations rained down upon her and her husband. He was weeping in disbelief.

Marie-Louise had feared producing a daughter, which might diminish her standing in her husband's eyes and fall foul of her homeland's expectations. She had written to her father the day following her wedding that she hoped to see him again within the year, by which time she also hoped, with God's help, to have produced a son. She had even asked Dr. Corvisart if there was anything she could do to predetermine a male heir. The Duchess of Montebello had told her not to worry – the whole of Paris spoke with one voice: "We are so used to seeing the Emperor's wishes fulfilled that no-one here doubts that the Empress will be delivered of a son."

And so it was. Marie-Louise felt grateful to have the companionship of the Duchess of Montebello, of whom she was now extremely fond. It seemed to her that she was assiduous in her duties, had been an impeccable wife and citizen, and was endowed with every grace and virtue. She was also an exemplary mother. When Catherine, Queen of Westphalia, had asked on honeymoon whether she still cared for the Duchess, Marie-Louise countered "My dear, I do not change my friends like my chemises! After two months' acquaintance I am quite attached to her!"[6]

As the cannon boomed away, there was a sudden burst of noise from outside. Napoleon ran to the window and drew the curtain a fraction away from the window so that he could see what was happening below. News had travelled fast that night, and by the early hours, everyone knew that the Empress was in labour. Immense crowds of all ages across the social spectrum had converged on the Tuileries gardens. Most were standing in respectful silence well behind the cordon placed along the terrace to prevent ingress through the lower windows. As the first shot of cannon was heard, everyone fell silent, many counting each strike under their breath. At the twenty-first cannon blast there was a sharp intake of breadth. On the twenty-second, hats flew into the air, people danced with joy and shouted loud applause.

> In one second, the great city of Paris was dumbstruck as if by enchantment. The most important business, the most deliriously absorbed lovers, everything was held in suspense, and without the echoing of the cannon, one would have thought oneself in the City of One Hundred Nights . . . then the twenty-second blast, then a huge cry of a million voices resounded in Paris so that the wall of the very palace in which the prince

THE BIRTH OF AN HEIR, MARCH 1811

had just been born shook, as crowds flocked. To the hero a son was born.

For once, Napoleon was awed by the public response, unable to check his tears. Marie-Louise had crowned his dreams. If only time had stood still.

THREE

The firm alliance, May 1812

Basking in his adulation, Marie-Louise was charmed by Napoleon, particularly by his wit and thoughtfulness. She loved the climbing vine installed for her at Compiègne, the miniature views by Isabey he had commissioned for her of Schönbrunn and the Laxenburg. To hear him sing, as he did frequently, in his terrible voice *"Si le roi m'avait donné sa grand'ville!"* made her giggle, and she relished his frequent bursts of laughter, audible from several hundred metres, his presence announced by the scent of cologne with which he patted himself every day after his bath. She loved it when he mimicked characters from the comedies of Beaumarchais and Molière.

Marie-Louise loved the way Napoleon teased her and everyone else. The Empress's lady-in-waiting, Mme Sophie Durand watched and memorised for the sake of her memoirs. Marie-Louise would tell him to leave her alone and go to his room when he came up behind her and pinched her neck. When she lost patience, he would take her in his arms, kiss and worship her until she gave in. Unseen, he would put his hands over the eyes of an unsuspecting victim, usually an uninitiated chambermaid, and tease her. On one occasion, Napoleon entered Marie-Louise's apartments when she was getting dressed. Unwittingly, he stepped on the foot of the lady presiding over her toilette, and instantly let out a loud scream. "What's the matter?" Marie-Louise asked with concern. "Nothing," he replied in a fit of laughter, "I stepped on Madame's foot and cried out in order to prevent her doing so, and as you see, it has worked!" On another occasion, when Napoleon had gone down to Marie-Louise's rooms, he had forgotten his handkerchief. Taking out and inspecting closely the intricate embroidery and lacework of the substitute supplied by his empress, he asked how much it cost. "Eighty to one hundred francs," the lady-in-waiting replied. "If I were a lady-in-waiting, I would steal one of these every day!" The lady-in-waiting retorted, quick as a flash, "It is a jolly good thing that we have more probity than Your Majesty." Peals of laughter followed. "Well done!" Marie-Louise said, "That is exactly what you deserve!" "And how much does the pâté I am eating cost?" "Twelve francs for Your Majesty, and six francs for a Parisian townsman." "That means I am being fleeced!" "No, – it is commonly accepted that a king pays more than his subjects." "I can see I am going to have to put a few things straight . . . this defies comprehension!" Napoleon declared.

Once he caught her with a burner, frying pan and ingredients brought to her so she could make an omelette. Taking over to show her how it should be done, he promptly tossed the omelette out of the frying pan onto the carpet. They had both laughed to the point of tears.[1]

Marie-Louise loved to play rounders, hunt, ride on horseback and to relax with him. Unlike many of her ladies-in-waiting, she had no difficulty keeping up with her husband's exhilarating pace.

Napoleon was good with everyone, charming but firm to his staff, courtiers, friends and family. He particularly loved playing tricks on children, diverting their attention away from the dinner-table and removing their food while they were not looking, or otherwise provoking them. He adored a spirited retort which demonstrated force of personality. Josephine's daughter Hortense and her children often dined with Marie-Louise and Napoleon. He loved to provoke the serious five-year-old Princess Elisa. "I have heard some wonderful things about you," he said to the serious five-year-old Princess Elisa, "so what is this I hear about you doing a wee-wee in your bed last night?" The little girl sat bolt upright in her chair: "Uncle, if you have only silly things to say, I'm off!" Napoleon fell about laughing. On another occasion, he teased her again. She leant over to her governess and whispered so that he could hear her: "Let's go back to

Florence – here I am not appreciated." Marie-Louise enjoyed every moment of her husband's company, each day filled with love and laughter.

Marie-Louise was particularly thrilled when Napoleon announced one afternoon that he was taking her to Dresden to see her family. The main purpose of the trip was not to be pleasure, but a summit meeting with Napoleon's so-called allies in anticipation of hostilities with Russia. War with the Great Bear had seemed probable ever since Napoleon had entered Marie-Louise's apartments in angry mood and removed the marble bust of Emperor Alexander from the piano. Brought up to fear Russia, and particularly its expansion westward which the Ottomans were relied upon to stop, Marie-Louise felt sick at the prospect of a fresh conflagration. Nonetheless, a good hiding from Napoleon, undaunted by the vastness of territory he would have to conquer, would do the Russians no harm at all. They would soon live to regret violating his continental blockade of England. Victory over Russia would give Napoleon and France access to the lucrative trade of the Indies, enabling him to deal a final economic blow to Albion and to devote his energies to her military subjugation.

"The Emperor will take me to Dresden where I will stay for a month or two. He hopes to see you there," Marie-Louise wrote to her father. Emperor Francis would come to Dresden with his wife. He invited her to Prague to see her siblings, aunts and uncles, feeling it too much of an imposition on the King and Queen of Saxony, the Dresden hosts, to receive the Habsburgs *en masse*.

The French Emperor and Empress set out for Dresden in high spirits as soon as the sun rose on a perfect May morning. Napoleon was richer than he had ever been before, and no expense was spared. The party was accompanied by a brilliant suite, a full retinue complete with chamber, table, pantry, kitchen and livery services, and wagons of presents for their hosts along the route and more importantly, his wife's family. Napoleon had also requisitioned the entire company of the Théâtre Français to perform for him.

As instructed by her father and Mme Lazansky, Marie-Louise reposed all confidence in her husband. She did not fear him, as she knew others did. She was sure people in Vienna thought she was subjected to daily tribulations, but it was not true. Instead, the most powerful man in all of Europe went in awe of her, anxious to please her in every respect. One very cold night, Napoleon ordered Mme Rabusson to light a fire in his wife's room. Marie-Louise, hating overnight heating and content with bedpans, immediately countermanded the order. Napoleon departed in a huff. From then on, Marie-Louise sent him back to his room after sexual intimacy so that he would not disturb her during the night. As a young girl, Marie-Louise had spent her days receiving instruction in languages, art, history (from a peculiarly Habsburg perspective) and geography. Few women in Europe enjoyed anything approaching the breadth of an Austrian imperial education, which was very advanced by the standards of the day. By her early teens, she spoke French, German, Czech and Hungarian fluently and had sufficient knowledge of Greek, Latin and English to be able to read the classics in those languages. Napoleon could not but have been impressed by the fact that she could communicate with far more of his subjects than he could. "Her tastes were simple, her mind cultivated ... Calm, reflective, good-hearted and sensitive, though not demonstrative, she had all agreeable qualities."[2] Napoleon adored her.

Fearful of contracting the stomach cancer from which his father had died, before Marie-Louise's advent, Napoleon had eaten only minuscule amounts of food with drops of wine, disdaining the delicacies with which his table was frequently laden. He preferred the leaner dishes, grilled breast of lamb, lamb cutlets, roast chicken, lentil or haricot beans. Preoccupied by his work, his breakfast would wait often for several hours. He would down his food at speed and leave the table without heed to his companions, demanding his *demitasse* of coffee, having completely forgotten he had already drunk it. Marie-Louise saw none of this. Enamoured by his bride, the former power-house languished over meals, indulging in everything, soup, beef, cheese and desserts, particularly the *viennoiserie* prepared each day by the pastry chef she had installed in the Tuileries. After two years of marriage, the weight he had put on since their first encounter, often a sign of marital contentment, was visible in his face and belly. He would sit at table for as long as Marie-Louise was eating, watching her, never becoming impatient. She took her time. Often, he sent staff to tell couriers who had arrived with dispatches for him, and ministers or family members who wanted him, to wait. He often turned up to meetings he had convened two hours after everyone else had assembled. At Versailles, he rowed his empress down the Grand Canal in a gondola named after her as water fountains cascaded along its length, and ambled in the extensive gardens alongside their son in a calèche drawn by goats. He attended reluctantly and only after a prolonged post-prandial walk to his duties, which he lately found tedious, and would return to take tea, cakes, compotes and fruits, tarrying with his beloved long after tea was over. Then he would return to her for a plentiful dinner, and billiards, at which she would beat him by a mile. When he cheated, she would reprimand him. Concerned not to come across as too serious, Napoleon wanted to be as much lover as husband. Marie-Louise heard how there were many things that he had sworn he would never do for anyone, and now did for her without a second thought. He was, from many perspectives, the perfect husband.

Everyone thought it was only a matter of time before his enthusiasm abated. They were wrong. Since the birth of their son, with whom he was besotted, the French Emperor's attentions to Marie-Louise were even more assiduous. He showed none of the nerves she felt in handling the newborn. Brought up by ajas, she had been formally presented to her parents before dinner. No etiquette stood between Napoleon and his son. Mother rejoiced as the adoring father held the King of Rome in his arms, teasing and tickling him, bouncing him on his knee in his study, in the nursery, at table or bathing. Napoleon loved nothing more than to lie on the floor and let the toddler crawl and climb all over him and would continue to do so while ministers tried to converse with their ruler about matters of state. He loved to hold his child aloft in front of the mirror and to make funny faces, provoking tears and laughter, or to dangle his son's fingers in sauces at the dining table and let him smear it all over his father's face. The imperial couple loved to relax under the chestnut trees on the lawns of the Tuileries Palace, the French emperor throwing his darling up and down on his lap, tickling him and pinching his nose. Above all, he loved to show off his son to his Guard of Honour.

For Marie-Louise's saint's day, 25 August, Napoleon had organised the most extravagant party ever given by him. Once more, he paraded Marie-Louise on his arm before the nobility of France on a cloudless summer's day. The whole of Paris seemed to be in Versailles vying for oxygen. Festooned in lamps of different colours, the Grand Trianon and gardens of Versailles were resplendent. Marie-Louise chatted amiably with some of the six hundred bejewelled young women gathered in the long gallery. One could hardly believe she had only been in France for little over fifteen months. Napoleon's secretary, Méneval, considered the event one of the most splendid and agreeable of all festivities. He described the staging of Alissan de Chazet's play, *Le Jardinier de Schönbrunn*, at the restored theatre, the ballet and cantatas devised by court composer Paër, against the backdrop of gleaming facades, lakes, islands and parkland, as Napoleon, hat in hand, strolled with Marie-Louise on his arm, followed by members of the court among the various attractions dotted over the gardens. Affectionately demonstrative to his bride, he seemed happy. Whenever he found Marie-Louise serious, he would try to amuse her with playful banter or foil her reserve with spontaneous, warm hugs and kisses. Méneval thought the familiarity, consideration and deference Napoleon showed towards her noble. The couple enjoyed a magnificent dinner in the *Grande galerie*, only retiring to bed at one o'clock in the morning.

Over the course of the journey from Paris to Dresden, the horses galloped relentlessly along streets lined with enthusiastic crowds waving the tricolour flag and throwing flowers in their path. Along the way, Napoleon ordered stops to inspect troops and fortifications. Local rulers and their entourages joined the party at Munich, Aschaffenbourg and Freibourg. Tried by heat and bad roads, the convoy finally reached Dresden at ten o'clock in the evening, a week after leaving Paris.

To Marie-Louise's disappointment, Napoleon considered it inappropriate for his exalted wife to go out to greet the parents she had not seen for over two years. He wished to receive, embrace and converse with them as family for a good quarter of an hour to inquire after their health and journey before inviting his wife to join them. Marie-Louise made her entrance in grand gala dress covered in precious gems, accompanied by her full retinue. Marie-Louise had longed for this moment, having missed her family desperately, but as her dearest Papa and Mama stood before her unaccompanied by any retinue, she felt awkward and embarrassed by the presence of so many French spectators. Empress Marie-Ludovica came to her rescue, facilitating conversation.

A sumptuous feast was held in the Queen of Saxony's apartments. Marie-Louise was overjoyed as her parents and husband engaged with ease and affection, exchanging details of Habsburg and Bonaparte family life. Marie-Louise adored the man her father had chosen for her and wanted her family to love him as she did.

It seemed to the French Empress that everyone was captivated by her emperor. The company assembled in Dresden all appeared charmed as he made solicitous enquiries and responded with warmth and good humour to theirs. Socially, he was both masterful and deferential, far from the *parvenu* the world beyond France believed him to be. Napoleon was particularly respectful to his mother-in-law. Every day, everyone spent several hours standing, and Marie-Ludovica was far too proud to accept chairs offered. The pretty but consumptive empress had great difficulty making her way along the long corridors and across the immense rooms of the royal palace, and was forced to succumb to a sedan chair. Napoleon walked beside her smiling benevolently stopping from time to time to whisper to her. Marie-Ludovica teased him, "Are you trying to woo me?" The strains on her physique of the on-going receptions, spectacles, concerts and visits were exacerbated by her deteriorating hearing.

No longer the adolescent archduchess, Marie-Louise appeared before her family with a new-found confidence, radiant in her husband's aura. Here she could prove to her Austrian family her devotion to him and to the Franco-Austrian alliance of which she was the central symbol. The following evening, a throng of kings and princes mingled with courtiers coming to pay their respects to Napoleon at his *levée* in the grand apartments of the Dresden castle commandeered for his visit. Many more presented themselves in the following days. Marie-Louise watched from her throne as the rulers of Württemburg, of Baden, of Saxe-Weimar, of Saxe-Coburg, of Nassau, of Westphalia and Würzburg fell on bended knee and lowered their heads, taking Napoleon's gloved imperial hand extended towards them. Each swore fealty to her husband and performed the *baise-main*. Their political alliance seemed steadfast, impregnable.

When free to talk in confidence, the former archduchess said how far superior her life in Paris and France was than it had been in her former homeland. She told Marie-Ludovica, who was struck by the transformation in her stepdaughter, that she believed only in Paris did people really know how to dress, confessing to an antipathy for anything Austrian in clothes. The only glaring omission had been the absence of pantaloons that she had rectified by ordering them in from Austria and introducing them to the French. She presented Marie-Ludovica to Mme de Luçay who would lay out the outfits for day, evening and night which her mistress had selected each morning by marking the exhaustive inventory of her wardrobe with a pin. Marie-Louise also introduced her stepmother to her hairdresser, M. Duplan, who had been induced to give up all other clients to serve her and her entourage exclusively for the fantastical salary of twelve thousand francs and a bonus of the same, plus a guaranteed pension of six thousand francs a year. Marie-Louise thought the investment indispensible. She was not acquainted with most of her suppliers, who came only in her absence, providing drawings and models for her approval. She told Marie-Ludovica of the court painters and sculptors for whom she sat, Isabey, Prud'hon and Canova. Taking the Austrian Empress to her rooms, Marie-Louise ran around opening trunks, jewellery, boxes, cupboards, wardrobes and drawers, showing her the vast range of clothes she had brought with her, the pearls and diamonds which Napoleon insisted she wear while with her family, and invited her to help herself. Marie-Ludovica did not hesitate to avail herself of the opportunity. Meanwhile, the French Empress's ladies-in-waiting thought they detected a hint of jealousy.

Marie-Louise declined most of the daily invitations by her parents to join them on tours of Dresden or to go shopping. She would be able to spend time with them in Prague. She preferred to be with Napoleon, from whom she would shortly have to part. To compensate, Marie-Louise and Marie-Ludovica exchanged daily letters running to several pages. Her stepmother's powerful intellect and sharp observations, which even the great Goethe held in awe, were invaluable. Marie-Ludovica's sensitive advice, her little *bons mots*, were so generously and dispassionately given to assist Marie-Louise in her role as fledgling French empress that she could be forgiven for being convinced of her stepmother's good intentions.

As far as Marie-Louise knew, and all the evidence suggested, Austria and France were firmly united. Emperor Francis, reluctant to lead the army in person, had handed over an auxiliary corps of the Austrian army to Napoleon to do as he wished. In exchange, Napoleon had promised him strategically valuable territories in the Balkans, and the restoration of the Illyrian provinces seized from him in conquest. Napoleon told her how impressed by her father's wisdom he had been and that he had much to learn from him. Both father and husband told Marie-Louise independently and confidentially that they were pleased with their time together and appreciated the other's talents. They had talked long and hard and each had expressed himself with the greatest candour, engendering a deep sense of trust which promised fertile cooperation.

As May drew to a close in glorious warm weather, Marie-Louise and Napoleon attended Mass with the Habsburg family. Napoleon did not go to bed after dinner, planning to set out to inspect troops amassed on the Vistula River at three o'clock the following morning. Marie-Louise's tears in anticipation and following his departure were enough to convince even the sceptical that she loved Napoleon sincerely. Pending his departure, postponed to four thirty in the morning, he paced up and down restlessly, embracing her tenderly, showering her with kisses, promising to return to her very soon. She did not fear for her husband's personal safety but she did not like to contemplate the war or its impact, or Napoleon's indefinite absence. Save for Napoleon's short trip to the island of Walcheren, he and Marie-Louise had barely spent a night apart since their wedding two years earlier. An hour and a half after Napoleon had gone, Marie-Louise wrote to Mme de Luçay: "You know me sufficiently well to understand how sad and unhappy I am."[3] She feared she would be miserable until Napoleon's return, and that she would be incapable of tolerating any extended absence. "May God preserve you from such a separation!" Nothing could console her for his absence and the absence of his caresses, not even the presence of the family she had so longed to see. Upon her return to Paris after her sojourn in Prague, she commissioned a painting by Gérard of the King of Rome to remind her beloved what awaited him at home. She wrote back to Napoleon following the official reports in Paris from the Russian front and news from her aunt, Marie-Thérèse, Queen of Saschen. "Nothing has happened to our armies apart from *bagatelles*, and the Russians are still retreating! What joy! If only peace could be obtained by retreating and without a single drop of blood shed!"[4] Her father tried to reassure her – the Russians must have lost their heads at St Petersburg to wish to measure themselves against a power as great as France, at least one hundred thousand men stronger.

FOUR

Napoleon Indomitable, December 1812

From the moment Napoleon left Marie-Louise in Dresden, he wrote daily loving letters which fortified her. He told her not to allow herself to become morose, to keep cheerful and to present a happy exterior. He would keep every promise ever made to her. "You know how much I love you, how important it is to me that I know you to be well and at peace."[1] He instructed her to reward officers conveying messages to her with diamond rings, the value of which was to be commensurate with the news they carried. Her letters to him arrived erratically, three or more letters arriving together after several days of drought. "Two days without word from you test my endurance. Love well he who loves you so much."[2] Marie-Louise wept to read "Addio, mio dolce amore." What could be more natural for a woman who was carrying her husband's second baby? He heard that she was vomiting. It was true. Marie-Louise could not contain her joy, and she was sure that Napoleon must feel the same, despite the doctor's warning after her first pregnancy that it might be dangerous for her to attempt to have another baby. When she was in Prague, Napoleon sent her instructions. "Heap your father with compliments. Tell the Empress that I kneel at her feet. Tell her how much I wish to please her at every opportunity . . . heap your sisters with compliments – I would have loved to have seen Leopoldine and all your brothers and sisters whom I love because I love you."[3] These outpourings convinced Marie-Louise that her husband was sincerely fond of her family and that her marriage was growing stronger by the day.

Napoleon sent his wife orders as to the distribution of gifts for her host, Prince Clary, and his household.

It is important to be generous and to give much in every sense. I have given directions for the dispatch of gifts for Empress Marie-Ludovica's ladies-in-waiting, and for Mme Lazansky who should receive fifty thousand livres. You must make her a similar gift so that she leaves with diamonds worth one hundred thousand livres. One should never give gold snuff-boxes which is in poor taste. You may give rings with your initials to a value of one thousand two hundred livres, two thousand livres, three thousand livres and six thousand livres. Give large donations to those who have served you in the past and your former teachers. Be agreeable to your father and to all your family. Find out whether there are any ancient customs which sovereigns should respect when they pass through Prague. Give a collection of books and sketches from my library to the university which will cost nothing but be very acceptable to them. See what you can give the city of Prague as a souvenir of your visit. Tell me that you have finally got rid of that nasty cold.

Marie-Louise read every word of Napoleon's letters carefully, learning each day how a caring sovereign spared no attention to detail. And his love of France and the well-being of its people were his guiding light. "Never allow anyone to say in front of you anything equivocal about France or politics."[4] Marie-Louise regretted accusing him of being lazy when a few days passed without his letter. When her pregnancy miscarried, he commiserated. "It is with pain that I see that for which I had hoped will not take place. We will have to postpone this to the autumn . . . I seal your beautiful lips with a tender kiss."[5] "You know how much I love you, I want to have you by my side; the habit of seeing you and spending my life with you is indeed very sweet."[6] He told her to take night walks to combat her insomnia. His letters suggested that his march towards Moscow was uneventful, a string of inspection of troops.

Marie-Louise left Prague feeling deeply saddened. Napoleon vetoed her wish to travel incognito in order to avoid the heavy load of scheduled public appearances. Once more, she feared it would be a long time before she saw her family again. She would see her father in Paris sooner than she knew.

Marie-Louise had longed to return to the child, fast becoming an adorable toddler, who alone could provide small consolation for the absence of his father. But the homecoming was not what she had anticipated. Marie-Louise confessed to her sister-in-law Catherine that she could not boast at the reception she had received from her son. He had cried and fought against her when she had tried to take him in her arms. He stubbornly refused to say anything other than Papa. Marie-Louise found herself eclipsed by her son's zealous governess who coveted the King of Rome as if he were her own and took full advantage of his behaviour towards his mother. There was no kindness or attention spared in the upbringing of her charge. Unlike the Duchess of Montebello, she came from an illustrious family, the old nobility. Madame de Montesquiou was well-educated, polite, pious, enlightened and assiduous in the performance of her duties. Knowing that Napoleon considered her irreplaceable. Consequently, Marie-Louise never complained at the lack of access granted her to her son and listened quietly from the ante-room as Mme de Montesquiou chanted prayers she was teaching him to recite day and night: "May God inspire Papa to make peace for the house of France and us all." From Gloubokoé, Napoleon wrote wanting to know what effect seeing her son again had had on Marie-Louise, whether he had begun to talk or to walk, whether she was happy with his progress. "The Parisians must be pleased to see you!"[7] Marie-Louise said nothing of her pain. At least he sympathised with her migraines, colds, stomach and rheumatic pains, colics and cramps with which she seemed to be beset since giving birth. Corvisart, the imperial physician, ignored her complaints, and treated her as a hypochondriac.

"Medicine is very fashionable," Corvisart liked to boast privately.

It has to be. It is the amusement of the idle and unoccupied who, not knowing what to do with their time, spend it trying to preserve it. Were they to have had the misfortune to be born immortal, they would be the most miserable of all beings. A life which they would have no fear of losing would not be for them at any price. These people have to have doctors who threaten to flatter them, and give them each day the only pleasure to which they are susceptible – that of not being dead!

In the interminable days alone, Marie-Louise roamed around the large rooms of the palaces of Compiègne and Saint-Cloud which previously echoed with the voices of her husband, his marshalls and the palace staff, and buzzed with the frenetic energy he exuded. In his absence, furniture sat unused, and the palace staff seemed less in evidence, less needed. Before his departure, Napoleon had ordered reinstatement of the old Imperial Code of Etiquette of the Palace by which Marie-Louise was obliged to have a large retinue in attendance whenever she went out, even to ride or walk. Napoleon had assumed that Marie-Louise had been brought up under strictest surveillance, and insisted that she never be left alone. From the moment she came to France, he had never allowed anyone access to her without prior written authorisation, and a red silk uniformed maid being present. He even applied the restriction to himself, requesting permission of her maid to visit her, and was angry when an attendant left the room for an instant to give orders to a servant. When the French Empress went out, her carriage was always accompanied by an equerry and a page on horseback, one to the right, the other to the left. Wherever she went, one of her ladies acted as her reader and writer. Wherever she slept, such a lady slept outside her room. Count Metternich, whom Marie-Louise had never liked but who was an important conduit for public relations, was the only man granted a private audience with his bride by Napoleon shortly after her arrival on French soil, in order to send the message back to Vienna that she was happily married. The former Austrian archduchess missed the excursions she had taken with Countess Colloredo, her governess in Vienna, when she used to wander in the meadows around Schönbrunn and pick flowers. These simple pleasures were clearly a thing of the past. As time wore on, Marie-Louise became increasingly reclusive, venturing out only when absolutely essential. The familial intimacy she enjoyed with her Habsburg clan was lacking in the Bonaparte foyer. To Marie-Louise's surprise, her closest friend and support in France turned out to be Napoleon's stepdaughter by Josephine, Queen Hortense, who often invited Marie-Louise to dinner at her home, the Palace of St Leu.

In her imperial residences, Marie-Louise enjoyed the pastimes she had learnt in Vienna, playing the piano and harp daily, embroidering and taking drawing and painting lessons. She developed an interest in arboriculture, botany, wildlife and ornithology, keeping the birdseller in modest commission. She gave orders to Mme de Luçay to ensure that her apartments were constantly provided with the rarest flowers, and sporadically sent instructions directly to the florists herself, paying for them from her own private purse. The freshness, fragrance and incomparable beauty of flowers lifted her spirits.

Marie-Louise was shocked by the coarse language of her art teacher appointed at Napoleon's behest by Denon, Napoleon's Director General of Museums. Prud'hon had distinguished himself painting many portraits and allegorical paintings of the Bonaparte family and designing the interiors of important public buildings and monuments. However, despite his fertile imagination and excellence at everything, Marie-Louise found his lessons dull. She found ungracious his pedantry in pointing out her every minute mistake after she had laboured for hours over a Virgin by Guido or Innocence by Greuze. For her, these lessons provided a distraction and a means of whiling away the hours of virtual imprisonment. She intended to have her husband replace him as soon as he returned home.

With Napoleon, Marie-Louise loved to indulge in confectionery, buying in large quantities of sweets and chocolate from the leading *chocolatiers*, savouring exotic teas and hot chocolate, ordering Viennese cakes. She had so many tea services, it was impossible to use all of them. In Napoleon's absence, these indulgences lost their appeal.

Marie-Louise cared little for the scandal which reached her involving many of the ladies at court. She tried, whenever possible, to avoid passing through the salon where they descended, entering the Duchess of Montebello's room in the morning through a clothes closet. She noticed that the ladies-in-waiting were becoming colder towards her and could feel their scorn. No matter: it freed her from having to spend more time with them.

As Marie-Louise's daily commitments reduced, so her entourage took the opportunity to request leave or plead sickness. The Duchess of Montebello was regularly ill, and Mme de Luçay often rushed off to attend to her husband. When the Duchess of Montebello was away, whole days passed during which Marie-Louise found herself alone, without the warmth of human contact, without a friend with whom she could take meals, share walks, share life's daily tribulations. Precluded either by protocol or discernment from conversing with her most intimate acquaintances, she began to realize that she was becoming isolated. She tried to stave off the gloom of unaccompanied nights by playing patience and solitaire. Napoleon asked in his letters that she write letting him know what people were talking about in Paris, but in truth, she really could not say. She received news neither from the guests who Napoleon had her invite in the evenings to alleviate her loneliness, nor from her Austrian family whose communications were confined to the banal.

Napoleon had promised that his Russian campaign would be over in three months. He would crush the Russians at the first encounter between the Niemen and Duna rivers at Vilna or Vitebsk. But time and his Russian Campaign dragged on. Marie-Louise received bulletins from Méneval, one of Napoleon's private secretaries. His reports informed her that Napoleon's affairs were going well. At Vilna, a beautiful city of forty thousand souls, the Russian army was outmanoeuvred. Napoleon stayed in a charming little house which, seemingly, Tsar Alexander had just vacated to avoid Napoleon's advance. As storms and torrential rain alternated with baking hot days, Napoleon was in high spirits, approving Marie-Louise's list of waiting staff for the following trimester. "You never say anything about the Duchess [of Montebello] Is she well? You must never pay any attention to Paris gossip."[8] Marie-Louise kept silent, not liking to confess to him that she too had found the duchess wanting in the performance of duty.

Marie-Louise delighted in the King of Rome's every movement. He seemed to her exceptional and provided light relief as Marie-Louise laboured under the heavy burden of solitude. Every day, morning, noon and night, she bestowed kisses on his forehead on Napoleon's behalf. She wrote to her husband telling him his son was a wonderful child, extremely strong. He never walked, but ran without assistance everywhere – rather like his father. He had already fifteen teeth, but so far he seemed not to want to talk.

In the middle of August, Marie-Louise was pleased to hear of Napoleon's victory at Smolensk in blistering heat, if saddened that three thousand of the enemy had perished and nine thousand had been wounded. How she hated war! She was proud of the Austrian demonstration of commitment: General Schwarzenberg had beaten Russians two hundred leagues from Smolensk, Napoleon reported. At Napoleon's request, Marie-Louise sat for portraits commissioned from the brothers Gérard and Robert Lefèvre. She hoped he would be pleased with the present she had sent him, a portrait by Isabey of their son, which she had dispatched to the front. She had a map of Russia in one of the books she had studied as a young girl, and she followed Napoleon's trajectory as he moved eastwards. Every day, he seemed to move further and further away. Napoleon complained of the discomfort of the heat and dust. She longed for him to be back in the mild Paris summer. As Napoleon approached Moscow, the granaries were full and the fields were carpeted in vegetables. His soldiers were well armed and well fed. Napoleon's optimism infected Marie-Louise. To cap it all, Gérard's large portrait of the King of Rome arrived. "It's a masterpiece. Thank you so much for your care. It is beautiful like you . . ."[9]

Next came news of another triumph over the Russians, this one more costly than the previous, but still a victory for all that. Napoleon gave brief account of French fatalities, specifying the few nobles known to Marie-Louise. Within sight of Moscow, Napoleon seemed buoyant. Marie-Louise was not. She was in such distress and felt so isolated that she turned through correspondence to those to whom she could talk without fear of reproach, her father and her mother-in-law, bemoaning how her lack of courage increased her anxiety.

Consoling herself with memories at the Trianon in late summer, Marie-Louise, together with Hortense, rejoiced at the victorious march of the Grande Armée into Moscow. Napoleon had taken a city as large as Paris, with one thousand six hundred steeples and over a thousand beautiful palaces, many of which were even more luxuriously furnished and appointed than the best in Paris. Even the army barracks and hospitals were magnificent, built in the French style. It seemed the nobility had fled, taking with them the traders who supplied the needs of their daily lives. Only the common people remained. The enemy had withdrawn, Napoleon wrote with satisfaction.

For little more than forty-eight hours, Marie-Louise began to dream of accompanying Napoleon to Moscow to see for herself its beauty and prosperity. Her musings were dashed when she received Napoleon's letter telling her of the vengeful fires started by the governor of the city who had given orders for the city to be torched. For four days the fire consumed the magnificence which Napoleon had admired a few days earlier. Vengeance was so ruthless that even the pumps to put out the fires had been taken away or destroyed, so there was little hope of combating the flames. All that could be done was to wait until they burnt out. Napoleon bemoaned Russian brutality and primitive behaviour, though Marie-Louise would soon discover if she had not already, that he was no stranger to torching the villages of his opponents. In the chaos, the new homeless wandered the streets destitute and pillaging flourished. Marie-Louise reeled in shock that anyone would wreak such devastation on their own homeland, but was heartened to hear that the French army had ample food, brandy and lodgings.

Napoleon wrote that things were going as planned, despite the setbacks. The arsonists responsible for the fires had been put before a firing squad. Everything was fine. He gave Marie-Louise one word of caution: she must not pay any heed to gossip regarding Russia in Paris. Marie-Louise thought nothing of it, used to avoiding idle prattle. Napoleon reported that the weather had become cooler, pleasantly warm. His letters, less frequent, remained positive, always solicitous of Marie-Louise's and her son's health, encouraging her to go out, to go to the theatre and the opera for which she had lately little appetite. "You are perfect," he wrote.[10] He always signed off telling her to give kisses to his son for him and affirming his undying love for her.

Just when Marie-Louise expected notification of Napoleon's return to Paris now that he seemed to have achieved his objective, he wrote to tell her that he was abandoning Moscow to withdraw to winter accommodation outside the city. There had been a light snowfall, he wrote, but he had seen nothing of the hostile climate he had been led to expect. "The weather continues to be superb like in Paris, a beautiful sunshine and not at all cold."[11] He told her she had nothing to worry about. He was leaving Moscow on schedule, he said, pursuing the plan to move westward, towards France. If he was unable to return to Paris that winter, he would send for her to join him in Poland.

Marie-Louise took comfort that Napoleon had finally subdued Russia though it had taken far longer than she had expected. She had spent many days over the course of his absence celebrating Masses to give thanks for the prevalence of his arms in his numerous glorious battles and she wanted him home. But he did not appear. Instead, she received constant nudges from Napoleon to write more often to her father. "Send him special couriers to get him to reinforce Schwarzenberg's corps so that he can earn honour."[12] She supposed her father and husband to share the same outlook as regards Russia and that she had only to do as Napoleon asked and her father would oblige. Two weeks later, Napoleon asked her to beg her father to think of Schwarzenberg and to have him supported by troops from Galicia. Marie-Louise thought her father remiss in leaving a man as important as Schwarzenberg exposed to danger. It must have been an oversight. Napoleon rarely mentioned battles – perhaps there was very little to do for the time being. Napoleon told her to see if her father might like to come and join her in Poland. The proposal that Marie-Louise and Emperor Francis should get together for a family tête-à-tête was further evidence to Marie-Louise that Russia had been subdued and Europe was tranquil enough for sovereigns to travel. But as November wore on, Marie-Louise began to believe that Napoleon had little intention of returning to her, and she berated him. He protested: how could she doubt him, knowing how much he loved her?

    Marie-Louise remarked that Méneval's army bulletins seemed to have dried up, and, worryingly, Napoleon's letters, speaking of the pleasure of marching in relatively mild temperatures under a glorious sun, became far less frequent. It was hardly comforting to learn that French communications had been intercepted by Cossacks. Things at home in Paris were unsettling too. One morning in late October, Marie-Louise received a note from Archchancellor Cambacérès to inform her that a riot of brigands had taken place in Paris during the previous night. It was in fact a daring attempted coup by Malet, a long-time opponent of Napoleon and others aiming to overthrow him. The conspirators spread a rumour that Napoleon had died in Russia and provided forged 'proof' which convinced several senior officials. Marie-Louise, unaware of the serious nature of Malet's initiative, was surprised at the terror it had provoked. The three conspirators were executed by firing squad a few days later. "They were brigands. What harm could they have done us?" General Malet, the madman, had been overpowered and shot. It all seemed to Marie-Louise a storm in a teacup. She had no idea it was far from it.

Napoleon wrote saying he counted on her character and courage to be able to bear further communication breakdowns. "Write fairly frequently to your father, I beg you. If you will come to Poland, where do you think your father would like to come to see you for a few days?"[13] But then, "Be gay and contented. Your wishes will be fulfilled earlier than you think . . . never doubt the affectionate feelings of your faithful husband."[14]

On the evening of 18 December 1812, Marie-Louise retired, miserable and suffering. It had been six months since she had last seen Napoleon. She had begun to wonder if she would ever see him again. She heard a noise at her door, and leapt out of bed. The lady-in-waiting who held watch outside her room refused admittance to the apparent stranger wrapped in a heavy fur coat who tried to force his way past her. Napoleon ran towards Marie-Louise and enveloped her in his arms. Marie-Louise nestled in his embrace, sobbing with joy. It would never have entered her mind that the panic spread by Malet's highly damaging machinations had prompted her husband's speedy return. To celebrate the new year of 1813 and the recent triumphs, Napoleon ordered constant celebrations and parties at court. France rallied to him, moving Marie-Louise to tears. This notwithstanding, she noted that not everyone was in the mood for jollity. But she was reunited with her love and that seemed the only thing which truly mattered.

FIVE

Marie-Louise, Regent of France 1813

Now there came a second separation, more painful than the first. On 15 April 1813, Napoleon set out after a blissful week with Marie-Louise, for Mainz, travelling via Metz, to carry out inspections of fortifications and troops, and to bring an end to war which he had been compelled to declare on Russia and Prussia a few weeks earlier, so he said. There were certain dissident elements which he wished to quell along the way, and this would take an unpredictable amount of time. He was in ebullient mood and proud that he would be forcing the enemy to a lasting peace.

In anticipation of his absence, Napoleon appointed Marie-Louise as Regent of France, bestowing upon her powers to govern in his absence. This awesome responsibility was tempered by Napoleon's explicit written directions telling her exactly whom to summon and what to say to achieve his objectives. He had left instructions with his ministers Cambacérès, Champagny and his private secretary Méneval (who had spent the past ten years deciphering Napoleon's hieroglyphs, as the Duchess d'Abrantes was wont to call his hand-writing), so that all Marie-Louise's job entailed was to preside over meetings of the Council of State once a month and to appear at all public ceremonies demanding the head of state. He appointed, Méneval, recuperating from post traumatic stress from the Russian Campaign, to look after the Empress. Napoleon hired a substantial house close to the Palace of Saint Cloud for the use of Méneval's family and included Méneval and his wife in Marie-Louise's daily soirées. Napoleon provided Marie-Louise with speeches he had written for her to deliver and gave her guidance as to how she should manage thorny issues and personalities. He sent regular instructions to both Marie-Louise and his ministers from abroad, sending news from the army for Archchancellor Cambacérès to insert in the official newspaper, *Le Moniteur,* with careful stipulations as to the timing of publication. He directed that prayers should be recited for battle and for fallen soldiers, though he warned praying for each and every battle would be excessive, undermining particularly important encounters. Marie-Louise's official life continued, just as Napoleon dictated.

Napoleon boasted to Emperor Francis that Marie-Louise had become his prime minister. Marie-Louise was sure her father would be impressed at this further proof of Napoleon's love for her and of his commitment to the Franco-Austrian alliance, placing an Austrian princess at the helm of his government.

"You must treat this decision by your husband as the greatest and most flattering proof of confidence in you! But if destiny demands it, follow the example of your ancestors, follow the advice of your already rather old father who possesses a certain experience in matters of government." Her father told her.

> Seek above all happiness in the love of the people entrusted to you, by guaranteeing them tranquillity at home and abroad. By this love you will safeguard the rights of your son and will guarantee him the heritage which his father has created and will bequeath to him. My only and unique desire for the time being is this tranquillity and that of being able to discard, as far as possible, everything which might expose your husband to danger and place you in this miserable situation of which I have just spoken. Assure him of my friendship and my gratitude for the confidence which he has placed in you.[1]

Marie-Louise intended to follow his advice. Sadly, the maintenance of tranquillity was not in her hands.

Napoleon's ministers constantly reassured the Empress that Austria's intentions towards France were peaceful and friendly and she was reassured by some of her courtiers that they were friends of Austria. Napoleon told her to take advantage of the diversions offered by Paris, to be cheerful and courageous. Marie-Louise dreaded another long absence. She retired to Saint Cloud where she could avoid the Tuileries court which she found so oppressive. Week in week out, unfamiliar faces came before her. After three years, she still had difficulty with grades, uniforms and ranks, and found them all confusing. It was a relief not to have to hold these tiresome receptions. She was miserable that she was still not pregnant; she confessed that she envied her childhood friend, Victoria de Crenneville who was with child again. Countess Lazansky hoped that Marie-Louise would soon conceive a second son. Marie-Louise felt all eyes were upon her, yet without Napoleon, there was no chance of conceiving. She read as much as she could, a few novels, but generally weighty historical tomes, travelogues and memoirs. She read the *Moniteur* avidly and considered herself well informed.

Napoleon continued to encourage Marie-Louise to correspond regularly with her father, whom he called "Papa Francis" in conversation with her. Marie-Louise assured her father that Napoleon loved him, a love which had deepened at their meeting in Dresden. She was distressed when her letters to him frequently went unanswered. She loved the titbits of family news, updates on everyone's wellbeing, on Marie-Ludovica's health, hearing about her siblings the archdukes and archduchesses, hearing about their travels. It seemed to her that Emperor Francis must have been pleased with Napoleon's triumph in Russia and that he must be awaiting news of Napoleon's further successes. In Napoleon's second letter to her from Mainz, he urged her to write to her father every eight days to give him details of military manoeuvres of the French army. She sensed that this openness with regard to highly sensitive information regarding national security was further evidence that a deep trust existed between the two men. Her father had often repeated his assurance to her and Napoleon when in Dresden that the Bonaparte-Habsburg marriage had changed the face of things in Europe and that blood ties leant a special character to any proposed action. Napoleon had continued sending presents, including a full porcelain dinner service decorated with scenes of their various palaces, to her family and Metternich in Vienna, and encouraged Marie-Louise to do the same.

Marie-Louise knew that any war in central Europe could not fail to touch on her father's territories. She also knew that Austria could ill afford the devastation of another war. Just before Napoleon's departure, Marie-Louise sent a letter to her father:

> I hope to receive news from you soon. It is so long since I have had any that I am beginning to feel concerned ... Thought of war would be terrible for me due to the terrible consequences which would ensue for you ... May God grant that we will soon have a lasting peace and that you will always accord me your good grace in the same way that the Emperor gives you his friendship.

In the spring of 1813, there seemed to be nothing of any consequence to report. Napoleon wrote that he had defeated a regiment of Prussian hussars and taken about fifty or so men prisoner, including an aide-de-camp of the leading Prussian general, Blücher, and that there had been minor skirmishes between the Elbe and Weser rivers. General Souham had overwhelmed a Russian division of five or six thousand men and killed many of them outside the town of Weissenfels. One of the fatalities was Bessières, who had welcomed Marie-Louise onto French soil and of whom she had grown fond. She went with a heavy heart to comfort his widow. These minor brushes seemed hardly worth mentioning to her father. Marie-Louise exulted in Napoleon's continuing protestations of love: "Love me, for you know how much I love you."[2] He feared that his son had forgotten him, and begged Marie-Louise to give his little king two kisses for him. "You must have heard from Vienna – there are still couriers," he continued casually, before letting her know that he was thinking of heading for Erfurt the following day.

The letter Marie-Louise received from Vienna was quite different in tone to previous letters. She immediately passed its contents to her husband. Napoleon wrote back by return.

> I am surprised that Papa Francis says that peace depends on me. For four months he has been unable to obtain any reply [to me] and Russia have only lately finally agreed to open negotiations. Write to him in these terms. Tell him that it is wrong to suggest that I do not want peace, when they have not even consented to negotiations. If they wish to impose conditions upon me without negotiation and force my capitulation, they are wide of the mark. Tell him that such a demand would only lead to war. If they want peace, they must open negotiations. Indeed, I told him three months ago I was ready to talk and I have had no response. Let him see that this country will not allow itself to be maltreated or to have shameful conditions imposed upon it by Russia or by England. Let him see that I have right now a million men under arms and I can have as many as I want, if the French find out that we are to be sacrificed to the anger of the English. Have your letter delivered by the Austrians so that there can be no doubt as to its source.[3]

Marie-Louise's conviction that all was well between Napoleon and her father was quickly dispelled by a further succession of letters. Napoleon, still in Mainz, pleaded, "I beg you to write to Papa Francis telling him not to allow himself to be led astray by others."[4] Another letter two days later: "Write to Papa Francis telling him not to allow himself to be misled by the hatred which his wife bears us. This will lead to dire consequences for him and create much misery."[5]

Marie-Louise had known all along that Marie-Ludovica was no friend of Napoleon, ever since Napoleon had evicted her family from the Italian dukedoms of Este, their family seat. Marie-Ludovica had attributed to Napoleon not only her family's exile but also the premature death of her father, who had never recovered from the humiliation. Marie-Ludovica's advice to Marie-Louise to cleave to Napoleon and to do everything to please him had always made Marie-Louise feel that Marie-Ludovica had put the past behind her. The reunion at Dresden had seemed to Marie-Louise a success, and she had hoped that past acrimonies had been laid to rest. Clearly, things were not so simple.

Now came news which Marie-Louise rushed to communicate to her father. Napoleon had secured a complete victory over the Russian and Prussian armies, led respectively by Emperor Alexander and the King of Prussia. Ten thousand of Napoleon's men had either died or were wounded. His troops were covered in glory, having given proof of their love of him, which touched him to the core. He sent Marie-Louise the details of the battle and told her to have them inserted in the *Moniteur*. He seemed to keep everyone on the run.

The next sentence made uncomfortable reading:

"Papa Francis is not behaving very well – he has removed his contingent." Marie-Louise was not yet aware that the auxiliary corps which Emperor Francis had promised to provide had never materialised. "They are trying to get him to turn against me. Call M. Floret, the Austrian Chargé d'Affaires in Paris, and tell him that they are trying to turn him against us. Tell him that the Emperor is ready. He has a million men under arms and I foresee that if my father listens to the Empress's tittle-tattle, he is heading for real disaster." Napoleon's letter continued:

> As his beloved daughter who cares deeply for his interests, and for the country of my birth, tell my father from me that if he allows himself to be led astray, the French will enter Vienna before July and that he will have lost the friendship of a man who is deeply fond of him. Write to him in these terms for his sake more than for mine, for I have seen this coming for a long time and I am ready.[6]

Letters from her father and the rest of her family had dried up. What was happening? Never had it occurred to Marie-Louise that she would have to write to her father in such terms. Though she had little appetite for the task, she felt it was her responsibility to avert the tempest. She was now painfully aware of her inexperience. How could a girl of twenty-two be expected to steer such a tortuous path? She did her best to tone down Napoleon's sarcasm and anger. She summoned Floret, the French ambassador to Vienna and told him how upset she was to hear that Austria intended to declare war against the Emperor. Floret told her not to be taken in by scaremongers.

> The Emperor himself seems to fear he has lost my father's friendship. He would be distraught to make war against Austria, not only because he knows how unhappy that would make me, but because he is sincerely fond of my father whom he got to know in Dresden. The Emperor would be even more irritated, and his resentment against my father would be irreconcilable. If my father were to declare against him, he would forget all his other enemies and turn all his forces against him. If that were to happen, judge for yourself how unhappy that would make me, and how dreadful my position would become.

She begged Floret to lay what she believed to be the facts before her father: "Convince him of the lack of wisdom of such a course of action." Marie-Louise knew Napoleon could not be expected to surrender so much as one province without compromising himself and upsetting the nation. Having dispatched Floret with clear instructions, she prepared her own letter to her father:

> You can rest assured that the Emperor sincerely desires peace. How many times has he said to me: Once this war is over, he will never start another and will no longer devote his attentions to anything other than domestic politics and family life. But he cannot sign a peace which dishonours him in the eyes of France... There is a rumour bandied about here, which I hope is neither true nor with any foundation. People say, my dearest

Papa, that you have removed your corps of troops from the Emperor and that you wish to make war against us. You cannot imagine how much pain this news causes me. It would be dreadful for me and make no mistake, dearest Papa, that, based on everything I see here, you would never have any advantage. I firmly believe, strictly between us, that the Emperor will soon have a million soldiers under arms. Knowing this nation and their love for the emperor, they would supply twice as many again if he so desired.

Marie-Louise had seen for herself the enthusiasm of Napoleon's soldiers, champing at the bit to demonstrate their valour. Every day, deputations from around the country arrived in the French capital to offer men, horses and funds for the war effort. Each week witnessed reviews at the Place du Carrousel of newly formed regiments. Napoleon's determination and genius guaranteed his ultimate victory which would lead to lasting peace. Were France and Austria to be at war, Marie-Louise knew that her position would be unenviable. Desirous of being candid with her father and loyal to her husband, she continued:

"I am sure that declaring war against the Emperor is repugnant to my father, and I am convinced that Metternich would not advise it. What I fear is that there are others,"[7] Marie-Louise avoided direct reference to her stepmother, "who, blinded by their passion to the dangers which war would unleash on the monarchy, do not perceive that they too would be swept along with it." And there might be "others" besides her stepmother, unknown to her, who exercised pernicious influence over her father.

The following day, the army notice set out details of Napoleon's triumph at Lützen. Marie-Louise conveyed Napoleon's order to the Ministers of War and to the Minister of Religion to have one hundred blasts of cannon fired and all places of worship celebrate his victory. Napoleon wanted his public to learn news of the war first from the *Moniteur*, never from Marie-Louise. Save in extraordinary circumstances, Marie-Louise should never mention military matters in conversation. She must never read anything other than the official notification which Napoleon had ordered her to publish. Any other report, particularly rumours, were dangerous and unreliable. The roads along which she travelled to Nôtre Dame to recite thanks for the Battle of Lützen were lined with troops and draped in coronation tapestries, flags overhanging the balconies and galleries. She listened earnestly to the Archbishop who led the prayers: "The people were called to acknowledge the thanksgiving which Germany offers the God of Armies to have delivered them, by giving their support to their august protector, from the spirit of revolt and anarchy with which the enemy embraced their cause." She returned home to the Tuileries bursting with emotion, having witnessed yet again how much the people loved their Emperor.

Writing to Marie-Louise from Dresden, however, Napoleon's language was unmistakeably curt:

"I think that the battle of Lützen and my arrival in Dresden has really confounded my enemies in Vienna. Give these good tidings to Maman Beatrice and tell her I have one million two hundred thousand equally good soldiers."[8] Enemies in Vienna? Enemies? Marie-Louise could not but be stung by the ironic reference to Marie-Ludovica as Maman Beatrice, the term of endearment Marie-Louise used for her. Marie-Louise prayed that her father would never find himself facing her husband's vast troops.

Marie-Louise rejoiced at Napoleon's successes – he was now master of both banks of the Elbe River, he said. With news of each triumph, her health seemed to improve, her headaches subsiding and her nervous state evaporating. Marie-Louise felt pride reading Napoleon's praise of her letter to her father: "I love you as the dearest of all wives. People say you are as fresh as the spring, I would love to be with you."[9]

By the time she received Napoleon's next letters, following another victory at Bautzen, Marie-Louise knew that Napoleon was mobilizing his army in the Italian peninsula against her father, and that he had written to him to acquaint him with this fact. She was distraught to hear that Marshal Duroc, the grand marshal of the Palace, had fallen, knowing that Napoleon would be devastated. She wept, raging inside against the enemy who persisted in prosecuting war, the enemy who now included her own father. She wept when she felt how much Napoleon longed to be with the son who was growing up without him, who had not been granted the leisure to hear the King of Rome's first words. "He must be becoming quite a chatterbox,"[10] Napoleon wrote from the front. She hated the powers who would have him constantly fighting, never allowing him a moment's respite with his family.

Marie-Louise felt isolated again without Napoleon. She had not been pleased to be woken in the middle of the night in the Tuileries palace by Mme de Montesquiou, whose son had brought news of another victory from the army. The following morning she was suffering from a terrible migraine and felt in no mood or condition to attend mass and the audience for which government and court officials were queuing up. She wanted to cancel it and send away the arrivals. Carriages were turned back by the gendarmes, posted on the bridge of St Cloud. Countermanding the orders of Mme de Montesquiou, who had insisted that the audience should go ahead, the Duchess of Montebello told her sternly it was the court who were at Marie-Louise's beck and call, not the other way round. Archchancellor Cambacérès intervened and ordered Marie-Louise to pull herself together. Marie-Louise complained in correspondence to Napoleon, who took her part after the event. To her gratification, he scolded the Archchancellor: "You are a child to think that anyone could have thought it bad behaviour not to receive when a person is tired. Everyone should have found that straightforward. Those that complained were fools."[11]

Marie-Louise was sorry, on the other hand, to have incurred her husband's displeasure by receiving the Archchancellor while she was in bed. "Not under any circumstances should you receive anyone in bed."[12] Such behaviour was only permissible once she was past the age of thirty. "If I correct you, it is to train you for the future. You know how pleased I am with you, even were you to do something which did not suit me." Marie-Louise was upset at Napoleon's scolding, but took it in good part. "I would find it all very simple. You can never do anything to make me angry, you are too good, too perfect for that."[13] This was not quite true. He had lectured her severely when she had not been ready to receive the Duke and Duchess of Darmstadt upon their arrival. She would sooner have died than give him the pleasure of witnessing her pain on account of his reproaches. On that occasion, she had restrained her grief until Napoleon had left the room. He had not been pleased that she had cancelled the evening entertainment at court because she had been feeling unwell. He told her she must never cancel a performance, even at home, to which others are invited. If he did not wish to attend, he would have an announcement made that he would not be attending, but would invite guests to tarry for as long as they wished, an invitation which would avoid any bad feeling. Receiving such sensible instructions, it would be hardly surprising for Marie-Louise to deduce that her husband was a reliable, rational and reasonable individual who was sensitive to other people's feelings.

Marie-Louise exulted when she read that an armistice had been agreed between her husband and his enemies. Napoleon told Marie-Louise he was lodged in a charming little house with a delightful garden, belonging to Count Marcolini in one of Dresden's prettier outlying districts. She was glad to hear he was back in Dresden receiving the hospitality of the King of Saxony and his queen, Marie-Louise's aunt Marie-Thérèse, of whom they were both fond. Her aunt regularly complained to Napoleon at Marie-Louise's lack of correspondence, telling him that his wife was lazy. This hurt Marie-Louise, who felt a pang of jealousy that Napoleon could be with her loved ones when she found it so hard to communicate with them from afar. The queen also wrote about her fears that Dresden would suffer destruction and death as the Russians, Prussians and French fought out their differences on her territory. Wary of generating political antagonism, Marie-Louise felt unable to set pen to paper. Banalities seemed out of place when there was so much at stake, and her position prevented her from addressing the burning issues of the day. Her situation was painful, her best course to show unswerving loyalty to her husband. Marie-Louise cleaved to her husband's family, spending time at the country homes of Hortense at St Leu, and of Napoleon's brother, Joseph at the Château of Mortefontaine.

Marie-Louise was pleased to hear from Napoleon that Metternich, her father's foreign minister, had arrived in Dresden to meet him. She wrote to her father: "I am extremely touched and cannot thank you enough. No news has given me as much pleasure, putting an end to all my fears, all my concerns. I am convinced that the Emperor will learn that you still have for him the same friendship."

Marie-Louise believed that, as long as there was frank communication between her husband and her father, the Franco-Austrian alliance held firm. Marie-Louise may not at first have noted any animosity in Napoleon's letter: "We'll see what Metternich has to say and what Papa Francis wants. Papa Francis is reinforcing his army in Bohemia; I am strengthening mine in Italy."[14] As June was drawing to a close, Marie-Louise read with joy that Napoleon and Metternich had spoken at length – she did not yet know that at length meant nine hours and that it had not been an amicable conversation. Napoleon wrote nothing of the detail of their discussions, and Marie-Louise concluded that they must have been fruitful, two seasoned statesmen speaking on equal terms. She had no idea that her husband's bargaining stock had fallen dramatically since she had last seen him. Napoleon seemed ready to make peace, but only on an honourable basis, which seemed right and just to her.

The tension which oppressed Marie-Louise seemed to lift, only for her to learn that reunion with Napoleon had to be postponed again. Almost three months had elapsed. Her nervous headaches and cramps returned. Despondent, Marie-Louise allowed the Duchess of Montebello free rein over her social schedule. This proved to be a mistake. Marie-Louise found herself the target of a rising tide of resentment. Archchancellor Cambacérès summoned the Duchess and upbraided her for her conduct. Napoleon was furious.

> The Duchess is issuing invitations outside the scope of her authority, which is generating a lot of bad feeling. She invites people who are known to have been absent from Paris for a month or even three, which makes people feel the whole thing is a mockery, and think that the invitations are issued by a humble lackey, and no-one feels flattered any longer by being in receipt of an invitation. Put this right. Make your own list, for your darling duchess is no longer any good for anything![15]

Marie-Louise could not believe this last criticism. On Napoleon's instruction, Marie-Louise had made the Duchess her closest friend, the only person in whom she could confide over the past three years. Suddenly, this woman was no longer reliable. This outburst against the Duchess must be a symptom of the stress Napoleon was under, she decided. She consulted Cambacérès for guidance, and continued to treat the Duchess exactly as she had before. Napoleon had realised his mistake all too late. From now on, he referred to her as "that blackguard of Montebello."

As June drew to a close, Parisian humidity at its height, another letter arrived from Napoleon.

> Peace will come about if Austria decides not to go fishing in troubled waters. The emperor is deceived by Metternich, who has sold himself for money to the Russians. He believes that politics is about lying. There will be a congress in Prague in two days time. We will see what he will do. If they want to impose upon me dishonourable terms, I will make war against them. Austria will pay for it all. I am angry at the pain this will cause you, but injustice must be rejected.

Marie-Louise again trembled for her former countrymen, particularly for her father and family – and for herself. Napoleon's parting shot alerted her to the fact that this dispute was no longer just between him and her father, but had taken on a wider significance. It was England, the thorn in Napoleon's side, which was causing trouble again: "The English have disembarked your grandmother at Constantinople from where she will go to Buda."[16] Marie-Louise knew that her grandmother, Queen Maria-Carolina of the Two Sicilies, had upset Napoleon, by trying to mount military campaigns against him, and had lost her throne, forced from Naples to her Sicilian seat of Palermo which she hated. Had Napoleon evicted her from here too? Marie-Louise did not know, did not understand. All she felt was that the world was reverting to the madness she had known in the years before her marriage to Napoleon.

Things were not going the way Marie-Louise had hoped. Pending the outcome in Prague, Napoleon was bringing together his armies in Italy and in Bavaria. "If there were to be a fight, if your father were sufficiently foolish to allow himself to be led astray, he would make his own states into the theatre of battle. Write to your father making clear he understands this."[17]

With a heavy heart, Marie-Louise took up her quill:

I hope to receive news of you soon. It has been so long since I had any that I have become very concerned. I hope that your first letters will give me some good news about you and the course of your affairs. The thought of a war would be dreadful for me due to the terrible consequences which it would have for you. Please God we should have soon lasting peace. Please God too, you will accord me your good grace in the same way that the emperor gives you his friendship . . . Have the goodness, dear Papa, to write to me soon and to tell me what you think of me. Then I will be the happiest person on this earth!

It was inconceivable that she should have to beg for a letter from her adoring father. Why was he antagonizing this man by whom he had been defeated repeatedly and who had twice occupied his own capital? Did her position not prevent family dissent?

After three long months of separation, Marie-Louise finally received summons to join Napoleon in Mainz for a few days. Napoleon set out full instructions as to the entourage which was to accompany her.

> You are to sleep in Châlons, then Metz and finally Mainz where I will join you. You are to travel with four carriages on first duty, four of the second, four of the third. You are to bring with you the Duchess, two ladies-in-waiting, a prefect of the palace, two chamberlains, two pages, a doctor and two red-uniformed maids, two black-uniformed maids and your table staff.[18]

Your last letter caused me Marie-Louise began her preparations hoping that war might still be averted.

Then hope was dispelled by her father's letter on the eve of her departure for Mainz. War between France and Austria was inevitable. Marie-Louise wrote in desperation:

> Your last letter caused me great pain because I see that the last hope for peace is lost. This thought must be as unbearable to you as it is to me. In my heart of hearts, I pity you, my dear Papa. I am convinced that this war will bring in its train much misery. Count on me, my dearest Papa, if I can be of service to you once events have run their course, to do whatever I can for you. The Emperor would not hold me dear if he was not assured of the feelings I have for you, but you would not hold me dear if my first wishes were not for the happiness of the Emperor and my son.

It was a terrible choice. Marie-Louise wept at the words she had written. Never had she imagined when she set out on the road to Braunau from Vienna as a dove of peace that her fate would unravel this way. Now a French empress to a French emperor whose love of her evidenced itself daily, it was his side she must take. It was all she could do to offer her help to her father once Austria was inevitably defeated once again by Napoleon.

Marie-Louise set out along the route prescribed, receiving delegations, flower-girls and garlands, attending masses for the success of her husband's arms against her father. She was deeply saddened, the whole of the French nation firmly committed to her husband and to the downfall of her father. But her sadness was eclipsed by her excitement at the thought of seeing her husband – she feared she had betrayed a heart of stone to the zealous Mme Montesquiou when parting from her son without a tear. Everywhere, there were manifestations of her husband's genius: the new fine roads had dramatically reduced travelling times – one could barely go any distance without coming across some benefit introduced at her husband's instigation. But her excitement was dampened when the Duchess of Montebello pointed out a piece of land to which she intended to retire once Marie-Louise no longer needed her services. It was undiplomatic, if not pure arrogance for a lady-in-waiting to anticipate the termination of her employment. Perhaps their recent altercations might have led the Duchess to think of handing in her notice. She noted in her diary,

> One cannot deny that in this beautiful country in which we live, one is never sure where one will be from one day to the next. The sovereign who offers you his hospitality today and calls you his friend, exiles you and forgets you the following day. The only wish I make is that Heaven preserve me from ever having the heart of a sovereign. I feel at least until now that if one of my friends were to fall from favour today, he would only become dearer to me thereafter.

Marie-Louise was irritated by Prince Aldobrandini, who insisted on starting out at six in the morning and not at four, allowing insufficient time, in her view, to cover the forty-six leagues to arrive at their destination before Napoleon.

Marie-Louise arrived in Mainz, set among the mountains of Rheingau and Hunsrück, on 26 July at three-thirty in the morning. The roads along which she travelled in the German territories were in a dreadful state. Her head pounded with a worsening migraine, following unsatisfactory bouts of sleep. Distracted, she tried to deflect conversation by responding to every question with "why?" until it was pointed out to great amusement that she was speaking nonsense. Sometimes she really detested conversation. Napoleon had told her that she would be different at forty. "So much the better, by then I shall have acquired a little amiability which is sadly lacking in me at present!" Marie-Louise recorded in her diary. The party was so much later than anticipated that no-one was awake to greet them, which was a relief to Marie-Louise. She longed to feel Napoleon's embrace. After fitful sleep, she waited, scribbling letters to Mme Luçay to send the things she had left behind, chocolate saveloys and some stimulating books. All her reading material had been selected for her from the catalogues of the leading Parisian publishers by her husband. He did not approve of novels which, in his view, trivialised and sentimentalised reality. A sovereign should constantly be on the quest for knowledge. It was not until eleven o'clock that night that Napoleon arrived, having ridden since three o'clock that morning from Dresden. He too entered the palace to find everyone asleep and entered Marie-Louise's room without anyone remarking his entry. Marie-Louise could not even begin to describe the joy she felt on seeing him again.

The following day, Napoleon rose early from bed and got down to business, inspecting troops, attending military parades, receiving the local dignitaries and authorities, issuing the accolade of the Légion d'Honneur liberally. Marie-Louise saw that the man of action, master military strategist in control of all he surveyed, was unchanged. Ultimate victory was assuredly his. While he worked Marie-Louise sent instructions to Paris for Isabey to paint a miniature of her and her son for Napoleon's saint's day, and rode on the banks of the Rhine in Biberich, Wiesbaden and Cassel. For company, she was surrounded by the wives of her husband's generals who had taken the opportunity of seeing their husbands during the armistice. Marie-Louise particularly liked being with Mme Berthier who was gentle and kind. These pastoral indulgences soothed her troubled mind. In the late afternoon, she was sometimes joined by Napoleon who treated her, as usual, with great tenderness and affection.

Despite the forbidding background, Marie-Louise's five-day stay in Mainz was fast assuming all the attributes of festivity. The imperial couple entertained a slew of local aristocrats, generals and ministers, the Prince of Nassau, the Grand-Duke and Grand-Duchess of Hesse-Darmstadt, and the Grand-Duke of Baden and the Baron of Dalberg, Governor of Frankfurt. Marie-Louise found them tiresome and feared that her true feelings could be read in her face. With her friends, she knew that she was quite a chatterbox, but with others, she had the greatest difficulty in the world to find just one phrase.

At mealtimes, Marie-Louise noticed that Napoleon was uncharacteristically silent, failing to engage in what was going on around him, paying no attention to answers given to questions he had asked of companions. This behaviour contrasted with the rest of company, who indulged in the generous supply of wine from Marshal Kellermann's Rhine vineyards. He was a little brusque with his interlocutors, especially when they wanted to bring the conversation round to increases in invasions. The irritations which had irked her three years earlier on honeymoon, his peremptoriness, impatience with mealtimes and intolerance, resurfaced. However, he was charming and permissive with her. He reassured her that peace would be brokered, that she should not worry. He would win Papa Francis round in the end. No longer the unworldly wide-eyed debutante, Marie-Louise found this hard to believe, it seeming to run counter to her father's letter. Napoleon also reassured her that whatever happened between him and Papa Francis, nothing would change his love and adoration of her. To bolster his assertion, he told Marie-Louise that he had made a list of projects which he wanted to complete over the course of the next few years, changes he wanted to the furnishings and paintings in the imperial palaces, construction works of houses, a church and barracks, kitchens and stabling.

Napoleon was putting in place arrangements for Marie-Louise to inaugurate the expanded port of Cherbourg in Brittany, soon to be renamed Napoleonbourg, which was now nearing completion. The readiness of Cherbourg was an essential component in the plan to invade England. The opening ceremony would send a signal to the world that Napoleon was mobilized to carry out his next acquisition.

When Napoleon left Mainz to join his troops, Marie-Louise could see that he was in so much pain parting from her that she had to be robust. He reassured her that soon everyone would be good friends again and told her to keep cheerful. With supreme effort, she managed to hold back the emotion which bubbled inside as she watched him cross the bridge over the Rhine and disappear into the distance in the late afternoon sun.

Napoleon had arranged for his wife to take a sailing trip down the Rhine on a luxurious yacht lent by the Prince of Nassau. The first yacht was followed by a second and two small craft, a carriage following their course on the left bank of the river. The towers and other remains of castles from the Middle Ages, with which the Rhine's banks were littered, provided distraction for Marie-Louise and her entourage. They sailed alongside an island where, in medieval times, pregnant women had been confined in a triangular chamber where one would not even lodge one's waiting maid. How miserable was the condition of women in the age of barbarism! They passed a convent in an obscure, picturesque valley in supreme solitude, a retreat for meditation and in times of distress. "I feel that were I to experience great misfortunes or losses, I would willingly buy myself this convent." Times of misfortune and distress seemed a long way off. The ladies dressed in floating chiffons and silks, hats and gloves in pastel summer shades under a summer sun and sky provided a perfect lazy picture which encouraged oblivion. To her embarrassment, several of her entourage took the opportunity to poke fun at the ugly daughters of the Prince of Nassau, one of her hosts. She reprimanded them.

Marie-Louise disembarked the yacht at Coblenz, by which time she was growing weary of the beauties of nature, missing her son. The noise of cannon fired to celebrate her arrival was always irksome to her, but on this occasion even more so, when she learnt of the injuries that befell two unfortunate gunners who should have formed part of her guard: one had lost one his arm, the other both wrists in endeavouring to discharge the cannon for this purpose. Such ceremony was senseless. The movement of royals caused great imposition. "I believe our journeys are a perfect nuisance to the peasants, who are obliged to provide horses to draw the carriages of the suite. Sometimes, a quarter of them break down. When this happens, all they receive is a measly fifty francs by way of compensation." It upset her that so often the motives for good deeds were questionable, and their impact mercenary, as in the case of the little girl shamefully abandoned by her parents to a foster mother, whom Marie-Louise had adopted a year earlier. As soon as the parents learned that Marie-Louise intended to give her an allowance, they came to collect her. The Empress could have wept.

Back in the Palace of Compiègne a few days later, Marie-Louise wondered if the happy days she had spent there with her husband would ever return. Once more she found comfort in her son, who had made considerable advances in her absence, and in Napoleon's love. In successive letters, he told her how he thought constantly of her and never wanted to have to leave her again, to rest before setting out for Cherbourg which he promised her she would love. By the middle of August, nothing seemed to have changed. Neither mentioned the negotiations at Prague and she imagined that all must be going well.

In the meantime, Marie-Louise received a letter from her father after many weeks of silence which set her straight:

> You know that our negotiators are gathered in Prague: may God bless this salutary enterprise! My duties are so varied, the interests which I must consider not only in my personal

> capacity, but in my capacity as monarch, are such that if peace is not concluded in the next few days, I will be, as little as I desire it, implicated in a war the outcome of which cannot be predicted by either of the two parties. I cannot be blamed if peace is not concluded. My intentions are reasonable, all are equitable. I have originated no proposal which might compromise in any way the interests of another power. Your husband's first desire like mine is tranquillity, and to achieve it no sacrifice is too great. I have the best hope, insofar as one can imagine hope of peace and flatter myself that those who take part in these peace negotiations will not refuse to bring it about.[19]

Emperor Francis was stating that it was not he but Napoleon who was the obstacle to a satisfactory arrangement. Marie-Louise could not accept this. Her husband's cause she thought sacred. Her father seemed blind to the writing on the wall. Holding her head high, though internally conflicted, she wrote:

> Rest assured, dear Papa, that, without taking into account the events, I will always feel towards you the most respectful filial love and I always ask God that he brings you happiness and good health. I am seized by a terrifying worry regarding the outcome of negotiations. God preserve us from war, and if there is one, may God ensure that you are not part of it, for I could not bear to imagine the consequences for you.

Adding a few words about her recent trip and forthcoming journey to Cherbourg, she concluded by saying that she had heard that he would like some dahlias, and ordered flowers to be taken with her letter by the courier.

Shortly before Marie-Louise set out for Cherbourg, she received a further letter from her father notifying her that he had had no choice but to declare war on Napoleon. Marie-Louise's fears were now realized. She was forced to take sides between father and husband, Austria and France. It was a painful choice, if choice she had.

She loved the husband she had been told by her father to obey and revere, to whose son she had given birth at her father's urging to consolidate the Austro-French alliance, and whom she had grown to love and admire over the past three years. She had no doubt that she, an Austrian archduchess, would have to assert publicly her solidarity with France and her condemnation of Austria, a position to which she had hoped never to be reduced. She immediately wrote to Napoleon. He insisted that it was not he but her father who wanted war, out of sheer unbridled ambition and avidity. Metternich was leading him astray "This man's head is not equal to his role."[20] "Do not get too upset about your father's behaviour, he has been betrayed as has happened before. Never doubt my love for you," he told her. Napoleon had already defeated Russian and Prussian troops and had chased an Austrian division led by a General, a certain Adam de Neipperg, from the mountains of Bohemia.

Marie-Louise wrote to her father. The outbreak of war must be as painful for him as it was for her. She reiterated her fear for her father and his nation and her reassurance as to her continuing filial love. She begged him to keep communication lines open. "Write assiduously, for this will be my only consolation in these sad circumstances. I am too unhappy to write a longer letter. I have the feeling that if I were to continue further it would only increase your sadness." Emperor Francis in response said he had done everything to try and avert the war, and hoped even before hostilities commenced that there might be a change in line with his wishes.

Marie-Louise delivered her first political pronouncement as Regent with determination and conviction. She had a severe cough and cold. Ignoring her ailments, she presented a charming sight in a low-cut dress, flowers and diamonds in her hair:

> Gentlemen, the Emperor, my august and beloved husband, knows that my heart holds dear love and affection for France. The proofs of devotion that the nation shows us each day increase the good opinion which I have of the character and

greatness of your nation. My soul is indeed oppressed to see that still this sweet peace eludes us which alone would make me happy.

How could anyone mistake her sincerity? "The Emperor is particularly afflicted by the numerous sacrifices which he must needs demand from his peoples. But as the enemy, rather than making peace, wishes to impose upon us shameful conditions and preaches everywhere civil war, treason and disobedience, it is indeed necessary that the Emperor has recourse to his arms which have always proved victorious in confounding his enemies and have saved civilized Europe and its sovereigns from the anarchy which threatens it." Each word had been carefully selected by Napoleon, but Marie-Louise believed in each word, and pronounced each with care, ensuring that every nuance of the message reached its audience.

Marie-Louise might appear to her subjects serene on the outside, but inside she was in turmoil. Her father's recommendations that she should stay calm were of little comfort: "The war which we prosecute is quite different from the earlier wars: it is entirely political." What her father meant by this was unclear. "I am not and never will be your husband's enemy; and I count on him never being mine."[21] It was hard to imagine how the two men could be friends, leading large armies against each other.

> Extraordinary forces find themselves pitched against one another. It is likely that a short space of time will decide by arms what we were unable to obtain by negotiation. I will keep up continuous correspondence with you by the army's advanced posts. I specifically invite your husband to have your letters sent to me and I will always send mine to him.[22]

Marie-Louise was desperate not to be cut off from Vienna. This last reassurance was invaluable.

Marie-Louise was in no mood to celebrate her saint's day as it loomed in August, the date set for the inauguration, the sun shining along the roads leading to Cherbourg. Hostilities had commenced, Napoleon defeating the enemy at various places, just as Marie-Louise had foreseen. Already the enemy seemed to be retreating. The Grande Armée had flooded into Bohemia, into Prague, into Berlin, marching on Dresden to attack Russians, Prussians and Austrians. Marie-Louise could not believe that it had come to this. It would all be over soon, she tried to reassure herself. Napoleon insisted she go to Cherbourg. "The flooding of the docks is a unique spectacle and I envy you – write to me telling me everything about it."[23] She found the journey tedious, and was pained to have to part with her son, with whom she had been reunited only briefly after her return from Mainz. His aunt, Queen Caroline of Naples, had brought him a little calèche pulled by two charming little sheep dressed by the stablehand, in which he could go out for rides in the gardens of the palace. At least the King of Rome would be absorbed in his new toy.

Marie-Louise kept a diary of her journey, noting down meticulously each village and town she passed, describing the countryside in detail. But she had no enthusiasm for the task, and her notes sat dryly on the page, reflections of her inner sadness. At least being in a carriage on a long journey spared her the merry-go-round of public appearances. Since her earliest youth, Marie-Louise had heard protestations of loyalty and devotion across Austria and now France, and knew that they were the stuff of ceremony, not of sincerity. She hated the eulogies which extolled her beauty, when she felt that she was rather plain. She preferred people to say, "I am pleased with you," which exhorted her to do greater good. Prince Aldobrandini and General Caffarelli who accompanied Marie-Louise to Cherbourg irritated her immensely, countermanding her orders. Sometimes, she felt so frustrated she wanted to beat them up, she confessed. The more she was prevented from doing something, the more she wanted to do it. She fought to go sailing when the sea was blowing a gale, even though she knew that it was an absurdity. Dr Corvisart's proscription of cream, which she loved, made her irritable. She was half dead from fatigue and churned up by the poor roads, suffocated by the dust, tired by a chesty cold. The day after her arrival, she went to the port with the Minister of the Marine, to inspect three openings in the breakwater through which the seawater would penetrate. A pavilion had been erected giving onto the dam from which Marie-Louise would watch the great event. Either side of the pavilion were tents from which dignitaries would watch. Seawater was expected to flood the new harbours in the late afternoon. The wind sending the ribbons fastening her hat flying across her face, Marie-Louise made her public appearance to great fanfares and artillery salvoes at around five in the afternoon. She was accompanied by her entourage, and an archbishop from the local diocese who recited a eulogy and blessings for the new harbour. Patiently, the party waited for the tide to come in, making polite conversation to while away the time. It was a good hour before the sea level rose sufficiently and the waves crashed into the port. Everyone laughed and congratulated themselves as cement gave way to seawater. The waters had yet to spill over to effect the rupture of the centre of the dam. The party waited and waited, the sunlight and its warmth fading into evening. Marie-Louise was beginning to feel the cold. She announced that the party should retire for a while to have dinner and that they should return thereafter. Many seemed surprised, but acceded to her wishes. When they returned an hour later, the Empress swathed in shawls, the final breaking of the waters had already taken place. She and they had missed the critical event.

Thankfully, there was some good news awaiting her by Chappe's telegraph. Such news would do more for her than all the medicines in the world. Napoleon had defeated all three nations at a brilliant battle at Dresden. Marie-Louise cried for joy and wept for her father, who, unlike the Russian and Prussian sovereigns, had had the good sense not to lead his army, and for the widows and mothers she would have to inform personally of the loss of French officers on the field of honour. Her father's troops were, according to Napoleon, in complete disarray, poorly equipped and almost naked.

Napoleon scored one triumph after another, taking prisoners, standards and cannon, sending her flags with orders to attend prayers for the recitation of the obligatory Te Deum in thanksgiving.

"We were all in extremely high spirits. News of Napoleon's defeat of Austria was met throughout France with enthusiasm." She wrote in her diary, regretting that only she could not rejoice with a full heart. "We have won a battle, but that will not bring my husband back to me. This thought alone contaminates my happiness." It was barely a year since she had parted from her father in Prague. She complained to Mme de Luçay that Napoleon's letters now barely amounted to a few brief words.

Goaded on by Dresden, Napoleon's troops were converging on Leipzig. Once this battle was won, Napoleon would devote himself to the final struggle, launching his fleet across the Channel from Napoleonbourg.

SIX

Invasion and Flight, Spring 1814

By late March 1814, Marie-Louise was in a constant state of agitation, suffering unbearable stomach cramps. She and Napoleon had exchanged letters sometimes twice a day over the course of the present campaign which had commenced in the third week of January. The latest letter from her father offered little to soothe her nerves.

> Peace can only come about on the basis of the proposed terms. Without these there is no salvation in Europe and even less so in France. You, more than anyone have an interest in there finally being peace. Once negotiations are reopened with a system of government built on peace, your husband will reap the blessings of the most beautiful state in Europe. He will make his people revere his memory and put his dynasty on a sure footing. All the people who advise him differently do not want what is best for him. No-one desires [what is best for him] more sincerely than I do and daily I give him proof of my opinion in this regard. Were I to stand alone against him on the battlefield, I would more easily sort things out, but peace only with Austria would only plunge him into fresh ruin. I will never break away from the Alliance which truly only desires the common good. The Emperor must therefore do what they require in order to obtain peace. The greatest duty you can ever perform for your husband, your son and your new Fatherland is to adhere to my sincerely friendly, paternal opinion and counsel. I have been ruling for twenty-two years, and your

husband should do me the justice of recognising that there is nobody who has spoken to him with greater honesty in all circumstances than I . . .[1]

At the beginning of March, Marie-Louise had written to Napoleon telling him how frightened many Parisians were, how convinced they were that the arrival of Cossacks was imminent. Then, she had reassured him. "Do believe me when I say, Darling, that I myself am not in the least worried. On the contrary, I have never felt so brave and so well, and if I *am* sad and distressed, it is simply and solely because you are away."[2]

Since then, she had good reason to feel far less robust. By the end of March, Marie-Louise had heard nothing from her husband for five days. She wrote nonetheless, unaware that her husband's letters to her, revealing his movements, were being intercepted by the enemy. "Here, you are constantly in our thoughts. Our son is always talking about you. The darling is dying to have you home. He remembers all the times you played with him and wants to know when he will do so again. If only I could give him a date in the very near future."[3]

The following day, a beautiful crisp, clear day, Marie-Louise and her son presided in the Place du Carroussel over the daily grand parade by the National Guard, to whom Napoleon, at his departure, had entrusted the welfare of his wife and child. It was a splendid three hours. The King of Rome, dressed in a military hat, always looked forward to it with great excitement, revelling in the pomp. Afterwards, Marie-Louise took her son to play in the gardens of the Tuileries Palace with his cousins, the children of Napoleon's siblings. Mme de Montesquiou had, as usual, to tear the little boy away to prepare him for dinner and bed. The King of Rome never stopped talking about his father and anticipating his return, hoping that Daddy's troops would defeat Grandpa's. Marie-Louise was instructed by Napoleon to keep cheerful in her exchanges with her household, never to address matters relating to the war with the privileged few authorized to grace her presence. She spent her evenings receiving guests in the drawing-room after dinner, playing her regular game of whist with her husband's oleaginous, heavily powdered minister Talleyrand, who seemed his usual relaxed self. The company were surprisingly light-hearted, given that France was at war with Austria, Prussia and Russia, and that matters did not appear to be going France's way. Assembled around the whist-table, they laughed at the ridiculous prophecies that Paris could ever fall under foreign occupation.

By Monday 28 March, the joke had worn off. Marie-Louise had received a visit in the early afternoon from Napoleon's brother Joseph and from Archchancellor Cambacérès. They came to tell her to leave Paris as a matter of urgency. The capital would be under siege any minute. Marie-Louise's first and prevailing instinct was that she should stand firm and stay where she was. If she confronted the invaders, at the head of whom was her father, they would not dare to take her and her son prisoner, nor would they dare to ransack Paris. Napoleon's family members and ministers had other ideas. Much of the aristocracy, including some of Marie-Louise's staff, had already fled Paris for, or evacuated their children to, the countryside. The Duchess of Montebello had sent her children to Meaux at Marie-Louise's urging. Provisional arrangements had already been made by Marie-Louise's entourage to prepare her and her son for a swift departure the following morning. If Paris were lost, there would be unremitting chaos. In the early evening, a courier arrived to inform Marie-Louise that the enemy had forty thousand men poised to take the city.

An emergency meeting of the Council of the Regency was hastily assembled in the Emperor's study to establish his instructions in such circumstances. Everyone of significance was summoned to attend. The main speakers were Napoleon's brother Joseph, the Archchancellor Cambacérès, the President of the Senate Lacépède and Napoleon's ministers Clarke, Savary, Boulay de la Meurthe, Talleyrand and Champagny. Joseph addressed the company: "Should the Empress and her son stay or should they leave?" Savary and Champagny begged Marie-Louise to remain in the capital. Boulay de la Meurthe went further, imploring her to go to the Town Hall to call the Parisians to arms to fight against her father. Talleyrand also backed the faction which wanted Marie-Louise to stand firm. Not so robust, Clarke and the Archchancellor favoured the immediate departure of the Empress and the King of Rome from Paris. In their view, the city lacked the means to defend itself against attack and did not want to see its sovereigns in the hands of Cossacks. After much exhausting debate, the matter was put to the vote. The majority were for Marie-Louise and her son staying in the capital. The losers demanded a second vote. The same thing happened: the assembly was unanimous bar Joseph and Clarke, who wanted Marie-Louise to leave. Just when everything seemed to Marie-Louise to be settled judiciously, her brother-in-law moved to take the floor. From his pocket, he extracted a letter he said he had received from the Emperor six weeks earlier and recited its terms.

> If, by any circumstances which I cannot foresee, I were to transfer to the Loire, I would not leave the Empress or my son far from me, because, in such event, both would be seized and taken to Vienna. If there is news of a lost battle or of my death, have the Empress and my son leave by way of Rambouillet. Order the Senate, the Council of State and all the troops to convene on the Loire. Leave in Paris either a prefect, an imperial commissioner or a mayor. Never leave the Empress or the King of Rome in the hands of the enemy.

Marie-Louise was incredulous.

> Brother, in accordance with the oral instructions I gave you and the spirit of all my letters, you must not allow in any circumstances the Empress and the King of Rome to fall into enemy hands. My plans may mean that you are without news of me for several days. If the enemy advances on Paris with

overwhelming forces which preclude any effective resistance, send towards the Loire the Regent, my son, the grand dignitaries, the functionaries of the Senate, the presidents of the Council of State, the grand officers of the Crown and the Treasury.

Then followed a most extraordinary statement, given that Napoleon expected the child's grandfather to take him to Vienna.

> Do not leave my son. Remember that I prefer to know him in the Seine than in the hands of the enemy of France. The fate of Astyanax, prisoner of the Greeks, has always seemed to me the saddest in history.[4]

Who did not recoil in horror, reading in Virgil's *Aeneid* the pronouncement of the Greek emissary at the fall of Troy, as Hector's wife Andromache held her baby to her breast: "The boy must die. He is to be thrown down from the towering wall of Troy. Now ... now, let it be done. Endure like a brave woman. Think. You are alone." At the dawn of the nineteenth century, Napoleon's was not a far-fetched image. It was not long ago that the Russian Tsar's father Paul had been assassinated, some said within his son's earshot. Marie-Louise was well aware that the fate of the son of her great aunt Queen Marie-Antoinette still remained unexplained. He had disappeared only twenty years ago – and here in Paris. A third vote was taken. Everyone was ordered to be up and ready to leave at six the following morning.

The emergency session, which had begun at eight-thirty, ended at one in the morning. The Empress then sat down to write to Napoleon in a state of nervous disbelief that he had not shared his instructions with her.

> Joseph read to us part of a letter in which you told him not to allow myself to be taken captive in Paris. He and the other gentlemen explained that there was no way that we could defend ourselves against such a large force, that there are very few

troops here and it was imperative that I did not expose myself to waiting for the Russian and Prussian armies. It has been decided that I must leave, at the latest, by tomorrow morning. It has also been decided that Joseph must remain here along with all your ministers and grand dignitaries, save the Archchancellor, the Duke of Cadore [Champagny] and King Louis who will accompany me. I confess to you that I am completely against this project. I am sure it will have a disastrous effect on the Parisians, robbing them of the courage they otherwise would have had to defend themselves. The National Guard will do nothing, and when you arrive to deliver us, you will find the capital in the enemy's power. You have always told me to follow the Archchancellor's advice, which I have done on this occasion so as not to expose my son.[5]

Marie-Louise wanted to follow her instinct, and yet she had been overruled, not just by the Council members, but by her husband. She could not take it upon herself, ignorant of so many relevant factors in the calculation, to gainsay him. If she were to contradict him and things were to turn out badly, he might never forgive her. She went to bed exhausted. Sleep, which for several nights had eluded her, now came and for just over five hours, she was released from her troubles. She awoke at seven, got dressed into travelling clothes, and had her son and ladies join her. From dawn, the drawing-rooms of the Tuileries Palace filled with people selected to follow her to the Loire. An eery silence prevailed, everyone jumping at the opening of a door or other unexpected noise. She sent a courier to find out what the night had brought. The news did not assist her. A deputation from the National Guard came to beg her to stay in Paris, promising to defend her. Extremely dejected, she thanked them for their devotion. Napoleon's brother Jérôme requested admittance and then delivered a curt order to Marie-Louise to stay in the capital. She wept, reading them the terms of Napoleon's letter. She kept postponing departure, looking mournfully through the windows at the berlin carriages lined up in the courtyard since eight o'clock in the morning, hoping against hope that Napoleon would have sent revised instructions which would not require her getting inside them.

Trembling with frustration, furious at her impotence as Regent, Marie-Louise again wrote to Napoleon:

> My departure is firmly desired by everyone, save M. Boulay, M. de Champagny and me. I would have had sufficient courage to stay, and I am very irritated that I have not been allowed to do so with all the resolve that the Parisians have demonstrated to defend themselves. But my opinion has little value in this matter, and the Arcchancellor told me that I must go. May God's will be done. But I am sure that you will not be pleased. This will demoralize the National Guard, and tomorrow the enemy will be in Paris. It is said that the enemy has made no advances this past night, but that partisans have been sent to Rambouillet. It seems it is better to be taken by the Cossacks than to sit calmly in Paris! Everyone has lost his head, apart from me. I hope that in a few days' time, you will tell me that I was right not to want to evacuate the capital for fifteen thousand cavalrymen who will never enter the streets. I am extremely angry to have to leave. My departure will be disastrous for you, but I have been told that my son could be in serious danger if he stays. With this in mind and since seeing your letter to Joseph, I have not dared to express my view again. Thus, I am placing myself in the hands of Providence, certain that it will all end in tears. I embrace you and love you with all my heart.[6]

Marie-Louise was sure that the narrow roads of Paris would provide insurmountable obstacles to the advancing enemy, and that the Parisians would have no difficulty in defending themselves. If she stayed behind, she could negotiate with her father and her allies for herself, her son, her husband, the city, for France. She would be in an immensely powerful position. She felt strong, capable of displaying all the heroism which the moment demanded of her. And yet everyone else would have it otherwise.

At around eleven, Clarke announced that if they did not set out immediately, the roads would be cut, and escape would be impossible. Within minutes, Marie-Louise's courtiers and family had made their way down the staircase and into the courtyard. Defiantly, the King of Rome tried to hold the doors of his room closed, then clung to the banisters, crying and screaming, hugging the furniture and sobbing: "I'm not going! I'm not going! I'm not leaving my house! I don't want to go to Rambouillet! As Daddy's not here, I'm the master!"[7] Mme de Montesquiou exhausted all her persuasive powers before taking him up into her arms as best she could and carting him off to the carriage. Marie-Louise had managed to stem her tears, but many of her courtiers and household could not restrain theirs.

Ten carriages bearing the imperial coat of arms rolled out of the Tuileries carrying Marie-Louise and her son, the Duchess of Montebello and Mme de Luçay, and several other ladies, chamberlains, prefects of the place, doctors Corvisart and Bourdier, and surgeons, equerries and the King of Rome's three governesses. Following them were the wagons loaded with silverware, the crown jewels, treasury funds, and trunks containing apparel of value, lace, cashmere shawls, dresses, hats, slippers, boots, and all manner of toilette and bathing accessories. Twelve hundred cavalry provided their escort. As the sun shone its ironic smile, the squares and streets were flooded with travellers going in both directions, many wandering around dazed by fear of imminent occupation. Villagers, farmers and country gentry were fleeing to Paris to escape imminent invasion. With them came wagons loaded with their possessions, furniture and furnishings, even cattle and other livestock. As they approached the city, the Parisians were wrapping up their most precious possessions to send together with their children and servants to their country estates along the Loire, which they perceived to be out of danger, far from the theatre of war.

The convoy arrived at Rambouillet at five-thirty in the afternoon. Marie-Louise did not know whether she should stay put or move on. She sent a courier to Joseph asking him whether the enemy had advanced any further, and to advise as to the safest place for her refuge. He told her to continue on her way.

Three days later, following instructions received from Napoleon as she was passing through Chartres, Marie-Louise set up temporary home in the city of Blois along the Loire. The outlook was very bleak. Marie-Louise could not stop shaking when she thought upon the consequences which would ensue from the abandonment of the capital, both for Napoleon and for France. All she asked in these terrible moments was to be able to prove to Napoleon how much she loved him. What really angered her was that she was a woman, a being of no importance, despite her elevated rank. The King of Rome steadied her nerves a little, being twice as affectionate as usual. Marie-Louise pulled him close to her, fearful of the Russian runners who were known to be marauding the countryside. The stable-horses were not as well-trained as the cavalry-horses, and could not travel at similar speed, which exacerbated her nerves. From Chartres, Marie-Louise wrote to Hortense to suggest she send her children to join the convoy. She awaited news as to whether she should make for Vendôme or Tours. Paris still seemed to be holding out, she wrote to Napoleon. The following day, Napoleon's letter, written at three o'clock in the morning, informed her that he had arrived too late to defend Paris. The city had already surrendered the preceding evening. He would make for Fontainebleau to assemble his army. He planned to come and collect Marie-Louise and his ministers from the Loire and mount a last stand.

Napoleon had told Marie-Louise to aim for either Orléans or Blois. Joseph suggested that she should go to Tours, which she refused to do, knowing that there were awful epidemics of prison fever which raged, taking out sixty people a day. Marie-Louise chose

Blois. But at Vendôme, General Caffarelli came to inform her that the little town of Blois had very few lodgings and was already squeezed, many Parisians having already fled there. If the imperial party were obliged to leave in a hurry, there might be the most terrible bottleneck. He was concerned also about the retinue of Napoleon's brother, Jerôme, and his wife Catherine of Westphalia, which comprised a dozen German officers. They might be excellent, decent people, but they could be adventurers or at worse spies. If the Bonapartes continued to travel as a party, Marie-Louise would have to foot the bill for feeding all of Napoleon's siblings and their retinues in addition to her own, which would put severe strain on her finances. Marie-Louise rejected General Caffarelli's proposal that all, save Joseph, be asked to find other places of refuge. Marie-Louise was angered to hear that Joseph had, without her authority, given instructions that a wagon containing substantial funds be left in Rambouillet, ostensibly for Napoleon's use.

On her fourth wedding anniversary, Marie-Louise took up residence in the Prefecture of Blois. The first cavalry detachments arrived, followed by luggage and fifteen wagons containing the treasures of the imperial court. The carriages gleamed, washed by rain which had thundered down upon the travellers, but the horses, exhausted, could go no further. It was a sad day, far from the husband with whom she had celebrated her previous anniversaries. The imperial party comprised Napoleon's mother, Mme Mère, her sons Joseph, Louis and Jerôme and their wives, the Archchancellor, ministers and heads of administration, and no less than eighteen thousand troops, for whom accommodation had to be found. It was said that there was barely a resident of the city who did not share his house, his bedroom and, in some cases, even his bed with the influx of refugees from the capital. Marie-Louise and her son emerged from their carriage to an immense crowd, all keeping a respectful, forbidding silence. This contrasted sharply with their reception in Orléans, where troops had shouted outside her window day and night, "Long live the Emperor".

A short letter from Napoleon told Marie-Louise that he hoped that they would soon be reunited. Blois was pleasant, her rooms giving a superb view of the turrets of the Château of Chambord, and at least here there was no disease. The following day being Sunday, she hosted a family dinner, an intimate reception and games. Though everyone was not quite as well attired as usual, court life seemed to resume as if there were no war. Marie-Louise's ministers pressed her to send someone to Napoleon to obtain answers to various questions and to address sensitive matters which could not be communicated in correspondence for fear of interception. She asked Napoleon to appoint a suitable intermediary. Marie-Louise held a meeting of the Council of Ministers to decide whether she should move on. She sent an envoy to find out whether the city of Orléans could accommodate her party, the city's population having increased by ten thousand since the invasion. Fearing that Orléans might prove too close to the theatre of war, it was agreed that she should await Napoleon's instructions. In the meantime, ministers would establish a newspaper in which Napoleon's future bulletins could be published. They were all of one mind: peace must be concluded immediately in the present circumstances at any cost. They would set out their views on paper and send them to Napoleon.

Many of Marie-Louise's entourage had started demanding advance payment for their services. Marie-Louise had no idea who and what she would need over the course of the next few days, never mind the coming months, and so said nothing. Many started to threaten that if she did not put them in funds, they would resign immediately, and demanded passports to return to Paris. Astonished by the disloyalty, her finances severely stretched, it was cheaper and easier to permit them to pursue their requests for passports from the Russian commissioner who now controlled passage. Her military escort began murmuring that they too were owed arrears of salary. She gave orders to Joseph that five hundred thousand livres should be allocated from the treasury and the debts settled. Joseph was also unhappy, having received assurances from Napoleon that two million francs would be made available for him which had not materialized, and demanded that Marie-Louise give to each of the nine members of the Bonaparte family one hundred thousand ecus to alleviate their destitution. Marie-Louise acceded to his wish, further depleting the treasury funds. She knew that the Bonaparte clan were making plans to find new pastures, and hoped they would do so soon, which would remove a great weight from her shoulders.

By the end of the first week of April, Marie-Louise had received only the briefest letters from Napoleon. They told her little, except not to worry and to look after herself. All she wanted was to be with him. Then, and only then, she felt, she would have more courage, more strength. She would console him as much as she could for his reverses and would try to be of use to him. "You know me well enough, my Friend," she wrote, "and I promise you that my perspective will not grieve you, quite the contrary. For goodness sake, have me come to you."[8] Did Napoleon doubt her loyalty to him? Why, when they were barely two days' ride from each other, had he not arranged with one of the couriers to have her and his son brought to him?

The allies were reported to have taken Chartres, and to be bearing down on Saintes, such that Tours no longer provided a safe haven. Where was there to go if she left Blois? She begged Napoleon to send her someone to tell her what to do. She had dispatched the Duke of Cadore to her father to advise him as to the situation, but nothing had been heard either from the Duke or from her father. This time she dispatched two ministers by way of Dijon, advising them that it was preferable to fall into Austrian, rather than Russian or Prussian hands. They took with them a letter in which she stated that she knew all the generous proposals which Napoleon had made for the good of France and that the enemy had not accepted them. She learned that the youngest surviving brother of the Bourbon King Louis XVI had already crossed into France to prepare for reinstatement of the old dynasty. Marie-Louise began to regret leaving Paris and was urged by her courtiers to return as quickly as possible to reassert herself as Regent in her capital. She readied herself for departure. By returning to Paris, perhaps she could reverse the tide, salvage something for herself and her son, take her fate into her own hands. The Duchess and Dr. Corvisart dissuaded her from this course. Marie-Louise spent her days vacillating between hope and fear, presiding over meetings of Councils of the Regency, evaluating the little news which reached them as it arrived. Their deliberations were pointless. The government in exile was impotent.

It was the saddest letter Marie-Louise had ever received. She was utterly distraught. Colonel Galbois apologized for having to be the bearer of news of her husband's abdication. Stifling tears, holding her head as high as she could manage, the fallen empress replied: "My father will not stand for this! He has repeatedly told me, over twenty times, that he has put me on the throne of France, and that he would keep me there forever, and my father is a good man."[9] She was sure that there had been some terrible, terrible mistake, misunderstanding, misadventure. "This marriage has changed the face of things in Europe and these blood ties lend a special character to any proposed action. I look forward to the opportunity of being able to prove my loyalty to the Emperor of the French." She had to go and sort it out. Her father would be shocked, she was sure. She announced to the members of her entourage that she would return with Colonel Galbois to Fontainebleau. She marched out of the Prefecture and into a waiting carriage which she had had prepared secretly. She begged Galbois to take her to her husband. As she mounted the carriage, the Duchess of Montebello rushed out to her and pulled at her arms, preventing her from entering it. She pleaded with Galbois: "It is not possible." "Why not?" Marie-Louise cried in a strangled voice. "You are going there anyway! My place is beside the Emperor at a time when he must be very unhappy. I want to join him, and I will be free wherever I am as long as I am with him!"[10]

Galbois did not flinch. He could not vouch for her safety, and would not have the temerity to assume a responsibility which had not been conferred upon him. Her Majesty would become a hostage to fortune by saddling herself with a Colonel without escort. The Duchess remonstrated with Marie-Louise, who tried to force herself forwards and into the carriage. Unable to resist either the duchess's physical force or the weight of her argument, and exasperated by Colonel Galbois' wooden restraint, she withdrew, running into the Prefecture, away from the eyes that bore down upon her. She went to her room and threw herself on the bed, pounding the mattress with her fists, crying her heart out.

The next letter Marie-Louise received from Napoleon was brought by Colonel Galbois, who came directly from Fontainebleau on a warm Good Friday. Its opening lines seemed extremely promising. "An armistice has been concluded and an aide-de-camp of the Emperor of Russia should be with you to escort you here." At long last! Then, "You must stop at Orléans, I myself being about to leave".

To leave? Just when she was hoping to join him? She did not understand. She read on.

> I am waiting while Caulaincourt arranges matters with the Allies. Russia desires that I am granted the sovereignty of Elba and that I stay there, and that you are granted Tuscany for your son after you, which will enable you to spend as much time with me as will not bore you or adversely affect your health.[11]

Napoleon had written in such haste that he had forgotten to sign the letter.

Slowly, it dawned on Marie-Louise that her husband was no longer master of all he surveyed, no longer Emperor of the French. She was no longer Empress. They had been deposed. A provisional government had taken over in Paris.

"Schwarzenberg opposes this arrangement in your father's name. It seems that your father is our most implacable enemy. So I do not know what has been decided." So not even Elba and Tuscany were certain. Were Napoleon, Marie-Louise and the King of Rome refugees? "I am angry that I can do nothing more than have you share my bad luck. I would have taken my life, if I had not thought that this would have exacerbated your troubles." The rest of Napoleon's letter set out instructions for the distribution of funds to ministers and to the Bonaparte family, whom he advised to head for Marseille and Nice by way of Limoges. He told her to take a million francs for herself from her own carriages and from Joseph's carriage. He told her to reduce her household to a bare minimum, asking Mme de Montesquiou to complete the King of Rome's education. She should pay all pages until the end of June and dismiss everyone else. They would need very little for their future existence. Napoleon closed by urging Marie-Louise to write to her father to ask for Tuscany for herself. For himself, he wanted nothing more than the island of Elba. "Adieu, my friend. Give your son a kiss." [12]

Marie-Louise emerged from her room a short while later, having washed her face. Waiting for her were her Bonaparte brothers-in-law Jerôme and Joseph. Gone was any deference to her. They told her that Blois could no longer be considered a place of safety, and they urged her to come with them towards the southern end of the Loire. There, they expected to be able to join the army returning from Spain, which they presumed still loyal to the fallen Emperor. Marie-Louise did not intend to flee. She wanted to join Napoleon. She was sure that her father would arrange everything and set matters straight. She did not need the Bonaparte siblings, who, Napoleon had often lamented, were always happy to enjoy benefits conferred but never the responsibilities which came with them. She told them that she wished them well, but that she would pursue her own course. They were furious. Joseph started shouting at her; Jerôme issued threats: if she did not come of her own free will, he would take her by force. Then Joseph tried to persuade her to put her mind to throwing herself at the first Austrian corps that she could find. Through them, the Bonapartes could petition her father to assure their safe passage and destiny. There was no time to lose, certainly no time to keep Napoleon informed, and still less to obtain his approval, which might not be forthcoming. "As long as I breathe, I shall stand by Napoleon!" she declared.

Marie-Louise said she would go as far as Rambouillet and no further. Jerôme gave orders in his usual pompous manner. No sooner had he done so than the officers of the Guard came into the courtyard and declared that they would not allow the Empress to leave. They would have themselves hacked to pieces for Napoleon, his son and for Marie-Louise. They knew that she was being forced to place herself in a situation where she would fall into Austrian hands and they would not assist in putting this disreputable plan into effect. Such an order they would only take from Marie-Louise or from Napoleon. If Napoleon's brothers were scared, they could leave. Marie-Louise thanked them for their loyalty and affection and praised their steadfastness in such dire circumstances. The officers saluted her, standing to attention as Marie-Louise announced that she would not be moving until she had received further instructions from her husband. Jerôme and Joseph were spitting with anger, but they could do nothing. They were, as Napoleon had said, opportunists. She would not be their ransom. Two days later, they bade Marie-Louise an angry farewell.

Marie-Louise's lady-in-waiting, Mme Durand, arrived from Paris with the newspapers and articles culled from journals from which Marie-Louise learned there was much of which she had been ignorant. She found Mme Durand, like Mme de Luçay, sympathetic to her plight, and supportive of her urge to escape to Napoleon: honour and duty demanded that she follow her husband into exile.

Marie-Louise wrote another letter to her father begging for his protection. There were those that told her to leave, others to stay. She wrote to the Emperor. Deflecting her questions, he told her to write to her father. She felt abandoned and placed her trust in the care of Providence. She feared that she might be a millstone around her husband's neck, that by rejoining him she might compromise his safety, that he might need to flee, that she might cause him to fall into enemy hands. She did not know what to think.

Marie-Louise begged Savary to go to her father. The Austrian Emperor kept an ominous silence. She had no idea where he was, where Napoleon was, and rumours abounded that the countryside was flooded with Russians. She wrote another letter to her father begging him to accord her Tuscany, access to the Italian coast essential for her communication with Elba. Nothing. Despite the lack of contact with her father, her faith in his steadfastness remained unswerving. He was a man of his word. Two emissaries arrived to her surprise, one Count Shuvalov sent by Tsar Alexander, the other Baron de Saint-Aignan, representing the provisional government of France. Their brief was to take her and her son to Orléans, the first stage of a journey to Fontainebleau, she imagined, where she hoped to join Napoleon. The two men confirmed that Napoleon had been granted by the Allies the island of Elba but said nothing as regards Tuscany. She immediately wrote to Napoleon telling him of this development and asking him for his views. His reply was ambiguous as to directions, but said how much he was looking forward to being with her, and how concerned he was for her mental and physical state. Before leaving Blois that evening, Marie-Louise made one last defiant proclamation to the French people, which, despite being aware of her impotence, she ordered to be disseminated throughout the country:

> The events of the war have placed the capital in the hands of the enemy. The Emperor, who has run to defend it, is at the head of his armies, so frequently victorious, and they are confronting the enemy at the walls of Paris. It is from the residence I have chosen and from the Emperor's ministers which emanate the only orders which you are to acknowledge. Any town in the hands of the enemy ceases to be free; any decree which issues from the enemy is the language of the foreigner or that which suits his hostile views to propagate. You will be loyal to your oaths. You will listen to the voice of a princess, whose custody was placed in your faith and who derives her glory from being French. My son was less sure of your hearts in the time of our prosperity. His rights and his person are in your safekeeping.[13]

Marie-Louise had no doubt that her French and Russian escort would convey her and her son and Méneval, who had insisted on accompanying her, safely towards her husband. She took with her jewels and the Crown diamonds. Anxious to rid herself of any potentially compromising weapon which she could not hide in her skirts, she sought Méneval's assistance to break the blade of the imperial sword from the hilt upon which was mounted the regency symbol, emblem of the empty power conferred on her. Méneval used one of the brass fire-dogs in the hearth to snap the two pieces apart before burning important family papers and other documentation which might fall into the wrong hands. Marie-Louise confessed her regret at not having risked everything to join Napoleon when it might have been possible to Mme Durand, the lady-in-waiting who had reminded her daily that honour and duty demanded that she follow Napoleon into exile. She reproached herself and then immediately bemoaned her youth and inexperience. At twenty-two, she was ill-equipped to weather the complexities of the politics in which she was embroiled. She would have done better to become a canoness as she had planned in her teens, rather than to come to France. Before mounting the carriage which awaited them, Méneval entrusted on Marie-Louise's behalf three thousand livres to the prefect of the city to distribute to the poor. Marie-Louise said goodbye to the bulk of her retinue and handed out gratuities to staff whom she had seen daily until now but might never see again.

The transit was not as uneventful as the deposed French Empress had hoped. The last wagons of her convoy were ransacked by Cossacks. She arrived at the Archbishop's Palace in Orléans at six o'clock in the evening after a harrowing journey. The Duchess of Montebello rushed forward to greet Mme de Montesquiou's son, recently arrived from Fontainebleau. "I can't wait for all this to be over! I want to be back with my children!" Marie-Louise could not believe the Duchess's insensitivity. Montesquiou brought a further letter from Napoleon containing further instructions as to the terms in which she should write to her father. She did as asked but, this time, qualifying them with her own considerations:

> Dearest Papa,
>
> I send you this letter with one of my officers to request permission to travel to see you. The Emperor is leaving for the island of Elba. I have told him that nothing will make me leave here without having first seen you and having taken your advice directly from you. I beg you to send me a reply. I am determined to do for my son everything within my power which you consider. I know that you have been asked in my name for the Grand Duchy of Tuscany. Be sure that this was done without my knowledge.

Napoleon might have forgotten conveniently that he had evicted Marie-Louise's aunt and uncle, her father's brother, from Tuscany. Marie-Louise had not.

> I know that you love us too much not to think of the fate which awaits my son and my own fate. All that I desire is peace, which is essential for my health. So I beg you, my dear father, to receive me and to allow me to see you . . . I beg you to send me a reply as soon as you are able, as I am dying of fear.[14]

Before her letter had reached her father, she received his reply to her earlier letter. They were not the words she wanted to hear.

> Unfortunately, I cannot give you the comfort you seek, however much I might want to. Everything has been concluded between your husband and the allies. I can only assure you that, no matter what happens, I will always love you as a tender father, and your child and also your husband, for he made you, as his wife, happy. If you need a refuge, take your people with you to my home.

His home, not hers.

More than this I cannot say ... I cannot allow you to hope for the other wish which it is the duty of a mother to desire, to help her son reach his father for I doubt it can be fulfilled. The circumstances seem to me of such a kind that I do not believe that it is possible for me to reach him for I have duties to my allies. I am sorry that your health is suffering ... but look after yourself for the sake of your husband, your child and your father, and show yourself to be my beloved daughter and of my blood even in your great misery ... in me you will always find the same loving father ... [15]

Her father, supposedly the foremost sovereign in Europe, expressed himself powerless to alleviate her husband's abasement, not even for his grandson. Marie-Louise found this inconceivable.

Méneval urged her to keep track of her father's movements, and to throw herself on his mercy. She wrote to her father in desperation, begging him to give her and her loyal servants refuge in his territories. She promised to send him every day a courier to tell him where she was, and asked him to send the courier back to her to tell her his whereabouts so that she could run to him should she be in dire straits. All she wanted was to live peacefully somewhere in his territories and to bring up her son. "God knows I will tell him not to be ambitious!" She felt an urgency to secure her son's future and was mindful of Napoleon's demand that she secure Tuscany: "I need somewhere worthy of my rank for me and especially for my son. I am persuaded that you do not want his only legacy to be the Island of Elba ... This miserable child, who is innocent of his father's failings, does not deserve to share with him such a sad situation." She told her father she would set out for Fontainebleau the following day, despite being extremely ill, suffering strong chest pains and spitting up blood which caused her to fear undertaking any long journey.

As if Marie-Louise were not sufficiently traumatized, more of her court now came forward demanding money and discharge. Acquitting them without rancour, she found their brutal abandonment of her both disgusting and humiliating. The Duchess and Corvisart declared that they would accompany her as far as Livorno, which she found rather peremptory, though she was grateful that they would stay with her for the time being. Countess of Brignole and General Caffarelli and five other members of staff would accompany her. As yet, it was not clear as to whether Mme de Montesquiou intended to stay indefinitely with the King of Rome. The loyal Ménéval would follow her to the ends of the earth, to set up home wherever life took her. His only reservation was that he was financially embarrassed, partially on account of arrears of unpaid salary due to him. Marie-Louise distributed further sums to keep those who were staying well-disposed towards her.

To make matters worse, a pompous official, Dudon, turned up, charged by the provisional government formed after her departure from Paris with the task of reclaiming the Crown diamonds and other treasures, and of returning them to Paris. The lady-in-waiting charged with safekeeping the imperial jewellery immediately ran to Marie-Louise, who was holding court in the drawing room. Marie-Louise told her to let Dudon take everything. Marie-Louise had worn her most valuable jewellery on the journey from Blois to Orléans, confident that no one would interfere with her person. The lady-in-waiting stammered that he demanded the string of pearls she was wearing. Marie-Louise calmly unfastened the necklace which had been given her by Napoleon as a personal gift shortly after the birth of the King of Rome. It had never been part of the Crown jewels. Marie-Louise gave it, still warm from the warmth of her body, to the lady-in-waiting, who was awestruck by this demonstration of nobility. M. Dudon left Orléans with twenty-two wagons heaped with dinner services, ceremonial porcelain, vast quantities of silverware and thirty barrels each containing a million gold coins. Marie-Louise later heard that the chattels had been safely returned, but that the gold had never reached its destination, intercepted by the Comte d'Artois, who organised their distribution to his own retinue.

Morally and physically depleted by the past two weeks, and in need of rest, which she hoped she would get from awaiting an interview with her father, she wrote to Napoleon: "I still harbour hope that when I see my father, such a good man, he will allow himself to be moved by my tears and you will have a better fate. Though you will go and stay on the island of Elba, you will reign too over the possessions which may be given to us, by which I mean Tuscany."[16]

The events of the past fortnight were taking their toll. Marie-Louise was suffering terrible headaches, fevers and was still spitting blood. When her mother-in-law, Mme Mère, and Cardinal Fesch parted from her to journey to Rome where they hoped to set up home, Marie-Louise told them that they would all be together soon. Like Marie-Louise, Mme Mère wanted only to share her son's fate.

Marie-Louise continued to wait for news from Napoleon. She wrote again, begging him for his orders to come and join him, hoping that she had the strength to manage the journey, asking him to indulge her by allowing a break of a few days for her to rest her ailing chest. When finally Napoleon's letters arrived, he advised her that she and her son had been granted by the allies not Tuscany but the duchies of Parma, Piacenza and Guastalla on the Italian peninsula. These duchies comprised four hundred thousand souls and three to four million francs in revenue. She would have at the very least a house and a wonderful country, which would be a perfect sanctuary when she had tired of being with Napoleon on Elba. He said that she should still ask her father for Tuscany, or if not for the principalities of Lucca, Massa, Carrara and their enclaves so that her territories would have access to the sea. He wanted to travel with her to Parma. They would meet up in Briare or Gien and travel together by way of Nevers, Moulins and the Mont-Cénis to La Spezia, where they would board ship for Livorno and travel on to her territories. Napoleon told her to have courage. She should not worry. He would allow her as many breaks as she considered necessary. In any event, she would soon be able to take the waters of

Lucca or Pisa, which would restore her health. He would go on to Elba and make ready for her arrival.

Napoleon's information regarding the award of the Parman duchies was confirmed by a letter Marie-Louise received from Metternich. The Austrian Chancellor told her that she and her august son would be guaranteed an independent existence. Once possessed of her new territories, she would be able to divide her time between Napoleon's kingdom and her own establishment. Pending conclusion of arrangements for the transfer of her duchies to her, Metternich invited her to Austria.

Marie-Louise wrote to Napoleon reiterating Metternich's letter and asking Napoleon whether she should await the interview with her father and join Napoleon immediately thereafter. She needed a response as soon as possible. Metternich's proposals, which seemed to grant her latitude to make her own decisions, did not seem unreasonable. It seemed that the considerations he was addressing were wholly practical. Nonetheless, she wanted to join Napoleon, not return to Austria.

Pending Napoleon's determination, Marie-Louise continued to release members of staff who were not to join her in exile from France. It made her heart bleed to have to part with retainers who had genuine affection for her and her son. Taking a careful look at her finances, she advanced herself her income for March and April so that she could defray expenses and send money to those in Paris who complained that they could not even afford to buy bread. She told Napoleon that Corvisart had advised that she must, once arrived at Parma, rest there and follow a strict diet. He did not think the baths of either Lucca or Pisa suitable for her condition.

The following day, Prince Esterhazy and Prince Liechtenstein, nobles both known to Marie-Louise before her departure from Vienna, came to accompany her from Orléans to Rambouillet where, she was told, she would be able to speak to her father. Napoleon's confidant and foreign minister, Caulaincourt, confirmed that the Austrian Emperor was expecting her. They demanded that she leave immediately. Marie-Louise did not want to leave without first having received Napoleon's consent. They said that they could not wait and that they were instructed to prevent her leaving with Napoleon without her father's consent. Acquiescing with reluctance, she had a dark presentiment that things were already hopeless. She begged Napoleon not to be annoyed with her. There was nothing she could do. She loved him so much that her heart was torn in two. "I fear that you will think that I and my father are conspiring against you. But once I have seen him, I will come and join you. They would have to be barbarians to stand in my way."[17]

Thankfully, the King of Rome did not understand the catastrophe which was unfolding around him. Marie-Louise would take him with her to his grandfather. His grandfather's heart would melt, seeing such a charming, innocent grandson for the first time. Then she would take him to his father with whom he must live. The more they might try to keep father, mother and son apart, the more she felt the need to be close to Napoleon and to take care of him.

General Caffarelli took his leave of Marie-Louise to return to Paris. He told her that, from now on, she belonged to posterity. Pompously, he told her to ennoble adversity: her conduct would determine public opinion in France, Germany and the rest of Europe. Marie-Louise would prove that she had no need for lessons in morality – from him, or from anyone else.

SEVEN

The Mountains of Savoy, Summer 1814

Marie-Louise asked the leader of her team of nineteen guides for a few moments to rest and admire the view. The party were making their way on foot through the Alps towards Chamonix and Geneva. She climbed a little higher using her leather handled long iron pole to hoist herself up a crag. There, she could sit on her own, away from her travelling companions. To one side rose the peak of Dru, a great pyramidal obelisk reaching towards the heavens, its tip lost in the clouds. At its foot of pasture, herds grazed, oblivious to the frozen sea around them. In the distance presided the colossal snow-capped Mont Blanc which seemed to look down on the follies of man as if he were as ephemeral as an insect. Existence seemed timeless, suspended. The silence was broken only intermittently by the sudden fall of an avalanche or the crack of a glacier which could be heard but not seen.

Ever since leaving Paris, the fallen empress had been in tears, the cambric handkerchiefs having made her skin dry and raw. Napoleon had not once sent word to her to make her way to him or planned any rendezvous. On the contrary, he had specifically instructed her to await instructions from her father. She had been convinced that he would be at Rambouillet and would orchestrate an early reunion of mother, father and child. As she had approached the gates of the turreted Palace of Rambouillet, she realised that she had fallen into a trap. Her former servants and guards had been replaced by Cossacks who stood menacingly along the approaching avenues and around the grounds.

"You will already know that they forced me to leave Orléans and that an order has been given to restrain me, by force if necessary, from joining you. Take care, my dear friend, for they are deceiving us, and I am terrified to death for you," she wrote to the deposed emperor on arrival, informing him that her father was expected in the next couple of days and that she could not wait to see him, the interview the only impediment to her joining her husband. "I will be resolute when I speak to my father. I will tell him in no uncertain terms that I want to live close to you and that I cannot understand why this alone should justify the shoddy treatment I am now receiving."[1] She felt antipathetic towards mankind and the world in general, given the ingratitude and falsity she had encountered lately. The island of Elba seemed the only place which might offer her and her husband an agreeable existence. There, by his side, she could be happy. Nothing in the world would persuade her to go to Austria.

Emperor Francis arranged for the Tsar of Russia and King of Prussia to come to her, against her will, to enable her to plead her and her husband's cause, and to seek permission from the Great Powers for her to travel to Aix-en-Savoie, where she hoped the waters might go some way to restoring her ailing health. Emperor Francis advised her firmly to restrain herself from doing anything precipitate. She should act as advised by Metternich, his most loyal servant and friend (on whom he had recently conferred the title of Prince), who, he assured her, was extremely concerned to protect his principal's daughter and grandson.

As Marie-Louise cursed the deceptions played upon her, Hortense suddenly appeared out of nowhere and urged her to hasten into the waiting carriage she had arranged to whisk her off to Napoleon. In a state of near hysteria, the Austrian archduchess begged her friend to give her a moment to reflect. This opportunity, possibly her last, to join Napoleon forthwith ran counter to his express instructions. Overwhelmed by the prospect of excommunication from a familiar world and abandonment to a hostile, inconsequential island, Marie-Louise burst into a succession of questions. Did Hortense think she would be banished from society? Would she be left without means? would she be forced to share her husband's fate on Elba? Shocked and disgusted, Hortense strode out of the palace with curt farewell and into her carriage. Distraught, the deposed Empress penned frenetically numerous letters of thanks to the staff who had served her as empress, expressing her regret that she had not had the time to thank them in person.

To her relief, the awkward, unhappy King of Prussia declined Marie-Louise's summons. Emperor Alexander came running to help, always eager to assist a damsel in distress. He listened patiently, his head bent slightly to one side to compensate for being hard of hearing, showing sympathy and understanding which Marie-Louise had found lacking in others. Ménéval, who was present at the interview, was impressed by her composure and lack of self-pity as she recited her sorry tale. The Tsar, no doubt, more than anyone else, fully appreciated the perilous ambiguity of her situation, having refused to countenance a Romanov-Bonaparte dynastic marriage five years earlier.

Marie-Louise thrust her son into his grandfather's arms upon his arrival at Rambouillet. It was the first time the Emperor had set eyes on his grandson. Emperor Francis was clearly distressed by the agonies his daughter had suffered. In floods of tears, she pleaded with her father to allow her and her son to go to the child's father on Elba. The family reunion her father planned was not in the quiet harbour of Portoferraio but in the cosmopolitan hub for which Marie-Louise had long yearned. He told her that it would do her good to return to Vienna and spend time with the clan there. She was glad that he had declined an invitation extended to Marie-Louise to return to Paris to say a last farewell to her adopted countrymen before journeying to Austria. Speaking for her father, Metternich told her that she would be allocated apartments at the Palace of Schönbrunn and funds to sustain her. She could go to Aix from there to recover. As soon as she was well enough, she could go and take possession of her states, from which she would be able to make arrangements to spend time with her husband, who would be free to visit her and their child in Parma. Her father had already reassured his son-in-law that his son would be warmly welcomed as part of the family. Marie-Louise would retain her title of empress and would be free to correspond with her husband. Metternich spoke warmly of his former long-time opponent: he would have handled things very differently had other coalition partners Russia and England not behaved mercilessly.

Marie-Louise was exasperated. Her father's promises seemed to amount to indefinite postponement of her joining her beloved. Setting out towards Vienna surrounded by an Austrian guard of honour, she felt dejected, regretting her failure to seize opportunities to join Napoleon when it might have been possible. At least her father had fallen in love with their son, she wrote with pride to Napoleon. "He is Daddy's enemy – I do not wish to see him!" After such outbursts, she had great difficulty getting him to behave agreeably towards his grandfather. She commended Napoleon on his fortitude and said how deeply moved she was to hear how bravely he was bearing his misfortunes in a letter written the day before his departure for the port of Fréjus, ignorant of his failed suicide attempt.

Particularly painful for Marie-Louise was the inexplicable lack of letters from Napoleon as she moved closer to Austria. At Emperor Francis's direction, she passed her own letters to him to Metternich, supposedly the best guarantor of their safe passage. She worried increasingly about her persistent chest pains, unceasing cough and spitting of blood, her dramatic weight loss – she doubted her husband would recognise her. She lay all her store by the waters of Aix.

Oblivious to the political changes which had destroyed his future, the feted King of Rome found the journey to his mother's homeland great fun. Relentless compliments raised her morale. Both she and his governess, Mme de Montesquiou, were pained by his constant questions after his father and by his distressing realisation that they were not getting closer to him. Mme de Montesquiou was extremely bitter about the fact that she had not been consulted on the fateful night before the flight from Paris, and had been forced to keep silent thereafter. Had she thought for one moment that the child might have to leave France without seeing his father, she would have got him to Fontainebleau, come hell or high water. At Rambouillet, the little King had begged her to stay as most of his entourage resigned. She promised never to abandon him, though she foresaw that her services might no longer needed. As each day passed, the toddler became more attached to her, one of the few last links to the father he missed.

The imperial party travelled via the awesome beauty of Zurich, Lake Constance and Waldsee. Marie-Louise's face ran constantly with tears. Her chronic insomnia was not helped by particularly painful menstruation. Concerns about passing through the Tyrol, prone to violent political disturbances, proved unfounded. Enthusiastic crowds acclaimed her deliriously, unharnessing and leading her carriage through every little town. Although heartened, she refused to be cast as the freed hostage. To show more than mildest approval would be to betray her husband. Finally, at Basel and at Schaffhaus letters awaited her from Napoleon. Both were depressing, expressing his disenchantment with former friends who now deserted him, and with countrymen who blasted him with insults.

"I find men so repugnant that all I want is for them to grant me that little for which I am dependent upon them." The only thing which would weaken him, he said, was the thought that his love no longer loved him. "It is only you who can bring me happiness."[2] Marie-Louise assured him that he was constantly in her thoughts, that she was constantly assailing her father with demands to alleviate his financial position and the conditions of his exile of which he complained. She was relieved to hear that his sister Pauline would be joining him on Elba.

Empress Marie-Ludovica had driven out to the town of Mölk, four leagues from Vienna, to greet her stepdaughter, a moment of triumph for the Bonaparte-hater. She received her warmly, as did Count Trauttmansdorff, once more kissing her hands in tears, just as he had four years earlier. Waiting for her in the courtyard of

Schönbrunn in a state of great excitement were Marie-Louise's siblings and two hundred and thirty carriages filled with prurient spectators. In the early evening sunshine of late May, Marie-Louise emerged from her carriage, her faced framed by a large travelling hat, to resounding applause. The brothers and sisters she had missed so much flung their arms around her neck with joy, congratulating her upon her return as if her ordeal had come to an end. "What an agonizing fate mine is! To have slipped from the hands of the Emperor and left France miserable!" she noted in her diary on her arrival. "God alone knows my suffering! Oh, my impotence in this vortex of intrigues and betrayals!"

For the next six weeks, Marie-Louise relished the company of her sisters: Leopoldine approaching seventeen and Marie-Clementine sixteen, both dangerously marriageable ages; Caroline-Ferdinande was thirteen and Marie-Anne ten years old. Gentle and kind as always to her simple brother Ferdinand, her father's heir, she was pleased to find a ready playmate for her son in her ten-year-old brother, Francis Charles. She spent the mornings with the King of Rome, whom all, save the French, referred to as Prince of Parma, a charming term which gave her confidence that she would soon be in the duchies promised her by her husband's abdication. It was a great comfort to be part of a milieu in which she had always felt easy, her father and stepmother, her uncles Albert Duke of Saxe-Teschen and Archdukes Rudolph and Karl whose company she particularly adored. Initially, she received the aristocrats with whom she had been used to socialize before her departure in 1810, the Trauttmansdorffs, the Metternichs, Countess Colloredo and her daughter Victoria de Crenneville, her close confidante, and other members admitted to the imperial inner circle such as the Wrbnas, Dietrichsteins, Sickingens, Witzecks, de Lignes and Esterhazys.

Marie-Louise was free to move about as she wished, but preferred seclusion to public appearance. Though overjoyed to see her Habsburg kin again, she wanted to keep a certain distance and dignity, insisting that she and her son have their own adjoining quarters where she could live independently with her entourage without the regimentation of etiquette, a refuge from the atmosphere of celebrations of victory. She quickly established a routine, timetabling painting, music, piano and harp lessons, horse-riding and the walks she had enjoyed in her youth with Countess Colloredo. Italian lessons in preparation for her departure for Parma were also scheduled. Whenever she went out, she was conscious of silent, respectful crowds following her, avidly watching her and her generally admired son. Both mother and son had become curiosities. The former empress took her meals alone with the remnants of her French entourage, Countess of Brignole, De Bausset and Ménéval, whose affection for her, her husband and her son often moved her to tears. After mealtimes, she had Mme Montesquiou bring the King of Rome, spoiling him with desserts and caramels.

To Marie-Louise's consternation, Countess of Brignole, one of the intriguers who, unbeknown to her empress, had been part of the cabale to facilitate Napoleon's downfall, proposed in conversation that Marie-Louise should seek a divorce from her husband, given the circumstances. Marie-Ludovica seized upon this idea with enthusiasm. Filled with indignation, Marie-Louise declared that she had no intention of doing any such thing. Supporting Countess of Brignole's proposal, De Bausset, until recently Napoleon's trusted imperial prefect, told the young bride to forget what he considered to be the sentimental inanity of a relationship which had outgrown its use. Marie-Louise was amazed at his effrontery, but her position was far too precarious to rise to the assembled company's provocation. Loose cannon he might be, but De Bausset managed her financial affairs and knew details regarding daily life at the French court. To alienate him and lose his goodwill might be foolish at a time when observers were looking for chinks in her armour. Ménéval despised De Bausset's behaviour.

Paradoxically, Marie-Louise found her greatest ally in her ageing maternal grandmother. At a weary sixty-three, Queen Maria-Carolina had lost none of her fight. She had taken a close interest in her precious grandchild from the moment of her birth, sending her generous gifts from Naples, and had insisted that her daughter send her Marie-Louises's first milk tooth. Marie-Louise had first met her grandmother in the year 1800, when she appeared with great pomp in Vienna in the company of Vice-Admiral Nelson, the toast of all civilized society following his destruction of the French fleet on the Nile. Four years later, she was back in Vienna once more, but this time, not consorting with heroes. Napoleon had sent French troops to occupy Naples when she refused to enforce his continental blockade against Britain, forcing her and her family to flee to Palermo on Nelson's ship, the *Vanguard*. Upon this second visit to Vienna, Queen Maria-Carolina caused general embarrassment with her hysterical, ultimately fruitless tirades against the French Emperor, referring openly to Napoleon as the Corsican cur or the Corsican bastard. He was a ferocious animal who would bring about the fall of the House of Habsburg. His elevation was a stain upon the name of sovereignty, an indictment of the weakness of humanity, of the barbarians who had first written vast libraries on "liberté, égalité, fraternité". Her hatred of the French, an obsession ever since the execution of her brother-in-law, Louis XVI and sister, Queen Marie-Antoinette, became compulsive. From the moment Napoleon had demanded her evacuation from Sicily to save her husband's crown, she announced that she was and never would be on good terms with the French. "I should like this infamous nation to be cut to pieces, annihilated, dishonoured, reduced to nothing for a least fifty years."[3] France should be pulverized and all her inhabitants along with her, preferably by the glorious arms of Austria. Her daughter, Marie-Louise's mother, was equally contemptuous, particularly after the crushing Austrian defeat of Austerlitz in 1805, unable to bring herself to write his name or to use or allow any acknowledgement of his title of Emperor to be made in her presence. The man lacked even a shred of humanity. She refused to call him 'the Corsican usurper', which many dubbed him, believing it to cast an unfair slur on the island.

Maria-Carolina had been horrified when her son-in-law announced in his eldest daughter's presence at a family dinner in Schönbrunn the year that Napoleon declared himself emperor, "Whatever you say, if Bonaparte were to ask to marry my daughter, I would give her to him, and if he offered me this proposal tomorrow, I would undoubtedly accept it."[4] She could not countenance any Habsburg Bonaparte marriage either during her lifetime or for two centuries thereafter. "That is the last thing missing in my misery, to become the devil's grandmother," she is said to have exclaimed on receipt of news of her granddaughter's marriage.[5] As the years passed, however, her hatred for the French Emperor transmuted into genuine admiration. It was clear to her that Europe's leaders lacked Napoleon's vigour, firmness and energy, his political conviction "more impossible to acquire than grabbing the moon with one's teeth". He was the greatest man several centuries had produced.

> In this man, everything is great . . . though I deplored that this grandeur was attached to so infernal a cause as the phoenix of the French Revolution. I have always wished for his personal happiness and glory so long as it was not at our expense. When he dies, they should reduce him to powder and give a dose of it to each ruling sovereign, and two to each of their ministers. Then things would improve.[6]

At Marie-Louise's return, the old Queen of the Two Sicilies, short with small eyes and colourless skin, was lodged in the Castle of Hetzendorf, the grounds of which adjoined Schönbrunn. Marie-Louise would later say that her grandmother was, before her father's arrival, the only humane being in Vienna to declare her goodwill towards her. Putting the past behind her, Queen Maria-Carolina urged her granddaughter to join her husband. Marie-Louise found her sympathy and concern genuine. Indignant at the Allies' treatment of the vanquished titan, Maria-Carolina thanked the French entourage for their loyalty to her granddaughter.

In spite of all the harm he had done to us in Italy, I must admit that I hold a high opinion of him, as I love the great in all things and everywhere, even when I find it turned against me. I foresee that this world will resound with his name, and that history will immortalize him.[7]

She loved to caress her great-grandson and to hear from Marie-Louise what a good husband and father Napoleon had been. In her harsh, rasping voice, Maria-Carolina chatted at length with Méneval in French, which she used to call "that murderous language". She expressed her contempt for the spineless men who kept wife from husband, depriving him of the sweetest consolation after the ignominy they had forced him to suffer. Marie-Louise and the King of Rome should be allowed to join Napoleon without delay. "Take the sheets from your bed and escape in disguise out of the window. That is what I would do in your shoes. When you are married, it is for life."[8] Marie-Louise found no such sympathy elsewhere.

Most of the time, the deposed empress found herself parrying slights of Napoleon, and withstanding the hurt of snide comments. Convinced that the allies had no intention of granting her a shadow of sovereignty, Méneval warned her against snares set by intriguers. Avoiding direct accusation, he implied that he feared that the Austrian court's real agenda was to have her remain in Austria for the rest of her life. Metternich was claiming Parma in her name merely to seize control of another Italian territory. He had no doubt that the allies had no desire to facilitate the former empress reaching her husband. She told him she would be firm and would not allow herself to be taken in. However much she wanted to escape her present uncomfortable situation, her grandmother's advice appealed neither to her character nor sense of propriety. Attempts at heroism would have been reckless to say the least, her great-aunt and uncle's ill-fated flight from Paris a stark warning.

Anticipating interception, Marie-Louise had carefully numbered each of her letters to Napoleon. Of over a dozen sent since her departure from Rambouillet, he had received only two letters numbered '8' and '11'. Having heard nothing from him since his letter of 10th May, she feared that he had not received her letters and would think that she had forgotton him. "This thought is the most cruel of all. I have had no word from you, despite the arrival of General Koller from Elba who must have brought a letter from you to me which no doubt Metternich has chosen to keep on his desk."[9] Nothing would deter her from writing. She would rather the letters never reached him than that she might have to reproach herself for failing to send him her and her son's news. Their son was on excellent form, better than ever, beginning every sentence "When we see Papa . . .". "Your son, beautiful as the day, often speaks of you to me, making surprising observations for his age, which makes me tremble. They say that children who are so precocious do not live long. Heaven forfend that this tragedy awaits me!"[10] Marie-Louise had been spitting with anger when her son had asked for news of his father in the presence of his great-grandmother, who told him firmly that he would never see his father again. Marie-Louise grabbed her little boy and, on the verge of tears, cried passionately, "You will see him! I promise you, you will see him!"[11] Whenever mother and son manifested the slightest sign of affection for Napoleon, they met with hostility.

In the middle of June, Marie-Louise set out to meet her father returning from Paris at the village of Siegratkirchen two miles outside Vienna. He had signed the Treaty of Paris, which was intended to seal Marie-Louise's entitlement to Parma. She greeted him on bended knee, her eyes wet with emotion, convinced that her loyalty and obedience would secure her early transfer to her duchies. It was a strange moment, the fact undeniable that he had collaborated in her fall and in the exile of her husband. The sacred interest of the House of Habsburg had forced him to be her conqueror and to reduce her and her son to be mere refugees. She would have to fight her own corner alone.

"There is a cabal formed to stop me going to Aix to take the waters." Members of the family were trying to persuade her to go instead to Karlsbad in Germany. "Some are scheming to deprive me of the Duchy of Parma and to find a way of disenfranchising our son. I am extremely tormented by these developments, particularly as I am told that my every word is the subject of the closest scrutiny."[12] She told Napoleon she would not give ground in relation either to Parma or to Aix. She would pretend to be ill to get herself and her son to Aix even if she felt better, Vienna having become a prison. Dejected, she waited for another letter from her love.

Marie-Louise bitterly regretted not standing her ground in Paris two months earlier. She was sure that her father's soldiers would never have chased her away and that she would now be with Napoleon. She had no need to pretend to be ill. She was suffering intolerable ongoing pains at the nape of her neck, radiating into her head and down her back, across her chest, through her arms and legs. The violent emotions which had assailed her since leaving France had brought her to a virtually convulsive nervous state. She knew not whether the sweats she suffered each sleepless night were symptoms of disease or purely a reaction to her trauma.

Marie-Louise railed against her father when he demanded that she leave her son in Vienna during her trip to Aix. To her surprise, he suggested she write to Napoleon for guidance.

> People might interpret my trip across the French border as an attempt to disturb the tranquillity of Europe, which might place me and my son in difficulties. My father even went so far as to say: "If Napoleon does not agree with me, he is the master – have the boy come with you." I would like your advice. Place prudence and my wishes in the balance. I know that there are no safer hands in which my son could be than here, but you know how mothers torment themselves far from their children.[13]

She had started some needlepoint, she told him, so that he would have a canvas for his upholstery embroidered entirely by her own hand for his bedroom on Elba.

There was little chance that any response from Napoleon would reach her before departure for Aix. Emperor Francis finally dissuaded Marie-Louise from taking the Prince of Parma and his household with her on the grounds of economy. He warned her that the financial affairs of Parma were in a precarious state. She could not expect any revenue from her duchies for the coming year, and thereafter things would be tight. She would have to live as frugally as possible for the foreseeable future. Marie-Louise yielded. Her father told her that Napoleon had sent a detachment of fifty Polish light cavalry and a hundred horses to Parma in anticipation of her arrival. "I have offered them employment, since their presence in [Parma] would be harmful both to Austria and to other countries."[14] Lacking the resources to feed them all, she would have to select the healthiest and sell the rest, she wrote to Napoleon. Still without direct communication from him, she sent him her itinerary for her journey to Aix. She would travel under a pseudonym, 'the Duchess of Colorno', adopting the name of one of her Parman country residences. She planned to travel on from Aix directly to Parma and to arrange for her son and his governess to meet her so that Napoleon could join them both there. She began to persuade herself that Napoleon would be happier were she to have a separate existence, which would give both him and her the freedom to come together at will. She asked him to allocate a modest lodging in the pretty country house he was building on Elba where she would stay as often as time allowed. In the meantime, she asked him to send her his requirements for cuttings of plants and flowers for his gardens, Paris having refused, despicably in her view, to oblige him.

At the close of June, Marie-Louise finally embarked incognito, nonetheless accompanied by a retinue of thirty-three, for a brief excursion to the Alps of Savoy, before taking the waters of Aix-en-Savoie. She was accompanied by Ménéval, her greatest source of comfort, who promised to write a poetic account of their trip.

Together they looked out over the glaciers of Bossons, Montanvert and the Mer de Glace. Both found their spirits uplifted by the marvelous contrast of ice and flowers which seemed to hold tribulations at bay. They crossed from Savoy to Le Valais following mountain paths of dried-up beds of torrents, strewn all about with sky-blue gentians. Ménéval walked alongside her talking to her, reminding her of the joyous times she had spent with Napoleon, the early morning rides in the summer while the household slept, the afternoon riding lessons when Napoleon, on horseback still in silk stockings and slippers with oval gold buckles, goaded her horse on so that she would scream with fear and beg him to stop. Those times would never return.

After six days in the Alps of Savoy, Marie-Louise set out from Sécherons for Aix. Two stations away from the town, an officer-general and his aide-de-camp, both in Austrian uniform, came to lead her to the lodgings prepared for her. She felt an instant antipathy for the officer-general. Two days later, she bade a sad farewell to Ménéval, wondering how she would manage without him over the six-week break he was taking to be with his wife in France. She hungered for a letter from Napoleon – nothing had arrived for two months. "If you might have the goodness to reply," Marie-Louise wrote with an overriding sense of impotence, "I beg you to send your reply to Aix. Write often for it is my only consolation – rest assured that nothing in the world will ever change the tender feelings I have for you."[15]

EIGHT

The untimely visit, September 1814

As wife of a usurper, diplomacy dictated that Marie-Louise's presence would be inappropriate at the public funeral held at the request of the restored Bourbon king, Louis XVIII, for his brother, Louis XVI. The first memorial of its kind took place on 21 January 1815 in Vienna's St Stephen's Cathedral, exactly twenty-two years after the late monarch's severed head had been shown to jubilant crowds. Emperor Francis insisted that the event be celebrated in his capital with extraordinary pomp, taking upon the Austrian Imperial Treasury the cost of one hundred thousand florins. Empress Marie-Ludovica, too ill to attend, confined to her bed, begged her stepdaughter to bleed her.

Marie-Louise had last nursed her stepmother in 1809. Then, Vienna had been in a state of panic as Napoleon marched towards Austria. Even the young archduchess, who hardly exerted any political influence, was approached by terrified French emigrés for help in arranging passports for hazardous passage across the Mediterranean to the Ottoman empire still beyond his reach.

Marie-Louise wrote from Vienna to congratulate her father on the great victory he had won against the French.

> When news first broke and spread about the city, the sense of elation was extremely touching ... We were particularly thrilled to hear that Napoleon had been present, for we hoped that, having lost such a battle, he might also lose his head. Here, everyone makes countless predictions as to his end. A

claim has been made that . . . he will die this year in Cologne . . . would that it were true!¹

Marie-Louise had grown up playing war games with wooden soldiers with her brothers. The unfortunate effigies chosen to represent Napoleon were habitually stabbed, mutilated, torn to pieces or burnt to a cinder. Clairvoyants had regularly predicted Napoleon's early death, the only prospect for Europe's tranquillity. His assassination, for which everyone hoped, would be regarded as an act of heroism.

Napoleon was far from dead and declaration of Austrian victory premature. Marie-Louise was swiftly evacuated with other Habsburg family members to the safety of Buda. When Napoleon had first invaded Austria in 1805, Marie-Louise, aged fourteen, had been sent on endless journeys back and forth across her father's Hungarian territories to avoid capture by Napoleon's troops, a rude awakening from the sheltered existence of pet animals and patisserie. This time, the Hungarian capital promised a safe refuge. As she travelled eastward, Marie-Louise witnessed droves of people in flight, risking insurgents and highwaymen. They fled the cities to avoid French heavy artillery and the countryside to avoid Cossacks, French troops and Turkish robbers who burned, sacked and pillaged. There were rumours from the Tyrol that the French cut off the beards of priests and monks, stripped and defrocked them and then slung them on burning pyres, threw out the hosts and stole church vessels or crushed them underfoot. The loyal Austrian archduchess deplored the depravity and cursed the French Emperor a thousand times.

Napoleon blasted Vienna with cannon by day and entertained his mistresses and aides-de-camp in the Habsburg residences by night. His onslaught had been so brutal, the atrocities perpetrated by his armies so gratuitous, and the fatalities and wounded so numerous at the battles of Aspern-Essling and Wagram that it had proved necessary to convert Vienna's famous Riding School, the city's convents and entertainment halls into hospitals. The bombardment of

Pressburg, where Emperor Francis was lodged during the hostilities, particularly incensed Marie-Louise and Marie-Ludovica. French troops detonated a sixty-two pound bomb aimed directly at him that pierced his room from which he chanced to be momentarily absent. The young archduchess thought then that Bonaparte was nothing other than the Antichrist and his war Armageddon. "Just to set eyes on this monster would be a torment worse than any other martyrdom,"[2] she wrote to her friend Victoria. Emperor Francis's letter to her after visiting the seventy thousand sick and wounded in tents which had become makeshift hospitals following the bloody toll of conflict, told how touched he was that several Frenchmen had promised not to fight him again. He had spoken kindly to everyone, Austrian, Prussian and French without discrimination. As often happened when large numbers of troops were together, disease had spread, so contagious that hoards of civilians were fatally sick. Marie-Louise would never forget the stench of decomposing French corpses which had floated past her and Marie-Ludovica as they took their promenade one afternoon in the Orczy gardens, the usually grey-blue waters of the Danube turned to the dark burgundy of congealing blood.

There had been a dreadful state of agitation. Few people opened a letter without trembling, so probable was news of death or mutilation. The slightest unfamiliar noise, an unscheduled arrival, the noise of postillions taking out one of the carriages for fun, had been enough to cause panic. The announcement of an armistice came as a relief to her.

The Austrian archduchess acknowledged bitterly that a peace treaty with Bonaparte was unavoidable, a *fait accompli*, however ignominious its terms. If her father did not make peace, the Habsburg Empire would cease to exist and be subsumed into France. She and her family would be forced into exile, in all likelihood to England where Bourbon Louis, rightful heir to France, had taken refuge. In any event, Austria was on the verge of bankruptcy. Forced back to metal currency after financing her wars against

Napoleon by the issue of paper money, this was not the time to entertain delusions. Everyone knew that a peace treaty signed by the French emperor was practically worthless – he had breached the terms of the treaties he had signed* after previous amnesties. Austria had to accept it.

Marie-Ludovica, supporter of the Austrian war party, or 'Anglomaniacs' as they were known, could not contain her anger and ranted between coughing and spluttering. The ogre who had chased her family out of Modena and brought about her father's premature death was the very devil. The destruction of Bonaparte and his country became an obsession. The Austrians were not prepared to countenance despatch of the contents of Habsburg granaries and coffers to the zealots in Paris who purported to teach the conquered the rights of man. They would not be forced to live as paupers, reduced to tallow for light, to feet for transport, horses and men requisitioned to do *his* battles. The Austrian Emperor, as erstwhile Holy Roman Emperor and Defender of the Faith, could not turn a blind eye to Bonaparte's kidnap and imprisonment of the Head of the Catholic Church Pope Pius VII, to leave him to languish in a dark dungeon in Savona while the despot presided from St Peter's in the Eternal City. Vienna was already smarting under Napoleon's domination, all inhabitants without exception obliged to pay their rents between one hundred and one thousand florins directly to the French. So far, the Viennese had expressed their contempt for Napoleon by disdaining the theatre performances he had substituted. Only the second rank nobility had dared to take up opera-tickets refused by the high nobility. They also ignored his fortieth birthday as he paraded on horseback with his troops through the city. No-one emerged onto his balcony or into the street, ignoring the illuminations that evening organised by the French. A loyal Austrian had

---

* By the Lunéville Treaty, Bonaparte had contracted to evacuate Holland, the Kingdom of Naples, Switzerland and Piedmont. By the Peace of Amiens, he had contracted to evacuate Malta. Instead, he had helped himself to Hanover, and goaded the English into confrontation by promising Malta to Russia.

put up a banner reading "Zur Weihe An Napoleons Geburtsfest [in dedication of Napoleon's birthday]" – of course, any German reading the acronym writ large in crimson red could see the word "ZWANG" – force, compulsion! Other banners read ambiguously: "The Emperor lives!" and "Oh, Napoleon! Your power entrances, give us back our Emperor Francis!" The imperial family wept to learn of the death of Haydn, his days cut short witnessing the destruction of his beloved city. He had been a frequent visitor to Schönbrunn, playing incessantly with his bone rosary accessible in a jacket pocket.

The failed assassination attempt* in the autumn of 1809 when Napoleon was parading his troops in the courtyard of Schönbrunn was met by deep dismay. Just before Christmas, Marie-Louise read in the newspapers of Napoleon's divorce from Josephine. Aware that she might be selected as Josephine's successor, she confided to her father that she had discovered in her cousin Francis, brother of Marie-Ludovica, all the qualities to make her happy. She left the decision to him, acknowledging that she could not place her future happiness in better hands than his. She wrote to her friend Victoria that Napoleon would be far too fearful of rejection to venture a marriage proposal. In any event, her father was far too good to impose such a restraint upon her on a matter of such importance. She pitied the poor princess ultimately to be chosen. Her sense of foreboding deepened as she scoured daily the *Frankfurter Allgemeine* but found no official announcement of Josephine's replacement. She tried to distract herself with the harpsichord or duets with her Uncle Rudolph. Music-making helped to settle nerves, particularly those of Marie-Ludovica. Marie-Louise begged her music teacher to send her from Vienna a new fascinating duet for two pianos which she

---

* Friedrich Stapps was a devout eighteen-year-old Saxon who considered Napoleon's occupation to be the root of all German misery and planned to knife him at a parade in Schonbrunn's courtyard on 12 October 1809. Arrested, he wanted no pardon, only expressing regret at his failure. Declared mad by a military tribunal, he was executed on 16 October.

had discovered, not put off by the dedication by the composer to Mme Bonaparte.

She wrote to Victoria to tell her that she placed her fate in the hands of divine Providence, but if unhappy fortune demanded it, she would be ready to sacrifice her personal happiness for the good of the State. True felicity was to be found in the fulfilment of one's duty, even to the detriment of one's own inclinations. She did not want to think about it and asked her friend to pray that she would not be called upon.

After Christmas, Marie-Louise returned to Vienna and to her father. She prayed that she would never again be separated from him for so long. Days later, she was startled to overhear her piano teacher, Koželuch, talking about the Emperor Napoleon's casting list for a new wife, headed by her own name. When her father summoned her to tell her that he was expecting the victor's marriage proposal, she knew it was her duty, however odious, to accept. Though she had refrained from the common ferocious outpourings against her suitor, she had never felt anything but contempt for him. She told herself that she would be the only person not to rejoice in the arrangement, and looked forward to divine recompense.

There was a distinct shift in attitudes over the course of the few weeks following the announcement of her engagement. The many letters of congratulation sent by aunts and uncles stressed the happiness that her union would bring to so many individuals, regarded as a benefit conferred by kind Providence for the entire human race. Napoleon was no longer the enemy, the vitriol in which everyone had indulged with such gusto conveniently forgotten. As her betrothed, he was both friend and kin. Marie-Ludovica who, but a few moments ago, had sworn eternal damnation to the victor of Wagram, promised her stepdaughter how happy she would be living as empress to one of the most powerful men in Europe. Papa Francis remembered how, four years earlier, after his ignominious defeat at the Battle of Austerlitz, Moravia, he had first met Napoleon: "With Bonaparte himself, I was quite fairly content, insofar as one can be content with a victor who has sequestered a large part of my monarchy. He was not sparing in his expression of respect for me and my family."[3]

Marie-Louise was told that she must not be downcast, but must celebrate her suit. She had once told her father how absurd she thought it that the Emperor Napoleon was included in the volume of the Great Men of History, and that her father was not. Following her engagement, the Austrian Emperor told his daughter to start appreciating the fine qualities of a man whom misfortune had forced her to regard in an unfavourable light. Suddenly, Napoleon was no longer a child of the regicidal French Revolution, but the man who had brought an end to the anarchy the revolutionaries had set in train. He was praised for the grandeur of his court and empire, for the love he inspired in his generals, his troops and his countrymen. He was lauded for his hard work, self-discipline and approachability.

Marie-Louise was not able to change her feelings quite so easily. Like the rest of Austria, she was not in party mood. Used to having her measurements taken, she found it a penance for a man and a wardrobe she had never sought. Many of the preparations and ceremonies in anticipation of the wedding were carried out in sadness, despite everyone's best efforts to display a gay exterior to the public or to any French guest.

Marie-Louise had done as her father had asked. From the moment she had set eyes on Napoleon, she had followed her stepmother's counsel. Marie-Ludovica started her extraordinary letter – longer than those from the Apostles,

> My dear child, to harvest the fruits of a sacrifice, the sacrifice must be total. If it is otherwise, it loses merit. By detaching yourself from everything, you will cleave all the more to your Husband who alone must possess both your heart and your confidence. This is nothing new. You will remember, my darling, that I have always told you this. For goodness sake, never

allow a third party, whoever it is, to meddle in your marriage or to presume to give you advice. Talk candidly to your Husband about your concerns. He will prefer your questions to the opinion of a stranger. I adopted this principle when I got married and it has never failed me. You will want for nothing if you stick steadfastly to your principles in all that you do. This is the essence of existence which the world will not teach you.[4]

Marie-Ludovica claimed to have guessed everything that was going on in Marie-Louise's soul as she made her way towards her groom, and asked her not to close the door which she had opened to her and from which she had derived so much pleasure. Only open conversation would console her for her stepdaughter's absence.

Marie-Louise had always been entirely open with Napoleon and with her father and stepmother, never once suspecting a lack of candour. She had listened only to her husband, placing her trust in him, never questioning his motives she believed commendable. She had produced the child whose birth was supposed to guarantee many long years of peace between Austria and France. Alas, her cooperation had not achieved this. As far as Marie-Louise could see, she had not given any third party any empire over her, though the Duchess of Montebello might have thought otherwise.

For her journey to Aix, after which she looked forward to joining Napoleon as soon as might be permitted, Marie-Louise's father had assigned her an equerry, the Bohemian General Neipperg, to be her escort for her stay. Well built, with a ruddy complexion, blond-tinged auburn hair and a black bandeau concealing his right eye, he was less than appealing. She kept him at arm's length. Despite her ambivalence as to the company, she enjoyed the baths. Aix's hospital had only been open a year, inaugurated by Hortense, to whom Marie-Louise would now be a stranger. Its charges modest compared to other fashionable baths making them affordable to the ordinary gentry as well as the impoverished aristocracy, the lack of ornamentation, marble basins and fluted columns suited Marie-Louise's understated style. She bathed daily, walking briskly to her appointments in a flannel dressing-gown, refusing to be carried as some demanded, and rested afterwards on a comfortable sofa. Going about under the pseudonym of Duchess of Colorno, she had no desire to attend the races, pigeon matches and other amusements on offer, for fear of being recognised. She enjoyed boating on the delightful Lac du Bourget, perch, trout, carp and other local fish visible in its calm transparent depths. She disdained the tamer lakeside promenades for forays into the hill of Tresserves and the mountains. As she climbed higher, the views of the lake, mass of sandstone, luxuriant vegetation, broad chestnut and fruit trees between crops of cereal became more dramatic. She loved the Gorges of Sierroz, Mouxy and the Cascade of Gresy with its angora rabbits. She enjoyed her outings so much that she was often taken by surprise by nightfall and found herself terrified returning home on horseback in the dark. Most of her evenings were spent quietly, save when she invited select guests and some of the stars of the French stage who appeared on Aix's boards to perform for her privately.

When indoors during the day, the Duchess of Colorno would write her journal and embroider canvasses which she planned for Napoleon's study or living room. From the window of her villa, occupied by Hortense in previous years, she had a marvellous view of the Lac de Bourget and the mountains beyond. Isabey produced charming vignettes which she intended to send to Parma to have copied. She received visits from Dr. Corvisart, and from the Duchess of Montebello. Blind to her insidious behaviour, Marie-Louise did not suspect that she might well be exultant at Napoleon and her own fall. Within a month of parting from Marie-Louise at Aix, she would be writing to her to tell her how sad the poor gardens of Malmaison were, feeling Josephine's absence, and asking Marie-Louise whether there was any truth in what people were saying, that Her Majesty had just given birth to a son.

The Duchess of Montebello had kept her hatred of Napoleon well hidden. Her husband, Marshal Lannes, had been one of Napoleon's greatest marshals. He had fought valiantly despite serious wounds to provide the foundation for the Empire at the head of which his 'friend' had stood. Lannes had become disillusioned with Napoleon and his inveterate warmongering, and warned him not to engage Austria in battle in the summer of 1809. He begged him to make peace, which, universally desired, might not make him more powerful, but would make him infinitely more loved. Napoleon ignored him. Lannes fell at the Battle of Essling. Napoleon dismissed his twenty-seven year old widow's request that he appoint someone else to the most prestigious position at court for a woman. Reluctantly, the Duchess left her five children and set out to meet Marie-Louise at Braunau. She was filled with indignation when she was forced, along with the Duchess of Bassano, to yield her necklace, earrings and other jewels to swell the pot available for distribution as gifts for the Austrian entourage who had turned up in far greater numbers than anticipated, and for the hosts en route. When Marie-Louise's retinue passed through Strasbourg, the Duchess, against advice, visited the crypt where her husband lay before transfer to Paris. Nothing could have prepared her for the sight of his mutilated remains awaiting embalmment. Napoleon had ordered that her husband, his so-called best friend, receive a state funeral at Les Invalides and that he be buried in the Pantheon. Crowds lined the streets of Paris as Lannes' body was carried to its burial place, but his so-called best friend had chosen to spend the day hunting with his bride. The Duchess's anger was not assuaged when Napoleon created the Quai de Montebello between the Pont Saint Michel and Pont de la Tourrelle, or the erection of her husband's statue on the Pont de la Concorde, or the commissioning from Guérin and Bourgeois of paintings of his last moments for the imperial palaces. She could not abide Napoleon's use of the familiar "tu" to which she had never invited him,[5] or him touching her in his usual jocular manner.

Marie-Louise represented everything that the late Marshal and his widow despised. Their hatred of nobles, particularly émigrés who had fled the justice of the revolution to return to Paris to resume their estates and elevated positions, was such that they had done everything in their power to stop Napoleon recalling them. Lannes' warning that the émigrés would prove false friends to his Emperor resulted in his exile from Paris for a brief period. The Lannes were also fond of Napoleon's first empress, having been introduced to each other by her at one of the many receptions at the Château de Malmaison, to which they were frequent visitors. The widowed Duchess was not alone in her condemnation of the Emperor for his abandonment of his first wife for the sake of a dynastic heir.

De Bausset, Prefect of the Palace, had drilled the newly appointed Lady of Honour as to the remit of her duties, foremost of which was to instil in the new Empress a love of France and the French. Marie-Louise arrived from Austria with an immense resource of goodwill which was ripe for harvesting. She was ideal material to become the well-informed, socially able consort who could oil wheels politically, foster and strengthen affection for her husband. Relaxed with intimate family, Marie-Louise could be garrulous, witty, light-hearted. She was quite the opposite before the French public. Bucking under duress, the Duchess devoted just enough time and obliging compliance to her mistress to cause her to act unsuspectingly in ways which scuppered public affection for Napoleon and herself. Montebello's privileged access to Marie-Louise prevented others from mitigating her influence. The newcomer Marie-Louise felt lost at imperial receptions and public appearances without the quick word in her ear, physical gesture or signal which the Duchess should have furnished to assist her in working overwhelming crowds. The Duchess failed to keep Marie-Louise informed as to important political or family connections and outstanding achievements. Marie-Louise never knew when to praise, to commiserate, to offer her personal intervention before her husband, or when to temper refusal of petitions. Unsure as to what she should say, words failed her. To her mortification, she addressed visitors by the wrong name. All she could do was move on as quickly as possible. French visitors, impatient with self-effacement, came away often with a negative lasting impression, feeling their empress was either haughty or an imbecile. She found her audiences so trying that the Duchess encouraged her, in Napoleon's absence, to retire to her apartments alone, disappointing expectant visitors. "What does it matter? Her Majesty is not a curiosity on display at the fair! If she does not feel like being on view, it is her right!"[6] The Duchess would say, as she closed the door on visitors who, Marie-Louise did not know, had invested their life's savings to see their empress and had travelled for days, sleeping overnight in their carriages. At a loss to understand how the initial enthusiasm at her accession had turned to scorn, she prayed that she would get used to French ways and that, in time, everything would come naturally to her.

Told by Napoleon to confide only in the Duchess, Marie-Louise believed her Lady of Honour to be entirely honourable, and became increasingly dependent upon her. There were many occasions when Marie-Louise felt homesick and had, at the Duchess's promptings, talked about the comforts of Vienna and her family. She was unaware that the Duchess, when not in her mistress's company, would drop into conversation with others Marie-Louise's generous allocation of her private purse to the payment of pensions of Viennese who had been in her service in Austria. The Duchess embroidered the truth for more sensational impact, adding details of regular shipments of porcelain, tapestries, dresses, lingerie, hats, flowers, toys, sweets, prints and small items of furniture to Austria, describing graphically the armies of wardrobe lackeys constantly employed to wrap everything, all overseen by the Ambassador to Austria. Exploiting the rigorous protocol which Napoleon had introduced to make his empress invulnerable, the Duchess demanded favours to accrue as much personal wealth as possible to ensure that when Napoleon's reign had reached its term, she would be sitting pretty. Her tenure at Marie-Louise's court would ensure that she would die leaving one of the largest fortunes in France.

Marie-Louise might spend double the amount Josephine allocated to charitable donations, but even in this she could not reap affection. The Duchess, improperly, delegated the administration of Marie-Louise's benevolence to a secretary, M. Lisigny, for a generous percentage to feather his and her own nests. Marie-Louise's money found its way to Lisigny's mistresses and relatives rather than to the intended beneficiaries – members of the clergy and victims of public accident, fire and mine explosion. Members of the public complained. Mme Mère, Napoleon's mother, tried to make her son see what the Duchess was up to, but to no effect. The Duchess looked forward to early retirement in luxury.

These derogations did not escape the notice of other less powerful members of Marie-Louise's household. Mme Durand, another lady-in-waiting to the Empress, recalled how one unseasonably warm autumn afternoon after the birth of the King of Rome, Marie-Louise decided to take a stroll with the Duchess of Montebello in the Jardin des Plantes. She loved the scenic paths, the rotunda, the menageries, the maze and the bear pit, which provided great amusement, and was particularly eager to learn more about the thousands of medicinal plants and herbs cultivated. She had grown to like the gardener who always answered her numerous questions affably and at length. Upon her return to the Tuileries, Marie-Louise asked the Duchess to give him five hundred francs for his pains. A few days later, the gardener asked the Duchess, accompanied this time only by Mme Durand, to convey his gratitude to Her Majesty the Empress for her gift of two hundred francs. Marie-Louise was told of the gardener's gratitude, but not of the destination of the three hundred franc balance of the original five hundred she had set down in her accounts.

Located in the corridors of power, the Duchess had her ear to private conversations. There were others whom Napoleon had included in Marie-Louise's entourage who were not so well disposed towards him. The Duchess of Dalberg and Countesses of Périgord and Brignole were married to three of the most politically astute men of their generation, intriguers from families represented at the most important courts of Europe. Their strategy and contacts would bring an end to his dreams of dynastic succession.

The only person who had status and access equal to the Duchess in the Empress's entourage was Mme de Luçay, Marie-Louise's Lady of the Wardrobe. The Duchess had never liked Mme de Luçay, who counted herself one of Napoleon's most loyal supporters. Fortunately for the Duchess, keeping Marie-Louise suitably dressed for every occasion was a very demanding task. Selecting outfits to be worn over the course of the day, choosing fabrics, accessories, models, slippers and underwear for new creations and making consequent alterations was a gargantuan undertaking which consumed all the hours in the day and allowed no time for intimate exchanges. Mme de Luçay barely had time to breathe. Besides, all she wanted was to get home to her invalid husband as soon as she could. Far from being aware of court intrigues, she was always fraught, poorly organised and frequently late. The Duchess found plenty of opportunity to exploit Mme Luçay's failings to undermine her, pointing them out to Marie-Louise, and laying the blame for her own failings at Mme de Luçay's door.

Marie-Louise would never know of her confidante's betrayal. In her ignorance, she bemoaned the brevity of her visit and that they might never see each other another again.

From Aix, Corvisart sent Napoleon a report of his wife's health, telling him that she was coughing and spitting blood rarely, and no longer had the sense that she was suffocating. Marie-Louise attributed the dramatic improvement to her bathing regime and to freedom from the harassment to which she had been subjected in her natal city. Colour had returned to her cheeks, her appetite had resumed and she was sleeping well. She was exercising regularly without tiring both on horseback and on foot. The night sweats she had suffered had abated. Corvisart ended his report by saying that although there had been a dramatic improvement in a short space of time, her naturally delicate, weak constitution was still vulnerable to unforeseeable upheavals which might yet assail her.

Marie-Louise missed Méneval and could not wait for his return, accepting reluctantly that he preferred to be with his wife and family. She confessed to him that, despite the improvements in her health, she was still in a state of cruel uncertainty, incapable of being happy, far from the two people she loved most. "I need to exercise a good deal of prudence in the way I conduct myself. There are times when my head spins so much that I believe that the best step I could take is to die."[7] She yearned for her son, who Mme de Montesquieu informed her from Vienna, was on wonderful form, more amiable with each new day. Her father had not responded to her request for permission to set up home in Parma in early September, a silence which seemed to bode ill. She planned, once the bathing season was over, to await the close of the Vienna Congress in Geneva or Parma and would not return to the Austrian capital until all the allied sovereigns had vacated it. She had given orders for her son to be brought to her as soon as her father gave her the go-ahead for Parma. Napoleon's birthday, 15 August, celebrated in the three preceding years with great ceremony and joy, passed with sadness. She sent him a locket containing a cutting of her hair. It was to be her last gift to him. Miserable at the ongoing separation, she chided her husband for spoiling her over the course of their marriage, sparing her the worries which had led to their situation. Knowing him to be unhappy, suffering and abandoned by all the people who had served him when fortune had smiled upon him distressed her. She did not for a moment regret the empire.

Finally, Marie-Louise received a response as regards departure for Parma at the beginning of September: from Metternich on behalf of Emperor Francis. According to Count Stefano Sanvitale's report on the situation in Parma, public debt was rising daily, suppliers of daily necessities and accommodation begging for help. It was impossible to levy taxes, everyone unable to pay them, and the duchies had no means of raising revenue of any kind. Creditors and priests who had not received their pensions for over a year, magistrates who had gone unpaid for over three months and financially exhausted suppliers all flooded the antechambers of the government to press their claims. The ducal palaces had been looted and were without furniture, linen and silverware, carriages and harnesses for horses. The only transportation available was two old gala carriages, small diligences and country traps without seats. If Marie-Louise were to go to Parma, she would find she had nothing to live on and that she would be without many of the basic comforts. To describe Parma as the abyss was no exaggeration.

The economic situation, however, was not the major impediment. Metternich continued:

> The presence of Your Majesty in Parma before the end of the Congress will put you in a perpetual compromise. According to my intimate conviction, it is even possible that this might prejudice your possession of the duchy. The branch of the House of Bourbon long in possession of Parma is extremely exercised; this branch finds great support in France and in Spain. The slightest disturbance in Italy may even lend their cause unpredictable further support. The presence of Your Majesty in this precise moment in provinces provisionally administered may further complicate the issues in an extreme manner. Thus the royalist and Jacobin causes may derive advantage from a step which has no utility. The Emperor has given orders to provide as much relief as possible to the people of Parma, reducing the number of troops which are a drain on its meagre resources. This is necessary for the maintenance of public order. It is only when the matter has been finally determined that Your Majesty can go and take possession of her domains. Your Majesty must rely on my judgment on this matter, reposing in the confidence that I regard my duty towards Her as sacred. Only when the business of the Congress

is concluded, which should be in November, will she be able to go home with the fullest security.

In order to promote local public satisfaction with new administrators and to prevent the return of former Bourbon functionaries, the Emperor had passed a new law in Parma excluding all foreigners from employment in its government.

The news that the duchies she believed to be hers might never be and that they were being administered in her name without reference to her came as a dreadful shock. Assuming her entitlement, she had already dispatched De Bausset to assess the relative merits of the ducal residences for her. She railed against the intolerable prospect of return to Vienna. She decided she would go from Aix to Geneva and Berne for a fortnight. She would ask her father if she could winter in Florence and would promise him that she would write to Napoleon only through her uncle, the reinstated Grand Duke of Tuscany. Desperate to have Méneval back by her side, she begged him to come and share her exile, passing on the many compliments Napoleon had expressed in his latest letter, while also warning her not to believe everything people might say against her husband. She also begged her lady-in-waiting, Countess de Brignole, who longed to return to Genoa, to stay with her. Marie-Louise had no option but to submit patiently to Metternich's advice. In any event, General Neipperg counselled, only this course would best serve her own interests, allowing her time to cultivate the sympathies of the allied sovereigns converging on Vienna to convince them to secure for her own establishment, crown and independence. She wrote to Napoleon telling him that her equerry talked about her husband in a manner which reflected her heart's desire. Neipperg knew her feelings for Napoleon sufficiently, she wrote, never to doubt her affection for him. She longed to set out to join her husband at the earliest opportunity, now convinced that Elba, Napoleon's fortunate island, would be paradise. She would, she said, overcome any obstacles placed in her way.

THE UNTIMELY VISIT, SEPTEMBER 1814

The moment for flight had passed. A week after Napoleon's birthday, Captain Hurault de Sorbée came from Elba to Aix ostensibly to visit his wife, Marie-Louise's personal reader. He brought with him a letter from Napoleon which told Marie-Louise to set out at once with Hurault for Genoa, where the brig *Inconstant* awaited her. It had not occurred to Marie-Louise that General Neipperg's seemingly sincere admiration for her husband and the strategic assistance he lent her were devices intended to lull her into a false sense of security, consistent with Vienna's orders. Accordingly, it was entirely to be expected that when Marie-Louise asked his advice, Neipperg immediately sent word to Emperor Francis and arranged Hurault's arrest and despatch under escort to Paris. Orders had been given to Neipperg, to the Austrian, Russian and French police and counter-police surrounding her for Marie-Louise's arrest should she attempt to set out for Elba. Henceforward, she could be in no doubt that she was already caught up in a political web from which she would never be able to extricate herself. She must do nothing which might lead to forfeiture of her duchies. On Neipperg's advice, Marie-Louise wrote to her father to reassure him that she had had no intention of acting on Napoleon's letter. Her reply to Napoleon marked a turning point, barely perceptible at that moment, in their future relationship, Neipperg having gained her confidence if not her affection. She had tried to organise her journey for the near future, but had received instructions from her father to return forthwith to Vienna.

Her constant, often sole companion, the General had plenty of time to talk to her at length about Napoleon's campaigns and his own diplomatic career in Sweden working with Crown Prince Bernadotte to bring about Napoleon's downfall. Marie-Louise would learn about the reasons for the disintegration of the relationship between France and Austria, that Austria had never seconded France's offensive against Russia, which had proved an unmitigated disaster. Far from the victory Napoleon had proclaimed, his miscalculated Russian Campaign had resulted in the deaths of the majority of his Grande Armée and their cavalry, most defeated not in the glory of battle but by starvation and hypothermia. She came to learn that Napoleon's German Campaign had been opposed by the most powerful coalition of unified allies he had ever faced, and which he was unable to divide. The Dresden interview between Metternich and Napoleon had been far from the friendly affair she had thought it to be, the occasion when Napoleon confessed his cataclysmic mistake taking a Habsburg bride, a step which had not achieved his objective of guaranteeing Austria's complicity in his policies and conquests. It would become patently clear to her that Napoleon had lied to her, had tried to manipulate her to try and scare her father into submission. Napoleon had refused numerous opportunities to make peace, preferring to squander lives instead. In the first quarter of 1814, Marie-Louise had written often to Napoleon without hiding that Paris and the provinces were crying out loud for peace. It seemed that her own commitment to act in the interests of France had been more sincere than her husband's. The impact of Napoleon's warmongering on the French economy, bled dry despite the injection of so-called indemnities from countries he had defeated, had been disastrous. By the approach of the end of March, a succession of allied victories had cut off Napoleon and his troops from Paris. Marshals Marmont and Mortier and their twenty-five thousand strong troops had fallen into enemy hands.

Marie-Louise had wept rivers of tears over the past few weeks, and yet there was still more misery of which she had not been aware. Over the past eighteen months in France alone, one million five hundred thousand men had been conscripted, the vast majority fatalities on Napoleon's battlegrounds. His megalomania had coalesced the enemy and forced them to rise *en masse* to put a brake on his destruction. It was terrifying for an innocent wife to have to confront these irrefutable realities, to try to comprehend why it had not been enough to maintain France as the most prosperous empire of the universe. It was practically impossible to reconcile the truth with the man who professed constant love to her and behaved with such charm and humanity in his interior. He had treated her extremely well sexually and emotionally, but he had seemingly never changed from the egotistical monster he had been before their marriage.

The reason why Marie-Louise had been placed under such pressure on her last evening at the Tuileries, essentially given no option but to abandon Paris, was because, unlike her, all Napoleon's ministers and the National Guard knew the reality of the scale of defeats and reverses which Napoleon had concealed from her. She had nothing to reproach herself for. She had acted impeccably. Only the daughter of the Austrian Emperor could have stood her ground against the allied enemy without armaments and barricades. Her continued presence would have enabled a peaceful transition to good governance and would have guaranteed an end to hostilities, sparing the toll of eighteen thousand lives consequent upon the attack on Paris. Few of these had been lost in combat. Cossacks marched into private homes and exacted brutal revenge for the Russian Campaign. The knowledge that Marie-Louise had abandoned the Parisians and the French just when they needed her most caused her immeasurable anguish. She reproached Napoleon for preferring to have his son dead at the bottom of the Seine than raised in the bosom of his loving Austrian family. Her husband's order to evacuate, weakening his own position and bringing down his wife and child along with him, had proved a tactical disaster, and he, the master military tactician, should have known better. Once more, Napoleon had prolonged bloodshed unnecessarily.

Since leaving France, Marie-Louise always found her letters from Napoleon arrived well after the date they were written, but extraordinary news reached her at this critical time with uncharacteristic speed. This news, combined with recent revelations, was to alter her perception of her husband and to change her feelings towards him irreversibly. On the first day of September, a rowing boat had been sighted approaching the pier at Procchio on the island of Elba. On arrival, three women and an infant alighted, greeted warmly by

Napoleon. The party transferred to a carriage and then to mules, to a hermitage above the hamlet of Marciana. Spies initially mistook for Marie-Louise and the King of Rome the Polish Countess Marie-Walewska and her son Alexandre, the blond child conceived by Napoleon in Marie-Louise's Palace of Schönbrunn during his occupation of Vienna. During the four years spent with Marie-Louise, Napoleon had made careful, extensive financial provision for his illegitimate son, conferring on him funds and a title, so that both he and his mother would be provided for in the event of Napoleon's fall in battle.

Upon her return to Vienna, Marie-Louise found herself no longer Empress or Her Majesty, just plain Duchess of Parma, though she remained far from recognised as such. As Metternich had warned, the French government of Louis XVIII and Spanish government of Ferdinand VII launched an aggressive attack on the allied grant of the former Bourbon duchies to the usurper's spouse. The Spanish Bourbons, who wished to be restored to Parma, proposed that Marie-Louise be offered accommodation in the Legations on the northern fringe of the Papal States. The Spanish Bourbon claim to Parma was championed by Talleyrand, her husband's alienated minister. Talleyrand, who had posed as her ally only six months earlier, had become her implacable enemy. Like Napoleon, Marie-Louise could not abide Talleyrand. She had always ignored his compliments and tried to avoid him in Paris. She felt sick in his presence, the smell of his heavily-powdered hair so overwhelming. His machinations were more dangerous than his powder. Taking his revenge on her husband, Talleyrand insisted that she be reduced to an annuity and total dependence upon allied goodwill. He declared that it would be iniquitous for the despot's wife to gain any benefit as a result of her association with Napoleon. Marie-Louise knew that without her own territory, she and her son would be at the mercy of the allies for the rest of their lives. Fighting off French and Spanish claims, she demanded that the allies adhere strictly to the terms of her husband's abdication.

Emperor Francis advised her that she would elicit the sympathy of the Austrians and Russians, particularly Tsar Alexander, if she were to demonstrate unequivocally that she wanted an existence independent of, not shared with Napoleon. Her father, obliged at all times to demonstrate his neutrality, would be able to convince the Powers of her good faith if she were, from now on, to pass all Napoleon's letters to her father. This injunction, an inevitable consequence of Captain Hurault's sally, would eliminate any meaningful communication between her and her husband by the use of trusted messengers with whom the Austrian spies were powerless to interfere. Impotent, she yielded. Napoleon's letters all arrived safely in Vienna. Metternich's secretary Friedrich Gentz lamented privately the reading of this correspondence to the raucous laughter of the vindictive monarchs and plenipotentiaries of the Congress, negligent of the difficult task for which they had convened. Oblivious to this pusillanimity, Marie-Louise still wrote regularly to the sovereign of Elba, even though she doubted her letters would reach their destination. When she realised reading Napoleon's delayed letter in late November that her letters had not been sent, she complained to her father. He promised to look into things. The situation did not improve. Her correspondence with other Bonaparte family members was even more strongly discouraged than before by her father. Catherine, Marie-Louise's closest friend in Paris, had been refused asylum by her own father for having failed to abandon Napoleon's brother, Jérôme. Probably at Marie-Louise's prompting, Emperor Francis allowed them to live in Styria. Catherine regarded this as a temporary measure and in her warm, fortifying exchanges with Marie-Louise, asked whether she might be pleased were Catherine and her husband to come and live in her capital. Marie-Louise said that she would ask her father's permission when the time came and bemoaned the sad century in which they lived. "At least you have a husband who loves you tenderly and who tries to make you forget all the pains you experience . . . " Marie-Louise thanked Catherine for her next letter giving news of Napoleon, but apologised for the brevity of her own, possibly her last to Catherine, on account of a terrible migraine. She felt her isolation deeply.

> I live as a recluse . . . I do not attend any parties and I do not even hear them described. My former acquaintances do not come to see me. There are only two of my old friends who have the courage to come virtually daily, and the society of Vienna reproaches them for it . . . it is in such circumstances that one learns to recognise who are one's true enemies.[8]

Vienna filled with revellers exulting at her and her husband's downfall was hardly a comfortable place to be. She and her son were treated like curiosities. Though received everywhere with deference, the prurient were desperate to catch a glimpse of them and to spread sensationalist gossip. The lack of tact made her angry. Marie-Louise was deeply distressed on one particular visit to her stepmother when a rabble stationed themselves in front of her carriage and started barking insults at her, chastising her for maintaining the imperial coat of arms and green livery of France on the side of her carriages.

"You would do better to return to your husband, instead of staying here and spying for your own ends!" they jeered at her. She immediately gave orders to have the carriages repainted and the livery picked out in a neutral blue.[9]

Marie-Louise received frequent visits from Metternich, who posed as her protector, informing her as to the state of negotiations. Despite his fawning, she was far from convinced that her interests were his motivation. Having elicited the support of the Tsar and, this time, also of the King of Prussia, she went with Neipperg as often as time permitted, to gauge political temperatures and gain valuable insights from Gentz, who, as secretary both to Metternich and to the Vienna Congress, understood all the dynamics and personalities with influence. Gentz sympathised with her plight. Unlike the rest of the population, he had been unable to celebrate her wedding-day, returning home to cry for her and her country. He knew that the temporary union would achieve its objective, and had, by the eve of her betrothal in 1810, already prepared the programme for the redistribution of lands conquered by the former French Emperor. She tried her best to ignore the vitriol which poured down upon Napoleon and which even Gentz found intolerable. Much to Ménéval's irritation, she kept a stoic silence, the stakes too high to risk her and her son's future by speaking in her husband's defence.

Time seemed to pass unbearably slowly. On some days, it seemed Parma would be hers, on others, Bourbon. The tension was intolerable. Marie-Louise and her small French entourage preferred to remain cloistered in the Palace of Schönbrunn. They were not alone there, the palace lodging many of the sovereigns and grand-dukes and –duchesses attending the Congress. She received many visitors discreetly so as to avoid attracting attention. She always presented immaculately, devoting much time to her toilette, receiving regular orders of gowns and bonnets from Paris. She avoided the parties and celebrations of the Vienna Congress hosted by her father, attending rehearsals of the grander performances when opportunity allowed. Unable to dispel overriding melancholy, Marie-Louise found greatest distraction spending daytime hours playing with her son. On mild mornings, Marie-Louise liked to accompany Emperor Francis, who walked two hours a day whatever the weather. Her uncle Rainer, to whom she remained close, came to see her every day. Sporadically, she received Parman administrators who had come to Vienna to report on conditions in the duchies. On most days, she dined alone with Countess de Brignole, Ménéval, General Neipperg and, at his return from Parma, with De Bausset, her former Prefect of the Palace. Conversation was often strained, many subjects potentially politically hazardous. Most evenings were spent in the same intimate company, playing the piano and singing.

Over the past few months, a rumour had gathered momentum that Marie-Louise intended to seek a divorce from Napoleon and to remarry, possibly even one of her bachelor uncles. Marie-Louise scoffed at such ridiculous notions. Not for her were the absurd acrobatics which Napoleon had indulged in to obtain a divorce from Josephine, a favourite preserve of autocratic leaders who had found Catholic doctrine so unnecessarily restrictive. Napoleon had set up his own synod to approve his conduct when the Holy See refused to annul a tie it regarded as indissoluble. Count Hohenwart, Archbishop of Vienna, had initially expressed himself unable to consecrate his union with Marie-Louise, "lest I should place the Holy Sacrament in danger of being annulled, and the bridal pair in a position at once dangerous and insecure, in which they would be exposed to cavilling and witticisms."[10] The archbishop's conscience had been silenced by the greater good of the nation. At the ceremony in 1810 in the Salon Carré, the empty seats which had incensed Napoleon were those of Cardinals who had chosen to sabotage the wedding in sympathy with the deposed Pope who refused to grant Napoleon a divorce. In Paris, Marie-Louise had been deeply upset when she discovered Napoleon had been visiting Josephine at Malmaison, the home he had shared with her and which she had since kept as a shrine to him. Alive to the widespread sympathy for this wronged woman hurtfully cast aside and the affection in which she was held by her own Lady of Honour and son's governess, Marie-Louise wanted to establish herself as solely entitled to Napoleon's affections. Prepared for an abatement of romance which Mme de Montebello had told her to expect after the birth of her husband's heir, she would not facilitate a revival of feelings he might once have had for his first wife. Marie-Louise could not obliterate her predecessor, of whom she was in some ways a beneficiary, the exquisite floral panels in the intimate *salon des fleurs* adjoining her bedroom originally intended for Josephine to remind her of Martinique. She had always been fond of Josephine's children, Hortense and Eugène de Beauharnais, who came to visit her in Vienna. Marie-Louise could never acknowledge that her marriage was a sham or bigamous, nor that her son was not legitimate. Josephine's death, news of which Marie-Louise read with shock in a Swiss newspaper in July of 1814, closed the subject. The Habsburg monarchy had never countenanced divorce. Neither would she. Her marriage had always been valid and subsisting. As 1814 drew to a close, Emperor Francis handed her Napoleon's letter dated the beginning of November. It was the first scrap of news she had had of her husband for months. She sent him New Year's greetings:

"I hope this year will be a happier one for you. At least you will be at peace in your island, and will live there happily for many, many years to the joy of all who love you and who are, as I am, deeply devoted to you."[11]

Marie-Louise visited St. Stephen's Cathedral with Marie-Ludovica the day before the commemoration service for her great-uncle and -aunt. In the centre of the old basilica, an immense canopy decorated with symbols of royalty rose sixty feet high. Four colossal statues, placed at the four corners of the cenotaph, represented France shedding tears, Europe bringing in tribute its regrets, Hope guiding the soul of the virtuous monarch in the sojourn of immortality, Religion holding in its hand its sublime testament, model of charity and pardon. The nave had all but disappeared under immense black drapes of material embroidered in silver. From every column hung the coat of arms of the house of France. Countless candles and tapers had been placed to illuminate the dark vaulted edifice. The sovereigns were to sit on a rostrum draped in black velvet edged in silver fringing. Every Frenchman and woman in Vienna, whatever their rank, had been summoned to attend, the nave and choir-stalls had been reserved for distinguished guests and the sides for the general public.

As stepmother and -daughter kept each other company, the Emperor and Empress of Russia, the Kings and Queens of Prussia, Bavaria and of Denmark, and the immense gathering of guests and members of the public gathered in solemn assembly. The women, shrouded anonymously in black, long veils, had set aside the flowers, diamonds and precious gems which were the uniform for the parties of the Vienna Congress for this day on which all entertainments were suspended. According to custom, Emperor Francis had arranged a detachment of the Regiments of the Guard and of the Hungarian Noble Guard who stood around the royal sarcophagus. The sovereigns knelt piously before the tomb symbolic of one of the greatest crimes in history. It was impossible to tell what sentiments were cloaked by the universal expression of humility, whether some felt guilt or repentance, or others a sense of self-congratulation at shared absolution. With the fall of Bonaparte, who had risen on the crest of the war which Louis's execution had triggered, the world gathered in Vienna perceived that the dark ages were at an end. The aged Archbishop Hohenwarth, his ministry having been blemished by the intransigence of the fallen dictator, could at least take heart that Napoleon had not created another schism in the Catholic Church. Only God erected and destroyed thrones. Divine intervention had finally reinstated the power and glory of the French monarchy, which had known over fourteen centuries of legitimacy.

Not far from the portrait of Marie-Antoinette by Vigée-le-Brun in Emperor Francis's apartments were ranged on the wall much smaller portable portraits of the late queen's children commissioned for the Empress Maria Theresa. Young earnest faces sparkled with innocent eyes and the vitality of life. All but one had perished. The spectres of the royal victims permeated Schönbrunn and the Tuileries alike.

Four years later, the parallels between Marie-Louise's and her great aunt's experience of France were striking. Like Marie-Antoinette, Marie-Louise had only become aware of the reality beyond her palaces when she was evicted from them. Until then, like Marie-Antoinette, she had been kept away from the workings of government, with neither real power nor influence. Like Marie-Antoinette, Marie-Louise had obeyed instructions from her Austrian family to stay away from politics to avoid any opportunity for conflict, and in the event of conflict, to take her husband's part being loyal to France. When the time came, Marie-Louise, like Marie-Antoinette, had stood against her Austrian family with compassion and loyalty to her countrymen. Napoleon had dismissed the prospect of a Habsburg replacement for Josephine after his defeat of Austria at Austerlitz in 1805, "An Austrian, never!" The sad reality was that the French had never regarded either woman as French. In both cases, the words "the Austrian" were interpreted in a pejorative intended to destroy reputation.

The fact that Marie-Louise had been very different from her great-aunt had not availed her. The laziness and dissipation against which Empress Maria-Theresa had warned her daughter, Marie-Antoinette, had characterised her queenship. Illiterate until the age of twelve, Marie-Antoinette dedicated herself to the sole pursuit of pleasure. Marie-Louise prioritised her responsibilities above all else and was a stranger to idleness. In France, she had fiercely defended and acted in furtherance of French interests. She had wanted to stand in solidarity with her subjects, never once countenancing flight. Had she stayed, so much would have been for the better, her reputation and status as heroine immortalized in the history books. She might then have created her legitimate claim to the French throne where none had existed before. With the veto, that opportunity had evaporated.

There were no grounds on which Marie-Louise could oppose the reinstatement of her Bourbon cousin, heir to her murdered relatives, or the return of Marie-Antoinette's only surviving child, her first cousin once removed, to the place of her birth. Marie-Thérèse had lived as a refugee in the Palace of Schönbrunn, afflicted day and night by the horrors of her family's imprisonment and execution. There was no basis upon which Marie-Louise could argue against the principle of legitimacy, which now witnessed the return of many other family members to the thrones from which her husband had evicted them. It was an act of international charity that he had been accorded sovereignty of Elba.

Used to the modern facilities of Parisian imperial residences, her French entourage did not like their new lodgings, which they found always cold. Doors did not close properly, letting in draughts which extinguished the candles. Ménéval complained that it was like living in open parkland. Marie-Louise did not miss the splendour of her former palaces. She could have access to the tradesmen of Paris from the safety of Parma, which looked for the moment as if it really might be hers. However, the allied sovereigns, courtiers and ambassadors were enjoying themselves so much in Vienna at Emperor Francis's expense that they showed no signs of being in a hurry to finalise new political and territorial arrangements.

NINE

Hopes pinned on Blücher and Wellington, June 1815

On 16 April 1815, Emperor Francis led public prayers at St Stephen's Cathedral for Austria's success in war against Napoleon. Many clamoured for Marie-Louise to make her position and allegiance public. Mercifully, Emperor Francis counselled against it. Once more, she sat with her ailing stepmother as the whole population of Vienna flocked to their houses of worship. For four days, youths bore aloft flags and banners in a rainbow of colours, marching through the streets of Vienna, starting in the city centre and moving in increasing concentric circles into the suburbs. A year earlier, the French empress had had little doubt that Napoleon's arms would prevail. Now she had no doubt that he was heading for a devastating defeat.

Marie-Louise was furious when Napoleon fled Elba. Lord Burghersh, English ambassador at Florence communicated her husband's disappearance to Lord Stuart, one of the English plenipotentiaries at the Vienna Congress. Everyone would forever remember the electrifying moment they heard of his escape. In Vienna, even those supposed to be "in the know" stopped in the streets several times a day and asked passers-by whether there was any further news. Like everyone else, Marie-Louise preferred to believe there had been some mistake, that Napoleon would suddenly reappear on his island. She was told to give her entourage strict instructions that her son must not know of his father's escape.

Marie-Ludovica felt for her stepdaughter:

My dearest beloved, you cannot, alas, be unaware, as everyone of every rank in society talks of it, that the Emperor Napoleon left his island with one thousand two hundred men on 26 February. We do not know where he is aiming for, but you will understand that we have to take a hostile position. In a few days' time, it will all be over. May the heavens ensure that it is done in the least afflicting way for you. I beg you to burn this letter this instant.[1]

When it became clear Napoleon was making for Paris, no-one thought for a moment he would get there without first being captured. Rumours ran that Masséna had killed him in combat, a merciful ending for both him and France. Talleyrand called Napoleon "organically mad". They soon stood corrected. Within days, Napoleon was installed in the Tuileries and demanding that his "august" father-in-law return his wife and child. Once more, émigrés abandoned Paris for Vienna.

Thunder-struck by Napoleon's reckless initiative, Marie-Louise was terrified that the assurances she had received regarding Parma might now be retracted. She had no idea that her husband had justifiable grievances, the commitments made to him to induce his abdication still unmet. He had not received the income of two million francs promised him and lacked the means of survival on Elba. Marie-Louise had no idea that, starved of communication with his loved ones, he feared for his own uncertain future. He had discovered plans to kill him, by others to kidnap him and to remove him from Elba to the Azores or to Saint Lucia. Nor did she know how indignant he was that the allies were shirking their obligation to settle his wife and child properly in their own state. He had learnt from his informers that Marie-Louise's entitlement was challenged and that she would receive nothing if he stayed on Elba. He heard that his own family was constantly under threat, that the pensions granted to staff and military personnel, purportedly guaranteed by the Paris Treaty, had not been honoured. Had Austria cared to protect his position, Napoleon might never have left Elba.

The coalition armies immediately mobilized to go back on campaign. Abruptly awakened from the endless frenzy of parties, people in Vienna put away their diamonds and satins in favour of more sedate clothing. Thomas Lawrence, the portrait painter, who had mined a rich seam during the spendthrift days of the Vienna Congress, returned discreetly to London.

When Marie-Louise refused to receive from Méneval Napoleon's letters to her, he read her their contents. She could do little to stop him.

"I am master of all of France." Having reinstalled himself in the French capital, Napoleon wrote, "All the people and armed forces are full of enthusiasm. The self-styled King has left for England. I spend the whole day reviewing twenty five thousand strong troops." He had written to her many times. "All I lack is you, my good Louise, and my son . . . meet me in Strasbourg between 15 and 20 April. The bearer of this letter will tell you how to reach me."[2]

Napoleon had totally misjudged his status in Marie-Louise's affections. During the fourteen months that had passed since she had last seen him, the landscape of her world had changed beyond recognition, revelation forcing her to revisit the past five years and to reassess her alignments. Until the preceding autumn, she had been desperate to join her husband. Marie-Ludovica had instructed her stepdaughter, upon her betrothal, that loyalty to one's husband is the greatest gift a woman can give a man. Marie-Antoinette's devotion to her husband had been to her eternal credit. Louis XVI might have been foolish or misguided, but he had not intentionally deceived his wife or demanded the sacrifice of two hundred thousand young men every year of his tenure. For over twenty years, the fields of Flanders and the Low Countries had been irrigated with human blood. All Napoleon could promise now was misadventure and more bloodshed; the very thought of him filled her with horror. Under the Bourbons, France, set within its natural borders, the Atlantic and Mediterranean seas, the Pyrenées, the Alps and the Rhine, could be great and strong without the need for conquest.

Safe in Vienna, the thought of returning to France and to the most hated man on earth was inconceivable.

Tsar Alexander came to her to discuss the regency theory. A year ago this might have been possible, but now it was pure fantasy. In April 1814, her father had come to the rescue, welcoming her back to the Habsburg hearth, and had promised her a resumption of family life with Napoleon once the situation had normalised. In the meantime, she and her son were safe. Marie-Louise could not count on this magnanimity a second time. Preservation of her and her son's future, particularly his security, was uppermost in her mind. The disappearance of her cousin, poor Louis XVII, whose body had never been found, was still well within living memory. This year, circumstances might conspire to place her and/or her child beyond her father's reach. The outcome of the inevitable looming confrontation was far too uncertain for her to place herself and her child where terror had reigned unchecked.

Everyone marvelled at the fact that Napoleon had marched from Fréjus to Paris unopposed. In all probability, battle fatigue, more than deep affection for him, accounted for the fact. The Tsar, still Marie-Louise's firm supporter, was determined not to allow the genius of evil to reconstruct his tyranny, which might be worse in the future than it had been in the past. Europe would pay dearly for flinching from the urgent task of bringing him down once and for all. It must act with one voice and persevere until the bitter end. Tsar Alexander did not care what form of government France was left with, democratic, monarchical, aristocratic, so long as it was not Napoleon. Napoleon and his men must be destroyed. Making his views known to Marie-Louise with as much diplomacy as he could muster, he assured her Parma would be hers.

Emperor Francis declared that he would not release his charges, and publicly renounced any claim Marie-Louise or her son might have to the French throne. He advised Marie-Louise to distance herself from Napoleon by issuing a statement making it clear that neither she nor her entourage had played any part in assisting his escape from Elba. By a declaration prepared by Metternich, she placed herself and her son under the protection of her father and the allied monarchs. Metternich also drafted a letter to Napoleon declaring that she did not wish to return to Paris until Napoleon had definitively renounced his bellicose intentions and peace was restored. Once peace reigned, there would be no obstacles to the family being reunited. Concerned that Marie-Louise and the Prince of Parma might be the target of abduction or assassination attempts, Talleyrand, on behalf of the allied sovereigns, prevailed upon Emperor Francis to transfer them from Schönbrunn to the Hofburg palace, protected by a warren of streets in Vienna's Baroque centre. Numerous guards swarmed around the doors of their apartments and under their windows.

Marie-Louise duly signed the declaration Metternich had prepared:

> At this moment of renewed crisis which threatens the tranquillity of Europe and which presages new miseries which accumulate over my head, I cannot hope for a safer refuge, a more beneficent protection than that which I request for myself and for my son of your paternal affection. It is in your arms, my dear Father, that I seek refuge – with the being who holds me the most dearly in all the world. I place myself in your hands, and our destiny under your paternal safeguard. There is no more sacred aegis. We know no greater will than yours with which you deign affectionately to direct all your steps in such a difficult moment.
>
> Submission without limits will be the first homage of my gratitude and of the respectful affection with which I have the pleasure of being, My very dear Father, your most obedient daughter.[3]

Marie-Louise, like the allied monarchs, received Napoleon's assurances that his intentions were pacific with scepticism. This time, the allies would disarm him forever. At the end of March, the

Duke of Wellington left Vienna to reassemble his forces in the Low Countries, while the other allied armies took up their strategic positions for a final assault on Paris.

When Napoleon's brother-in-law, King Murat of Naples, declared war on Austria in April, two months after Napoleon's reinstatement in Paris, the allied sovereigns mobilised their armies for action. Austria, bled dry by waging a decade of war against Napoleon and by the expenses of hosting the Vienna Congress, was in a parlous financial state yet again. The prospect of another war against Napoleon had an immediate effect on the economy. Four hundred and fifty paper florins were worth only one hundred florins in money, the depreciation hitting the Viennese hard.

This time, the allies would have to come home victorious. They published the following statement.

> By breaking the convention established at Elba, Bonaparte has destroyed the only legal title to which his existence could lay claim. By returning to France, he has deprived himself of this protection and shown himself incapable of peace or truce. In so doing, he has placed himself outside any civil or social relations and as an enemy and disruptor of the world's peace of mind, has delivered himself into the hands of public vindication.[4]

The excommunication from society was unprecedented. Henceforward, Marie-Louise's husband and father of her child was a non-person without rights. It was painful attending dinners at which her husband's march on Paris was discussed with general consternation and united venom. He was called the scourge, the destroyer, the infernal genius, barbarous though the real Barbarians had typically shown greater restraint, people said. He had inherited the most prosperous country in the universe only to lay it waste and leave it destitute, ravaging its gigantic armies, desecrating its institutions, altars and thrones indiscriminately, worshipping no other god than himself. Napoleon was a monstrous tyrant who put the likes of Nero and Caligula in the shade. Marie-Louise's uncle Archduke Johann, never short on directness, told her that he hoped Napoleon would break his neck before it was too late. Malicious shafts of wit were particularly hurtful.

Relations between Marie-Louise and Méneval became increasingly strained. When she told him that she had resolved never to return to France, Méneval sought to dissuade her, pressing her to avoid partiality. He regretted the declaration she had made and begged her not to sign anything which might commit her one way or another to the allies or against the Emperor, and to maintain strict neutrality.

As with Napoleon's previous letters, she passed the latest to her father. She had become increasingly distressed, fearing accusations by the secret police of her non-disclosure of letters which they knew to exist, when she noticed that Méneval and Mme de Montesquiou were burning letters she had read so as to avoid their onward transmission. For a long time, she had been unable to communicate freely, and now it was best she avoid any contact with her husband. Méneval tried to force Napoleon's letters upon her. Marie-Louise asked him to desist, and to treat those to which she could make no meaningful reply as never having arrived. He continued to remonstrate with her, urging her to rethink her decision never to return to Paris, constantly reminding her of Napoleon's unstinting affection for her and the pain he suffered on account of their continuing separation. She might say her decision was irrevocable, but both she and he knew that no decision was irrevocable.

Méneval accused the Austrian imperial family of failing her, refusing to abandon their neutrality among the allied powers on the issue of Parma, and of being disloyal, deserting her when she badly needed them. Marie-Louise did not share Méneval's perspective. Her family's detachment from her situation enhanced the justice of her claim. She was embarrassed before him, but she dared not speak out in her husband's defence. Her former people were, according to his friends and relatives, watching daily to see if she might arrive, petrified at the thought of her staying in Vienna. His assertions that she would be received as an angel of peace, earning the eternal gratitude of the French people, were hardly convincing.

Ménéval accused her of consulting neither her heart nor her own true interests in her violent resolution. She told him firmly that, fearful of relying on her own judgment at this stressful time, she had discussed the matter with her advisors and was convinced of the wisdom of the course she had decided upon. Marie-Louise found his lack of understanding of her position profoundly irritating. Ménéval had proved loyal, but lightweight and ineffectual. It would be easier once he left. Besides, neither he nor she could tolerate the oppressive spies who constantly prowled around him, observing his every word, his every gesture.

With Austria and France at war, the position of all Marie-Louise's residual French entourage was untenable. As retainers of Napoleon, they were potential threats. De Bausset, former chamberlain of the French Imperial palace, insisted that Marie-Louise issue a formal statement to exonerate her entourage from any blame in relation to Napoleon's actions. Marie-Louise did as asked. The formal statement did not help them. They could no longer be tolerated on Austrian soil. Emperor Francis summoned Marie-Louise to tell her that she must tell her and her son's French staff that they were no longer needed.

Ménéval, who had gone to Vienna specifically to safeguard Napoleon's charges, could not get his bags packed fast enough. The rest of the party was well aware of the ambiguity of their status and talked with enthusiasm about returning home to France. But it was not so easy to leave. Metternich intentionally delayed Marie-Louise's requests for passports. Ideally, Napoleon had to be disabled before his supporters with potentially valuable secrets from Vienna could return to Paris.

By May, Marie-Louise was in such a nervous state that words seemed to issue from her mouth unbidden. A future predicated on Napoleon's victory was too frightening to countenance. His defeat, although terrifying, promised a resolution to her problems, a reprieve from the abyss into which his first defeat had cast her. She talked about her plans for the future in Parma as if everything were settled, as if there were no doubt that her husband would be defeated by her father. She planned to live, she said, in the Garden Palace in the winter and in the Palace of Colorno in spring, and to spend the summer with her son in Vienna.

Passports finally arrived for Méneval and for Mme de Montesquiou. Wretched at the thought of their private exchanges, Marie-Louise could barely make even the most banal conversation with them in the days preceding their departure. The instruction to leave Vienna was issued to Mme Montesquiou on her charge's fourth birthday, the very same day that Napoleon entered the Tuileries, vacated by the fleeing Louis XVIII. The governess was bitter, praying, begging, protesting to be allowed to stay. Her entreaties went unheeded. She had overstepped the mark, feeding the child news of his father and current events in France, constantly promising him accession to the French throne. This could not be allowed to continue. Once she knew she would have to leave her little king and Vienna, she wept constantly. The letter of thanks and sapphire necklace from the Austrian Emperor were small compensation for the pain of abandonment of a charge whom she had barely left since his birth. The surgery was particularly brutal for the little King. Her regime, though strict, was kind, and *"le petit roi"* as he called himself, had become strongly attached to her as a second mother. It was she who had brought him up to sing French nursery rhymes and patriotic hymns, to read the fables of La Fontaine and to say prayers for the welfare of his father and of France as she put him to bed at night. She could be playful and tactile, kissing and cuddling him, but she refused to indulge him. She had never allowed him the slightest shred of arrogance. To her credit, the child was polite, well-mannered, quick-witted and humorous. Marie-Louise was distraught watching her son shed floods of tears, clinging to his dear Quiou-quiou, begging her to stay.

Marie-Louise had never liked Mme de Montesquiou and, although she suffered for her son's loss, she was glad to see the back of her. But her feelings were much more ambivalent at the departure of Méneval, save for herself the last substantial link between Napoleon and his son. At least for her, there would be an alleviation of the intolerable tension which had persisted since the beginning of March between her and her French entourage. Nonetheless, she wept tears to hear that her son had told Méneval on parting from him to tell Napoleon that he still loved very much the father whom he might never see again, were the allies to prevail. Marie-Louise dared not think about the dreadful retribution which would rain down on Napoleon's head once he had been subdued.

Within a month of the French exit from Vienna, news arrived of a major defeat of Napoleon's troops outside the village of Waterloo in the Low Countries. Marie-Louise incarcerated herself and her son at Schönbrunn, avoiding the Viennese municipal celebrations to which the townsfolk flocked. The hall in the Hofburg in which Marie-Louise had been betrothed to Napoleon was now filled with revellers celebrating his downfall. Beethoven's *Victory of Wellington*, later known as *the Battle Symphony*, with its loud drumbeats and cymbals of triumph, was played repeatedly.

"May God ensure that soon a general repose will follow the tempests which have so tossed you about,"[5] Archduke Uncle Karl wrote to Marie-Louise. The imperial family rallied to her.

Had Marie-Louise known that Napoleon had returned on 23 June after the Battle of Waterloo to Paris to try and coerce his government to accept his second abdication in favour of his son, she would have regarded this as yet further proof of his insanity. There were far less dangerous mortals locked away in the Salpetrière, Paris's lunatic asylum.

Following victory in the Low Countries and the imposition of punitive measures on the French, the allies converged on London to raise their glasses in triumph and self-congratulation at Apsley

House on the capital's Hyde Park Corner, home of the Duke of Wellington. Marie-Louise was in Baden, a short distance from Vienna, trying to settle her nerves with the town's well known sulphurous waters, when she learnt of her husband's fall.

"I am happy with the outcome of the war," she wrote to her father.

I learnt with joy that King Louis XVIII has re-entered his capital, scotching the dreadful rumours which had been circulating. I would like Napoleon to be treated with gentleness and clemency and beg you, my dear Papa, to arrange this. This is the only prayer for him I address to you and it is the last time I will concern myself with his fate. Without doubt, I owe him gratitude for the serenity in which he allowed me to live and for trying to shield me from unhappiness.

Marie-Louise still had cause to be nervous, Napoleon at large, the allies unsure of his whereabouts. A month later, she received from Metternich a letter from which she could deduce that her husband was most unlikely ever to disturb her again. "You can see by the attached article, an extract from *le Moniteur*, that, having tried in vain to escape the surveillance of the cruisers established in front of Rochefort, Napoleon has just taken himself aboard the English vessel the *Bellerophon*."[6]

Unbidden and unrecognised, Napoleon had climbed aboard his old enemy's ship, grossly miscalculating that England's benign government would afford him a second comfortable exile. Ignoring his brother Joseph's advice and refusing offers by American captains to cross the Atlantic, Napoleon felt sure he would fare better in England. He flattered himself that he would be tolerated, indeed welcomed in England as a private individual. He addressed himself directly to the Prince Regent, "the most powerful, the most constant and the most generous of my enemies", through the *Bellerophon*'s Captain Maitland: "Exposed to the factions which divide my people, and to the enmity of the greatest powers in Europe, I have terminated my political career, and I come, like Themistocles, to seat myself at the hearth of the people of Britain."[7]

On hearing that the former French Emperor had reached Brixham Harbour on the English south coast, Marie-Louise's younger sister and joker, Leopoldine, wrote to Marie-Louise: "Napoleon is in England in safety and likes it very much. In two years, we will receive another visit from him!"[8] No-one in Europe wanted that. It seemed never to have occurred to this master of strategy that his arrival in England would coincide with that of news of the casualties of Waterloo. Napoleon's sally from Elba had cost the French twenty-five thousand, the English fifteen thousand (including half of Wellington's officers) and the Prussians seven thousand in dead and wounded, a terrible waste of life, but a drop in the ocean as compared to that he had brought about during his reign. It never seems to have crossed his mind that these losses had fed a bubbling cauldron of anger and incited over the years his long-time enemy not to embrace him with open arms but to clamour for his death.

Napoleon should have seized the opportunity to go to America. He would be interned at Fort Saint George in the North of Scotland, Metternich wrote. From Marie-Louise's standpoint, this was very much further away than Elba, making resumption of any kind of family life impossible. A subsequent letter from Metternich reported that in Scotland "he will be placed under the surveillance of Russian, Austrian, French and Prussian superintendents. There he will receive very good treatment and all the freedom compatible with the most comprehensive security which he will not be able to escape."[9]

Napoleon's behaviour over the past two years had caused Marie-Louise such a nightmare that it was best for her as much as for Europe to have him removed from the scene. Marie-Louise maintained her composure. Her new lady-in-waiting Mme Scarampi, closely followed by the Baronne de Montet, arrived to present her with a letter from her stepmother, Empress Marie-Ludovica. According to the Baronne's record, Marie-Louise asked them to wait outside her rooms while she read it. When she emerged a few minutes later, she could see that they had hoped to gauge her reaction. "I thank you, I knew the news that you have just announced. I would like to go riding at Merkenstein – do you think the weather will be good enough for it?"

Demonstrating total self-possession, Marie-Louise indicated without causing offence that she had no need of condescension. She could not wait to get back on her horse. After an early lunch at eleven, she set out, cutting a romantic silhouette, her stole floating in the breeze. As the elements caressed her, her life as a prisoner, as a fairground curiosity, was suspended.

Marie-Louise had her uncle Archduke Rainer to thank for her readiness on this occasion. Thoughtfully, he had foreseen the general voyeurism, and had pre-empted attempts to wrong-foot his niece.

> This moment a courier has arrived: Napoleon has given himself up freely to the English on the island of Aix. The Empress is travelling to Baden to tell you herself, though I fear she will arrive too late, so I have sent this in the greatest haste and beg you in the name of heaven not to divulge my letter to her.[10]

Archduke Rainer saw Marie-Louise daily, often walking with her, going to the theatre and to concerts. She found in her uncle, patron of Beethoven, lover of music, the arts and nature, a kindred spirit and a sensitive ear, and adopted the habit of consulting him about her situation. Though they would often part late in the evening, they would send each other notes in the morning, Archduke Rainer sharing valuable pieces of information which might not otherwise come Marie-Louise's way. Such morsels often, as now, enabled her to react in private and to appear untrammelled in public. Alive to the ramifications of her predicament, he ensured that her social engagements were managed so as to spare her any awkwardness: "I think that whenever there are strangers dining, it would be best for you to stay away. On these occasions, it is all too inevitable that your husband will be brought up in conversation."[11] Marie-Louise was grateful.*

Resilient and strong when in company, Marie-Louise surrendered to her feelings when alone. When she cast her mind back over the past two years, she could not believe that she had actually survived them. The shocking news of what appeared to be Berthier's suicide by throwing himself out of a window disturbed her greatly. Berthier, the Marshal chosen by Napoleon to come to Vienna as his representative for Marie-Louise's betrothal to him, had gone over to Louis XVIII after Napoleon's first abdication and had been rewarded with a peerage. He had been Napoleon's confidant as regards tactics and strategy, and had always proved himself to be precise, prompt, willing and indefatigable. Both she and Napoleon had been immensely fond of him.

Marie-Louise tried to keep herself constantly occupied. It was not as easy as it had been in the past. She had lost her French entourage and had not developed any degree of intimacy with her new retainers. Her father and many of her male friends were away in Paris, London, or in Austria's Italian possessions. She missed her rebellious grandmother, Queen Maria-Carolina, who had suffered a fatal heart attack the previous September, the only person to have some grasp of Marie-Louise's irreconcilable struggle.

At Napoleon's capture, the allies agreed to relax security measures such that his son was allowed to return from the Hofburg to his mother at Schönbrunn. Knowing her husband to be out of harm's way, Marie-Louise found her sleeping improved. She woke at six or seven in the morning and summoned one of her amaranthine uniformed maids to open the shutters and bring her writing desk. She spent the next few hours dealing with correspondence which

---

* She was often taken aback by unbridled effrontery and had complained to her uncle about the Grand Duchess Catherine of Russia who never hesitated to try to pry into the intimate details of her private life with Napoleon, demanding to know how often she had confessed in Paris and to whom.

came in from family and friends. The arrival of letters from her young uncle, Archduke Johann, who was travelling in England and Scotland, provided amusing distraction,* particularly his witty disparaging remarks about English food and girls. Letters arrived from Paris from her father and from the Duchess of Montebello which were less cheerful. Emperor Francis reported that France was in a terrible state, that the French harked back to the days when Marie-Louise was Regent. There was very little to be done, "for the King wavers with rogues all around him on his throne."[12]

The Duchess of Montebello shamelessly bemoaned the situation in Paris to Marie-Louise. "We are most unhappy here. My poor home has been plundered by the Prussians. We are managing now with requisitions. War has always seemed such a horrible thing to me. I have to suffer seeing my poor country desolated yet again by foreigners."[13] Only when the Duchess was personally touched did she feel the desecration of defeat.

In Emperor Francis's absence, Archduke Rainer continued to provide Marie-Louise with practical and trustworthy advice. Meticulous in his consideration of matters relating to Parma, discussing exhaustively with her issues relating to succession, possession, the employment of staff, financial and administrative matters and questions regarding her son's eventual transfer there, his friendship invaluable. Archduke Rainer took a particular interest in the little Prince of Parma, ensuring that the boy's new male German tutors were giving him plenty of attention and care. He also constantly reassured her of her father's affection for her.

"Always at the forefront of your father's mind are his daughter's feelings and convictions," he told her. "He is good and loves you sincerely. He certainly does not want to sacrifice you any more for the sake of politics." Terminology had changed noticeably since

---

* He reported that he had got to know all the English royal family, particularly the princesses. He was thrilled by the vast array of luxury goods, steel-ware, tin-ware, paper of every kind, inkpens, Wedgwood utensils, cotton cloth, tea and East India goods, the super-abundance of flowers everywhere.

Marie-Louise's departure from Paris. None of the family refrained from referring to her marriage to Napoleon as "her sacrifice."

Emperor Francis advised her to spend more time at the summer spa resort of Baden, away from the capital. Once there, determined not to give any outward signs of her inner struggle, Marie-Louise offered generous, meticulous hospitality. She prided herself on the good-natured service of her entourage. People commented that her ladies attended her with solicitude and studied refinement that belonged to the realm of art. Departing from the Habsburg parsimonious understatement, she adhered to the standards of toilette and dress she had learnt in Paris, taking great pride in her appearance, and held herself with dignity.

Metternich's information in his letter to Marie-Louise had been superseded. It seemed that the British government was torn as to the whether Napoleon should be exiled or hanged. The King of Rome had understood that his father had been vanquished, euphemisms inadequate to prevent him getting the gist of what had occurred.

"Is my father a naughty man?" the innocent toddler had inquired. During the long intermission between defeat and the determination of Napoleon's fate, he asked, "are they going to kill him?" as England's Lord Holland pressed for Napoleon's execution before a firing squad, arguably a more humane, more honourable end for the fallen emperor. Marie-Louise and his tutors fielded the child's questions with the greatest sensitivity. But unlike Elba, some realities are inescapable. The King of Rome was no longer called such. No-one wanted to call him Napoleon, so it was agreed that he be addressed by his second name, Francis, which he declared openly he did not like. It cut no ice that it was the name of his grandfather whom he was growing to love more deeply each day.

The allies relented, flattering themselves that they were far too civilised to terminate Napoleon's life, a barbaric act. Some thought that the prisoner afloat in Plymouth harbour should be handed over to the French King. Finally, permanent confinement seemed the only realistic option, either in Great Britain, Gibraltar, Malta, St Helena, the Cape of Good Hope, or any other British colony assessed to be sufficiently secure. Most inclined to a destination at a distance from Europe, such as the Cape of Good Hope or St Helena.

Three and a half weeks later, Marie-Louise discovered her husband's fate. Metternich wrote:

> Napoleon is on board the *Northumberland,* and on his way to St Helena. We have no news of his departure from Torbay other than by telegraph. But we know that it was on the open sea that he left one vessel for the other. He was put out to sea on the *Bellerophon* because there were so many craft crowded with curious onlookers around the vessel that it was impossible to be completely sure that there might not be some commotion.[14]

Marie-Louise had no idea where St Helena was. She was informed that it was an inhospitable island somewhere off the coast of Africa. Africa sounded a very long way off. "He will never return from there, that we can guarantee." Metternich promised.[15]

Not content to have banished Napoleon to an island from which escape was impossible, Louis XVIII issued an edict that Napoleon's family be exiled permanently from France. Conceding that they in themselves represented no personal danger, he nonetheless feared that they might be manipulated by others. Every member of the family, particularly the non-person's wife and son, should be subject to the strictest control of movement, and if possible, immobilised. From now on, all Bonaparte family members were required, when granted refuge in one of the allied States, to make a solemn declaration that he or she would commit to residing in the place assigned to him or her and would abide by all pertinent laws and rules for foreigners in force or specifically applicable to the persons listed and ordered as seen fit by His Majesty King Louis XVIII. At the head of this list, drafted by the allied plenipotentiaries, Prussia's Hardenberg, England's Castlereagh, Russia's Nesselrode and Metternich, stood Marie-Louise and her son. She found the imposition of such constraints upon her and her son deeply humiliating. Mercifully, her father stood as guarantor so that she was never asked to sign the requisite solemn declaration. The formality of renouncing for herself and for her son the title of Majesty and any pretension to the French throne was a further humiliation. From now on, she would be known as Archduchess of Austria Marie-Louise and Duchess of Parma, Piacenza and Guastalla. When Marie-Louise next saw Metternich, he was distinctly cooler towards her and her son. With Bonaparte on St Helena, Marie-Louise and her son had no longer any bargaining status. Metternich wanted them to be nothing more than impotent spectators of politics, mere hostages who must be grateful for the crumbs he cared to throw them.

Marie-Louise's severance of ties with Napoleon was finally rewarded. As promised her, the Tsar insisted upon the implementation of the terms of the First Treaty of Paris signed on Napoleon's first abdication insofar as they related to Marie-Louise, and refused to agree to any arrangement which departed from them. Over the course of the duration of the Vienna Congress, the Tsar visited Marie-Louise frequently at Schönbrunn. Often unannounced, he would breeze in and show great affability, courtesy, and sensitivity to Marie-Louise's plight. To compensate for his deafness, Marie-Louise found herself shouting, especially when there was ambient noise. Her efforts paid off. To her relief, she received a solemn assurance of her entitlement to the duchies of Parma, and an income of twelve hundred thousand francs until she could administer her States. England's Duke of Wellington and Lord Castlereagh had also backed her claim. This confirmation, so long desired, had come in the second week of June before Napoleon had been subdued. She had feared that things might unravel. With Napoleon now decisively defeated and disposed of, her entitlement, it seemed, could no longer be challenged.

There were two stings in the tail. Firstly, Marie-Louise would have, for the time being, to leave her son in Vienna. Secondly, she would be allowed to occupy the duchies only pending final determination of the claim by the Spanish Bourbons. The solemn assurance of her entitlement to Parma, Piacenza and Guastalla was just that. Papers had yet to be signed. Only when the allies had put their signatures to the final deed would Marie-Louise know her exact status. Metternich and Tsar Alexander assured her matters were settled and that neither would allow any further negotiation. Marie-Louise was horrified at the prospect of being separated from her son and remonstrated with her father. He told her that she must wait for memories to fade, for the allies to relent. Fearful of being denied her new territories, she had no option but to accept that, at least in the first instance, she would have to go and live in Parma without her little boy. She asked her father if she might live permanently in Vienna and be sovereign from afar. Without sovereignty, she could do nothing for her son. Her father told her that she must go and inhabit her hard-fought-for territories: the Parmans were waiting for her impatiently. At least with Parma, she could save five hundred thousand francs of her ducal income a year, which, added to the revenues of the fiefdoms of Bohemia which her father planned to devolve upon her son, would ensure he could lead an independent existence after her death. Méneval had laughed at her — how could the son of the great Napoleon be compensated for his loss of status by mere money? He had accused her of being complicit in the disinheritance of her son, who, already deprived of his father's inheritance by the Congress, was now deprived of his mother's inheritance. He had pitied the poor boy, forced to live outside the protection of the law, without a homeland, a title, even his Christian name. At least he had been spared his father's execution and could grow up in Europe's most important city among his loving Austrian family, far from the desolate rock where his emasculated father would have only to wait for death. With Napoleon out of sight of the European world, Marie-Louise hoped that the venom which Napoleon had inspired would simmer down over the course of time and that the censure which pursued the Bonaparte clan, including her and her son, would abate. Her father, having set out from Paris for Vienna, told her to instruct the child's household not to talk about "his previous situation" and

> not to anticipate his wishes in such a way that he does not have to help himself...so that arrogance and stubbornness will not grow in him from a young age. God knows that I wish for him to become an honest, virtuous and brave man. Given that he has been endowed with the sterling talents, he should grow up to be the happiness of the people that are entrusted to him and not the misfortune of the world. Give him a hug from me. I have demanded a hard sacrifice from you in having him stay with me.[16]

Marie-Louise would bide her time and get her boy to Parma.

TEN

Parma, 1816

The winter of 1815/1816 spent waiting to leave for Parma, knowing she would have to leave her son, were excruciating. She immersed herself in preparation for her new responsibilities, taking lessons to perfect her Tuscan Italian, though few in her duchies spoke it, the local dialect being the natural language of communication as elsewhere throughout the peninsula. She read extensively about the life, conditions, institutions and economy of her territories, and received regular briefings on them. She plunged into the works of Vasari, Cicognara, Rumohr, Sismondi and Guiccardini to learn about the country's wonderful art, architecture, history and genius, and to have a sense of its morals, manners and opinions. She looked forward to the freedom she would enjoy as sovereign, beyond the surveillance of Viennese spies.

Lying to the south of Milan, west of Genoa and north of Tuscany, the duchies granted to Marie-Louise comprised gently undulating hills along the plains of the rivers Po, Taro and Trebbia and their various tributaries, and numerous small Alpine lakes. Parma, Piacenza and Guastalla had enjoyed a chequered history. Their strategic position between Milan, Genoa, the cities of the Romagna and Tuscany facilitated flourishing trade in times of prosperity. Though prone to inundation, the rivers irrigated the rich fertile soil, allowing the inhabitants to live in relative affluence. In times of darkness, the cities were vulnerable to the advance of foreign armies, typically Spanish, Austrian and French, which used them as thoroughfares for troops in transit, if not as bloody battlefield.

The intelligence the new Duchess of Parma received suggested that she was not about to lie on a bed of roses. Emperor Francis had ordered an investigation into complaints of administration, seeing little chance of the duchy's revenues ever being remitted to Marie-Louise. "I would not wish my worst enemy to reign or live here. The only means of keeping order is by force...we have to try to make the next generation better and to keep the current one quiet and obedient with severity," he told his daughter.[1] Neipperg, appointed to be her chief administrator, had carried out a short survey of Parma. He could not hide from her the fact that people feared her arrival. For reasons beyond his comprehension, Marie-Louise had been cast as having a reputation for being completely in agreement with the old French administration and Napoleonic principles. Thus, Parmans feared a repetition of Napoleonic occupation. Nobles and commoners were greatly impoverished and everyone dreaded bankrupting themselves completely if they were to be required to appear at court.

Napoleon's régime had been unbearable for most in Marie-Louise's duchies. Requisitioning of goods, of livestock and tools had been so severe that many, particularly those who lived in the Piacentine mountains, were left with no means of earning a living or cultivating their land, and faced starvation. Promises by Napoleon's Viceroy Eugène de Beauharnais, that there would be no forced conscription, that country-folk would receive comparable value for animals requisitioned for French troops, that their wishes would be heard and accommodated, were never honoured. Insurrection seemed the only weapon. Napoleon ordered his Governor General of the States of Parma and Piacenza, General Junot, whom Marie-Louise had known subsequently in Paris, to burn towns to the ground and to shoot the insurgents as a deterrent to others. He gave specific orders that the village of Bobbio, which had led the insurgency, be razed first, that the priests who had supported their parishioners be put in front of a firing squad, and that three or four hundred of the guilty be sent to the galleys. The village of Mezzano in the Trebbia valley was also razed to the ground, with its feudal mansions and parish church, the French having first removed the bronze bells from the bell-tower to melt down for weaponry. "Torrents of blood will be needed to ensure the tranquillity of Italy," Napoleon told Junot.* "Spare no-one."

Conscription became more onerous, encompassing an ever broader proportion of the male population; taxes became unbearable. French demands were implemented mercilessly, the addressees told of the privilege conferred upon them to be able to associate themselves with the destiny of a great nation, opening to them fountains of glory, greatness and prosperity. Life and the possessions of ordinary citizens became precarious, particularly in the countryside. Thefts, highway robberies, murder and incidents of arson filled police reports. Begging festered. Napoleon ordered the construction of four houses of correction with pertinent workshops, each with a capacity to accommodate seven or eight hundred inmates who could be put to work to root out mendacity. For months, trials of suspected rebels dragged on under the Military Commission of Parma which Napoleon had established, almost a quarter of the eighty-eight guilty eventually condemned to death. Napoleon congratulated himself that his methods had subjugated the population and that it would remain subjugated for a very long time. "This salutary measure will put a brake on this people's natural inconstancy."[2]

Parma suffered Napoleon's degradations along with the rest of the Italian peninsula. Napoleon promoted French trade to the detriment of the former Italian states, diverting suppliers and customers away from Italian producers to the French. If the silk factories of Lyons were highly profitable, it was because their counterparts in Lombardy and other Italian regions were being squeezed out. If French factories were at the forefront of technology, it was because Napoleon blocked the financing and import of new machinery to

---

* Those found in possession of firearms were arrested, placed in iron shackles and displayed at the stocks with a notice bearing the word 'Rebel'. The French Emperor arranged for a panel of adjudication headed by the Procurator General of the Court of Appeal in Genoa to make its way to Parma to carry out anticipated trials.

prevent industrial development in the Italian peninsula. Parma had long worked in wine production in association with Reggio, whose borders were only seven miles distant. Napoleon stopped this. Parma and Reggio lost out, while French wines flourished. The Italians were forced back on supplying agricultural products for low revenues. The continental blockade meant that inferior French products replaced the English raw materials upon which the Italians relied. Napoleon demanded interest rates higher than those paid in France on capital, which made the cost of raising capital for industrial and commercial development prohibitive. Due to reduced volumes of trade, and commandeering of valuable trading partners, there was catastrophic decline in the Italian ports. Trieste, Venice and Livorno, once barometers of the generation of wealth, did a fraction of the trade under Napoleon that they had enjoyed previously. To add insult to injury, Napoleon imposed customs tariffs on French goods destined for Italy, but exempted French producers from paying the same on Italian goods. Then came the imposition of charges on Italian hosts for the upkeep of French troops and for armaments needed to protect French occupation. These charges were quite separate from the regular contributions which were levied throughout the Italian peninsula as a general charge for the benefit of enjoying the association with France.* Many feared that their new sovereign, although Austrian, might continue some of Napoleon's repressive methods.

Marie-Louise had examined thoroughly the bundle of papers relating to Parma's financial affairs, which, following French exploitation, were in a lamentable state. She was no stranger to accounting and management of finances. Napoleon had been particularly strict in accounting and made his staff stick to budgets, which he constantly reduced, forcing staff and ministers to make do. Marie-Louise heard complaints, oblique criticisms of her husband's

---

* As the cost of Napoleon's wars on the Spanish Peninsula increased, so conscription and taxation in his Italian dominions worsened.

policy. "If everyone makes savings, we will all have sufficient," she used to say. She had never considered herself exonerated from economising. Just as she had done in Vienna, she wanted not only to operate within budget but to have money left over. Knowing the terrible dread Napoleon had suffered with Josephine, trying to reconcile her insatiable appetite for clothes and sex with her financial resources, and of the ensuing arguments and tantrums, Marie-Louise became obsessed with accounting, classification and order. She knew the cost of every item in her wardrobe, the total of her laundry bill in each of her residences, and which items had been mislaid or were lost.* She kept every bill and signed them off. She was astonished when one of her staff asked her why she bothered to have things repaired when Josephine would just have replaced them.

Marie-Louise spent no more than a fraction of the allowance she had allocated herself. Brought up to regard philanthropy as a primary duty, she assigned typically four-fifths of it for benevolent purposes, which pleased Napoleon who abhorred avarice and delighted in the generous acts of others. Her self-restraint was exemplified when presented with a set of jewels comprising diadem, necklace, comb, earrings, hairpiece and belt of Brazilian rubies by the Crown jewellers for her approval. As much as she hankered after this marvel of modern design, she declined it because the forty-six thousand francs which it cost would leave her out of pocket once she had bought her family presents. Shortly thereafter, Napoleon presented her with a much more valuable replica. Napoleon learnt of this incident directly from the member of staff charged with returning the set to the jewellers. Loving more than anything else to see his wife covered in precious stones, he wanted to get it for her. Marie-Louise was livid at the betrayal. Her self-control and close administration would serve her in good stead.

Marie-Louise was to govern much more wisely than her husband,

---

* In Paris, it seemed she had had an uncanny knack of losing valuable gems and pearls which went missing with disturbing frequency, despite her best efforts to keep track of them.

informed by family instruction manuals written by her great-uncle Joseph II, who had introduced the concept of the equality of all before the law, and by her paternal grandfather Leopold. Her grandfather had produced in 1774 Points for the Education of Children, among which was the following advice,

> No pains must be spared to acquaint princes with their country and make them respect the proprieties. Establish in them an aversion to taxation and make clear to them that their sole passion should be humanitarianism, compassion, the desire to advance the happiness of their people. Stir their sensibilities on behalf of the poor and make plain that the rich must never be favoured over the poor. Explain that the greatest misfortune for a prince lies in not having seen with his own eyes and not being informed of the true state of his country's affairs.[3]

Guided by advisers, the new Duchess of Parma soon distilled definite ideas as to how her duchies were to be ruled. Parma had benefited from much enlightened administration under Bourbon administrator Du Tillot which the new Duchess hoped to resume and refine. Fifty years earlier, Du Tillot had carried out numerous reforms, considerably reducing ecclesiastical power and privileges. Property in mortmain* was abolished, monasteries and convents suppressed, the Jesuits expelled. Marie-Louise gave strict instructions that the Church and specifically the Benedictines and Jesuits were not to be restored to their former positions of power under the Bourbons. The recent French administration had not been all bad. The reforms introduced by Napoleon's appointee Moreau de St Méry, an enlightened humanist, brought the positive reforms of the French Revolution to Parma. There had been advances in agriculture, industry and commerce. The central administration was reorganised, criminal and civil jurisdiction separated, law courts

---

* Property held in mortmain refers to property, ownership of which is perpetual and inalienable. This mechanism allowed land to remain forever in the hands of leading noble families and the Church.

reformed, the Napoleonic Code introduced, and customs barriers between Parma and neighbouring states abolished. All these, Marie-Louise intended to retain with necessary adjustments. She proposed the creation of a commission to amalgamate, take over, and create a scheme to repay the crushing debts paralyzing her states. She set about streamlining her court, reducing the number of civil servants to a bare minimum and their salaries to a scale more suited to such a small state. Most of the positions at court would henceforward be honorary, without financial reward. With the money saved, she could arrange widespread distribution of corn to the starving and financial subsidies to the poor and needy, fund free inoculation programmes and arrange assistance for artisans. She was prepared to make drastic cuts in her own lifestyle to match the cuts she would be meting out in her court. She would have to act slowly and cautiously in order not to incur local disaffection. Some expenses could not be negotiated. Ruthlessly, the allies required her to repay in full the nine hundred thousand gulden which her unwanted sojourn in Vienna between the summer of 1814 and the spring of 1816 was assessed at. She would somehow have to service this heavy debt from revenues from Parma, which she could ill afford.

Marie-Louise had been given the order to prepare to leave for Parma in February 1816. Her Prime Minister in Parma, Count Magawli-Cerati, put her in funds for the journey. She was not to be accompanied by any French staff, save the wives of non-French staff. French staff would only lower her in the esteem of her subjects, who, like everyone else in the Italian peninsula, feared and detested the French.

"You have seen for yourself in Schönbrunn that these people do not know how to value anything except France,"[4] her father told her. Marie-Louise was heart-broken to have to dismiss the few loyal members of staff who had survived the cull following her husband's return to the Tuileries a year earlier, but she did her father's bidding, forced to accept the prevailing political enmity. She insisted, however, that she must retain chamber-servants, cooks, stablehands and security personnel whom she had known for a long time and for whose behaviour she could vouch. These she would never let go, save by natural wastage.

Emperor Francis proved impervious to her tears and imprecations to allow her son to accompany her, and constantly repeated the same reasoning which she was powerless to deny. In granting his grandson the 'gift' of security, he was forced to deprive the child of his mother's invaluable presence. Until such time as the current frenzy in the world had settled down, he would be safe only among those who, out of love, would not allow any harm to come to him. She would understand that her husband had many enemies.

Marie-Louise had feared that she would not survive the parting from her son, and anticipated the unspeakable day by gradually reducing the amount of time she spent with little Franz over the preceding months to try to soften the inevitable blow. In abject pain, she attended mass several times daily, attracting criticism that she was demonstrating an excess of piety. It was all she could do to contain herself, to cope with the hours she longed to spend in his company but which she judged would only make the parting harsher. It was impossible to put her feelings into words. Little Franz did not want to say farewell and hid in his bed under a shawl he had appropriated from her cupboard. How she had managed to tear herself away, she did not know. She had held back her tears with the greatest difficulty, only releasing them once Vienna and onlookers were out of sight. It was a dreadful humiliation.*

Having nursed her stepmother, Empress Marie-Ludovica, until her death at Verona, Marie-Louise entered her duchies in trepidation on a sunny April day in 1816. Her journey from Austria had taken her through Venice, Padua, Vicenza and Verona, all cities new

---

* The imperial family went to great lengths to spoil little Franz on his fifth birthday shortly after her departure and took him in the evening to a children's performance at the Theater an der Wien where he had jumped up and down with excitement. Both he and Marie-Louise would have to get used to birthdays and many more traditionally family occasions without each other.

to her, but which would soon become familiar as she journeyed back and forth. Just beyond the town of Casalmaggiore, she crossed the stagnant, muddy waters of the Po over a large pontoon of boats dominated by two triumphal pyramids. Jubilant crowds greeted her.

The following day, Marie-Louise and Neipperg emerged from the first of eighteen carriages into the sunlight in Parma's main square. The horses drew up level with the magnificent doors of the city's grey, cream and rose marble cathedral, where incense, holy water and unctuous compliments were dispensed by the local clergy. The enthusiasm of Marie-Louise's new subjects, who had cheered her along her route and clapped wildly, moved her to tears. She stood beneath Correggio's frescoed cupola, barely discernible in the half-light, as benedictions for her good governance were recited. Bells rang out in continual celebratory cacophony from all of Parma's sixty churches. The goodwill seemed endorsed after a few hours rest in her new palace, when she went out for a ride in an open *calèche* to enjoy the fireworks display to fête her arrival. Before going to bed that day, she wrote to her father,

> This welcome instilled in me ever more deeply the sacred duty which falls upon me and has fortified me in my resolution to do everything within my power for the happiness of this dominion. I hope that I will be happy and tranquil here and that I will be able to take care of my son's future.[5]

Marie-Louise wrote to her friend Victoria de Crenneville that she found the country in which she was living a veritable garden, that she had within her grasp the means to make happy her four hundred thousand souls, to protect the arts and sciences. Her ambitions were only to leave to posterity works and institutions of public utility rather than extravagant self-proclaiming monuments. She harboured the humble hope that she would be able to stay put for many years which might all resemble each other but which would be gentle and tranquil. No turbulent sentiments would unsettle her mind. Assuming she could see her son every year for long stretches, she was leading an enviable life. But the past had scarred her. She dared not live more than each day for itself, so disgusted was she with how horrid and perverse life could be.

Marie-Louise was content with her modest palace, with her small but elegant apartment, the delightful little study in which she could write and entertain her small circle of friends in the evening. She soon got into a routine, spending the mornings attending to business, to household accounts and other sundry matters, and the afternoons riding in the surrounding hills which she was growing to love. On arrival, she appended portraits of her son. It was to be hoped that he would soon be running around her corridors, toppling over jardinières and causing children's havoc. Sometimes in the long evenings, she would take one of her miniature portraits of him and carry it around with her, admiring it from time to time, planting a kiss on the cherubic lips which looked out at her from the glaze. On such occasions, her eyes welling with tears, she would tell the company that it was only a matter of time before he would be joining her.

Each day, the new Duchess looked forward to the arrival of post from Vienna, particularly letters on pink paper edged in gold, sent in the name of little Franz. At first, his letters were drafted with substantial assistance from his tutors: "Believe, my dear Mama, that your departure upset me a great deal, and that I will love you and respect you forever. I will not cease to beg the Good Lord . . . for your prompt return into the arms of your dear son."[6]

Collin, one of Franz's newly appointed German tutors, reassured Marie-Louise that Franz often thought of his dear mother and that he loved her infinitely. He promised to be a good boy, pleading for her to love him always. Marie-Louise wept to read that Collin himself had been reduced to tears by those of her son.

In the terrible June and July of 1815, after the difficult departures of Méneval and Mme de Montesquiou and the bulk of her and her son's French entourage, German replacements were selected for him. Mme Soufflot and her daughter Fanny who had nursed the

King of Rome since his birth were allowed to stay for the time being, as was Mme Marchand. Marie-Louise agreed that summer to the provisional appointment of Count Dietrichstein pending her anticipated departure for Parma. In his forties, Count Dietrichstein had many qualities to commend him. His father had been close to Marie-Louise's great-uncle Emperor Joseph II, and his mother to the Empress Maria Theresa. Aged eighteen, he had served for five years in the Austrian campaigns alongside Marie-Louise's chief administrator General Neipperg and in Naples against the French before being taken prisoner by them and taken to Paris. Upon release at the turn of the century, he returned to Vienna to marry and pursue a civilian career in the arts and science, becoming one of the luminaries of his age. He adored music and counted among his friends the leading musicians of Vienna, including Beethoven, who was known to be a regular visitor to his family home, and Schubert. Marie-Louise had made his appointment temporary only, at first not convinced that he was the right man for her son. She was particularly concerned when her son's childish insensitivities reduced the Count to tears. The Soufflots were playful and affectionate with the boy, but disgraced themselves by referring to him only as their little prince, constantly reminding him of the magnificence of his father's court, and encouraging his habit of calling everyone else, particularly Austrians, enemies. Count Dietrichstein looked on with disapproval as they allowed him to win at all military games at the end of which they declared him Emperor. Having fought the French from the commencement of the revolutionary wars, the Count had an acute understanding of the political sensitivities regarding the education of the only heir to Napoleon.

Marie-Louise appointed a second tutor, originally from Trieste, Captain Foresti, when she saw the aggressive way her son treated Count Dietrichstein. Like the Count, Foresti had had a long military career fighting the French. Marie-Louise liked him for his modesty and for the fact that he was an unmarried observant Catholic, qualities which would incline him towards faithful devotion to duty. Dietrichstein, Foresti and Collin educated in the Austrian style, which required the student to read, rather than be taught. Under his French governess, the little Napoleon had learnt much by rote, able to recite reams of fables and to perform fantastically long memory exercises. Little Franz did not immediately warm to the new curriculum set by his tutors or their methods, and expressed his disapproval in constant dejection.

It was clear to Marie-Louise that her little prince could not continue to throw his weight about in regal fashion, that arrogant ideas implanted in his mind in France would have to be subtly and imperceptibly removed. The French women would have to go to give the Germans a clear rein. She agreed to the dismissal of the Soufflots, but asked that Mme Marchand, a good woman who never meddled in matters which did not concern her, be allowed to continue. She breathed a sigh of relief that little Franz seemed only momentarily out of sorts at the Soufflots' departure in late October. Four months later, Marie-Louise was obliged to let go of Chanchan, as little Franz called her affectionately, the poor illiterate woman's constant innocent references to Paris, her only subject of conversation, proving too provocative to be tolerated. With subtlety and discretion, the trappings of the King of Rome were gradually removed. Lingerie and possessions embroidered with a capital "N", bees and eagle were replaced by those bearing a simple "F". Toys which the little Napoleon had been given by French aunts and courtiers which recalled them with fondness to little Franz's excellent memory were disappeared. Count Dietrichstein carefully removed medals which had been conferred by the boy's father, leaving only the Cross of the Order of St Stephen conferred by his grandfather for him to wear on rare formal occasions. He informed Marie-Louise that he had also removed books, albums, engravings and prints which recalled the French past. Mild attempts to dissuade Franz from excessive filial devotion to his father were made but then abandoned at Marie-

Louise's insistence, and he was allowed to continue his daily prayers for the welfare of his father as well as his mother.

"Now that I know Count Dietrichstein more intimately," Marie-Louise wrote to her father, "I like him very much, and I cannot but congratulate myself upon the zeal and trouble that he devotes to my son."[7] He soon endeared himself to her, keeping her abreast of musical developments in Austria, his letters often enclosing sheet music of the latest compositions published, the most recent waltzes and cotillions for orchestra and, over the years, introduced her to the new rising stars, such as, among others, the new sensation Johann Strauss.

Marie-Louise appreciated the Count's lack of self-interest in the performance of his duties. She could count on him to convey a faithful picture of her son's daily life, and anticipate wise response to the fears and concerns ever-present in her mind. He assured her that he would take care of everything concerning the Duke with the same exactitude, the same affection he lavished upon his own children. She could not have asked more than that he should grow to love her son as if he were his own.

Marie-Louise's departure signalled a complete change in Franz's regime and a commitment to relentless hours of instruction. A brief lunch with tutors replaced the leisurely hours spent with Marie-Louise. Under Count Dietrichstein, Captain Foresti and Master Collin taught Franz on alternate days. The French grammar and Catechism, long soliloquies from Racine's tragedies and various tracts from Lafontaine fables learnt by heart which had earned the King of Rome so much praise in the past were no longer of any relevance. From now on, all instruction would be designed to make him a German.

"I don't want to be a German, I want – I want to be French!" he had cried, in hot temper stamping his feet long before Marie-Louise left Vienna. Marie-Louise took him on her lap and told him that if he did not speak German, his grandfather would not want to see him. He yielded grudgingly. His German household had been ordered to address him in German only, and to resort to French only when there was clear misunderstanding. The poor child could barely speak a word, never mind express his basic needs in this alien language. After intensive instruction over three months, arduous for both teachers and pupil, the prince was capable of understanding virtually everything, but it would take a lot longer for him to enjoy the fluency in German which he had in French. Habsburgs were expected to be polyglots. Once he had mastered French and German, he would have to learn Italian, English and Czech.

The Duke's physician, Dr Frank, reported to Marie-Louise,

"If the beauty and firmness of the prince's body have made rare advances in his growth, his intellectual faculties are developed well beyond his age and I have never seen anyone learn so promptly as he a language as difficult as German."[8]

Archduke Rainer wrote regularly to his niece to keep her abreast of her son's progress, personal idiosyncrasies, haircuts and table-manners. He had been little Franz's first visitor on his fifth birthday, giving him a puppy basset hound. He marvelled that a child so young had remembered so much from his former life and about his father whom he had last seen aged two and a half, and about whom everyone was barred from speaking, on pain of dismissal. Undoubtedly, little Franz was endowed with remarkable intelligence, he reported.

No longer the obliging child he had been to the indulgent French retainers, little Franz was surly with his German superiors. His mother gone, he railed against the new discipline forced upon him, bursting into uncontrollable tears or erupting into a dreadful temper. He affected a limp in his left leg to irritate his superiors. His mother was exasperated to hear that remonstrating with him was ineffectual, as were punishments, and bemoaned the extended separation from her beloved child, the root cause of his dysfunction.

However painful, Marie-Louise had no choice but to raise her child from a distance. From afar, she would have to instil in him a sense of virtue, to exert a strong hand and discipline, demonstrating her love through her correspondence with him, with his tutors and with other members of her family who could be her eyes and ears. Marie-Louise eased her pain at first by dreaming about the eventual transfer of her son to Parma once she was properly established and the allies' paranoia had dissipated. Contrary to expectations, Parma had so much to commend it that she was convinced that she would want for nothing if only she could have little Franz with her.

Her duchies were much richer in terms of art, history, archaeology and scenic beauty than she had imagined. Even though they were small, they offered plenty to keep her busy and to admire. The centrepiece of the city of Parma was undoubtedly the Palazzo della Pilotta, a gloomy, forbidding, rambling building, started at the end of the sixteenth century by the Farnese Ranuccio I but never completed. Though substantially in a poor state of repair, its magnificent indoor amphitheatre constructed entirely of wood, its Museum of Antiquities, its Royal Library and the Academy and Gallery of Fine Arts, all institutions created or enhanced by Du Tillot, were still places of pilgrimage for those on the grand tour. Since the twelfth century Parma had been a centre of learning, with its University and Noble College of Theologians, attracting young men from illustrious Italian and European families. The city was littered with baroque churches, municipal buildings and monuments of architectural merit designed by the great architects of the Renaissance. Domes, walls and vaults were richly decorated, and sculpture, stucco and inlay gilded every corner of the city. Work by the master-craftsmen Correggio, Parmigianino, Anselmi and Araldi were abundant. Marie-Louise hoped to restore as much of the now faded grandeur to its former elegance and refinement. The Royal Press and the newspaper *La Gazzetta di Parma* flourished.

The Farnese art collection, once one of the finest in Europe, had been drastically depleted. Seventy years earlier, Bourbon king

Charles III had taken the finest pieces of the art collection and library to the Palace of Caserta in Naples, which he adopted as his royal seat. Now these were the property of Marie-Louise's maternal grandfather. More recently, it was Marie-Louise's husband who had made off with the jewels which remained. It was a travesty to think of the long corridors of the Louvre where she had seen countless treasures stacked indiscriminately as if they were bags of flour. They might never see the light of day, floor and wall space inadequate to display them. Following Napoleon's second defeat, the allies punished the French for their complicity in his return by demanding restitution of his plunder. Strenuous efforts were made under the Duchess's aegis to repatriate Parman treasures, but few items were returned. Marie-Louise planned to build up her own art collection, which over time might compensate Parma for some of its losses. She intended by degrees to enrich and increase the international stature of all the institutions she had inherited. However, this could only be done once Parma's financial affairs had improved.

Over the course of the next few months, Marie-Louise became acquainted with her veritable garden. Parma's Apennine ridges were covered with vast forests of ash, beech, oak, walnut and chestnut trees. On the lower slopes were elms, poplars, elders and willows. Hogs and wild boar roamed the forests in large herds. All kinds of game, hares, partridges, quails, ducks and other water-fowl were also plentiful. The hills were a sea of orchards and vineyards furnishing excellent local wine and exquisite fruits, mulberry yielding particularly valuable returns. The Parman plains were remarkably fertile and well irrigated, cultivated with cereals, maize, beans, tobacco and hemp. The cattle famed for the quality of the cheese from their milk were everywhere, looking infinitely healthier than their human co-habitants. When the rains had come in their season, the Po and its tributaries were full of fish. There was copper, salt and marble. There were factories producing silk, linen and cotton goods, paper, gunpowder, hides, tobacco, brass and earthenware, candles, soap and refined wax. There seemed to be enough natural resources to provide her and her subjects with a very agreeable lifestyle.

The temperate climate suited her much better than France or Vienna. In unbearably hot summer, she could retreat to the hills of Sala Baganza or to the sea breeze along the Tuscan coast.

It was not long before the harsh reality set in. Marie-Louise found many Parmans inveterately lazy and shallow. They showed no inclination for work, preferring to beg, even though she made every effort to demonstrate that work would lift them out of poverty. Catastrophic flooding had wrecked recent harvests, leading inevitably to famine. People lay dying and corpses remained for days on the streets. Despite her father's assurances, no steps had been taken prior to her arrival to spare her some of the more unpleasant sights which famine and disease offered. There was much more for her to do than she had anticipated. Shortly after her arrival, she organised the distribution of four thousand stacks of corn to the poor. The most urgent project was to eradicate typhus and to get the sick back to good health. She implemented legislation for the prevention, care and treatment of typhus and funded a free vaccination programme held at Parma's Maternity Hospital, for which she recruited final year medical students. She reduced the ducal army to thirty thousand men, releasing expenditure saved to fund schools, museums, the academies of arts and of sciences, the theatres and the university, all neglected during the Napoleonic period and in desperate need of investment of resources. Drawing on plans conceived under the previous French administration, she implemented a public works programme. Her first priority was the construction of a permanent bridge over the River Taro, capable of withstanding regional adverse weather conditions which had taken away so many of its wooden precursors and effectively prevented geographical mobility. Marie-Louise hoped that these initiatives, providing gainful employment, would eventually put an end to the proliferation of beggars who flooded the capital from the countryside.

As regards freedom of the press, Marie-Louise accepted that some censorship was expedient, but she saw no need for active suppression. In her view, it was better to allow a certain amount of freedom of expression, especially of justified grievances. Her reasonable tax regime was a holiday compared to her husband's oppressive fiscal measures. There was no conscription. Within a short space of time, Marie-Louise demonstrated to her subjects that they had nothing to fear from her rule and much in which to rejoice.

Culturally and socially, Parma was worlds apart from Vienna and Paris. The local opera and orchestra were disappointing, at best mediocre. She planned to improve it. Other things were less malleable. Marie-Louise confessed that she found society in Parma tedious beyond imagination. "It is quite impossible to get any intelligent word out of any of the women." She had got to know some of her Parman household in Vienna during the Congress at her receptions on Tuesdays and Saturdays. The Parmans made only a superficial impression, save that they were generally considered to smell of a blend of their local cheese and the heavy *Eau de Portugal* which they seemed to apply to excess. Undiluted in Parma, Marie-Louise's courtiers seemed rather drab. The most important members of her small Parman entourage, trimmed to her limited budget, were Count and Countess Scarampi, her lady-in-waiting of whom Marie-Louise was becoming increasingly fond despite her earlier *faux pas*, Count Stefano Sanvitale, Count and Countess Magawli, and her chief administrator, General Neipperg, who applied himself with all the zeal of friendship.

The oxygen of family and friends visiting from Vienna and Tuscany was indispensable for intellectual stimulation. Even Count Metternich's visit was a breath of fresh air, coming full of compliments with the way in which she had organised everything: "[Madame l'Archiduchesse] has hit the right tone, neither too much nor too little of anything."[9]

Soon after her arrival in Parma, Marie-Louise received the eccentric, outspoken Germaine de Staël, whom she found highly entertaining.* Since leaving France, Marie-Louise had read many of her books, most recently, her studies on the quest for the happiness of individuals and nations and on the social importance of literature, *On Germany, Ten Years of Exile,* and her novel *Corinne, or Italy.* Said to write like a man and to act like a woman, De Staël had a woman's insight and was extremely accurate in her judgments of people and places. She had strong views and was afraid of no-one when it came to expressing them. De Staël's intellect clearly frightened men. Marie-Louise's brother Ludwig wrote to say how glad he was that he had not been in Parma: "Mme de Staël's arrival would certainly make me want to leave instantly!"[10]

Marie-Louise was immensely pleased when she heard that Archduke Rainer had been appointed Viceroy of Lombardy, relocating him from Vienna to nearby Milan. She hoped that in time he would come to like the Italian peninsula and his subjects and she tried to persuade him as to their merits when he came to visit her in her first autumn at the seventeenth century Palace of Colorno. Marie-Louise loved Colorno, its spacious rooms well suited to entertaining guests,

---

* Marie-Louise had last seen her at her father's wedding to Marie-Ludovica in January 1808. De Staël parents had believed that it was the absurdity of women's inferior education which led to their inferiority, and gave her an instruction on how not just to manage a home but to govern an empire. De Staël had chosen the empire of reason, a dangerous choice as long as France had been in the grip of revolution and Bonaparte. The Habsburg imperial family had a high regard for the Swiss aristocrat, and for her courage in speaking out and writing her impassioned plea in defence of Queen Marie-Antoinette, dubbed "the Austrian bitch" by the French press, who was blamed for all the ills of France. The British Ambassador to Naples presented it to Marie-Louise's grandmother, Queen Maria-Carolina, who sent it to Marie-Louise's mother, Empress Marie-Thérèse. It was said that no-one had attended Sunday Mass in Paris whenever one of Germaine's books appeared in publication until Napoleon had taken a distinct dislike to her when he became the target of her criticism, and banned her books. He had referred to her as "a whore, and a filthy whore at that", and "the predator bird which bodes ill." The French newspapers referred to her as "the Genevan she-wolf, to be seen in short petticoat and stays dictating to her darling lover, her work as immoral as that of the incarcerated Marquis de Sade."

making music and playing billiards, chess and tric-trac in the evenings. It had the merit of being relatively well furnished and of having all its walls and its roof, which was more than could be said for her other residences in the duchy. Its beautiful gardens, vergers, miniature lake, white swans, tropical plants, enclosures of stags, deer and other animals enabled her to relive the joys of Versailles and Schönbrunn in miniature. The surrounding countryside was rich in delightful bridle-paths which offered plentiful hacks. She planned her own traditional English gardens, botanical hothouses for tropical plants and a kitchen garden. She invited the renowned Viennese gardener, Charles Barvitius, to direct the landscaping of her new project and asked the Duchess of Montebello to send her a comprehensive assortment of vegetables and salad from France, Belgium and Holland. Archduke Rainer had enjoyed his stay in Parma so much, he confessed, that he had found it hard to tear himself away. The feeling had been mutual. Marie-Louise longed for his long informative letters, despatched on his travels, from Venice, Genoa, Florence and Livorno, in which he described in detail the art, industry, landscape, living conditions and welfare issues of the places he visited. His Christian spirit, warmth and empathy with his subjects were well known. Marie-Louise felt a great harmony in their thinking and was constantly inspired by his good advice. Archduke Rainer's custodianship and management of Marie-Louise's personal finances, and arrangement of loans and currency transactions, were invaluable.

To Marie-Louise's great delight, Victoria de Crenneville descended on Parma to take her on a tour of the regions surrounding her duchies. Marie-Louise had heard much about these regions from her father, particularly Tuscany, where he had grown up. For the first time in her life, she would be able to see for herself the great masterpieces of the Renaissance. Travelling incognito with her childhood friend, Marie-Louise could talk of the troubles which afflicted her. She listened to her friend's counsel, taking care never to undermine her own dignity or self-esteem.

Marie-Louise could also speak openly with her uncle, the Grand Duke of Tuscany, who had enjoyed her and Napoleon's hospitality in Paris and now hosted her at the Pitti Palace. The Grand Duke lived and governed very much in the style and with the philosophy of his father, Marie-Louise's grandfather Leopold, who had worked tirelessly to improve the lives of his subjects, and had toyed with the novel notion of granting his own people a constitution. Marie-Louise chose to adopt his style of political liberality in her own duchies, and during her stay delighted in the company he kept and in the affection which he and his family showered upon her. She was quite astonished to find a drawing by her father, sketched in 1776, on one of the palace walls. In this cosmopolitan society where people of all faiths and provenance mingled, Marie-Louise had the good fortune to meet Lord and Lady Burghersh, for whom she quickly developed great affection. Lord Burghersh,* British Ambassador to the court of Florence in Tuscany, *chargé d'affaires* and therefore regular visitor to Parma, thoroughly appreciated the intellectual and artistic offerings Florence offered. Like Marie-Louise, he and his wife both loved, were extremely knowledgeable about and made music. In short, culturally and intellectually, she found herself with kindred spirits.

Over the winter, Marie-Louise could imagine her son's excitement, described by his tutors, as he woke up and ran to the window to see the snow, rushing to get dressed, disdaining breakfast to make snowmen and have snowball fights on Schönbrunn's ample lawns. It was painful waking each day without the prospect of

---

* Lord Burghersh had participated in the Spanish campaign for three years as Wellington's adjutant, and then in the German Campaign under General Schwarzenberg. Both he and his wife were also talented sketchers and painters. Having studied music in Lisbon and London, Lord Burghersh spent much of his spare time in the study and composition of operas, and ultimately founded an academy of music in London, the Royal Academy of Music on Regent's Park, on the model of the Italian academies, where he planned to enjoy his retirement. His portrait is to be found there.

seeing her little boy, the months passing with little prospect of reunion. She no longer felt susceptible to joy, sensing only pain, she told her brother Ludwig. She began to fear that little Franz might not recognise her and might refuse to talk to her, just as he had done to Ludwig upon his return from his travels abroad. When feeling particularly dejected, she called the world perverse and envied those who could retreat into a nunnery. It seemed that whatever she did would be misconstrued by idiots, that she was the target of evil tongues. She had to shelve a visit to Livorno to take the waters when she heard that Louis Bonaparte was already there, a man whose political conduct had never caused any concern. "Our meeting, however fortuitous, in Livorno would cause an outcry throughout Europe."[11] God only knew what nefarious motives would be attributed to her. She immersed herself in music, drawing and tapestry and took lessons on how to keep melancholy at bay from Mr. James Bielby, a young self-deprecating dry-witted Englishman.

"Fresh air and the occupations of your garden are excellent. The country furnishes a variety of new objects which dissipate the attention and draw the mind from the contemplation of itself."[12]

In an effort to raise the tone and her morale, Marie-Louise set about preparing a programme for improving the cultural life of her new states, though there was little prospect of her ever replicating even a fraction of the legendary efflorescence of music, literature and philosophy which she had always perceived as her cultural birthright. Her first birthday without little Francis was intolerable. How envious he was of his aunt, Marie-Louise's sister Marie-Clementine and uncle, Prince Leopold of Salerno, who would shortly be visiting her: "And I am deprived of this happiness! On your last birthday, I gave you a bouquet, and I can't now."[13] Welcome reports of his good behaviour from his tutors were a poor substitute for the bouquets he would love to place daily at her feet.

Leopoldine, Marie-Louise's capricious, witty younger sister, always brought Marie-Louise cheer, finding something to laugh about in even the blackest situation. In her first letter to Marie-

Louise in Parma, she teased her sister mercilessly by pretending that she had looked into her crystal ball: "I foresee darkness for the future and believe we will shortly have a visit from St Helena, since a person from this island has confirmed that many North-American ships stop there and I believe they have something in mind."[14] Marie-Louise laughed heartily, and at her sister's letters relaying newspapers' "reliable" reports about Marie-Louise's "impending divorce" and the gossip in Viennese society as to the men they were marrying her off to. Leopoldine reported that she and Franz had enjoyed themselves hugely at the *Opera Buffa*, before ending her letter in her usual fashion by reassuring Marie-Louise that she would visit little Franz as often as she could and take the greatest of care of him.

Marie-Louise would have loved to go and see her son in the summer of 1817, but there were good reasons why she had to postpone. There was nothing for it, she and her little Franz would have to wait another year. Having resigned herself to postponement, she again found herself under fire. Leopoldine was not laughing now. She had heard rumours of discussions afoot to try to unseat her elder sister: "I cannot tell you how much I fear that another sorrow is about to befall you."[15] The allies had decided without reference to her to divest her of Parma and to restore it to her Bourbon cousin as soon as this could be achieved. They were pressing for her to vacate Parma forthwith. Marie-Louise petitioned her father immediately.

> It seems that new difficulties have emerged against my possession of the Duchy of Parma. How is it possible that people are not content with the harsh sacrifices I have made for the common good! I will not lower myself to accept humiliating conditions and still less will I surrender anything granted to me unanimously by the whole of Europe, unless I and my son are given corresponding advantages in exchange. My dear father, in these sad circumstances, I place in your hands the fate of your very loving daughter and that of your grandson.[16]

Marie-Louise was as desperate as she was incredulous. Lady Priscilla Burghersh, to whom she had opened her heart, tried to calm her, promising to get herself to Parma as soon as she could:

> I can quite understand that Your Majesty is alarmed and worried at the very idea of new worries, but it seems impossible that these noises could have the least foundation. The injustice would be so glaring and so impolitic that I cannot imagine that anyone would *dare* to even hazard such an idea if there were people who desired it. The firmness of Your Majesty would soon put paid to their hopes![17]

Count Scarampi's words were particularly fortifying: "Your Majesty has shown so much courage thus far, She would not wish to lack courage in the future."[18]

Marie-Louise's migraines returned with a vengeance: "I take comfort from the fact that if the other powers wish to confer against my repose, you [my dear father] will come to my assistance. For me, nothing is important, save the future of my son."

Marie-Louise was isolated. Neipperg, her chief administrator, had gone to Vienna on her behalf to attend her father's betrothal to his fourth empress, Karoline-Auguste. Karoline-Auguste, Marie-Louise's coeval, had suffered seven years of miserable, unconsummated marriage before being repudiated by King Louis of Bavaria. She was an excellent choice from the many eligible brides who had volunteered themselves, some as young as fifteen and as old as eighty. Marie-Louise fell in love with her when she told her earnestly that she adored little Franz: "It is not that he deserves to be loved, it is that one cannot help it."[19]

Leopoldine reported that the new Empress had said that she wanted to love the Duke and take care of the Duke as if he were her own son. Karoline-Auguste, extremely thoughtful and understanding of Marie-Louise's difficult situation, certainly was a welcome replacement of her predecessor. Though unquestionably loving towards her stepchildren, Marie-Ludovica had been extremely difficult to live with, her politics and lack of diplomacy causing the Emperor constant embarrassment. Remarried after tuberculosis finally claimed his third wife and with peace in his realm, he seemed incredibly happy.

Count Dietrichstein reported that Karoline-Auguste, who could not have been more affectionate towards the Duke if she tried, gave a lunch on the occasion of his first communion, just one of the many rites of passage in his life of which his mother would be deprived. She told Marie-Louise that, whilst she thought it important to inculcate obedience in him, she made it her aim to obtain his trust so as to preserve it for his mother. Only a mother could inspire such a feeling. But it needed nurturing and maintaining. It would be a pleasure for her to contribute to this process. In her view, no man (with very few exceptions) could equal a woman in this respect. The Austrian Empress had converted the Chinese study into a garlanded temple of flowers with cages full of birds from the Indies, and had given him a silver basket and porcelain cup and, on Marie-Louise's behalf, a small telescope.

Knowing that her son was in loving hands did not enable Marie-Louise to find any peace of mind. The constant prurience of her Parman court coupled with the occasional local earth tremor was enough to drive her insane. It seemed her secrets were safe only with her spaniel, Lovely, and her parrot, Margharitina, a gift from Leopoldine. Without Neipperg, her chief administrator, who appreciated the precarious nature of her emotional state, she felt alone, at the mercy of her persecutors. Again Marie-Louise sought the chivalrous aid of Tsar Alexander. This time, he could not help.

And Marie-Louise had other worries. Her dearest sister Leopoldine had been bartered in a dynastic marriage to the eighteen-year-old prince Dom Pedro of the Portuguese royal family. Dom Pedro lived in Brazil, not in Portugal. Marie-Louise knew that the chances of seeing her sister ever again were getting slimmer by the day. Dom Pedro had promised the Austrian court that he would return with Leopoldine to Europe within two years, but in the unlikely event that the promise were to be fulfilled, Europe might mean Lisbon, not Vienna or Parma. Having never met her husband, but in love with the portrait Dom Pedro had sent and with the diamonds with which he had showered her, Leopoldine was excited but terrified. She faced the long hazardous sea-voyage with trepidation. Marie-Louise was upset to hear from Archduke Rainer that Metternich had specifically tried to organise matters to frustrate a meeting between the two sisters, despite knowing how very close they had always been. "Her departure is tantamount to a death sentence."[20]

"I am not allowed to go to Parma! It's not the Portuguese who would be incapable of this stupidity but dearest Papa! I cannot believe it – I am dreadfully upset."[21] Leopoldine begged Marie-Louise to come and join her at Poggio Imperiale outside Florence, and to accompany her to the port of Livorno, where her ship was anchored, while the party awaited favourable winds. Fortuitously, Marie-Louise's doctors had advised her to take a course of sea baths at Livorno in order to improve her severely strained health. Leopoldine, accompanied by Metternich and a large retinue, many of whom would accompany her to Brazil, waited in Florence for the arrival of Portuguese escorts sent to collect her, delayed by British ships as they passed through Lisbon. While the party waited, news came that there had been an uprising in Pernambuco in Brazil and that ships were to be commandeered to put down the revolt. Leopoldine sat sweating in Florence in soaring summer temperatures which she would soon have to endure all year round.

As soon as the escort arrived, the party set out for Livorno. The *Dom Joao VI*, a ship-of-the-line which was to be Leopoldine's conveyance across the high seas, was anchored in the bustling trading port of Livorno. Marie-Louise remarked upon the attractive lighthouse and the outline of the island of Elba, visible in the distance. A marquee had been erected on deck with an orchestra, brought from Brazil, which serenaded Leopoldine on her first visit to the ship. Sumptuous quarters for Leopoldine and her entourage, her cabins emblazoned with the Portuguese royal insignia, had replaced the vessel's sixty cannons. Marie-Louise listened to Leopoldine as she described how superior the Brazilians were to the Europeans, still children of nature uncorrupted by luxury and its terrible consequences. Having studied the language and the journals of Alexander von Humboldt recording his expedition to the Amazon, she looked forward to discovering the New World. She was convinced she would find more probity there than at home. She said that she was not, contrary to Marie-Louise's expectations, scared of the fate which awaited her. She was full of confidence, setting out for a future which she regarded as predestined. The Portuguese ambassador to Austria had filled Leopoldine's head with all sorts of ideas, very few of which Marie-Louise thought could have any foundation. However, there was no point trying to disabuse her of them at this stage. Reality would hit all too soon. Marie-Louise disapproved of the suit, but said nothing. Whether she liked it or not, fate had decreed that Leopoldine should marry Dom Pedro, just as she had had to marry Napoleon. To be born a Habsburg woman really was unenviable.

During the sisters' brief reunion, Leopoldine handed Marie-Louise a letter from their uncle Archduke Rainer, which he begged her to destroy immediately after reading. "There is another storm ahead of you as you read these lines." Metternich, who Leopoldine had cynically nicknamed 'Everyone's Darling', was accompanying Leopoldine officially to surrender her to the Portuguese,

> but his real mission is to make quite another surrender – your duchies to the Queen of Etruria.* The plan is to exchange Parma for Lucca and a substantial pension from Spain. People think that you favour this solution. I agree that this option

---

* The Queen of Etruria: Etruria was an artificial kingdom carved from Tuscany by Napoleon for Spanish Bourbon Maria Luisa's husband Louis following Napoleon's conquest of Parma, to which Louis was heir. In 1815, Maria Luisa lost her fight for Parma to Marie-Louise, "compensated" by the grant of the Duchy of Lucca pending Marie-Louise's death when her son would inherit Parma.

might have suited you better and given you peace of mind had you been granted it at the outset. But to agree to this option now is quite another matter. It is my duty as a friend to speak with your best interest at heart and to advise you that the most important thing at this moment is to stand firm and be steadfast. If you have to make any exchange, there would have to be exact equivalence of value. But I strongly advise against any such concession. In my view, it is far preferable for you to keep Parma for your lifetime, the Bourbons inheriting upon your death. I fear that if you do not concede the reversion of Parma at your death to the Bourbons, Spain and France will do everything they can to get rid of you. Be sure that eventually these immortal cabinets will find the means to oust you and you and your son will be left with absolutely nothing. If you now concede the enjoyment of the duchies only for your lifetime, you will be saved from constant threat and will be able to live out your days pleasantly in an earthly paradise. You must be extremely careful to safeguard your situation on every front as diplomacy does not always work in honest ways.[22]

Archduke Rainer told her to brief Neipperg to conduct matters on her behalf and not to budge without her express authority.

Archduke Johann, Marie-Louise's uncle, like all other members of the imperial family, put a brave face on Leopoldine's departure. In his letter to Marie-Louise, he expressed how happy he was that blue Austrian blood would mingle in the veins of a nascent tribe which, he predicted, would long outlast much of the Old World. "I will never give up hope of one day going to see Leopoldine and her adopted country."[23] Johann concluded.

Marie-Louise, as sovereign, would never have the freedom or time to embark on such a voyage. She embraced her sister, trying as best she could to reassure her that a rich future awaited her, desperately fighting back the tears. She had little doubt she would never see her blue eyes and blonde curls or hear her torrents of laughter again. She took her leave of her sister shortly before midnight when the *Dom Joao IV* and the remaining Portuguese fleet set sail in turbulent seas.

Marie-Louise remained in Livorno for a month after Leopoldine's departure. Lately, it had begun to be both fashionable and recognised as beneficial to health to take sea-baths. She immediately took to the sea air of Tuscany, far more gentle and inviting if less invigorating than that of the North Atlantic. The sun and saltwater, the wonderful country walks and rides, the excellent local theatre and opera where she heard *Tancredi* and *Aureliano in Palmira* by Gioacchino Rossini, the most celebrated composer of the day, immediately lifted her mood. Sadly, clear sunny days without storm clouds were to be a rarity.

ELEVEN

Absent Motherhood, 1818

Bad news from Vienna brought by Neipperg exacerbated her nerves. The Tsar and, incredibly, Marie-Louise's father had caved in to the British and Spanish. Marie-Louise was incredulous. Not only would her son not inherit Parma, the state to revert to the Spanish Bourbons after his mother's death, but he would have to remain forever in Austria.

> I do not hide from you, my dear father, that it is with a very heavy heart that I bend to the arrangements which have been made regarding my son's future. After the very great sacrifices to which I consented for the peace of Europe, I did not think I would be asked to make still more. By way of fresh proof of my filial love, and to show you how far I subordinate my own interest to that of the community, I accept the proposed terms subject to certain conditions which will assure my son, if he renounces the succession to the States of Parma, a position suited to his rank which is the most advantageous position in the Austrian States.[1]

Marie-Louise continued bitterly: "Accordingly, my Illustrious Father, I place my happiness in your hands, persuaded that your affection for your daughter and the consciousness of the sacred duties which are incumbent upon you as guardian of your grandson will encourage you to do what is best and most honourable for their performance."

Marie-Louise expressed her consent subject to several conditions, from which she was determined not to budge. She refused any exchange of land for pension. Duchies her son must have of equivalent importance to those she now occupied. Her father should also confer upon her son a ranking giving him status equal to the hereditary Habsburg princes. Her assertiveness provoked Chancellor Metternich's vindictive streak. Having engineered this departure from the Paris Treaty, he demanded that Marie-Louise be made to give her unconditional consent. The sad reality was that, without Marie-Louise's knowledge or consent, Emperor Francis had already, albeit reluctantly, made the magnanimous gesture of conceding the duchies unconditionally to the Spanish. Marie-Louise found her terms considerably watered-down in a protocol signed six months later. Upon his mother's death, her son would inherit territories in Bohemia producing revenues estimated at five hundred thousand francs and a large endowment. Until then, he would remain dependent on his mother's limited purse and his grandfather's largesse. Marie-Louise had never predicted such betrayal after the magnificent promises of Tsar Alexander. "I am completely distraught when I see that all my sacrifices are useless and that Europe is indifferent to the fate of my child. How happy are those who depend on others for nothing and the destiny of whose children depend only on their affection!"[2]

Archduke Johann advised Marie-Louise to fight the grief and displeasure of separation from loved ones and to drive away morbid thoughts by attending to the administration of her duchies. "Fulfilment of your duty and the pleasure of some good you may accomplish – it is in these that you must find adequate compensation."[3] Both he and Rainer cursed the dreadful political times they were living through. "Apply yourself with conviction and God will stay on your side," her father counselled. She held her tongue, clinging to Parma and her sovereignty. The protocol finally determining the succession made no mention of the little Napoleon, granting the duchies she now occupied to her for her life, thereafter to the Queen of Etruria and the Queen's son, Charles.

It was pointless to express anger at her father, who had been accused by the allies of excessive sentimentality towards his grandson. She had done everything she could for the peace of Europe and, she hoped, for the future of her child, though it was far less than the birth right in prospect when he was born. Marie-Louise must put up a robust front to the French who were out to find a chink in her armour. She wrote to the Duchess of Montebello, with whom she still corresponded, but whom she had long ceased to idealise that she wished to have her son educated according to the principles of her homeland, to make of him a loyal, honest German.

Grandfather Leopold had enunciated Habsburg philosophy: Habsburg offspring, even if destined for monarchy, were not to dream of grand establishments, but were to prepare for employment as merely ordinary private individuals and servants of the state. Marie-Louise's ideals were rooted in reality, not in the fantasy world of her husband.

"The destiny and future of my son have been decided. I admit that this gave me much pleasure, and I am convinced you will share my feelings. You know that it was never for thrones or for states that I nursed ambitions for my son. I have always hoped that he would be the richest and most likeable individual in Austria."[4]

Marie-Louise and the Duke of Reichstadt were reunited in June 1818 in the spa town of Baden, just outside Vienna, where Marie-Louise had received news of the outcome of the Battle of Waterloo three years earlier. They had not seen each other for two years. Marie-Louise reassured Franz, by her side from nine in the morning to ten at night, that she had not abandoned him, that she loved him more than anyone else in the world. It was a blissful eleven weeks. At last Marie-Louise could smother her seven year old, already almost her height, with kisses and caresses long overdue. There was nothing more seductive than the Duke's charming, rosy-cheeked face and blond curls, which Count Dietrichstein had prevented the barber from cutting before her arrival, and his constant chitter-chatter. Marie-Louise read stories to him, finding that he knew many of them already. She was impressed by his knowledge of the

Old and New Testaments, his powers of recall and comprehension several years ahead of his age. Like his tutors, Marie-Louise was taken by surprise by his clever insights and questions. It was true that he was mature beyond his age, rather too serious perhaps, not enough of the child about him. But there were few children who had had his experience of life. Marie-Louise had to use the short time allotted her to constantly reassure him of her and his father's love and affection for him, to bolster his inevitably undermined self-esteem. Just as she had had to learn to live with an impossible situation, so would he. At least he had on hand her own close family, headed by the most adored man in Austria, his grandfather. His upbringing was privileged, and there was nowhere more beautiful, no city more architecturally charming, more culturally rich or more scenically pleasing than Vienna. Marie-Louise would not exchange the palaces of the Laxenburg, of Schönbrunn, the Kahlenberg, Wienerwald or Dornbach for anything she had seen in France. And the little Franz was growing up in times of peace in an enlightened empire under a benign sovereign.

On a hot August morning in Vienna, an official ceremony took place in the Hofburg Palace to confer upon Marie-Louise's son the title of His Most Serene Highness Duke of Reichstadt. A new duchy had been created expressly for him. Marie-Louise had been sent a list of possible titles, of which Reichstadt seemed to convey the finest German aristocracy. She had thought a bad joke the proposal that he be made a count, the title conferred customarily on illegimate offspring. An emperor's son had at least to be a duke. The name of Reichstadt was innocuous, carrying no associations of kingship, or of ancient ruling households to which the child was not to consider himself born. One day, the boy had asked as he played in his grandfather's study, "What does it mean that I am called the King of Rome?" His grandfather replied adroitly that these terms were meaningless. One of his many titles was King of Jerusalem, a place far away, not his. Little Francis had looked momentarily perplexed. Not all of his grandfather's titles were meaningless.

Emperor Francis, resplendent in his white imperial costume, declared that he, Emperor Francis II of Austria, King of Jerusalem, of Hungary, of Bohemia and so on (all the lengthy "meaningless" titles recited in full), was empowered under the Final Act of the Congress of Vienna and by his negotiation with the principal allies to determine the title, rank, arms and personal relationships of Prince Francis Charles Joseph, son of his beloved daughter, Archduchess of Austria, Duchess of Parma, Piacenza and Guastalla. The Emperor conferred on his grandson the right to use a coat of arms embossed with lions in gold, an oval shield mounted between two golden griffins and ducal cloak both imprinted with a ducal crown. In addition to the duchy created expressly for little Franz, Emperor Francis granted him the enjoyment and income during his lifetime of additional Bohemian lands and property, together with fixtures and furnishings, other effects and pertinent rights, situated in the same region, all the domains of unknown, remote, politically inconsequent territory.

The new duke, in full military uniform, was oblivious to the postponement of his standing in line to the Austrian throne beyond the other princes and archdukes of the imperial family and cousins as yet unborn. No mention whatsoever had been made of the boy's father, the Christian name, Napoleon, given him on baptism, or his surname, Bonaparte. Emperor Francis hoped that this ceremony would dispense with the ambiguity of the child's position and root him fairly and squarely in the Austrian bosom, though he was not referred to as Habsburg. From now on, he would imbibe the best of Austro-German culture. His social environment, his schooling, his pleasures would be free of any Bonapartist taint. Everyone was convinced that the seven year old would grow up to be an Austrian citizen through and through.

Victoria de Crenneville wrote to Marie-Louise:

> I knew full well that your maternal heart would not rest until the title was certain, but I have become so sceptical having

experienced so many events that I constantly feared political postponements, which are so often designed to leave business unfinished. Finally everything is signed and sealed. I have the greatest pleasure in repeating to Your Majesty that he will be the most adored, the richest and, I may add, the handsomest Prince. His crown will be his achievements and the happiness he derives from what he enjoys doing.[5]

Victoria had lived through Marie-Louise's troubles and believed, without political prejudice, that a better future beckoned for the child whom she would visit as often as she could when in Vienna. Marie-Louise tried to persuade herself that her little boy now had many mothers rather than just one – his new grandmother, Empress Karoline-Auguste, his aunts, Victoria de Crenneville and many more in the imperial household who adored him. She hoped that, although no substitute for her, they would go some way to providing him with the female physical attention which his tutors could not provide.

Marie-Louise had no need to be persuaded that a happy peaceful existence was much to be preferred to the poisoned chalice of prestigious thrones. The allies were so neurotic about ensuring that Marie-Louise was prevented from acting otherwise than in their interests that they demanded that an Austrian garrison be maintained in Piacenza. Soon formidable defences were constructed and armaments flooded in to keep Marie-Louise, her government and her duchies under constant surveillance.

When Marie-Louise spoke of her anticipated departure, Franz cried for a whole week. He desperately wanted to go and live with her in Parma. After parting, Count Dietrichstein took the Duke out for a ride to go and get a cup of coffee to try and stem his tears. Eventually, he found himself forced to scold the poor boy in order to get him to calm down. It was pitiful to read the Duke's next letter: "It makes me sad whenever I think that at this hour the day before yesterday I was with you and now it is no longer so."[6]

On her journey from Vienna to Parma, Marie-Louise dismounted at each town to buy little presents to comfort him. She sent Franz gifts regularly, a collection of shells, a wallet, a model of her home, showing him the rooms in which she lived. Unlike Count Dietrichstein, she forgave his lack of expression of appreciation for a beautiful wooden horse she had sent for his birthday:

"You say that the prince is still so young. But I believe on the contrary that every toy, indeed everything which interests him should remind him how much he owes to his mother. I never cease to tell him this or to expound on the virtues of filial love."

"Ah, if only I were there with you! I love you beyond all expression!" the Duke frequently lamented. He told her how he constantly reread her letters, each time finding fresh tokens of her love. He talked about his mother, groaning as he reread her letters, praying fervently for her return, working himself up into such a lather that he would start screaming for her. In the middle of the night, he would wake up Collin and pretend he had lost his pillow, though it was under his head, or complain that his bed was too short, all little ruses which evidenced the torture of abandonment. On other nights, he would wet the bed. Count Dietrichstein tried every means at his disposal, including a few strikes of the whip, to shame him into stopping. Emperor Francis, absent for long stretches while travelling in his own dominions and on the Italian peninsula, had reluctantly authorised this punishment. When Marie-Louise heard about this, she begged the Count to spare her child. Thankfully, Count Dietrichstein, finding it both hateful and ineffective, soon gave up in exasperation. Little Franz had become so fond of the Count that he burst into tears when told that his misconduct had prevented the Count from sleeping. But Franz had begun to use swear words and to tell lies. He was severely reprimanded when he told his tutors they were "shits". Following such occasions, he would not appear at dinner with his grandfather and would show his contrition by penning letters to his mother apologizing for his shortcomings, promising to improve if only she would run to Vienna.

In one of many letters, the Duke wrote,

> I beg God above all to make you as happy as possible and to accord me the grace of being able to contribute to your happiness. Our separation seems a century. I am only truly happy when you write to me. How much do I envy the fate of this letter! I owe God the greatest gratitude for having given me such a good, loving mother.[7]

Marie-Louise prayed that God would remove all impediments to an early reunion. She despaired, hearing that the Duke was expressing his pain by lashing out at his tutors and rebelling against the strictures of his daily routine. He refused to study and do his homework, demonstrating total indifference to everything and everyone, hitting Foresti when challenged.

Marie-Louise did her best to appear serene in performing her public duties, but inside she was miserable at her son's severe affliction. Just how impossible her situation was the Duke of Reichstadt could not know. Not until he was adult would he realise the competing claims on his mother's time. Even in adulthood, he would be ignorant of the public charade of her life in her distant duchy.

TWELVE

Napoleon's heart, 1821

The year 1820 had started badly with the murder by an anti-royal Bonapartist of Marie-Louise's cousin and the French king's nephew, the Duke de Berry, who was expected to continue the Bourbon dynasty on the French throne. The assailant struck with a dagger as the Duke emerged with his pregnant wife from the opera house on the Rue de Richelieu. The news sent shock waves through the royal houses of Europe. Many were convinced that the assailant had acted not alone, as asserted, but as part of a much wider, international plot to bring down the monarchical order. Marie-Louise heard from Lady Priscilla Burghersh that those believed to be the authors had been caught in London. Some saw in this new regicidal drama vengeance for Napoleon's humiliation, and predicted his or his son's return to France.

Over the past few years, Marie-Louise and other rulers on the European continent had observed the political developments in the sparsely populated, largely undeveloped New World. From Argentina to Mexico, former Spanish and Portuguese colonies had broken and were breaking free of their imperial masters, to establish their own governments. These events inspired revolutions in Portugal and Spain, the latter forcing the Bourbon king to concede the Constitution of Cadiz, drafted by the Spanish government in exile in 1812 when Spain was occupied by Napoleon. These risings fuelled unrest in the Spanish Bourbon Kingdom of the Two Sicilies, and almost everywhere else on the Italian peninsula. The discarded flag which Napoleon had given his Italic Kingdom twenty years earlier was proudly flaunted from balconies and the tricolour cockade sported in direct defiance of Austrian masters. Austrian funds on the Frankfurt Stock exchange plummeted. The rebels in Turin and Genoa established their own governments. Insults were hurled at Victor Emmanuel I, King of Piedmont-Sardinia, as he fled, his carriage hurtling out of his capital towards Nice. The Duchy of Lombardy, vital to Austrian control over the northern peninsula, clamoured for independence from Austria and instigated a patriotic government. Under pressure from the rebels, Marie-Louise's grandfather, Ferdinand, King of Naples granted a constitution and then fled to Llubliana where a meeting of terrified allied European monarchs hastily convened to agree a response.

Fear of being ejected from her throne was never far from the mind of the twenty-eight-year-old duchess, whose small territories bordered both Piedmont and Lombardy. It was to be hoped that her own enlightened style of government, a complete contrast to the despotism everywhere else, would convince the Parmans not to join the mêlée. The world beyond her "little garden", as she liked to think of her lease, was a hostile, dangerous place. As a precautionary measure, she bolstered police powers and sent a battalion of her regiment to Piacenza, along with a warning to her subjects that any disturbance of the public tranquillity would not be tolerated. Any agitators were to be sent to the Fortress of Compiano not far from Parma, and to be kept there until her return. Should these injunctions prove inadequate for those individuals who believed that they would find happiness in trying to force change, she would arrange, on her father's advice, for their transfer to the Fortress of Mantua as prisoners of the Austrian State. This threat was unnecessary. She told her father that everything was as quiet as if nothing was happening beyond her borders. Though many Parmans had family, friends and business associates in the neighbouring states who proclaimed the gospel of independence, there was no general demand as yet in Marie-Louise's duchies for constitutional or regime change. To ease tensions, the Duchess lowered taxes. Her subjects' petition begging her not to leave for Llubliana, to which she had been summoned by the Austrian Court, confirmed her in her decision to sit out events in Parma.

Emperor Francis issued orders for the Austrian fleet in the port of Trieste to prepare itself for immediate service, and all Neapolitan and Sicilian vessels in the harbour were sequestered in retaliation for the arrest of Austrian vessels in Naples. All other ports on the Adriatic coast were put in a state of defence. In Llubliana, Metternich exhorted his European allies to join Austria in sending forces to suppress the constitutionalists. Russia mobilised its 100,000-strong army to march on the Italian peninsula, as Austria prepared to advance its 60,000-strong troops quartered on the right bank of the River Po.

Inflamed by this act of provocation, the new government of Piedmont declared war on Austria. Soon, most of the male population of Turin were under arms, braced for to take Milan from Austria. Sympathisers from other parts of the Italian peninsula flooded into Piedmont to swell the patriots' ranks, rallying to the cry of "The Constitution of Cadiz forever! War to the barbarians!" Austrian spies who tried to incite counter-revolution by bribing soldiers who thronged the thoroughfares were arrested and deported. Defecting Austrian officers were also known to have declared for the constitutionalists. The Piedmontese government announced: "The hour has arrived not only of the Constitution of Cadiz but of Italian independence!"

Her hands trembling like those of an old woman, Marie-Louise begged her father to excuse Neipperg from military service, were Austrian troops to be sent to Lombardy. The tranquillity of her duchies depended to a large extent on mutual confidence between him and her subjects. The Venetians and Tuscans rose against the Austrians. Archduke Johann sent Marie-Louise regular bulletins of troop movements, warning his niece that she should make no mistake – her father and Tsar Alexander would stop at nothing to regain control and root out dissent. Conflicting reports suggested that Russian troops had been diverted to Constantinople. Determined to replace the Ottomans as the dominant power over the Eastern Mediterranean, they fomented Greek discontent, pumping hundreds of roubles into subscriptions to fund the Greek struggle for the Ionian Islands against the Turks. In response to the Greek leader Ypsilanti's vow to spread fire and sword through all Ottoman ports, the Sultan ordered the desecration and destruction of all Christian churches. International pleas for revocation of the order were ignored and the Greek Patriarch tortured and killed, his corpse handed to the Jews with an order to cut it to pieces to throw to Constantinople's famished dogs. With the outbreak of insurrections in Moldavia and Wallachia, a general war in Europe seemed unavoidable to all, including Marie-Louise.

The Russian troops had not been diverted as rumoured. Austrian, Hungarian and Russian soldiers advanced down through the Italian states to restore the despotic Ferdinand to his decadent court.

By the end of April 1821, reactionary rulers on the Italian peninsula had, with Austrian backing, rounded up those revolutionaries and supporters who had not managed to board ship for the Iberian peninsula. To be caught bearing arms was enough to be condemned to death. By confessions extorted by torture, detainees were persuaded to incriminate kinsmen in their own and neighbouring states. Austrians, Bourbons and Papacy all acted without scruples. Family members found their heads at the end of a pistol butt or an unsheathed sword, even when their loved ones gave themselves up without resistance. Austrian procedure, which permitted up to forty lashings to be administered to detainees on alternate days over a finite period, was ignored in favour of two thousand to extort 'confessions'. Some lost limbs and even buttocks, lacerated to such a degree that they became infected and had to be amputated. Others were so badly crippled they could hardly move let alone walk; yet others were deprived of their manhood. The convictions obtained by the Austrians would all have been illegal according to the Napoleonic Code of laws recently cast aside by Napoleon's enemies.

Under the Code, lack of adherence to procedure in any trial or adjudication would invalidate the sentence and require a retrial. In theory at least, the defendant had freedom to be represented by the most able advocates, free inspection of documentary evidence to be used against him and every available means of putting to proof any discrepancy. There was no such protection of the human right under the Austrian code of laws. Though any trial in which legalities had not been fully observed was technically void, the accused had no means of identifying failures in procedure or of establishing proof of their occurrence, and so retrials were extremely rare. The best elements of the French system, which gave defendants every guarantee of a proper defence, were retained in Marie-Louise's duchies. The pillory, branding and confiscation of goods, all penalties still in force beyond her borders, were abolished in Parma. Thus, Marie-Louise's few citizens enjoyed an immense advantage over the remaining millions in the rest of the Italian peninsula. Her cruel cousin, the Duke, otherwise known as the Butcher of Modena, liked to refer to the duchess as the *Presidentessa* of the Republic of Parma. As spring wore on, fresh Austrian regiments continued to be despatched from Innsbruck into the Italian territories to maintain order. Trials in Milan led to trials in Brescia, those in Brescia to trials in Mantua, those in Mantua to Modena, those in Modena to insinuations in Parma.

Against this unstable background, Marie-Louise, having retreated from Parma to the mild air of Sala Baganza, chanced to read a perfunctory notice which appeared in the *Piedmont Gazette*:

> The death of Napoleon, reported by a courier from Rothschild, the Paris banker, to the Court of St James, was announced yesterday 13 July in Paris by the Gazette de France. The intelligence is generally regarded as of little significance. Hence the Court has not gone into mourning.

Few people lent credence to any of the frequent reports of the death of the former Emperor of France. This time, the nature of the notice and the details allowed little room for doubt. Marie-Louise, Duchess of Parma, reread the notice to be sure that her eyes had not deceived her. Confirmation came a few days later.

"I have been given an important piece of news. Emperor Napoleon is dead for certain," wrote Caroline Amelin de St. Marie, one of Marie-Louise's former ladies-in-waiting, her letter dated 16th July[1]. "They say he died from stomach cancer at seven o'clock in the evening on 6th May. Your Majesty will soon have a visit from a courier from Vienna."

Napoleon had died two and half months earlier and no-one had had the decency to inform her personally. The government of England, which must have known of his death at least six weeks earlier, had not written to her. France might have sent word but had not. Chancellor Metternich should at the very least have sent an official notice. Her Viennese family members must have known, but they too had kept silent. She was shocked at how little she could count on those from whom she was entitled to expect more interest and friendship. Simmering with anger at the world which was always ready to pounce on her and accuse her of ill-will, she addressed a curt letter to her father expressing her indignation at this humiliation, reminding him of the many sacrifices she had made in the past, of the silence she had kept in order to comply with his wishes, and demanding further details. She referred to her late husband not by his still unutterable name, but as "the poor soul" and "the deceased."

Six sleepless nights after reading of Napoleon's death, Marie-Louise received her father's cool reply. As yet no will had been found, only a codicil. This expressed Napoleon's last wish that his heart, preserved in alcohol in an eagle-topped silver reliquary, be transported to his good Louise, his dearest wife, so that she could dispose of it as she wished. The Austrian Emperor asked for her instructions and told her to adopt the measures stipulated by Metternich for mourning. There the letter ended. There was no expression of sympathy.

Neipperg issued instructions on Marie-Louise's behalf to the Parman court.

> Save for employees, all members of the court shall observe mourning for my august husband for a period of three months: none of those ceremonies should be forgotten which the piety of the living consecrates to the dead. Napoleon shall receive in death those sentiments of attachment and devotion which I have held for him during his lifetime.

Marie-Louise heard nothing officially. A communication from Parma dated 29th July in the foreign papers stated:

> The Court of Austria had not yet officially notified the Archduchess Marie-Louise, our Sovereign, of the death of her husband Napoleon Bonaparte. This Princess put on mourning on receipt of news of that event direct from England. It is not known whether her Imperial Highness will cause a notification of his decease to be made to Foreign Courts, as is the custom.

Marie-Louise replied to her father,

> I can no longer doubt that the Almighty has brought an end to the days of pain of Napoleon, my husband. The newspapers brought the news ahead of the letters which I received from Vienna and Paris. They went further and gave various versions as to where his sepulchre is to be located. If, since 1814, my voice has not been allowed to be heard with regard to the conjectures which decided his fate, I believe that it should be the same today and that, by persevering in the silence which your counsel and my situation have made a duty, it remains for me only to keep enclosed within me the feelings which I must naturally feel. Nonetheless, if, after so many vicissitudes, I were to have a wish to express, and for me, and as it seems to me for the Duke of Reichstadt, it would be that the mortal remains of my husband, of the father of my son be respected. By entrusting

with unlimited confidence this wish in the paternal heart of Your Majesty, I abandon to you the care of assessing whether my wish is appropriate and necessary.²

Napoleon declared in his last will, dictated close to death on St Helena: "I have always had reason to praise my very dear wife Marie-Louise. I harbour for her until the very last the tenderest feelings. I ask that she take pains to keep my son safe from the traps which still surround his childhood." He bequeathed to his son "the boxes, orders and other objects such as silverware, camp bed, weapons, saddles, swords, vases from my chapel, books, linen which have served my body and my utility. It is my wish that he cherish this meagre bequest which will allow him to retrace the memory of a father of which the whole world will keep him occupied." In a codicil, he asked his executors to set straight his son's knowledge of his father and to prevail upon him to take up his father's name as soon as his son was capable of reasoning and could take the step when fitting. "My memory will be the glory of his life." He asked that engravings, pictures, books and medals be brought together to give his son and his wife just ideas and to destroy the false ideas that might have been inculcated by the politics of foreign powers.

Napoleon made no specific financial legacy to Marie-Louise or to his son, though he left the latter lengthy advice, even as to potential spouses. If Napoleon knew that his son had been robbed of his Christian name, he possibly also knew his private assets of one hundred and eighteen million francs had been appropriated by Louis XVIII, transferred to the French treasury by royal decree of 1818. Whether or not Napoleon knew of the sequestration of his funds, he made legacies assuming their existence. He had even bequeathed the two million francs which Marie-Louise had taken when fleeing from Paris, over half of which she had used to defray the costs of her journey and that of her large Court entourage who had followed her from Paris to Blois and Orléans, and of the French household who had followed her to Vienna. The remaining nine hundred thousand francs had been returned to Napoleon.

Marie-Louise feared that the British government might deprive her son of his inheritance from Napoleon. Metternich couched his secret intercession to prevent the legacies reaching their specified legatees in "his concern for Mme the Duchess of Parma and her son", and instigated proceedings in Marie-Louise's name for half these funds to hold for her son until his majority. Napoleon's executors demanded access to Marie-Louise. They were refused, as was their request that she intervene to secure the return of Napoleon's remains to France. Instead, they were invited to hand over to the Austrian ambassador to France Napoleon's last gifts to his wife, embroidered linen and a bracelet woven with his hair for onward transmission to her.

Napoleon's offer of his heart was terribly misconceived. Marie-Louise had no intention of creating a shrine, as his first wife had done in Malmaison, to which those faithful to her late husband's memory could come and worship. There would be no burial of his heart in Parma which might revive her earlier traumas. Besides this, there were other reasons.

Marie-Louise told others that she had discharged her duties towards the father of her child and her conscience was clear. Inside, conflicting emotions and the excessive heat sapped her strength. A letter from her sister Leopoldine, dated before Marie-Louise herself knew of her husband's end, was particularly touching:

> Accept my heartfelt sympathy on the death of Napoleon, as I know your kind-heartedness and gentle way of thinking, I am convinced that you must be greatly aggrieved. I who love and treasure you sincerely like no-one else in this world, share in my heart all your troubles and worries. Unfortunately, there is now no hope of sailing to Europe, and to be honest, in the current critical situation in Europe, one must be thankful for being in Brazil, which is from every perspective such a rich land.[3]

NAPOLEON'S HEART, 1821

Aunt Marie-Thérèse, Queen of Saschen, was equally sympathetic,

The effect on you which the loss which you have just suffered has been such as I have always thought [it would be' . . . having seen you together in 1812 . . . you conducted yourself on that occasion as you always do on every occasion with great prudence, reflection and decency . . . and you were right to consult only your heart and to make of it a private affair, otherwise . . . everyone would have put the blame on you . . .[4]

From the moment Napoleon had entered her life, the now widowed Madame Bonaparte had found herself on the edge of a precipice, politically, socially and mentally. Even his death would not provide an escape. For the time being, at least, Marie-Louise was pleased to report to her father that the people of Parma had forgotten about politics and were obsessed with the opera, the ballet and the other entertainments planned for the coming carnival season.

THIRTEEN
Resisting the witch-hunt, 1822

Ever since the murders in Mannheim in 1819 of Kotzebue, a reactionary dramatist, and in Paris in 1820 of the Duke de Berry, Metternich had become increasingly aggressive in rooting out those he considered to be opponents of Austria. He cared little for labels. Constitutionalists, regenerationists, philanthropists, friends of the people, Jacobins, anarchists, demagogues, reformers, carbonari, radicals, atheists, deists, naturalists, materialists; he lumped them together and suspected them all. In the light of Kotzebue's murder, German students were to be allowed to visit Parma for a short period only to see places of interest. Throughout the Austrian Empire and its satellite states, association with a proscribed sect was a crime of high treason. Nonetheless, secret sects proliferated everywhere, meeting in local cafés and tavernas to plan ejection of foreign masters and self-government. All were preparing for future insurrection, though they were far from having common aims, and could be used as much for the promotion of evil as of good. It would be many years before they could all be persuaded towards unity of purpose.

Nonetheless, Austria, and no doubt Marie-Louise too, knew full well that their strength was not to be undermined, as was evident in the political changes set in train in Spain, Portugal, Piedmont, Naples and most of the Hispanic South American continent.

Dealing ruthlessly with dissident elements, Metternich had arrested, among other intellectuals, the liberal Federico Confalonieri, editor of the liberal journal *Il Conciliatore* which had been forcibly closed, and Silvio Pellico, celebrated playwright of, among other works with patriotic messages, *Francesca da Rimini*. Both men had been sentenced to death, their convictions commuted to indefinite detention in the Spielberg Fortress in Moravia, a hell in which few survived to emerge alive.

Since her arrival in Parma, Marie-Louise had been under relentless pressure to keep under close surveillance and to send to Vienna names and details of known or suspected agitators, and to carry out sporadic "cleansing" of secret societies in her duchies. The Milanese authorities sent Marie-Louise a list of names of regular attenders coming from within and without the duchies who were alleged to be attending political meetings in a specified private home in Parma. She took no action. In contrast to her father, who had demanded trials with scant regard to the availability of corroborated evidence, she refused to sanction a witch-hunt. She ignored Metternich's instructions, persistently denying any knowledge of dissidents or secret organizations within her lands, though several of her courtiers, loyal and sympathetic to her on a personal level, were widely known to desire emancipation from the Austrian yoke and were members of a sect created by Count Jacopo Sanvitale, nephew of her courtier Stefano Sanvitale.

Shortly after Marie-Louise's arrival in Parma in the spring of 1816, Jacopo Sanvitale had recited a cantata of praise to her, infused with warmth and appreciation of the tranquillity that he hoped her appointment would bring to her states. Like many in her territories, he had had personal experience of her husband. The flower of aristocratic Italian youth, Jacopo had been part of the Guard of Honour which had received Napoleon and Josephine on their visit to Parma in 1805. His uncle Count Stefano Sanvitale and cousin Luigi had hosted the French Emperor at the family's ancestral seat of Palazzo Sanvitale, the residence of choice for all illustrious visitors passing through the city. Napoleon had come as a public relations exercise after having himself crowned King of Italy in Milan's Cathedral, but also to empty the previously Bourbon treasury. He had gone away disappointed, the scant pages of accounts handed him by his administrator, Moreau de St Méry, a far cry from the twenty volumes Moreau de St Méry had produced in his previous post on the island of St Domingo. The incompetent Bourbons had never taken much interest in keeping records. For his hospitality, Count Sanvitale had received only a showy gilt-veneered but worthless lead snuffbox.

Jacopo believed passionately in the patriotic message conveyed by Dante, Petrarch, Boccaccio, Ariosto and Tasso (all writers, save Petrarch, excluded from institutional education in the Duchy), and refused to serve foreign masters with the apparent indifference and phlegmatic reserve of his uncle Stefano and cousin Luigi, Marie-Louise's courtiers. His appointment as superintendent of public health during the typhus outbreak had given him the opportunity to travel frequently to Turin and Milan, where secret societies proliferated. Returning to Parma, Jacopo founded his own group, the Liberal Italian Society of Sciences and Letters at his cousin's home the Palazzo dei Marchesi Dalla Rosa Prati*, situated across from Parma's Baptistery. Members of the police force, the army, the medical and legal professions and performers rallied to him. The French authorities were under strict orders to keep the press heavily censored, to strictly prohibit the dissemination of any Papal publication, to allow the circulation of only very few select foreign newspapers and to silence dissident voices. Alerted to the activities of Jacopo's new group, they immediately ordered him to disband it.

Jacopo next came to the notice of the French authorities in 1812 when he composed a provocative satirical poem on the birth of the King of Rome. Testament to its success, the Parmans learnt the poem by heart and repeated it until it reached the ears of Savary, Napoleon's Chief of Police, who chanced to be in Parma.

Savary informed Napoleon, who gave orders for Jacopo's immediate arrest and imprisonment in the infamous fortress of

---

* Now converted to Parma's most luxurious hotel.

Fenestrelle.* Eighteen months later, he managed to escape, and took refuge in Milan among the men who were to become household names in the struggle for Italian independence. He learnt of the Russian catastrophe, of Napoleon's defeats and of the wave of bankruptcies which Napoleon's economic policies had set in train on the Italian peninsula. The hope that Napoleon's Italic Kingdom, which extended across Northern Italy, might be granted the right to self-government vanished when the Viceroy Eugène de Beauharnais and his 'embroidered coat-tails', the Italians who had collaborated with his administration, capitulated to the Austrians. Men like Jacopo were disheartened but far from giving up their struggle. Though fond of Marie-Louise, he would not allow her to stand in his way.

In the spring of 1816 just before Marie-Louise's arrival, Jacopo was appointed Professor of High Eloquence and History of Literature by the provisional government. He gave his inaugural lecture on "The influence of literature on love of the homeland". His message was unambiguous. "Let us cultivate literature, and let us love our homeland above all else. We love our homeland and cultivate literature justifiably. For we feel righteous pride in the power which we feel when we repeat: We are Italians!"

He did not declaim in Latin as was customary, but in the Tuscan dialect, promoted by patriots as a national language. From that moment on, he started every lecture and tutorial by reminding his students that they were Italians, that they should take pride in their identity, that they must realize that they had the power to shape their future.

The Sublime Perfect Masters, one of the more recent sects, in coordination with their brotherhood in Turin, had planned that,

---

* Italy's gulag was carved into the deep solitary valleys of Chisone, seven hundred square metres above sea level in the mountains of Piedmont. The prison comprised buildings of over a million square metres, approached via a titanic staircase of four thousand steps, a massive cascade of high grey walls, ramparts and labyrinthine steps exposed to the icy, biting winds of the Alps.

following the risings in Piedmont in 1821, Piedmontese troops would assist the inhabitants of cities in the central swathe of the Italian peninsula to revolt. Jacopo was tasked with the preparation of a proclamation.* In December of 1821, Jacopo had together with Marie-Louise's courtier Claudio Linato, laboriously printed thousands of copies of it in the utmost secrecy, and his collaborators had placed it in the bag or on the pillow of every one of fifty thousand Hungarian soldiers who passed through Modena's barracks on their way to Naples.

Only many years later would the truth about these events emerge. By 1821, there was hardly a person of any status in Parman society who was not a member of a secret society. Its head, Giacomo Martini, a doctor and one of Marie-Louise's guards of honour, took his orders directly from Turin. Caderini, Parma's presiding judge highly respected by Marie-Louise, had seen Jacopo at the Parman chapter of the Sublime Perfect Masters. All devoted their energies to an intensive propaganda programme to advance their cause. Austria, like France before it, might proscribe these associations, but the engine of independence, with networks across the Italian peninsula and in France, could no longer be extinguished. No doubt aware of the existence though not necessarily the workings of these groups, Marie-Louise would have to exercise her sovereignty with subtlety, finesse and great ingenuity to maintain her position.

As troops marched towards Naples to restore order, the Milanese authorities sent a circular to all government leaders on the Italian peninsula, including to Parman chief administrator Neipperg, asking

---

* The proclamation, stated to be expressed on behalf of the people of Naples, read:
"You are nothing more than the blind instrument of Austrian tyranny. Following your example, we have claimed those rights which you have for so long defended from the unjust seizure of emperors. Do not desire, valorous soldiers, to descend into the arena to sustain a hated dynasty as parasites of a people warm with the saintly love of liberty, constrained to defend itself, its homeland and its sons to vanquish or die."

whether they had come across any notice address printed in Latin to Hungarian soldiers. Neipperg replied on behalf of Marie-Louise that indeed, some time ago, a Milanese traveller passing through Parma had talked about such a document distributed in Modena, and had even produced an example. However, despite thorough enquiries by the Chief of Police, it had not been possible to identify its originator or distributors. Dissatisfied with Marie-Louise's response, Metternich and the Duke of Modena threatened to send into Parma Austrian troops to hunt down the miscreants if she was not prepared to do the job herself. Marie-Louise told her father firmly that she did not want to do anything to upset the perfect tranquillity reigning in her duchies. She had taken every precaution to ensure that those whom it was suggested were implicated would not seek to evade justice. Were her father to send Vienna's appointees to conduct trials in her duchies and convict, she would not be prepared to carry out sentence and she would demand their retrial by him personally. She did not flinch from duty, but challenged those who sought to interfere with her administration and to foment fear and hatred. Irritated by the Duchess's disobedience, Vienna accused her of involvement in an international conspiracy, Austrian spies having intercepted packages sent to her from Naples and London. These were subsequently found upon inspection to be recently published novels sent by foreign friends.

Forced to take action, the Duchess of Parma invited Metternich and the Duke of Modena to submit to her names of Parman subjects against whom the accusers professed to have evidence. Meanwhile, she had Neipperg forewarn the most prominent suspects through trustworthy channels. Ambrogio Berchet, well loved by Marie-Louise and head of her Ducal Regiment, was asked to alert others to the impending danger. Despite Marie-Louise's protestations, Metternich sent Austrian judges to try the accused. Marie-Louise refused them entry. She had plenty of men in her duchies who were well qualified for the task, who would carry out their functions impartially with probity and strict adherence to the principles of justice laid down by her laws. To Vienna, she defended the accused. "Count Claudio Linati has been in Spain for over a year. Major Berchet might have known those involved, but he is a man of honour, incapable of any mischief." Her drawing teacher Boccaccio was also under suspicion, incriminated by his remark that the whole of the peninsula would soon be engulfed by revolution. Marie-Louise reassured Metternich that Boccaccio would not involve himself with any rebellious individuals. "Jacopo Sanvitale, Martini, Avv. Maestri, Captain Bacchi, Giordani, and Gioia are all known for their principles, they too would be incapable and fearful of any involvement. Furthermore, I have never let these men out of my sight."[1]

Neipperg wrote to Metternich to say that there existed no secret societies in the Parman duchies – he personally did not take the Italians seriously, believing them incapable of concord, action and sacrifice. By nature, they were addicted to gossiping in cafés and other public places. Testing Marie-Louise's allegiance to the fatherland, Metternich summoned Neipperg to take command of a division of the Austrian army to help in the dissolution of revolutionary forces assembled around Voghera south of Milan. Marie-Louise dared not countermand this summons, though the image which his participation in such repression would give to the Parmans was hardly attractive.

In the spring of 1822, news exploded across the central states that the Chief of Police of Modena, grand inquisitor of patriots, had been stabbed to death. The assassination was alleged to have been masterminded by patriotic collaborators in Parma. Away on business attending the Congress of Verona, Marie-Louise reluctantly directed the making of arrests, but refused to expedite the trials.

The Duke of Modena's prime suspect was Jacopo Sanvitale. Jacopo was arrested at his rooms in the university and immediately transferred to the prison of Sant'Elisabetta following the discovery of a seditious manuscript in his apartment and the production of a signed confession, obtained under duress, incriminating him.

Berchet, also accused of being a member of a proscribed sect, of organizing insurrections and proselytizing, asked Marie-Louise for permission to purge his honour and that of the Ducal Regiment. Marie-Louise reassured all the accused that they would receive Parman justice – a fair trial. She would allow nothing less than scrupulous adherence to procedure and that the travesties and abuses occurring elsewhere in the Italian peninsula would find no quarter in her duchies. She discouraged flight, reminding the accused that the Austrians were merciless, keeping political escapees constantly on the run, using diplomacy to have other countries on the European continent, particularly vauntedly neutral Switzerland, evict them. In their absence, they would be condemned to death, like Jacopo's friend Antonio Panizzi,* just one of many, condemned to death in absentia and hence, to eternal exile. Once captured, defectors would be summarily transferred to the black hole of the Spielberg. They would do better to face trial in Parma where she could protect them.

Upon her return from the Congress of Verona, at which the Great Powers discussed the reinforcement of Austrian rule in

---

* Panizzi graduated in law from the University of Parma in 1818. When in May 1822, the Duchy of Modena's Chief of Police, Giulio Besini, was assassinated, Panizzi was tipped off that he faced arrest and trial as a subversive, he fled to Switzerland. There, in 1823, he wrote a book decrying the repressive regime and trials against citizens of the Duchy of Modena which was ultimately published in Madrid. Following the book's publication, he was indicted, tried, and condemned to death *in absentia* in Modena, and pressure was brought to have him expelled from Switzerland. In May 1823, Panizzi moved to England, becoming a British subject in 1832. Upon arrival in London, Italian poet in exile Ugo Foscolo gave him a letter of introduction to Liverpool banker William Roscoe and he moved to that city, where he made a meager living teaching Italian. In 1826, Panizzi met lawyer and political figure Henry Brougham who later, as Lord Chancellor of England, obtained for Panizzi the Professorship of Italian at the newly-founded University of London and later a post at the British Museum Library. Panizzi held a string of posts there: first Assistant Librarian (1831–37), then Keeper of Printed Books (1837–56) and finally Principal Librarian (1856–66). In 1869, he was knighted by Queen Victoria for his extraordinary services as a librarian.

Northern Italy, Marie-Louise facilitated the prolongation of procedure, allowing every opportunity for exploitation of weaknesses in the prosecution case and of its procedural defects. When Vienna and Modena complained, she ignored them. She could not, however, prevent the trials from advancing.

Her detractors tried to interpret an underlying motive for her tolerance and leniency, the hallmarks of Marie-Louise's administration. They claimed that she fancied herself as the first – and her son as the second – monarch of a united Italy to recover the title of Queen of Italy, which she once held as Empress of France. They misjudged her. Marie-Louise, understandably interested in self-preservation, was a woman of principle, not of unbridled, machinating ambition. Her justice would demand a high standard of proof. Jacopo's evidence corroborated his alibi.

By the end of 1822, Marie-Louise had eighteen of her citizens under arrest. Fed up with Marie-Louise, the Duke of Modena, her cousin, demanded that all defendants still awaiting trial in Modena, Milan and Parma be tried together in one place, preferably under his nose in Modena, or in Milan, but definitely not in Marie-Louise's territories. Knowing her terms would not be met, Marie-Louise said that she would only allow this if he would agree to her conditions as to the conduct of the trials, such terms to be guaranteed to her subjects. One defendant, Martini, was sent as a token of her goodwill to be tried in Milan. As Marie-Louise might have anticipated, the evidence against the defendants took the form of confessions extorted under torture from prisoners from the Romagna, Lombardy and Modena. It was a matter of days before there were complaints that the tribunal was being offensive, riddled with prejudice, piling insults on the leniency of Parma's Duchess. When Marie-Louise heard, she demanded Martini's immediate return and declared that trials would be held in Piacenza, garrisoned by Austrian troops. The Parman tribunal would carry out their functions with exactitude such that there could be no complaints of bias or laxity. At the end of a lengthy trial, Jacopo was finally acquitted, along with most of his co-defendants. None of the facts could be established beyond reasonable doubt.

The Viennese cabinet's stance ran counter to the philosophy of Emperor Francis, who instructed his daughter "to allow the development of the law to take its own course unhindered in all legal and therefore also in criminal matters, and never to put moral constraints on the judge."[2] It was furious. The overwhelming number of acquittals contrasted sharply with the number of convictions secured in other states. Modena alone had convicted forty-seven defendants. Austria refused to accept that there had been true impartiality and accused the Parman judiciary of treating the trials with frivolity. Marie-Louise forwarded a memorandum from the judges setting out their defence to Vienna's accusations.

> If there have only been a small number of convictions compared with other states in the Italian peninsula, the reasons are twofold. Firstly, the laws in other states are very different from our own. Secondly, the laws applied by the judges in Parma are fair laws, based on probity, not on fear and extortion. Furthermore, the judges were issued with clear instructions by the Duchess in person that there be no derogation from them. The lack of availability of evidence relating to Lombard prisoners and the poor cooperation of the Austrian government have been striking. The convictions secured in Parma were based on confessions obtained in Parma without duress, and are therefore reliable and secure. The judges have carried out their duties in full loyalty to the Duchess. Political trials elsewhere have been conducted with questionable legality. In Parma, nothing but principles of humanity and justice have prevailed.[3]

Metternich demanded that Jacopo remain in custody, notwithstanding his acquittal, until extradition and retrial. Marie-Louise responded that there was no question of either. The man had been tried and acquitted. As far as she was concerned, justice had been done. To pacify Vienna, she agreed to detain Jacopo in the Fortress of Compiano, where he would continue to receive his academic's stipend from her treasury, and his family, while she carried out a review of the trials to satisfy herself that there had been no irregularities. Vienna's hawks were outraged, accusing her of cloaking him with a Messianic mantle. The Duchess, away in Persenbeug with her son, ignored them. The same harridans wrote again, demanding that Jacopo be moved to more secure incarceration, complaining that two allegedly inebriated fortress guards sympathetic to Jacopo had allowed him to wander in the fields beyond the fortress precincts. Neipperg wrote on the Duchess's behalf ordering that the fortress guards be temporarily suspended from duty. A month after ordering his detention, Marie-Louise ordered his immediate release.

Upon her return to Parma after a dressing-down in Austria, Marie-Louise formed her own commission to carry out a review of the sentences passed. The review found no way of avoiding the conclusion that Parmans Micali and Martini had incited insurrection and increased their sentences to the death penalty. Marie-Louise was deploying her own tactics to leave no doubt in absolutist minds that she flinched from applying the law in all its severity. Three days later, as Parmans reeled from the shock, their Duchess's halo was restored when she announced that she was commuting the death sentences to twenty years hard labour, a very far cry from its Austrian equivalent, to be served in her prisons. She charged the trial judge with the task of conveying to the prisoners the commutation of their sentences with the message: "Keep hoping, always hold on to hope."[4]

It was dangerous brinkmanship. Marie-Louise had shielded most of her subjects from harm. The trouble was that she needed to find some justification after the event for the reassessment she had made of evidence which had been available at the original trials. Far from diffusing the tension, Marie-Louise seemed to have increased it.

After two years and one hundred and fifty suspects tried, and a million and a half florins spent, the Austrians had achieved nothing. Metternich and the Duke of Modena were beside themselves with fury. In their view, Parman magistrates were operating a constitutional monarchy by default, and once this became known, the practice would spread to the rest of Europe.

Smarting from humiliation, they did not wait long to try and bring the errant duchess to heel. At the beginning of 1823, the Governor of Milan produced fresh documentation and witnesses implicating more Parmans, particularly those acquitted in the first trials, including Ambrogio Berchet.

Judge Caderini again wrote to Marie-Louise, his letter intended for onward transmission to Vienna, protesting that the death sentences passed elsewhere were unconscionable and unsustainable in law and in fact. Her subjects' loyalty towards their sovereign was beyond debate. The same could not be said of the Duke of Modena. The decisions handed down by the Duke manifested his expansionist plans, punishing the innocent and absolving the guilty to his order. Marie-Louise kept Caderini's letter to one side to use when it was needed. Again, she declared there would be no right to appeal these fresh trials. This would ensure containment of the political fall-out and provide the convicted with certainty. It would also prevent Vienna from demanding retrials and would allow her to exercise clemency as she saw fit. She reserved to herself the right to make modifications or clarifications to the criminal law insofar as the outcome of the trials demonstrated a need for it.

As storm clouds gathered, Marie-Louise published directives for the constitution of a special tribunal, comprising different judges from those who had tried the first group of defendants, to try the latest round of defendants. Foreign confessions based on hearsay would not be admissable for the purposes of obtaining the accused's confirmation or denial, but would be read by the commission. This time in Marie-Louise's absence, convictions secured were severe. Four men were sentenced to imprisonment, Berchet for a term of ten years, stripped of his military rank and position, of the Order of St Constantine which he had been awarded for his commendable work in the duchy, of his right to bear the *Légion d'Honneur* he had won under Napoleon, and of the Iron Cross he had been awarded by Austria. The regimental school of military training which he had created, now a breeding ground of sedition, was closed.

Following the convictions, the government made a list of citizens suspected of *carboneria*, involvement in secret societies. Marie-Louise called them to her and gave them a severe reprimand. Under pressure, she placed suspects under house arrest for a brief period, protecting the victims from facing charges which Vienna's ubiquitous police informants might try to manufacture. Shortly thereafter, she revoked the house arrests, ordered a stop to police harassment and provided subsidies to prisoners, their wives, children and parents, seeking out those she knew to have been disadvantaged financially by the recent spate of trials, paying for trial legal expenses, medical expenses, transportation costs and arranging restoration of goods sequestered by the authorities.

Two years after the end of the trials, Marie-Louise announced that, in celebration of her saint's day and to mark the inauguration of a new bridge over the River Trebbia attended by her father the Emperor, she was commuting the convicts' sentences by three years, offering them the opportunity to spend the remainder of their sentence in exile, beyond Italian, French and Austrian borders. She arranged for the many who opted for exile, most to liberal England*, to meet up with their families and relations and put them in funds for their journey and new life. In addition, she paid a substantial annual subsidy to families who remained in Parma of exiles and of prisoners who opted to spend the rest of their term in prison. For a few years, Marie-Louise enjoyed respite from Vienna's harassment, attention diverted temporarily from the struggles in the Italian peninsula to that for Greek independence. It was only a temporary moratorium. Everyone knew that if the Greeks were successful, Italian patriots would intensify their activities and Austria would fight back even harder.

* Opting for exile, Ambrogio Berchet found employment as an Italian teacher in Brighton, on the Sussex coast.

Generally, people with sympathies across the political spectrum congregated and bantered unhindered in Parma's cafés. Naturally, supporters of Spanish Bourbon claims to the duchy attracted close police scrutiny. They were to be treated with decency and courtesy, without causing any vexation or embarrassment. Marie-Louise's law enforcement agents were respectful, loyal and, above all, honest. Post was intercepted, but, it seemed, only those excerpts which demonstrated lack of culpability of persons suspected by Vienna were relayed back by her administrator Neipperg. Marie-Louise was always at pains to keep taxation and customs duties to a minimum, to find extenuating circumstances justifying her merciful intervention, to pardon and to grant greater freedom of movement and of doing business. Her wise moderation disarmed her opponents both in Vienna and close to home. Most in Parma hated the Austrians and loved the Duchess's liberal attitudes, her generosity, the instructions she had given to distribute money allocated for celebrations for her arrival to the poor, the fact that she perpetually ploughed back the revenues from her states into public projects which were transforming her subjects' living conditions.

From one perspective, Parma had done well under the Vienna Congress, awarded relative autonomy, unlike the former independent republics of Genoa and Venice which had been subsumed into larger Austrian territories. Unconstrained by reactionary absolutism, she forged ahead with her revisions to her new civil code notwithstanding accusations that some of its proposed terms were revolutionary and republican. Overtly obedient to Vienna, Marie-Louise kept the Parman press heavily censored. Newspapers in her duchies were barred from printing articles about insurrections in other states or supporters of previous regimes or about the Habsburgs. However, anyone could consult the foreign daily newspapers containing matters prohibited locally but available in private clubs in both Parma and Piacenza, and no steps were taken to limit their circulation. Careful to avoid grounds to fuel discontent on either side, she ignored Vienna's accusations that she was allowing anarchy in her states and banned reprinting of the Constitution of Cadiz. She had Neipperg send troublemakers letters asking them to keep their mouths shut and their pens still so as not to attract Austria's attention. With reluctance, she ordered banishment of particularly provocative elements who threatened her delicate strategy.

Discreet inquiries found that the Parmans had no desire for a Neapolitan-style revolution, which risked the intervention of Austria or any other foreign government in their internal affairs. Over four-fifths of the inhabitants backed constitutional reform, but few had desire or time to invest in its realization. Parma's university students were, like all young idealists, clamouring for a republic. The disaffected and dispossessed, as in every society, wanted change for the better. The clergy, who were not without influence over the general populace, had no time for either constitutions or republics, both of which typically reduced the Church's power. But nobody wanted foreign masters, however benign. At the moment, few were in a position to act, but it would not always be so. Further clashes were inevitable.

FOURTEEN

Bereavement and Revelation, 1829

During the trials for high treason, Napoleon's last doctor and taxidermist, Antommarchi, arrived in Parma from St Helena with the ex-emperor's heart and to scrounge a pension from Marie-Louise, presumably to be paid from the severely stretched Parman treasury. Neipperg told the doctor that Marie-Louise was too grief stricken to see him and despatched him without ceremony. The political unrest provided reason enough to reject the offering, but this was not the only nor the determining factor. Only eight years after his father's death would the Duke of Reichstadt be forced to realize the complexity of his mother's situation. Circumstances and contemporary mores had not permitted Marie-Louise to be honest with her son. It was inevitable that an unexpected turn of events would cause hurt.

When Napoleon died, Marie-Louise was deeply frustrated at the distance which separated her from their son. The Duke's tutor Collin went to the Duke in the quiet hour of evening and told him that his father had died on St Helena, an African island with a lovely climate, where he had spent his last years in the company of a few good friends. The political troubles throughout the Italian peninsula which had begun in the spring of 1821 had made it impossible for Marie-Louise to go to Vienna to be with her son that summer. The rest of the Austrian Imperial family had thought and hoped that the duke would retain only a dim memory of the father he had not seen since shortly before his third birthday. They were wrong. Napoleon's loyal Mme de Montesquiou had inspired in him an unflinching, indestructible adoration of his father. Marie-Louise had endorsed this adoration, reinforcing his affection for a father whose good qualities she had seen for herself and who had shown nothing but love for his son. Holding up Napoleon as a father who would always expect only the very best from his son, she exhorted Franz to good, decent, moral behaviour. She told him of the pride Napoleon would take, knowing his son to be worthy of him. His parents wanted him to be a fine, upstanding, hard-working, socially conscious contributor to the broad canvas of life.

Upon Napoleon's second exile, Marie-Louise had told the Duke that his father had been sent a long way away to a remote island because he had misbehaved very badly, and that it was unlikely that they would ever see him again.

"Was my father a criminal?" he asked Captain Foresti. "That is not for us to judge: continue to love your father and to pray for him."

The Duke asked how his father had misbehaved, and was told that it was very complicated and that he would understand the situation when he was a good deal older. Marie-Louise had tried to make the Duke understand that fundamentally his father had been a good man, of high ideals, who had wanted the best for his countrymen (though this was something Marie-Louise struggled with), and that it had been in the promotion of these goals that he had come to blows with Grandfather Francis and many other sovereigns. The Duke knew that it was part of the settlement following his father's imprisonment that his mother be given the sovereignty of Parma, and that he was obliged to remain in Vienna for his own safety. Marie-Louise told him how dull life was in her duchies and that she could never have given him the lifestyle or opportunities open to him in Vienna.

There were many lovely memories to share. There were the times spent by them both with Napoleon under the chestnut trees in the Tuileries Palace playing on the lawns, and at table, when Napoleon used to throw his son up and down on his knee, tickle him and pinch his nose. There were the occasions Napoleon used to get down on the floor with his little boy in his study while ministers tried to

Wedding trousseau, Napoleon's gift to Marie-Louise of Habsburg, which is 173 cm high, 134cm long and 83cm deep. Marie-Louise first saw her trousseau, the work of Atelier Louis-Hippolyte Le Roy, when she arrived at the border town of Branau where she was formally transferred from Austrian to French hands. The trousseau contained the finest jewellery, clothes and accessories Paris could offer.

Religious wedding ceremony of HM Napoleon the Great with HRH Marie-Louise of Habsburg, 1810. This etching by Italian engraver Carlo Lasinio shows the imperial wedding on 2nd April 1810 in the Salon Carré of the Louvre. The Salon Carré had been converted on Napoleon's orders into a chapel.

Empress Marie-Louise painted in 1812 by Robert Jacques François Lefèvre. The portrait provides a portrayal of Marie-Louise which suited Napoleon's public relations campaign for his second wife. Particularly noteworthy are her stunning necklace, earrings and crown, all gifts from Napoleon.

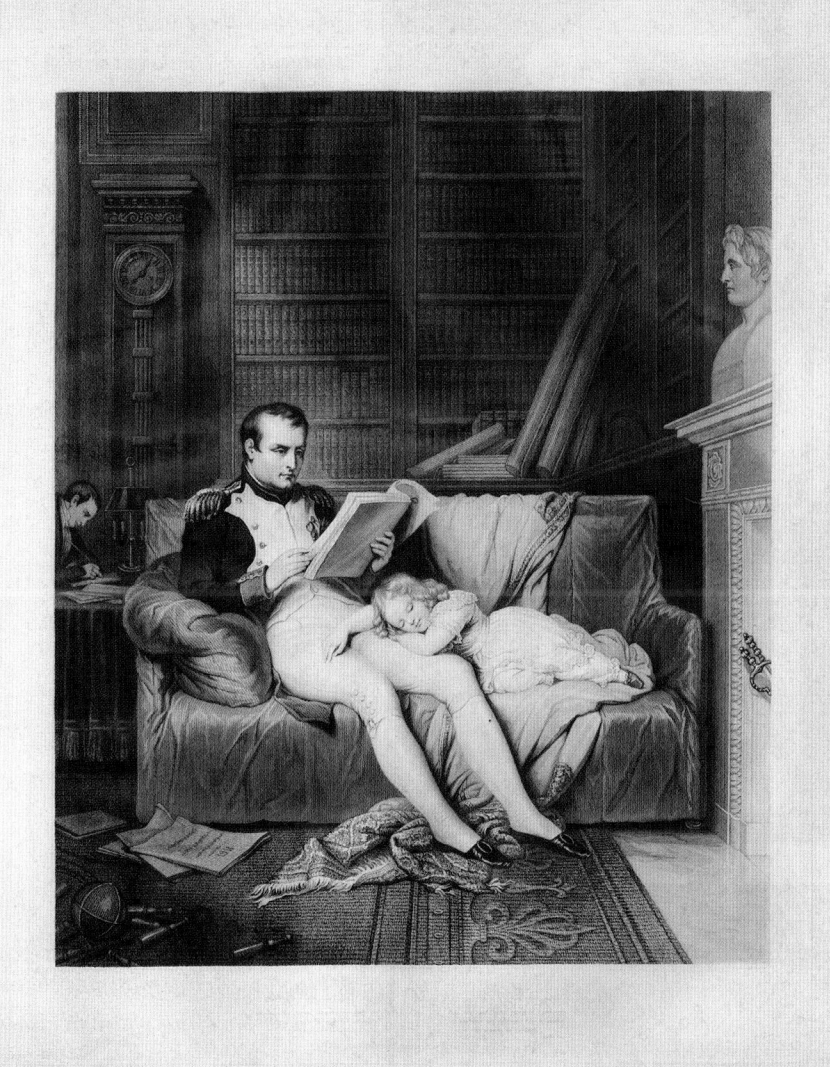

Napoleon and his son in Napoleon's study, drawn by German Romantic painter Carl von Steuben. Steuben's painting of the death of Napoleon on Saint Helena is well known.

Bust in biscuit of the King of Rome, son of Napoleon and ML, with the insignia of the Grand Aigle and the Légion d'Honneur. On the base is a disc in aluminiun showing the inventory no. 2494 relating to its listing by Prince Victor Napoleon, grandson of Napoleon's youngest brother, Jérôme.

Portrait of General Adam Albrecht Neipperg by Giovan Battista Callegari, a Parman painter known for his sparkling characterisations.

Portrait of Albertina Montenuovo Sanvitale, painted by a member of the Parman School of painters in the year of her marriage when she was sixteen years old.

Portrait of Count William Montenuovo by Sir Thomas Lawrence, painted in the last years of the painter's life.

Sketch of Marie-Louise at the piano by Paolo Toschi, a celebrated Parman draughtsman and engraver.

Drawing by Marie-Louise of Habsburg of an allegorical group featuring a love scene. This is one of many imaginary scenes Marie-Louise drew. There are many delightful watercolours by her in her notebooks in the Museo Glauco Lombardi.

The Ducal Palace of Parma, Marie-Louise's home for her tenure, in the 1840s painted by Giuseppe Alinovi. The building was finally destroyed following Allied bombing in 1944.

All illustrations lent by kind permission of the Museo Glauco Lombardi, Parma.

converse with their emperor about matters of state. Marie-Louise loved to make little Franz laugh by repeating things which Napoleon used to say, all the while artfully disguising her own ambiguous feelings towards him. The Duke loved and idolized his mother, believing her to be the perfect wife, faithful and devoted in her abandonment and widowhood. "I love you more than can be expressed and wish you the most perfect happiness." The Duke wrote to her in anticipation of her thirty-sixth birthday, "May I one day be like you."[1]

Upon Napoleon's death, Marie-Louise wrote at length to her son:

> I have heard, my darling son, that you were deeply upset by the misfortune which strikes us both, and I feel that it is a great source of consolation for me to write to you and to talk it over with you. Certainly you feel the same deep pain as I do: you would be an ungrateful son if you were to forget how many loving and good things he did for you when you were a child. You must endeavour to emulate his many virtues and to avoid the pitfalls which led him astray.[2]

Count Dietrichstein congratulated Marie-Louise on her letter: "It was truly a masterpiece."[3]

Marie-Louise instructed the Duke of Reichstadt to go into mourning and to say daily masses. Countess Lazansky reported that he had done as instructed, political considerations incapable of dispensing with duties towards a father, and that he no longer appeared in public nor anywhere where there was a large gathering. His tutors reported that he cried uncontrollably for a whole day virtually without interruption. Then he stopped, locking the pain within himself, making no mention of his father until several weeks later. Count Dietrichstein wanted to show the Duke that he was prepared to talk about his father, but, at every attempt, the Duke refused to engage. The Duke talked only to his mother about his father. He believed that he and she shared lifelong devotion to him. Bound together in solidarity, they could face the outside world with pride and dignity.

In 1829, the Duke, a tall and handsome eighteen year old, discovered that she was no longer the ideal he had imagined. Marie-Louise had never intended to mislead the apple of her eye. By the autumn of 1814, she was in little doubt that she had met the love of her life. At first, she had found the swarthy Austrian officer with bandeau across his right eye assigned by her father to accompany her to Aix-en-Savoie unappealing. She paid him little attention, nursing her own predicament and that of her son, longing to be reunited with her husband. Her journey to Aix had taken her through Munich, where she had paid a courtesy visit to Napoleon's stepson, the former Viceroy Eugène and his wife, and through Baden, Payerne and Allamau, where she dropped in to see Napoleon's brothers Louis, Jérôme and Joseph respectively.

Gradually Marie-Louise had warmed to Neipperg's charming, solicitous personality, and had found that his views and interests so closely matched hers that they were in many ways kindred spirits. They could talk together about Austria, Bohemia and about Paris. Neipperg had fond memories of the French capital, having been born and brought up at the court of King Louis XVI and Queen Marie-Antoinette, before embarking upon his career in the Austrian army. The French Revolution had prompted his family, like others, to abandon France for Austria. He had spent his career first fighting the French in Belgium, where a sabre blow had taken out his right eye. Disdaining a rather rudimentary prosthesis which threatened deterioration of his left eye, he assumed the black bandeau which had become his trademark for the rest of his life. Thereafter, he had served in the Tyrol, in Alessandria in Italy and in Galicia against Napoleon. In 1801, Metternich had sent him to Paris to table peace negotiations but with specific instructions not to conclude them, awaiting commitments of financial support from England to enable Austria to resume hostilities. By the Battle of Austerlitz, Neipperg had become well known to Napoleon's marshals as the most brazen intriguer that one could ever meet.

Neipperg had first seen Marie-Louise in Strasbourg on her

arrival in France, and a second time in Dresden and then in Prague, on both occasions forming part of Austrian retinues. Marie-Louise had no memory of him. He had spent his career thereafter forging diplomatic alliances to work against Napoleon. From 1811 to 1813, he had served his country as Austrian ambassador to Sweden. Having secured Sweden's participation in the coalition against the French Emperor, he left to take command of troops in early August 1813 and fought in the Battle of Leipzig, given the honour of conveying personally the news of the French defeat to Emperor Francis in Vienna. This conflagration, where Napoleon's teenage soldiers, enlisted following the devastation of the Grand Armée during the course of the Russian Campaign, were confronted by the coalesced armies of Russia, Prussia, Austria and Sweden, had marked a major turning point in Napoleon's fortunes which he had singularly failed to convey to his wife. The conflict, which came to be known as The Battle of the Nations, had involved over six hundred thousand soldiers, one hundred thousand of whom had been allied fatalities. It was the largest battle Europe had ever seen. Three days after it, Marie-Louise had forwarded to the Duchess of Montebello a letter from her husband from the outskirts of Leipzig with a covering note in which he said, "I think that this news will do you some good." Napoleon's defeat had forced him to return to France, leaving the allies, to whom were added Britain, Spain, Portugal and smaller German states, to penetrate France over the course of the next few months. Silent as to defeats, his letters were bullish, boasting of trouncing Bavarians and Russians and taking thousands of men prisoner along with their ensigns and cannon. As the reality of the recent past began to unfold, Marie-Louise must have realised just how Napoleon had exploited her.

In contrast to Napoleon, Neipperg was gracious, warm and infinitely patient, according not only to Marie-Louise but to everyone with whom he came into contact, giving them his full attention. Whenever she had been with Napoleon during waking hours, there were others present, maids, chamberlains, equerries, aides-de-camp and ladies-in-waiting. Life had been full of receptions, family obligations, entertainment programmes, military parades, state council meetings, interminable journeys. There was rarely place or time for heart-to-heart conversations. Staff knew the imperial couple's daily habits and sleeping patterns and were stationed to overhear their sexual exchanges. In both Austrian and French imperial households, she had rarely been allowed a moment alone, a lady always present to ensure her conduct was beyond reproach. She had never been alone with a member of the opposite sex, apart from her husband.

For the first time, Marie-Louise was alone with a man for much of the day. Diplomatically, Countess Brignole, the lady-in-waiting who had accompanied the empress from Paris and still remained with her, made herself scarce. Neipperg seemed never to be in a hurry and nothing would hurry him, even when there was business to attend to. He showed her respect, never presuming upon her, never overstepping the distance in rank between them, careful never to criticise Napoleon. Appreciating his discretion, Marie-Louise found herself increasingly more relaxed in his company, and began to confide in him. She soon began to regard and to refer to him as her mentor.

Marie-Louise had been effectively widowed since Napoleon's departure for his German campaign for the better part of sixteen months. The intervening few weeks she had spent with him had been fraught. She now understood why he had been in such a dreadful mood, demanding that everyone be joyful when they had nothing to be joyful about. Marie-Louise had not understood why the ladies of her entourage had behaved so distantly, why it had seemed that she could never get a word out of them beyond matters of total inconsequence. Now she knew that they could not have behaved differently, knowing their empress to be kept in ignorance of the pointless bereavements and humiliations they were forced by their emperor to suffer, knowing of the under-age conscripts, whom the public referred to as *"les Marie-Louises"*, whom Napoleon press-ganged into his army to feed the campaigns which should never have been fought. Marie-Louise's eminence placed her above such communication. When her husband's retainers, the Duchess of Montebello and Dr. Corvisart, finally left, she was relieved.

As the days passed in the delightful surroundings of Aix, she began to enjoy the freedom of being single again. The long picnics and afternoon rides took her mind away from her troubles. General Neipperg's company grew on her. Extremely discreet, he never bragged or boasted. She loved his witticisms and playful games. They had plenty in common, shared languages, shared culture, shared philosophy. They both adored music, the theatre, the countryside, Vienna, coffee, chocolate and patisserie. They both played the piano and soon spent the evenings singing the well-known arias and duets of Mozart, Beethoven, Gluck, Weber and Handel, which they both knew by heart. Neipperg composed waltzes which he dedicated to her.

In Aix, Marie-Louise missed her little boy, but save for this gaping absence, she had begun to feel the return of the *joie-de-vivre* of her natural disposition which had eluded her four years earlier when she had set out for Paris. She wanted to stay in Aix forever.

Marie-Louise's bubble burst abruptly when Metternich forwarded a notice from the new French administration. Bourbon King Louis XVIII declared that the presence on French soil of Napoleon's ex-empress was an embarrassment, Talleyrand having been displeased by Marie-Louise's brief contact with her Bonaparte brothers-in-law. The prospect of returning to the haughty disdain of the Viennese aristocracy filled Marie-Louise with dread. She convinced herself that she would not stay long in the Austrian capital. She was anxious to meet the grand chamberlain newly appointed to her court in Parma and to accompany him back to her duchies. It would only be a matter of time before the remainder of her French entourage were dismissed, all foreigners having been excluded from employment in the government of Parma. She packed her bags and mounted her carriage to set out back across Switzerland towards Austria, planning to spend a few weeks in Geneva and Berne.

Marie-Louise was in Switzerland when she heard the unpleasant news that Napoleon had received on Elba his mistress, the Polish Marie-Walewska and her son by him. There was no denying that the union between Napoleon and Marie-Louise had been blessed by genuine, deeply felt affection. Her affection, however, had been predicated upon an idealized image of her husband which she now knew bore little resemblance to his persona beyond his domestic interior. But Napoleon's feelings had not been about love, or at least, if they had been about love, he had had no compunction about lying to her, abusing her and her family, and leading her recklessly into disaster. The heady promises he had made to her in his love letters as she had made her way towards him in the spring of 1810, subsequently repeated, when he had said how inconsolable he would be were she to think that he could ever deal other than kindly with her and spare her any anxiety, were it to be in his power, had proved hollow. His protestations that he could only be contented and happy if he knew his Louise to be so had proved equally vacuous. Napoleon might have been a brilliant military strategist, but he had shown a phenomenal lack of judgment off the battlefield. Critically, he had not made a way for her to join him to share in his fate when he could have done, but had always insisted she await her father's order. It was not credible that a man who really wanted his wife and child with him had not arranged matters to achieve that end.

Marie-Louise had ignored allegations that Napoleon had been constantly unfaithful during the years of their marriage. The revelation of the betrayal with Marie-Walewska forced Marie-Louise to reconsider her place in Napoleon's affections. To play the tragic heroine would have been absurd. Aged twenty-two, she was badly in need of physical love. Leaving aside her son, the only person close to Marie-Louise who still believed in the sanctity of her marriage and her husband's glory was her grandmother, Queen Maria-Carolina, who had shown great sympathy and understanding upon her return from Paris. The old queen's death after an apoplectic fit was timeous in the wake of Marie-Louise's new alliance.

The Princess of Wales, Caroline of Brunswick, on her way to winter in Rome, chanced to be staying at the same hotel in Berne as the former empress and her party in the fourth week of September. The Princess introduced herself. Previously known to the company only by extensive newspaper articles which had been full of scandalous accusations, everyone was pleasantly surprised by how agreeable she proved to be. Accompanied by her adopted child, the Princess, swimming in silk train exuberantly adorned by magnificent pearl necklace and diamond crown, put everyone at ease. The two separated wives, shunned by the high society of Europe, felt no need to put on airs or to dissemble with each other. That evening, the gayest that the loyal Méneval had experienced in a long time, the charming if eccentric Princess joined Marie-Louise and Neipperg at the piano by singing their way through Mozart's *Don Giovanni*. Marie-Louise's voice was intoxicating, at its finest. She tried to catch Méneval's eye, but looked away with embarrassment, conscious of the bloom of new love etched over her face, which Méneval found unbearable to see.

Later that evening, after everyone had gone to bed, Neipperg crossed the landing between his and his charge's rooms, entering the latter with the key entrusted to him by Marie-Louise. It was around this time that Marie-Louise wrote to the Duchess of Montebello to say that she would never go to Elba – the Emperor was now of such inconsequence. She said she would explain all later.

Marie-Louise regretted having begged Méneval a month earlier, to come and share her exile. Then, she had wanted the only person she felt she could trust close to her at all times. Since then, she had tried to dissuade him by letter from leaving his wife for any length of time. She could see plainly that he was not enthralled to have come. Méneval found his former empress quite changed from the woman he had left after their sojourn in the Savoy mountains. She had put on weight, her appetite returning with her sense of self. Her complexion had turned from rather pasty to flushed with rude health. He could see why. Neipperg was full of romantic initiatives, on one occasion insisting that he had found in castle ruins on Lake Lucerne a fragment of the spear of Rudolph, progenitor of the Habsburg dynasty. She responded to Neipperg's suggestive smiles with coyness and self-conscious giggles, more like a naïve adolescent than an ex-empress. Marie-Louise was aware of her own behaviour but she revelled in every wonderful moment. She still treasured the ring she had had made from the relic upon her return to Vienna. Her attempts to put Méneval at ease, affectionately protesting deepest friendship and praising him to everyone, did nothing to dispel his fears that his master and hero had been displaced in her heart. Marie-Louise saw his distaste when he caught her and her loved one locked in embrace. There was no vestige of any inclination to go to Elba, Marie-Louise glad no longer to be referred to as Empress or her Majesty, but rather as Duchess of Parma. Méneval took his leave and made his own arrangements to travel separately to Vienna.

Throughout the course of the Vienna Congress, Méneval constantly tried to undermine Marie-Louise's association, and pleaded with her to have regard to her rank and duties. Marie-Louise would not allow rank to frustrate her new love. She had performed her duties as dynastic wife in good faith and to perfection, and she had been betrayed. The marriage had served the purposes for which it had been created: her womb had produced the heir for which Napoleon had yearned, giving the allies time to consolidate and unite to bring him down. The Austro-French alliance had run its course. Marie-Louise was determined to plead for clemency for Napoleon, but her father and Metternich had silenced her. She was best to stay out of the fray, leaving negotiations regarding her situation to be conducted by others. Méneval wanted Marie-Louise to rebel against her father, and accused her of refusing to assert her independence. It never occurred to him that she might be exercising her independence by forging a future without her husband, that her objectives did not conflict with her father's demands, that once she was installed as Duchess of Parma, she would have more independence than she had ever known before. Méneval was not living in the real world if he imagined that she had had any independence as his master's empress.

In France, Méneval had enjoyed immense status, though he had always been without political influence. In Vienna, he was nothing. His petition for restoration of Belgian lands granted him by Napoleon was viewed in a dim light, and made him seem to the allies rather small-minded. As chaperone, he had long outlived his use. Even he was aware of his own superfluity. Marie-Louise diverted him to the little King of Rome, one of the few people left who still regarded her son as such and could regale him in affectionate terms with wonderful anecdotes about his father.

When Napoleon staged a comeback in the February of 1815, husband's and wife's paths had diverged forever. For twenty years, France had been at war with Austria and others, and Napoleon by his actions provoked another.

Mme de Montesquiou and Méneval spoke in disparaging terms of Marie-Louise's new affections, accusing her of weakness, of being derailed by flattery, of giving in to vulnerability. She decided not to hide from them, not to act falsely. She banished constraints and with dignity and discretion made no secret of her *penchant* for the General, on walks obliging the French retainers to fall ten paces behind to allow her and Neipperg a *promenade sentimentale*. To her great relief, they soon declined to accompany her and went to bed early, leaving her alone with Neipperg. Méneval accused Marie-Louise of being a blind servile instrument of a policy without scruples. She held her tongue. The boot was on the other foot. With her renewed vigour came a renewed attention to her appearance. She ordered more dresses, bonnets, shoes and accessories from Paris to flaunt her femininity. She ignored the disapproving looks of her French entourage and of the Viennese, who remarked how she had changed over the past four years. Upon arrival in France, with little interest in fashion and fripperies, she had been struck by the vulgarity of the French their heavily powdered skin, elaborately coiffed hair and self-conscious deportment. The revealing décolletages she saw had been reserved in Vienna for the stage – or the bordello. She had hated the two hour process of purification and rededication to France which she had been forced to undergo, extensively remodelled, pomaded and perfumed as if she were an expensive piece of merchandise. Now she luxuriated in her toilette, was constantly attended by her hairdresser and disdained the staid if discreet Austrian hem- and necklines. She continued to correspond with Napoleon sporadically, taking less interest in his situation, precluding in her mind any joint future. Notwithstanding her resolve, she felt constantly afflicted, conscious of universal disapproval and contempt. Tables had turned. Her former lady-in-waiting, the Duchess of Sagan, now Metternich's mistress and Talleyrand's confidante, was the guest of honour. Excommunicated from the party of sovereigns, Marie-Louise abandoned herself to making music and song with her beloved General.

 Neipperg knew how to play a tactical game to avoid the snares set to dispossess Marie-Louise, and to extract the best advantage out of the frightening challenges that assailed her. Initially, Marie-Louise had feared that he would prefer her father's interests over her own, but she soon saw how loyal and dedicated he was to her. It did not take her long to appreciate just how indispensable he was. He knew everyone of any consequence. He knew their personalities, their strengths, their weaknesses and their inclinations, how best to approach them and how to massage them to achieve his ends. He had the dogged persistence and unfailing patience to see things through, however long this took. He was particularly liked by Gentz, now not only Metternich's secretary but also secretary to the Vienna Congress. Gentz had full mastery over all the various disputes and issues to be decided by the Congress, exerting considerable influence over Metternich. Neipperg visited Gentz daily to receive his invaluable advice to Marie-Louise on how to win out over Parma.

Gentz explained the reasons why Marie-Louise would have no hope of gaining Parma if she was not prepared to consent to leaving her son behind in Vienna. She had wanted to address an impassioned plea to the allied sovereigns to allow the child to accompany her. Gentz could see her anguish, but reminded her of the violent desire for retribution which he witnessed every day at sessions of the Vienna Congress. To his own distaste, she had been the unfortunate victim of trickery and disguise, forced to enter into a mock marriage as temporary expedient. The European allies had paid dearly for allowing Napoleon's sledges to pass by on his retreat from Russia, and it was partly on account of recognition at their ineffectiveness that the allies rained down their invective upon him and his family. Napoleon had been a fool, constantly refusing what he claimed were humiliating conditions for peace. And yet, after the peace, Metternich had in mind that Napoleon would still have been the most powerful sovereign in Europe, would still have at his side his wife and child. After Napoleon's abdication, when Gentz was supervising censorship of the Austrian newspapers, every day there came pouring in the most abominable diatribes against the fallen emperor, some to be printed in their own right, some intended for the theatre, others to be set to music and sung in public. In the first few months of 1814, it seemed to Gentz wholly absurd that at the very moment when the Austrians were negotiating with Napoleon that they should brand him unceasingly as the blackest criminal ever spewed forth by Hell. Appalled at the allies' treatment of Napoleon, Gentz had developed sympathy for him, admiring his patience and dignity when endlessly lectured, subjected to three or four hour monologues. He abhorred the opening of Napoleon's letters to Marie-Louise to great ridicule at sessions of the Vienna Congress.

These men were not going to be touched by a mother's pain. Many of them, their friends and families, had been separated from their children forever. Marie-Louise would have access to her child for several months at a time every summer. She must not treat this privilege lightly.

Gentz was convinced that Austria's true interest lay in re-establishing a regency, which would have doubled the influence and power of the Habsburg monarchy in Europe, but neither her father Emperor Francis nor Metternich had lent his view any credence. Perhaps they had been right. Marie-Louise had never had much appetite to be Regent at Napoleon's fall. The French hated the Austrians, and Marie-Louise had seen enough to know it. Gentz had admired her stance in Paris and told her that she had been right to try and stand firm. Without the backing of her father and his minister, without her husband's support, she had had no alternative but to leave Paris, fatal as her departure had been. Had she been able to stay, that would have been the time for impassioned pleas, but not now. Major players at the Vienna Congress did not want to see a little Napoleon in his own seat and would have found his disappearance – like that of Louis XVII – a suitable resolution to his situation. Had she tried to hold onto the reins of power in Paris, she would only have exacerbated her and her son's situation and would have attracted the imposition of more painful conditions, ultimately causing herself further humiliation. Marie-Louise found in Gentz an ally whom she could trust and who could advise her more disinterestedly than her father.

With Gentz's aid, Marie-Louise obtained the ear and support of Tsar Alexander. The Russian Emperor loved to come and visit her unannounced, sympathizing totally with her and her son's predicament. Arguably the most powerful sovereign at the Congress whose veto was determinative, the Tsar humbled everyone, so that in his company Marie-Louise found even her most implacable enemies charming towards her. The Tsar conversed regularly with Gentz, whom he called affectionately the *Chevalier de l'Europe*, enabling Marie-Louise and Neipperg to be able to read political temperatures at critical moments and to flatter or deflate egos accordingly. It was Gentz too who engaged Wellington and Castlereagh in Marie-

BEREAVEMENT AND REVELATION, 1829

Louise's cause, to which they began to demonstrate a favourable predisposition, Wellington not easily lured away from sitting for Marie-Louise's former court painter Isabey.

As time advanced, Marie-Louise soon realized that Neipperg was her soulmate. It was a relief when his wife Teresa, with whom he had eloped thirteen years earlier, had five children and only married the previous year, died in the spring of 1815. Marie-Louise was so thrilled at the news which freed her lover from any marital constraints that she announced the death at the dinner table with undisguised satisfaction, and was pleased to register the shock on Méneval's face. She had never known so much passion and devotion before.

Metternich assigned Neipperg to a mission in Turin but at Marie-Louise's pleas and pressure from the family, he countermanded the order. However, there was nothing Marie-Louise could do to stop Neipperg's assignment to the Italian peninsula when Murat, King of Naples and Marie-Louise's brother-in-law, took the initiative to assume the leadership in the struggle for Italian independence, a role for which very few regarded him as having any credentials. Only sixteen months earlier, Neipperg had gone to Naples and persuaded Murat to join the coalition against Napoleon. This betrayal by Murat of his brother-in-law attracted accusations that he was nothing more than an unscrupulous, unprincipled mercenary. Neipperg had spent four months in Naples enjoying the hospitality of Austria's latest, albeit opportunistic, ally. Before leaving Vienna in early spring 1815, he wrote Marie-Louise a long memorandum containing advice to assist her during his absence. After his departure, he sent daily letters, often nine or ten pages long so that Marie-Louise was sick with worry when she heard nothing from him for eighteen days. Then came news that he had forced Murat back to Rimini, then that he had defeated him after a long and bloody battle at Tolentino, Murat's troops deserting in their thousands. Marie-Louise was jubilant when she heard that Neipperg had entered Naples in May and recovered it on behalf of the Austrians, negotiating peace in the urbane, moderate and just manner which came naturally to him. Her late grandmother had been avenged. Marie-Louise's reunion with her beloved, a firm believer in religious tolerance, was delayed until late September. Metternich sent Neipperg in July to the department of the Gard in the Ardèche to reconcile previously implacable Catholics and Protestants. She consoled herself for his absence at the baths at Baden, where she received news of Napoleon's departure for St Helena. Once more, Neipperg had been triumphant. Neipperg was the true hero, the true conciliator of men!

Despite the pain she had lived through, Marie-Louise was far from having any regrets at the path down which she had been diverted. Her new chief administrator was a man of intellect, good sense, moderation and infinite patience. He had no need to dominate or impose. His good-natured disposition, equanimity and ease of conversation anchored Marie-Louise, prone to emotional mood-swings on account of her strains. Happy in himself, governing in her name with wisdom and justice, he was universally respected and loved. The same could never have been said of her first husband, whose personification of the enemy she had been expected to suspend for little over three years.

Despite Napoleon's failings, however terrible things he had done, the lies he had told, she had loved him and wished him well. Marie-Louise wrote to Count Dietrichstein, "Death erases all one's unpleasant memories, as I found on this occasion. I could think only of the good he had done me, of the agony of his death, and of his last unhappy years, and I wept bitter tears for him."[4]

Letters of condolence flooded in, Mme Lazansky writing,

"The wrongs of those who are no longer one forgets, and one thinks only of their misfortunes, even when they themselves have been the cause."[5]

Arrangements to take effect on Napoleon's death had been prescribed by Metternich in Parma three years earlier. Marie-Louise was to observe three months' mourning along with the rest of her household. The rest of the court, officials and soldiers did not. Attempts made to dissuade her from attending funeral ceremonies proved fruitless. He was still a part of her and would remain so for the rest of her life. Marie-Louise ordered that a thousand masses be recited in Parma, and another thousand in Vienna. A memorial service was held, a private affair, in the oratory at the Rocca di Sala Baganza, in a discreet, neoclassical chapel adjoining the thirteenth century home loaned her for the summer by Napoleon's former general, Michele Varron, pending the completion of works at the country residence of Casino dei Boschi which she had bought two years earlier. Simple, unadorned and cool, Marie-Louise could give herself over to sad contemplation without fear of interruption. The sanctuary, constructed twenty years earlier by the Bourbon Duke Ferdinand, was located next to the vaulted chamber known as the Room of Aeneas, the bedroom which Marie-Louise occupied. Here, she could go to weep under the canopy of magnificent Renaissance frescoes, one of which depicted the suicide of frenzied Dido falling on the blade of a sword before the sacrificial pyre she had constructed at Aeneas' departure, as the horrified people of Carthage tried in vain to restrain her. An announcement on 24th July in the *Gazzetta di Parma* of Napoleon's death did not refer to him by name, but as "the Most Serene Spouse of our August Sovereign". Unusually, the death notice was not edged in black.

Marie-Louise was outraged at the failure of the European courts to inform her immediately of her husband's death and at the refusal of her father's court to assume mourning dress, a fact which, she considered, gave ammunition to those who questioned the legitimacy of her marriage. The Baronne de Montet recorded in her diary that the day after the arrival of the courier announcing Napoleon's death, she was awoken early in the morning by the noise of horses and carriages. The Emperor and Empress and all the court were decked out in their finery for a splendid shooting party.

The years of enforced silence had caused Marie-Louise great pain: it had been unimaginable to have no contact with loved ones to whom she had become close in Paris. Her surrender of contact with Jérôme's wife, Catherine, particularly upset her. Over time, her anger at his irresponsibility had subsided. Stories of the brutal, absurdly restrictive conditions which he was forced to endure on St Helena reached her despite efforts to keep them from her. Her hands tied, she had declined to add her name to a petition by the Bonaparte family for an alleviation of the conditions of his imprisonment. Archduke Johann told her not to ignore rumours in the newspapers of Napoleon's return, the consequences of which she feared, and that it was impossible to escape St Helena. In any event, the French king was even more paranoid than she about another Elban style attempt at escape and considered St Helena neither far nor remote enough. Marie-Louise had no need to worry. Reports of Napoleon's sufferings, the nausea, vomiting, perspiration and incontinence as stomach cancer ravaged his body, tormented her. She did her best to respond cheerfully and loyally to the innocent inquiries of his son, thinking of him, bereft of comfort on the other side of the world.

Lady Priscilla Burghersh intuited Marie-Louise's ambiguous feelings:

> The occurrence which took place on 5 May last has just been announced to me. One really must not rejoice in an occurrence of this nature. But as there is nothing dearer to my heart than the happiness and peace of mind of Your Majesty, I hope that I may be permitted to perceive for Her Majesty a future in which there is more of both than She has known up until now.[6]

Comforted by Neipperg and his two sons, of whom she had become increasingly fond and who had come to regard her as mother, Marie-Louise found her new domestic life with the Count more banal but far better suited to her character than the years she had spent with her first husband. Matters had been arranged so that, ostensibly for ease of communication, Neipperg's apartment was located next to that of Marie-Louise, with only a servant's room between them. At night, her beloved would take the key to their apartments and lock the outside world out. She felt far more at ease in her humble states in Parma than she had ever been in the ostentatious grandeur of Paris. No longer awkward and tongue-tied, she felt liberated, free of suffocating etiquette and of prurient retinues ready to judge every inflection, every glance and every word. In Paris, the stress of receptions and public appearances had caused in her immediate conversational paralysis. In Parma with Neipperg, she was always in good humour, animated, enthusiastic, full of the joys of life. Her conversation sparkled and entertained. When Neipperg was absent, her anxieties began to eat away at her again. "I am so little accustomed to happiness that, until I see him near to me, and until I hear him speaking to me with soothing words, I will be overwhelmed by my worries," Marie-Louise wrote to Victoria de Crenneville.

Marie-Louise held her head high at the Congress of Verona a year after Napoleon's death, surrounded by all the monarchs who had looked down upon her eight years earlier. At the card table, Marie-Louise defeated Lord Wellington, who attended the Congress in place of Castlereagh, his recent suicide believed to have been prompted by political strain. She accepted payment of her gains in *Napoleons* before receiving his compliments on her former chef whom he had recently engaged. Not everyone was as agreeable. The humpbacked poet Châteaubriand, ludicrously accessorized by wide sash and Saracen sword, was dismissive. Neipperg struck up a friendship with Rossini, the Pesaran composer invited to the Congress to entertain, conducting by starlight in Verona's Roman amphitheatre.

Throughout their relationship, Neipperg had never ceased to show Marie-Louise the most profound tenderness. There were rumours that the world to which she had committed him was too narrow, that he hankered after the more varied existence he might have enjoyed had he not followed her to Parma. His appointment to her court had taken him away from the battlefields and international diplomacy, considered the fora for refining honour and character. If he had moments of disappointment or regret at the sacrifice of his military career, he kept them well hidden. It seemed to her that he enjoyed his existence and that he made the most of his new life. She came to rely on him as administrator, friend and lover, and it was with immense joy that she found herself free to wed him when news of Napoleon's death was confirmed.

The first signs of Neipperg's illness manifested themselves when he accompanied Marie-Louise in July 1824 from Genoa to Palermo, and on to Naples to see her grandfather. He had a dreadful cold, coughing and sputtering in a menacingly consumptive way, virtually collapsing from pains in his chest. Ever since then, it seemed he had not been the same, Marie-Louise constantly scolding him for not taking enough care of himself. In Vienna in the summer of 1828, his health began to deteriorate dramatically. Emperor Francis expressed concern at his shortness of breath. Marie-Louise summoned the renowned heart specialist Dr. Aglietti from Venice, whose prescriptions seemed to bring about a full recovery. It must have been military manoeuvres which he conducted in Parma later that year which undermined his strength. His condition was exacerbated by the journey to Vienna to see the Duke of Reichstadt. When Neipperg and Marie-Louise set out to return to Parma, Neipperg developed a high fever and could barely breathe. He refused to allow Marie-Louise to stay with him and insisted she continue onward without him. Charles Felix, King of Piedmont-Sardinia, invited him to recuperate at his castle at Aglie, two leagues from Turin. Marie-Louise received reports that his condition had worsened, that he could no longer breathe lying horizontally, obliged to sit upright. His legs had swollen horribly and he had become incontinent. By the time he reached Parma at the end of October, it was clear that the end would not be long. Leading doctors Tommassini, Rossi, Moriggi and Gili recommended he be bled and given quinine. After a brief rally, he suffered a relapse and forty-eight hours of coma before life departed.

Words were inadequate to convey the vacuum created in

Marie-Louise's life. She had hoped for many more than the fifty-four years the Almighty had allotted him. Neipperg's death was an irreparable loss for her, for the Duke of Reichstadt and also for Count Dietrichstein, who had lost his best friend. The Duke of Reichstadt arranged to see Neipperg's sons Gustav and Erwin immediately after receiving news of his death, in order that he might mingle his tears with theirs and alleviate their pain.

Marie-Louise gave her love of fifteen years a state funeral. Three days after his death, at four o'clock in the afternoon, Neipperg's body was carried to the ducal chapel of Saint Louis in Parma's Church of the Steccata, led by a squadron of dragoons and two batteries of artillery to the beat of drums, the hearse draped in black cloth preceded by the General's war-horse, the cortège flanked by thirty-six footmen bearing torches. The streets were lined by silent crowds. All were moved by the eulogy which listed the fine qualities of the deceased. Rectitude of mind, generosity of spirit, a passion for doing good. He had proved loyal, vigilant, indefatigable, magnanimous with inferiors, modest with his peers, sincere in love and kindness to all irrespective of wealth or rank, a valorous warrior softened by kindness. He always listened, wanting the best in everything for everyone. He always aimed for moderation and compromise, capable of reconciling the seemingly irreconcilable. The gifts so rarely encountered in one person had inspired in others universal reverence and love. Neipperg's funeral ended, as was the German custom, with the immolation of his battle-horse.

FIFTEEN

The beings, 1829

Count Dietrichstein wrote to Marie-Louise upon Neipperg's death: "I am not abreast of the troubles which the testament will set in train, but I can imagine."[1] The disclosure of Neipperg's will would open a Pandora's Box.

Unable to sleep fearing the Austrian Emperor's opprobrium, Marie-Louise waited for his reply as she wandered aimlessly through the rooms of the home she and Neipperg had shared, looking through a glaze of tears at the spaces and chairs the deceased would never occupy again.

The response came from Empress Karoline-Auguste, to whom Marie-Louise had addressed her letter of explanation, confident of her latest stepmother's ability to choose the right moment for the painful revelation which Marie-Louise's letter made. Unostentatiously pious, in the same tradition as her stepdaughter, she was sensitive and empathetic.

"You have lost all the happiness of your life," she commiserated warmly. Nonetheless, Marie-Louise must not allow herself to be indifferent to life. There were important duties which she must still fulfil. "I passed your letter to your father, for I could not be satisfied with talking to him of its contents, of altering your words which I knew would go straight to ... this dear heart which, although deeply afflicted, has never ceased to cherish you. It is not from an unhappy child that such a father can withdraw his affection."[2]

Marie-Louise had always known that he would be far from pleased when he realised that the two children, whose existence had been made known to him less than a year earlier, had been conceived out of wedlock.*

> If this disastrous secret had been disclosed eight months ago when the Emperor first heard of the existence of other children when approving the Parman loan, I do not know what would have happened. But now things are different. You have no need to fear that you have lost that place which you occupy in his heart, and you must not hesitate to come to Vienna this summer. I anticipate that the first moment will be horribly painful for you, but you will find consolation in the fact that his affection for you remains unchanged. Nor has he forgotten the immense sacrifice which you made for the state in 1810.³

Her father might not have forgotten her sacrifice but his reply was less charitable. Her crimes were to have borne children by Neipperg before Napoleon's death and to have married Neipperg, her social inferior. More than anything, Marie-Louise wanted her father to recognise her officially as the mother of her two children, Albertina and Wilhelm. As regards Neipperg's inferior status, Marie-Louise had loved Neipperg and wanted the world to know, though she was prepared to defer to her father on the matter of publication. Emperor Francis, who had been fond of the General, and grateful to him for banishing Napoleon from his daughter's affections, consented to his daughter's wish, despite Neipperg's non-conformity to pedigree. However, the Emperor could do nothing to perfect the children's illegitimacy. Marie-Louise had given birth to Albertina in 1817 and to Wilhelm in 1819, before marriage to their father. Another child had not survived long after birth. The Habsburg Imperial family did not approve of, but turned a blind eye to, extra-

---

* Marie-Louise wrote to Count Metternich on 17th March 1829 to advise him of the additions to her family and true dates of birth. According to de Bourgoing, the letter was only made public when found in 1918 amongst secret deeds in the archives of Vienna in an envelope bearing Emperor Francis's seal.

marital affairs. The metropolitan European public talked of little else. The arrival of progeny was quite another matter.

"I cannot hide the profound concern caused to me by this situation for which there is nothing that can be done and which should never have existed before God and the world."[4] Emperor Francis wrote to his daughter following his discovery of the Beings, as he called them.

Illegitimate children were hardly a rarity. Neipperg, sixteen years her senior, was himself an illegitimate child, the product of an adulterous love affair between Countess Neipperg and a young French nobleman. His putative father, an Austrian diplomat long dead, had been a spurious son of Empress Maria Theresa. All five of his children had been born illegitimate. He had died a pauper. The French Revolution had declared all children born equal. There was only one man who had ensured that illegitimate children should remain without legal status throughout their lives, who had encouraged the practice of infant abandonment to the Catholic Church. One man had promoted the concept of honour killing and legitimized the murder of a wife for conceiving a child out of wedlock, ensuring that men were freed of the burden of paternity recognition. That man was Napoleon.

In 1791, just as Marie-Louise was emerging from her mother's womb, citizen Cambacérès was asked by the National Assembly of France to produce a coherent unified code of civil laws to enshrine the rights of man as defined in the early days of the French Revolution. Over the course of the next eleven years, he produced four drafts faithfully representing these ideals. Truth, one and indivisible, was to be heralded as a beacon of light to the nations of Europe. The National Assembly asserted the principle of divorce on demand by mutual consent and the right of a child to seek judicial recognition of its natural parents in order to obtain the nourishment for its survival. In 1794, the French newspaper *Le Moniteur* published a statement by Cambacérès ruling out any justification for a parent repudiating a child.

"There must be no distinction between legitimate and illegitimate children. All children without exception have the right to succour and to succeed to those who have brought them into existence. Differences between them are the effect of pride and superstition. They are ignominious and contrary to justice."

Napoleon, as First Consul, devoured the heavy law books which Cambacérès gave him at his request in 1801, to speed up formulation of the new legal codes. His input at sessions debating their provisions was to erode, not to promote, human rights, reversing the tide of liberty, fraternity and equality which had swept across France for just over a decade. He denied divorce to a wife for a husband's adultery, but conceded divorce for a wife's adultery. His reasoning, alien to the most primitive of societies, was as follows:

The role of a woman is to honour her father and family and, after marriage, her husband and his family. She is to repose absolute confidence in her father and, after marriage, in her husband. She must believe her father and then her husband and not argue with him. She must prefer her husband over her father, for her husband magnanimously bestows his protection upon her. Her purpose is to reproduce, to sacrifice herself to duty and to her country. To prepare for a life of obedience, she must receive from an early age, comprehensive religious instruction. This will inculcate in her a constant resignation, a tender and yielding charity which compensates for the weakness of the female intellect and the volatility of her ideas. Throughout her life, she must be kept under close scrutiny and firm restraint.

Napoleon had very definite ideas as to the qualities required of the fairer sex.

"Essential in a woman are piety, chastity, perfect modesty in word, deed and thought, honesty to a fault. Then comes sobriety of conduct, industry, frugality, good humour. A man should be able to divorce his wife on the grounds of incompatibility of temperament. And beauty. Female beauty keeps a man happy."

Napoleon introduced clauses which gave a husband the right to have his adulterous wife detained in a house of correction. The husband and his children by her could murder her, her lover and any illegitimate issue with impunity.

In the autumn of 1801, Napoleon considered the legal capacity of the illegitimate child:

> A pious woman has no truck with conception outside matrimony. The illegitimate child is the product of a wayward mother, a libel on her own sex and on men too. Public morality requires that she and her issue be driven from conjugal society, not accommodated within it.
>
> "Pecuniary damages are sufficient compensation for rape for which there is corroborated proof. If it were possible to prove paternity, I would force the natural father to marry the mother. It is impossible. The man found guilty of having demoralized the mother of a child must not have attributed to him a child of which he may believe himself not to be the father. Society has no interest in the recognition of bastards. There can be no exception. I shall accord them special status: henceforward they shall be known as 'les enfants de la patrie.

An illegitimate child could not inherit, and his assets could be confiscated by church or state.

Henceforward, women were to be regarded as nothing more than sport, pleasure vehicles, and unwanted offspring cast-offs for whom men had no responsibility. Wives were venerated for bearing legitimate children, but were chattels of their husbands. The sight of an unwed mother was an affront to public morality. The *droit du seigneur* charmingly illustrated by Beaumarchais and Mozart was a delicacy most men found impossible to forgo. Unwanted babies thereby sired they did not want to know about. Family honour had to be maintained by keeping secret these little hazards of sexual congress. Midwives could be trusted to keep silent. Napoleon had seen to that, imposing a six-month jail term on midwives who compromised a woman's honour by revealing her identity to others. A responsible female knew to deposit anonymously her newborn at night in a cylindrical wooden box in the wall of her local convent foundling home. All she had to do was to ring a little bell and a nun would come running out to turn the handle on the other side of the wall, rotating the wheel to retrieve the superfluity. In all likelihood, the child would not live to see its first birthday, but the Catholic Church would ensure that he or she would be baptised and receive the last rites. If it was one of the two per cent who survived into adolescence, it would provide excellent cannon fodder. A responsible girl dare not keep the child and invite the censure of the Catholic Church and bring down the wrath of God upon herself and her family.

A God-fearing girl trusted to the nuns, servants of the Almighty. Better she should not venture inside the foundling home, for it was not a sight for the faint-hearted. They were wretched places, housed in derelict buildings, so-called havens of Christian mercy resembling punitive institutions. The poky, dark rooms were typically covered with straw which was sporadically changed but, in the interim, covered with human excrement and urine. In rural areas, farm animals often rested beside infants. The women drafted to wet-nurse the newborns were starving prostitutes infected with syphilis or malaria. They had all given birth to unwanted babies which they had either abandoned or brought with them to nurse along with others. Their milk was of poor quality so that the nourishment they produced was inadequate. The pay was meagre, not enough to attract anyone with healthy lactation. It was a cruel sight: a worn, emaciated peasant nursing two newborns at her breast, servicing six or eight in rotation, transmitting disease more often than sustenance. Even more painful was the sight of babies being torn from the breast so as to ensure a last drop for the next. In countries in Northern Europe where paternity suits were permitted, few children were abandoned or found their way to the foundling home, and infanticide was rare.

Slowly but surely, Napoleon had seen to it that the ideals of republicanism were being swept away to yield to the dictates of a dynasty which it had fallen to Marie-Louise to begin. The unified code came into force on 21 March 1804 in France and thereafter in Belgium, Luxembourg, the Low Countries, the German Confederation and in the Italian Peninsula. It had since been used as a model for legislation in much of independent Latin America. For his services to the French Empire, Napoleon conferred upon Cambacérès the title of Duke of Parma.

The immediate and long-term impact of Napoleon's legislation was to transform a woman's virtue into an ideal incapable of achievement. When, predictably, she fell short of the standard, she was placed beyond legal and moral redemption. It was an irony that his good Louise should have been trapped by his morality, that his own son's honour should have been so besmirched.

Marie-Louise had learnt from the Bible that rulers bear responsibility for their actions and their failings even when arising unwittingly. According to her religion, it was arguable that a ruler need be even more careful than ordinary people not to fall into ways of sin. The back-sliding archduchess was wracked by constant guilt, and resented the prevailing hypocrisies which had placed her in her impossible position. She could never have yielded her children to the wheel of misfortune, as the convents' contraptions were known, yearning to enjoy the active motherhood of which she had been deprived in Paris and Vienna, and was deeply hurt by her father's censure.

Marie-Louise often lamented that she had not been born a man. Only the word of the elusive virtuous woman carried weight. To be virtuous, a woman had either to shun men completely, or to be faithful in mind and body to the man whom fate had placed in her path, even if fate had also parted them for eternity. She should not have a mind independent of her husband's. Marriage, even loveless marriage, conferred respectability on a woman. Any other woman was by definition a charlatan. None of these rules applied to men. And a woman was powerless to change her own situation, economically totally dependent on her husband, and at his death, at the mercy of her sons or daughter's husband.

These were not immutable laws of nature. When Marie-Louise came to Parma she created a legislative commission of five Parman lawyers to craft her own code of legislation, blending the best of the Napoleonic and Austrian codes and introducing her own innovations. These were designed to improve the condition of women, bringing them as close to equality with men as her times and mores could countenance. In this, she was well in advance of her time.

As always, however, she had to come to a compromise, the disturbance of family structures and long held traditions potentially hazardous for her government and her ducal throne. In her world, a woman had no legal capacity in her own right. She could not prosecute her own legal proceeding or be heard in a court of law whether as prosecutor or accused, claimant or defendant. She could not make a will or accept an inheritance, assume a debt or free a slave. She could not receive a legacy from her husband but could from her father or brothers, but she could not transmit it to her children, neither ties of blood nor of affection relevant as regards the power of the family. The wealth of the *pater familias* was overriding. The family patrimony was invoked as a justification for the subordination of the wife to her husband. Family wealth had to devolve upon sons, who would keep alive the family line. Women had no more status than children and slaves and their survival was of little importance. Her abandonment or murder in infancy rarely attracted censure. Nonetheless, women were subject to taxation, and to controls aimed at reproduction of the family. She was juridically irrelevant. A daughter could marry only with her father's consent, which he could withdraw by simple unilateral declaration of will. The dowry which accompanied a wife immediately became the property of her husband. The Catholic Church had allowed women moral and spiritual equality with men, but had so distorted the original Roman law as it pertained to women that their position was much worse than it had been in ancient times. In antiquity, a woman without a male partner had been able to enjoy her own assets, administer her own affairs, sell and assume obligations. Napoleon could have improved the condition of women and children, particularly illegitimate children, but such improvement would not have suited the society he wished to create and the military policy he intended to pursue.

Reforms under enlightened absolutism had not trespassed on the territory of family law, regarded as the province of the Church, local legislation and secular habits. There were, however, two areas which were improved by the Napoleonic code: rights of succession and divorce. Daughters could not be disinherited without good reason and received a quota of the family wealth. A woman had a right to ownership of property in common on marriage, as long as she remained within the marriage. But a married woman still could, without her husband's consent, neither give, nor sell, nor place herself under obligation, nor incur credit. Napoleon's Italian subjects who could be heard (the men) naturally disapproved wholeheartedly of these changes. To them, male superiority was the natural law, not equality between the sexes. Such reasoning claimed that, far from being a demotion of woman, it was recognition of her primordial role as mother and daughter and as cornerstone of the family. Wedded to their time-honoured traditions, the Milanese patriarchs abhorred the liberality of the Austrian universal Civil Code of 1811, which adopted most of the substance of the *Code Napoléon*. Introduced in Lombardy-Veneto in 1816, it accorded the woman more independence by doing away with the need for her husband's consent in the management of her daily life, creating a time limit upon which paternal authority ceased, and allowing parity upon family succession.

At the fall of Napoleon, the *Code Napoléon* was provisionally confirmed in the duchies of Parma, Piacenza and Guastalla, although divorce and the right of holding property in common were eliminated. Marie-Louise's dictates and the efforts of her commission produced arguably the most advanced legislative provisions produced anywhere in the Catholic world.

The most dramatic changes were in the family sphere. Marie-Louise's legislation regarded as paramount not preservation of family wealth nor the means of production, but the education and protection of children. Her innovative code saw as imperative the fact that children both need and deserve in equal measure parents supportive of their choices. A daughter was an absolute equal to her brother. Having illegitimate children of her own had brought home to Marie-Louise the absurd disparities in legislative systems between children born within and without wedlock. The importance of blood ties of the family as oasis of love and affection, rather than as immutable institution, could not be over-emphasised. All family members were worthy, irrespective of their imperfections.

Marie-Louise broke the prevailing taboo. An unmarried mother with child was not an inferior, or anything less than a valuable mother. Marie-Louise's Code allowed a parent, or in his or her absence other family member (brother, sister, aunt, uncle, first cousins) who had reached majority, to object to an intended spouse only on the grounds of his or her imbecility, dementia or violent nature. A tutor or person standing in place of parents was allowed limited grounds upon which to object, such as an intended spouse's lack of means of subsistence, proven or widely known anti-social habits, contagious disease or other defects impeding the aim of the marriage or other similarly grave matters. Not only were the grounds of refusing consent dramatically limited, having previously been justifiable without statement of grounds, but any opponents to the marriage whose grounds were rejected by the courts would be obliged to pay damages and interest to the child seeking the consent. Where a marriage was opposed on the grounds of lack of means of subsistence, an opportunity was given for someone to come forward to assist. The child's right to challenge his parent's decision, even that of the father, by recourse to law, was an extraordinary innovation, overturning centuries of family crises.

By abolishing the obligation to provide a dowry upon marriage, Marie-Louise had given hope of marriage to many women who previously would have remained unmarried because their parents were unable to support a new family unit. Where a dowry was provided, the daughter was to give credit for it, deducting it from her ultimate inheritance. A woman could also make a will disposing of her assets as she chose without reference to and without the agreement of her husband.

Children were no longer subject to their parents' whims, obliged no longer to act in the family's interests, but in their own interests which might entail negative consequences for the family. In future, parents would have to earn their children's affection, the affection which would ensure that they would *want* to take their parents' interests into consideration. These provisions empowered a daughter, woman and wife as she had never been empowered before. She could assume responsibilities and express her own will, fully confident of society's protection. The role of the father, previously sacredly respected, was no longer as head and sole guide of the family. According to the Parman code, marriage produced rights and obligations just as reciprocal between husband and wife as between parents, children and descendants. A husband must help, protect and take care of his wife in his home and provide for her commensurate with her condition and her own means of subsistence. In return she must obey her husband, co-habit with him, follow him wherever he considers it opportune. She must co-operate in the maintenance of her husband when he does not have sufficient means. She must have no other home than that of her husband, save in the cases of separation.

Children of both sexes under the age of twenty-four had first to obtain their parents' consent to their marriage. In a revolutionary departure from pre-existing legislation, a parent could no longer withhold consent on any grounds and justifiable grounds were severely curtailed.

There still remained much legislation which subordinated the wife to her husband, and permitted the right of primogeniture, but only with the sovereign's approval. Exceptionally for her age, Marie-Louise had left her fortune to Albertina and Wilhelm in equal shares, dividing her obligations to third parties equally between them, taking care to ensure that pensions to people who had served her at various stages in Vienna, Paris and Parma were continued and carefully managed.

The father of the family, the husband, was still perceived as the ideal instrument for leading the family, a natural choice in a society which could not imagine having two equal juridical partners in one family. Marie-Louise aimed her innovations at enhancing the stability of the family unit and eliminating scope for abuse of women. The code made a clear delineation between first and second family units, a spouse marrying for a second time with surviving children losing the property of that portion which the spouse might otherwise have left him or her which would henceforward devolve upon the surviving children. Marie-Louise had inherited nothing from either Napoleon or Neipperg but she understood only too well the importance of providing for surviving children. No father in her duchies would enjoy his previously inalienable and absolute right to dispose of his assets as he chose. No magnanimous sentimental gestures would be permissable towards ex-veterans or towards undisclosed children until the primary family unit had been taken care of. A father – and a mother – must first administer family assets for minor children, for their education and maintenance. Loans from children to parents were permissible only with judicial consent.

Woman had come a long way from being no more than a chattel, and her husband the owner of that chattel. Additional new laws provided for the guardianship of children, the protection of maternity, and for popular education, including a college for women, both rich and poor, founded in the former convent of San Paolo. The women and children in Marie-Louise's duchies enjoyed more freedoms through her tenure than women anywhere else in the Catholic world, virtually all of whom were governed by variants of the Napoleonic Code, the variations made by men with little concern other than to preserve the status quo between the sexes.

Marie-Louise's codes established the publicity of trials, the abolition of the pillory and of confiscation of goods, and the denial of any civil status to the Church's ecclesiastical forum. In her states, there was honest freedom of the written word and of action. Civil liberties were guaranteed. The Duchess of Parma took no part in the Austrian policing and surveillance operated from Milan for the whole of the Italian peninsula, and protected her subjects against them. She was exasperated by the coercive and vexatory departures from her codes by unscrupulous officials. Injustice brought to her notice exasperated her. She tried to rectify matters wherever possible, and when it was not, ordered payment of compensation.

It would take many generations before legislation would change attitudes, and Vienna remained as traditional as ever. Even if the Duke of Reichstadt were not to feel the stigma of having illegitimate half-siblings from his mother – of course he had many through his father – intriguers at the Viennese court might do their level best to make him feel it. Marie-Louise could not bear the thought of possible rejection by her firstborn. A stranger to scheming, the domestic ménage she had been forced to adopt upon the birth of her second family gave her no joy. Her desire to acquaint her firstborn with everything to do with her own life, while keeping hidden the existence of his half-sister and –brother had made her wretched. For the time being, however unrealistic, Empress Karoline-Auguste advised that her best course was to keep the true ages of Albertina and Wilhelm from him.

> Your father desires as ardently as you that your son never learns the age of the two Beings of whose existence he is still unaware, or of whom he was unaware until very recently. For

his part, your father will do everything within his power to ease your situation, but you must not on any account introduce the two Beings in public until many years hence and until such time as you may do so without giving rise to ugly reproaches. We can only hope that nobody will have the indiscretion or the wickedness to tell your son that which he must never know. Such discovery would cause him – and you, my poor friend – too much unhappiness. Oh, this unfortunate will! Ah, if only the illness had not weakened the mind of the deceased, he would have foreseen the embarrassment into which he has thrown you and he would have spared you this![5]

The reception of her firstborn's arrival had been very different to those of Marie-Louise's second and third child. Her father's heart had swelled with pride at news of a grandchild, her siblings had rejoiced to become aunts and uncles, every courtier wanted to hold the baby, to bestow a kiss on the downy cheek or forehead. The world at large wanted the child paraded publicly so that they could catch a glimpse of the newborn. The same grandfather's heart, the same aunts and uncles felt no warmth for or connection with the two Beings, a hateful term which sought to rob the children of any nexus with the Imperial family and of any right to life itself. The very idea that Christian conduct demanded that a man of right mind would have spared his wife embarrassment by making no mention of his dear children in his will was an insult to common sense.

The impossibility of keeping the truth from the Duke of Reichstadt for any length of time became abundantly clear. Emperor Francis wrote telling Marie-Louise how he had told the Duke of Reichstadt of Marie-Louise's morganatic marriage to Neipperg and about the existence of two children.

"He asked me no questions about the children. If he had done, I would have discussed this further with him, without at any time mentioning their age. Unfortunately, this detail will not remain hidden long, and accordingly you naturally run the risk of not retaining the elevated feelings he has for you."⁶ Count Dietrichstein wrote to Marie-Louise telling her what an angel her father had been in conveying very gently to her son the terrible blow that the revelation must have been. Marie-Louise dared not countenance how far she might have fallen in her firstborn's affections.

SIXTEEN

The charade revealed

At long last, Marie-Louise's father knew the truth about her marriage and the children. For twelve years, Marie-Louise had lived in a ghastly no-man's land, heavily reliant on the loyalty of others to keep the secrets she dared not utter. A cohort comprising clerics, doctors, wet-nurses, maids, governesses, gardeners, household staff, traders, suppliers and manual workers had colluded in her clandestine life. A large but select clutch watched as Marie-Louise had no option but to play a ridiculous charade since shortly after her arrival in Parma when she had fallen pregnant for the second time. As her pregnancy advanced, she withdrew from public life. Marie-Louise confided the existence of her second and third children to her closest friend, Victoria de Crenneville, and her mother, Countess Colloredo, both of whom sent gifts to the children. Beyond this circle, no-one would have evidence of the Duchess's intimacy with her chief administrator or of the existence of offspring.

Houses were built and prepared for Albertina and Wilhelm in the vicinity of Marie-Louise's ducal palaces. In the midst of dense woodland, Marie-Louise had built the little house of Fedolfi, which she could access directly from the former Farnese hunting lodge of Casino dei Boschi, much loved by her great aunt Maria Amalia, sister of Queen Marie-Antoinette and wife of Ferdinand, the last Bourbon Duke of Parma. Both at Casino dei Boschi and in Parma, the children were brought up by Dr Rossi, a trusted courtier, whom Neipperg nicknamed *"le père nourricière"* and whom the children called "Papa", and by a Swiss governess, Marianna De Pury de Neuchâtel, whom the children addressed as "Mama". By the time

Albertina was nine, she knew that these were only terms of endearment to people whom she regarded as second parents. Every morning, Marie-Louise and Neipperg, in the early years posing to the outside world as their benefactors, would visit the children who addressed them as "Madame" and "Sir". These accommodations for society's benefit pained Marie-Louise unbearably. In the late afternoon, they would be admitted to the library in the company of the few people party to the secret. Neipperg's four sons came regularly to visit him in Parma, and he and Marie-Louise decided to appraise the boys of their recent marriage and, once Albertina was seven and Wilhelm five, to introduce the half-siblings to each other and to integrate them all as a family unit. Alfred Neipperg described how, at fifteen, he had learnt of his father's relationship with Marie-Louise.

> Only later did I understand that the affection and tenderness shown by Marie-Louise to me and my brother, Ferdinand, were something more than that which might be extended to a guest. Ignorant of the truth, I returned to Switzerland with Ferdinand where a friend's teasing made me suspicious. Only when my father revealed the mystery did I understand everything. It was during my stay of three or four months in Parma, when I first entered the imperial army, one Friday morning in September 1824. My father summoned me to his bedroom and, after having made me swear to keep secret what he was to tell me, revealed his clandestine relationship with the Duchess.

One of Marie-Louise's projects into which she poured her interest and resources was the excavation of Roman ruins at Veleia, not far from Parma. Eighty years earlier, the ruins had yielded a find fully documented in Roman history, the famous Tabula Alimentaria, the largest inscribed tablet from antiquity, drafted by the Emperor Trajan. Spread out over extensive hillside terraces, further excavation revealed a thermal spa, a forum which originally would have been entirely paved in sandstone flags and arcaded on three sides, a rectangular basilica and extensive living quarters. Marie-Louise directed the collection of artefacts from the site and the reorganization of Parma's archeological museum, begun shortly after the first findings but suspended during the French occupation, for which she designated a room in the Palazzo della Pilotta. One afternoon, not long after Alfred's talk with his father, Marie-Louise invited him to accompany her on one of her trips to Velleia. There, among the remnants of fallen empire, she told Alfred of her recent marriage to his father, confirming everything that he had already been told. A few days later, Marie-Louise again found a quiet time to tell him that he had a sister, Albertina, and a brother, Wilhelm (Guglielmo in Italian). Alfred recorded the event and its aftermath in his memoirs:

> On 28 September, I saw the two children for the first time, in the charge of a governess, Marianne de Pury Neuchâtel. They lived in a pavilion in the little garden of Parma's Ducal Palace. Accessible in a few steps without being seen, Her Majesty spent a large part of the day with her children. And then in the evening, they would come to the library located on the same side of the building. Every evening, I participated in these intimate reunions, as did sometimes a few of Her Majesty's ladies-in-waiting, or Dr. Rossi or my father's adjutant, M. Richer.

Alfred spent many stretches of time in Parma and things remained unchanged.

> It is impossible to imagine a happier union than that between my father and Her Majesty, and a more tender love for children by their parents. Every day, when my father woke up, he would write a few lines to Her Majesty. The reply arrived very soon thereafter. Sometimes her letter arrived before he had sent his, and sometimes they would exchange several notes. My father never went to Her Majesty's room until lunch was served, as mornings were reserved for affairs of state, and my father only got dressed very late. Her Majesty spent much of the morning

with her children, helping with their lessons. Lunch was served at one, then we all went to their apartment for half an hour. My father returned to his room and gave audience, attending as fast as he could to the business which his office required of him, and only after he had finished his work went to Her Majesty's room to go for a walk with her. When they returned, he went back to business and then discussed matters with Her Majesty until eight o'clock. Then the children would come to the library, where everyone would stay until about nine o'clock. Then the children would have dinner, and, half an hour later, Her Majesty and my father would have a light evening meal. Virtually the same routine was repeated when they were in the country, save that there were more carriage rides together and etiquette was far less rigid.

Never had Marie-Louise been able to venture out beyond her palaces in Parma and Piacenza with her children. Carriage rides *en famille* she could only contemplate in the woodlands of Sala Baganza. Never could she acknowledge her children publicly as her own. Whether present or absent, there was always a child from which she had to withhold the truth.

SEVENTEEN

Feeling widowhood

From the moment Marie-Louise parted from Albertina and Wilhelm to visit her firstborn or to attend to her duties as sovereign, she counted the distance in the number of days it would take her to return to them, yearning to retrace her steps back over the Alps. She begged each child to write to her often and never to forget how much she loved him or her. She was tormented at the thought that weeks, sometimes months lay ahead before she could embrace them again, and she would fall prey to interminable palpitations. She wrote letters daily on her distinctive letterhead, bearing her monogram framed by a crown in the left hand top corner, frequently defeated by streaming tears. Just as in conversation, she resorted to words and phrases in German and Italian which came to her more swiftly than the French which Albertina and Marie-Louise spoke together, often using capitals for nouns, transposing part of her German heritage. Typically, she addressed herself to Albertina, begging her also to write daily to enable her mother to bear her absence, passing on love to Wilhelm who rarely responded – he was a joker who never seemed to take anything seriously. Albertina wrote daily on her own initiative, whatever came into her head. Though often inelegantly phrased, Marie-Louise adored her daughter's simplicity and spontaneity and was sure she would grow up to be a sensitive empathetic woman. "You can always write whatever comes into your mind. My only wish is that you will always believe that I am your best friend."[1]

Marie-Louise had always signed herself by her Christian name, prefaced sometimes by the epithet "your friend", never "Mother".

From Vienna, her letters described her mornings bursting with visits and time spent with her family. She spoke affectionately of all her beloved relatives, *her* kinsmen, not those of her illegitimate children. Listing everyone present, she would frequently omit reference to her firstborn so that he remained a mystery figure to them. In Vienna, she would wait impatiently for the post, which arrived punctually at midday, for news of her children. On days when there was nothing for her, she hid her deep disappointment, imagining overturned carriages and other disasters, asking in her next letters whether her children still felt affection towards her: "Remember me daily, and love me a little hundredth part of the way in which I love you."[2] Her face ran with tears as the clock struck eight in the evening, the hour at which Albertina would be bouncing in to see her, were she in Parma.

She sent a profusion of gifts, toys, decorative fruits made out of sugar, sketches, berets, straw hats, whale-bones for new dresses, undergarments, material for summer dresses and winter coats and books, often accompanied by flowers she had dried and pressed.

In the afternoons, Marie-Louise took refuge in the Imperial library, a vast hall with frescoed dome. There were many gems in her father's collection of three thousand volumes which absorbed her. *Jerusalem Liberated* by Tasso, copies of which she procured to give as gifts, was her firm favourite.

After walks or a carriage ride in the countryside and dinner, she would spend her evenings playing Taroc. She spent hot evenings in Karoline-Auguste's apartments on the second floor of the palace, filled with beautiful plants, parrots, monkeys and birds.

Marie-Louise's favourite activities when in Vienna were to visit the botanical gardens, greenhouses and menageries of her childhood. She had been brought up to adore animals and took a particular interest in all the animals of her father's zoo and at the Prater, and followed their progress on each visit. A particularly momentous occasion was the arrival during her stay in Vienna of a Nubian giraffe, a gift to her father from the Pasha of Egypt. "The giraffe's appetite is enormous – she eats a minimum of four chickens, ten pigeons and a whole lamb a day, and drinks fifteen glasses of honey syrup, which makes thirty pints of wine a day."[3] The first giraffe did not last long and another was sent a few years after its demise.

Marie-Louise promised to bring home with her the offspring of the Brazilian doves sent by Leopoldine for Albertina to keep in a bird-cage indoors. She obtained Austrian butterflies for Wilhelm, Brazilian for Albertina. She told them about the lion with four cubs no more than thirty-six hours old, an elephant, a Brazilian leopard, two white foxes and a hyena, while sending strict instructions to her gardener in Parma not to allow the cats to eat the rabbits. There was alarm in the menagerie when the lady elephant seemed to be on the point of dying "- I wonder she did not write a will last night!"[4] Marie-Louise teased. There were tragedies too. One year an epidemic exterminated the monkeys. Another epidemic killed many deer and over sixty wild boar. She loved to see animals in the wild and remarked upon the environs of Pressburg where the deer and wild boar were numerous and extremely dangerous, zealously protecting their young. She had run into a decomposing dead boar swarming with worms during the day on one of her walks.

Marie-Louise was delighted at the beautiful little English puppy Neipperg had bought her, though she doubted the dog would happily co-habit with her Lovely and Diane who often accompanied her on trips, and which she confessed was not as pretty as Albertina's horse, Soletto, or Wilhelm's Otello. She talked of hunting partridges and hares, and picking raspberries with her father. Local folk music and dancing cheered her, Tyrolean yodelling sending her into fits of giggles. She described ribbon factories, sugar refineries, rum and vinegar distilleries.

Marie-Louise described her walks around the villages of the Kahlen and the Leopoldberg, the views across the Moravian plains and the tortuous path of the Danube, the hills around Vienna and the snow-capped high mountains of Austria and Styria. She described the flora and fauna, the beautiful butterflies, the wisteria, the Irish musk, the blue gentians, magnificent hortensias, the young violet and many more. She rarely got angry, in fits of laughter when adventures took her into brooks and streams, getting her wet and throwing mud all over her clothes.

In addition to the towns she visited in Austria, she described the port city of Genoa, and the coastal strip through Chiavari to Livorno, the routes through Piedmont and Lombardy-Venetia. In Milan, she described her visit to the stupendous Gothic Cathedral with its magnificent stained glass, how at Count Neipperg's insistence she climbed the hundred and twelve steps to the vertiginous tip of the dome, hanging on to the iron railings for dear life, closing her eyes, opening them to feast upon the richest, most fertile land imaginable across the plain of the river Po, the Apennines and Alps.

Marie-Louise's longest trip was her tour of her grandfather Ferdinand's Kingdom of the Two Sicilies in 1824. Having boarded ship at Livorno, she told Albertina, aged seven, and Wilhelm, not yet five, how a scirocco wind had made the sea so rough that the frigate on which her party was sailing had had to stay anchored close to the shores of the island of Elba, from which she had looked out with binoculars towards the islands of Montecristo and Corsica, "Think that we love you both so much."[5] As yet, the children could have no idea of the significance of Elba and Corsica to their mother.

Marie-Louise's grandfather was known by his subjects as *il Re Lazzarone*, the Rogue King, such were his despotic tendencies and his insatiable appetite for hunting, lewdness and the pleasures of the flesh. He had a soft spot for Marie-Louise and had planned extraordinarily lavish entertainment for her. For two and a half months, Marie-Louise was showered with attention, her presence constantly demanded at the Fondo and San Carlo theatres, at court receptions and hunting and boating parties. Naples, the most populous city in Europe, seemed to Marie-Louise to sprawl for miles. King Ferdinand had organised a particularly sumptuous 'party on the water' in the bay of Naples, framed by the city and the dormant but simmering giant of Mount Vesuvius, a host of musicians in shining livery on a golden candlelit barge, a huge topaz shell floating on a bed of sapphire. Marie-Louise and Neipperg watched, part of the royal party, on a second large gondola with silk canopy overhung with drapes, slightly parted to allow the ingress of balsamic air. Lady Blessington thought the Duchess of Parma looked like a modern day Cleopatra. Marie-Louise described her eight hour trek to the summit of the volcano Vesuvius, standing at the brink of the crater near glowing coals, the ash still hot from the eruption two years earlier. Running down in the ashes, fearful of getting a good foothold, she had abandoned her socks and shoes only to burn her feet. She collected lava which she had made into a bracelet and necklace for Albertina. From Naples, she began her tour of all the sights of Campania, including the recent excavations at Herculaneum and Paestum, going further south to the African aridity of Sicily, taking in the ancient temples of Segesta and Agrigento. Born with a natural curiosity for and wonder at life, she relished her trips, but always within her was a wrench around her heart.

Thankfully, Neipperg had urged Marie-Louise two years before his death to approach the man Werklein called "the Croesus Rothschild" to provide for her offspring in the event of her and his death. At this juncture, the offspring was impliedly only the Duke of Reichstadt, though the intended beneficiaries were her two Montenuovo children. Salomon Rothschild and Neipperg made financial arrangements, based on the year-on-year surplus from revenues in which Parma had begun to rejoice, to secure her secret children's future. In exchange for the sacrifices she had made for the peace of Europe and for the infrastructural works she had had executed for the benefit of her subjects without recovering the cost from taxation, property for her personal use constructed by her from Parman revenues would be considered her private property, to form part of her estate upon her death. A secret loan was created against this security. Negotiations were entered into with her Bourbon successors as regards her furniture, pictures, library, horses and jewels to avoid contest upon her death.

The Duchess could not have been more pleased with these arrangements, but was irked by Metternich's immediate deduction from the loan of funds spent by Austria on military expenditure and on the maintenance of Marie-Louise during the years 1814 to 1816. She particularly noted the tone of his instruction to refuse the conferral by her of the Knightly Order of Constantine for Rothschild's managing clerk on the grounds that the Order represented a genuine religious brotherhood from which the Jewish religion barred him from participating. The statutes of the Order prevented the admission of non-Christians. Like Goethe, Metternich had looked with scorn at the enactment at Frankfurt in 1823 of a new law permitting marriage between Christians and Jews, suspicious of bribery of corrupt legislators by the Rothschild empire. Metternich wrote to Marie-Louise,

> Temper your refusal with appropriate expressions of your extreme regret, and the matter will be ended. Do not mention my name. I myself have committed the great offence of refusing for all time to obtain an Austrian decoration for the Rothschild family. If he thought I was implicated he would regard me as a positive cannibal![6]

Rothschild's clerk was dispatched with a signet ring. Marie-Louise valued Rothschild, and relied upon him, deferring to him as regards not only the loan, but as regards income from the Bohemian estates intended for the Duke of Reichstadt. Shortly before Neipperg's death, a separate account, designated by an "M", was created for Albertina and Wilhelm, their first official appearance as part of the Montenuovo family. At Metternich's intercession, her father, acknowledging the invaluable service Neipperg had given to his daughter and to Austria, accorded his bastard grandchildren the official titles of Count and Countess.

In April 1829, about the same time that Marie-Louise received

Karoline-Auguste's letter relating to the Beings, she received a visit from the Baron de Vitrolles, ambassador of Charles X. The last time she had seen the Baron was when he had accompanied her on the fatal flight from the Tuileries to Blois. He had been one of the emissaries she had used to send messages to her father. Vitrolles had always been charming to her, having served Napoleon for many years and fought in his battles. Like many at her Parisian court, he had pursued self-interest at the critical moment and, at the earliest opportunity, had gone over to the new administration of Louis XVIII, expressing himself dedicated to the Bourbon cause. He had been part of the cabal at the Vienna Congress determined to defeat Marie-Louise's claim to Parma.

Vitrolles's visit came only six weeks after Neipperg's death, letters of condolence still flooding in. "Your Majesty performed Her duties until the very last moment. She sweetened the last moments of my friend, as she has made his happiness over the past fifteen years." Dr Aglietti, Neipperg's doctor, said too that she had done everything she could to try and save his life, "but unfortunately there are occasions when all the great talent which you possess to such a high degree and all the efforts of art are powerless, for it is impossible to fight against the divine will." Despite these and other reassurances the Duchess received daily from her courtiers and friends and family, she was guilt-ridden. She perpetually asked herself whether there was more she could have done for her beloved, things she should have asked him, things he might have wanted. He could not have known he was in mortal danger; had he done so he would have prepared her for the end. He was always so thoughtful, he would have advised her regarding the situation in which he had left her, "Advice I needed so badly and which he never gave me!" She wailed in frustration. Marie-Louise felt devoid of energy. She had been suffering from a dreadful migraine over the previous two weeks and had to make a considerable effort to put herself in the frame of mind of playing host. She had lost weight, and looked emaciated and wan. She clung to the Parmans who gave her tokens of their affection and devotion to her, particularly courtiers Sanvitale, Bianchi and Paveri-Fontana. Though she had no desire to accommodate Baron Vitrolles, she knew that it was important that she must. His advent was not fortuitous. The French and Spanish took every turn of events offered them to undermine her position. She invited him for a late dinner, three-thirty in the afternoon, which gave her time to attend to the morning's business and to invite a dozen members of her court to join her. She received them shrouded in long veils of mourning, which hid the tears which she found impossible to check.

Marie-Louise asked after the health of her Cousin, the French king, and after the Dauphin and the Dauphine, the Duchess of Angoulême whom she had known in her childhood in Vienna. She expressed particular interest in her second cousin, the poor Duchess of Berry, whose husband had been assassinated. She had heard that the little Duke of Bordeaux, born after his father's death, charmed everyone. Vitrolles tried unsuccessfully to take Marie-Louise back to the days she had spent in Paris. Everything besides Neipperg was a blur, she said. Appearing distracted, she asked him what had become of the Pantheon, and to remind her of the name of the metropolitan Church of Paris. When he started talking about members of Napoleon's family, it was as if he were talking about strangers. Vitrolles referred to women who had apparently been in service to her as ladies-in-waiting. Marie-Louise, who had disciplined herself long ago not to be drawn into conversations about her life in France, asked him to remind her, give her clues to help her identify who he was talking about. She had no recollection of them. To Marie-Louise, her short sojourn in Paris seemed as if it had taken place in some prehistoric epoch that was certainly no part of her present. Mercifully, her memories of France no longer troubled her. The figurehead Empress and the benevolent Duchess were two totally distinctly separate entities within her. The Bourbon minister overstepped the mark when he upbraided her indirectly for her lack of attachment to her first husband. Marie-Louise put him in his place:

We other princesses are not brought up like other women, we are not taught to have the same emotional ties, the same family sentiment. We are always prepared for events which break the link, which take us far from our relations and give us new and often conflicting interests. Look at my poor sister who died in Brazil, unhappy and far from her loved ones![7]

As Leopoldine had said, "We poor princesses are like dice which are thrown down for good or ill."[8]

Marie-Louise's tears were for her late second husband, whose loss she continued to lament to the humbled ambassador, and for the dishonour she had brought upon her first son. But they were also for herself and for her poor sister Leopoldine, her younger sister who had fallen asleep out of boredom during a recital performed by the great Beethoven. Leopoldine's lot seemed infinitely worse and unjust. At their sad parting at the port of Livorno in the summer of 1817, Leopoldine had had such high expectations of life in the Americas, on the verge of a new dawn, the old continent of Europe in decline. She had been impatient to set sail on her two month Atlantic crossing and to arrive in her new homeland. Leopoldine's first impressions were favourable. She was ecstatic.

"My husband is not only handsome, but he is good and understanding. I am really, really happy. Brazil is paradisical."[9] Husband and wife made music together. A few weeks later, she wrote, Furs and books can be readily obtained just as in Livorno as there are many foreigners here. I even have a tailor who worked a lot for you in Paris. I have one of your former cooks in Paris who remembers your beloved breakfasts. I have four darling saddle-horses. I have been dancing until I practically dropped dead from perspiration. I already look Portuguese and speak the language like a native."[10]

She found plenty to feed her interest in botany, butterflies, minerals, numismatics and natural history. She talked of long rides through Rio's Tijuca parklands and subtropical forests, of treks through waterfalls, mimosas and palms. She loved the mountains, the green fields, the birds of exquisite plumage. She described in detail all different aspects of life in Brazil, the people, the palaces, chaotic day-to-day living, the endless armies of slaves and courtiers, the gardens, flowers, seeds, plants, collections and libraries relating to her interests. Full of enthusiasm, she delighted in everything. Marie-Louise had always adored Leopoldine's letters, of which she received well over two hundred, in Vienna sharing them with the rest of the family to great laughter and tears.

The paradise had soon turned to a steaming hot wilderness, the heat and mosquitoes unbearably oppressive, the climate unforgiving. Rio resembled a rather bad Hungarian town. Leopoldine longed for the snows of Europe. The people, particularly the women, were primitive, barely literate, superstitiously religious though morally lax, generally capricious and not to be trusted. Brazilian court life bore no resemblance to that in Vienna. The Portuguese royal family were far from the *gemütlich* clan she had anticipated. "I no longer laugh as once I did in our family circle in my dear fatherland."[11] Her husband was boorish, habitually unfaithful and jealous. He spoke his mind with a certain brutality, did exactly what he wanted. Barely a year after she had arrived, she sent Marie-Louise a letter setting out her views on their brother-in-law's infidelity which sounded warning bells.

"Men will be men, we must be women and abandoned, must wait, through patient virtue, until the right time to take matters in hand. They always come back and then they treasure us so much more."[12] Three months later, Leopoldine wrote: "You are indeed right, Marie-Louise, true happiness does not exist in this world. I could say that I am alone for I see so often such contradictory dealings that I cannot rightly decide whether I have a friend in my husband and am truly loved by him."[13]

She had never got used to his earthy, sexually explicit language, to his practice of urinating and defecating in full public view, to his vulgar interest in pornography, to his beating the slaves on the slightest pretext with a silver-handled whip which he would take on walks wherever he went. A woman, Leopoldine was barred from enjoying the amusements and intellectual pursuits which had filled her life in Vienna and was forced to live the life of a hermit. Marie-Louise found her sister's sufferings excruciatingly painful. Yet again, Marie-Louise was powerless to help her. Leopoldine was just one more of the many Habsburg brides abandoned to a pitiless fate.

Leopoldine asked Marie-Louise to send her the details of her Paris shippers so that she could send her the beautiful birds and plants she had collected. Isolated in her palaces in St Christophe, Rio de Janeiro and Santa Cruz, bereft of true friends, she thought of Marie-Louise's constantly. Letters home signed "Your American" were her outlet. She complained constantly about the meagre post she received from Europe. Correspondence transported on Italian ships arrived, but nothing from London or Vienna. The birth of a daughter cheered her considerably, though the Portuguese surgeon had lacerated her so incompetently that she felt she would have done better to have given birth without assistance, like an animal in the wild. A son followed. It was at the time of the uprisings in Spain, Piedmont and Naples that she wrote to Marie-Louise telling her that a new Brazilian throne had been created, and that her father-in-law the King of Portugal had ceded this to her husband. He had pledged his oath to a constitution, so that Brazil was now a constitutional monarchy and he and she the first Emperor and Empress of Brazil.

Mutinies and massacres were becoming commonplace, all Europeans primary targets. Leopoldine feared carnage. "Here education, which is already better than it was where one who had an enlightened mind was considered a heretic, is abysmal."[14] She was soon forced to discharge the governess to her children, a charming English-woman, Lady Graham, on account of the prevailing political climate. Leopoldine reported that the South American rebels clamoured for Marie-Louise to acknowledge herself as Napoleon's bride and torchbearer of his supposed ideals.

"The yoke of marriage is in these terrible times more dangerous than ever."[15] She was increasingly depressed, seeing in the terrible spirit of cancerous rebellion tremendous darkness for the future. There would be more bloody struggles. The death of her son and a further pregnancy exacerbated her mood. "Black, black is the future for me! Would that I could return home!"[16] She begged Marie-Louise to intercede with their father and with Metternich to have Austria recognize the new Brazilian government in the hope of putting an end to the bloodshed.

"The word "politics" tortures me so much that I will hate it forever!"[17] Long ago, they had both privately agreed that they loathed Metternich. Though it would be impossible to deduce this from their correspondence with him, neither archduchess could bear his self-righteous exploitation of their weak position. Both had always known too how much they depended upon his goodwill, and how hard they needed to work to maintain it. "Happy are those who depend on others for nothing and the destiny of whose children depend only on their affection!" Marie-Louise wrote in exasperation.

Marie-Louise read and re-read Leopoldine's letters, which had sustained her since her parting from her son. One of the last letters she had written Marie-Louise before leaving Vienna for Brazil read: "Prince Anton insists that he has received letters from Parma which say that you are marrying a General Nova Monte, translated into German. I was half dead from laughing over this idiotic notion and ended up quarrelling with him because he firmly believed it. Isn't that a tease?!"[18] Poor Leopoldine had never known the truth. There was so much to cry about.

In Vienna, Marie-Louise had always thought that her sister would long outlive her siblings, Napoleon's invasion of Habsburg territories unable to dent her excellent sense of humour, but sadly she was mistaken. Leopoldine died three years before Neipperg in December 1826, not yet thirty years old. Three months pregnant, she had written to Vienna just over two weeks before she expired telling of her gall disease, insomnia, over-exhaustion, inability to eat. In desperation, he begged the family to pray for her for her meeting with the Almighty. She had no hope in Brazilian doctors, who were all barbarians. A letter in Portuguese addressed to Marie-Louise which she had written shortly before her death was found by her bedside:

> My health is very, very poor and I have reached the end of my life. It is a great sorrow to me that I am unable to convey to you all my feelings which have stirred my heart. I will never see you again! I beg that you will take sisterly pity on my poor children who will be left orphans by my death, left in the care of the people of Brazil who have proved my undoing. I have much more to tell you, but my strength fails me. I have debts which I incurred to help the poor who solicited my aid. The Marqueza d'Aguiar is instructed to inform you of the details of matters relating to my beloved daughter. Oh my daughter! What will become of you after my death! Farewell, my beloved sister, may God permit me to write to you again which would surely aid my recovery![19]

The Marqueza d'Aguiar wrote to inform Marie-Louise of Leopoldine's death, enclosing this last letter. During the course of her deterioration and when death finally came, the people of Brazil flocked to their churches to lament her passing. Every class and ethnic group wept for this young tragic life. The Portuguese, the Brazilians, the whites, the blacks, rich and poor, powerful and downtrodden made their pilgrimage on foot or on horseback to Sao Cristovao to pray for the soul of their dearly beloved Empress.

The family and Court in Vienna, particularly Marie-Louise's father, were distraught. Leopoldine would still be alive, had she married a young Austrian according to the dictates of her heart! The lot of a Habsburg bride was unenviable. Her place would be taken by Amélie von Leuchtenberg, daughter of Eugène de Beauharnais, Napoleon's stepson.

Taking care to protest the greatest friendship with the French Bourbon Court by flattering its envoy, Marie-Louise invited the Baron de Vitrolles to extend his stay to the following day when they could converse more informally. The Baron spoke about how he found not only the Duchess and her court in deepest mourning, but all her duchies who seemed to share her pain. He had not heard one voice raised in complaint against her administration. Marie-Louise told the Baron, lest he be tempted to think otherwise, that she had always kept a close eye on matters delegated to her former chief administrator, even when he decided matters otherwise than in accordance with her views. Since his death, she had become even more scrupulous in her supervision, holding regular audiences to listen to her subjects' grievances. The Baron thought perhaps she might prefer to be back in Vienna, which he was sure she missed. Marie-Louise told him that she missed her firstborn tremendously, that she had never got used to his absence, and of course she loved to see her kindly father. It was always painful leaving Vienna, but then it was always painful leaving Parma. The Baron expressed sympathy for her situation and took his leave.

Vitrolles had come with an agenda, not as friend or ally. The ruler might have changed, but the French were still smarting from losing out to Austria over Parma and the rest of Northern Italy. At some point, they would return to pounce on spoils of political turmoil. The Baron had spent the morning of his first day pressing French treasury claims to Parman assets. Purporting to be motivated by the concern of protecting the independence of the states within the Italian peninsula and the maintenance of their tranquility, he discussed with Werklein how he felt that Neipperg's death provided sufficient reason to think that Marie-Louise might wish to bring forward the transfer of her duchies to her successor. With her entitlement to Parma resting solely upon her connection to Napoleon, he and his successor now dead, Parma could hardly hold any charm for her, lacking the cultural and social diversions which she so enjoyed in Vienna. In exchange for the surrender of her sovereignty,

Vitrolles continued, she would receive an income of over a million francs, leaving her son free to come into possession of the income of his Bohemian fiefdoms. Doubtless the Austrian Imperial court would feel that this rearrangement would enhance its lustre and *éclat*. When Vitrolles asked how the Duchess would view such a proposal, Werklein dodged the question. He had no idea as to the Duchess's plans: "And what interest does the French King have in the early cession of Parma to the Duke of Lucca?"

In an effort to suggest that he had not intended the Duchess to take immediate steps, the Baron said that his Majesty's role was merely protective as regards the fourth branch of the House of Bourbon. As far as the Baron knew, His Majesty the King took no interest in the matter, and in his personal opinion, the Duke of Lucca had not yet demonstrated sufficient wisdom or maturity to place himself on such an important stage, though he was sure an early surrender would be warmly welcomed by the Duke of Modena and the Grand Duke of Tuscany, who would both thereby gain territorially.

Marie-Louise was not moving. Two months after Neipperg's death, she attended the inauguration of the Parma theatre, the Teatro Reggio, which they had planned together. The finest singers on the Italian peninsula had been summoned to perform Bellini's new composition, *La Zaira*, commissioned for the occasion. It was a grand public event to which Marie-Louise invited Charles Felix, King of Piedmont-Sardinia, who had been especially kind to Neipperg during his last illness. The opera was a disaster. Merciless in their criticism, the Parmans whistled their disapproval, prompting Bellini to flee the theatre and Parma before Marie-Louise had had a chance to confer upon him the usual honours. Marie-Louise put on a brave face, but her heart was in pieces.

Daily the Duchess wrestled with her conscience. She could not put off forever telling her firstborn the truth about the ages of his half-siblings. Her nerves were in a terrible state. As weeks passed, the thought of going to Vienna became increasingly frightening.

She decided to go to Geneva to breathe the restorative air of the Alps. Victoria de Crenneville offered to look after Albertina and Wilhelm, but Marie-Louise wanted them, her only consolation on the loss of their father, to be close to her. Taking the Montenuovo children with her obliged her to sacrifice being with the Duke. She had not been with the Duke at Napoleon's death, but there had been so many impediments, not least another advanced pregnancy which subsequently miscarried.

On the last day of July, Marie-Louise set out with a small retinue towards the Swiss Alps. She arranged for her children and a tutor and some of her court to stay at Gex, two steps from the French border, and rented a small castle nearby in Le Petit Savonneux for a month. Just as fifteen years earlier, she was constantly under surveillance, her motives for her sojourn suspect, though it must have been plain to see from her appearance that she was in desperate need of spa treatments, racked with rheumatism and melancholy. The woman who stared back at her in the mirror looked more like fifty-eight than thirty-eight.

Marie-Louise received Neipperg's son Gustav, a charming child, the one she felt more than any of the others would follow in his father's footsteps, of a rare solidity for his age with best heart and much wit. She loved to watch him play with his half-siblings, touched by the tenderness he displayed. She prayed that the world and bad society would not be granted the opportunity to corrupt him. Gustav loved and adored his second mother, and she was delighted that he was on intimate terms with the Duke of Reichstadt. Gustav could be relied on to set the record straight and enlighten the Duke with the greatest sensitivity in areas where the Viennese court might have been less than economical with the truth.

Marie-Louise returned to Parma as autumn waned. She found deciding what to wear extremely tiresome, no longer interested in her appearance. The fringes and feathers which had come into fashion seemed absurd. She tried to find distraction in her new theatre which relied upon her for her support. She rarely had an appetite for what was playing, finding that the opera singers often screamed: in *Tancredi* everyone seemed to be competing to shout the loudest. At the dawn of the new year and decade, her friends persuaded her to launch into a little comedy to bring some lightness and gaiety into her life. Marie-Louise played the leading roles in several comedies, including *"Les deux maris"* by Scribe, which reminded everyone that Marie-Louise was quite capable of taking herself less than seriously. She found herself carried away by emotion at performances by the renowned opera singer Giuditta Pasta, who took the starring roles in both *Othello* and *Romeo and Juliet*. "She performed in a way that has not only never been equalled," Marie-Louise wrote to Victoria de Crenneville, "but has never been conceived by the works' composers!" Pasta's portrayals of Desdemona and Juliet enhanced the tragedy of the wronged woman and of choices vitiated, in their purest, most perfect, unadulterated form. Touched to the very core, Marie-Louise returned home to fling herself on her sofa, weeping hysterically for several hours.

EIGHTEEN

Repercussions of the July Revolution, 1830

The Duke of Reichstadt's letters to his mother in Switzerland during the summer of 1829 were sensitive and loving, often moving her to tears. He showed no sign of rancour and told her to forget the past and to think only of the future.

Sometimes he found writing to his mother difficult. Count Dietrichstein remonstrated with him, depriving him of his riding lessons to try and focus his mind.

"Dear Mama, I ask you not to think that my long silence is caused by a lack of love and admiration, both of which will only end with my life." Sometimes, he delayed writing to her to avoid upsetting her, as when his grandfather had been so ill that everyone had feared for his life, and he had waited until the worse was over.

At the age of fourteen, he made a conscious decision to write to his mother in French, asserting his fierce loyalty to his father.

"You yourself have expressed the wish that I should always write to you in the language of the heart and my own feelings allow me nothing else. I have taken a firm resolution to apply myself to the French language so that by the time you get here this year, I will be able to speak it as fluently as German."[1] He was studying Italian, translating abstract, difficult extracts into German, hoping perhaps that one day he would have cause to use it when he finally got to Parma.

Marie-Louise recommended the Duke read the letters of Mme de Sévigné to try and correct his countless spelling and grammatical mistakes and to improve his letter-writing style. He instantly adored them, calling them "bonbons for the heart".

Count Dietrichstein had been at the end of his tether during the Duke's early teenage years. The Duke's increasing awareness of the uniqueness of his position had made him a very difficult adolescent. He refused to be taught in German. The Count had never known anyone as indolent, lying and opinionated. The Duke might be charming in society, but that was all a veneer. "His rebellious character and his system of eternal contradiction paralyses all measures and stops him in his instruction."[2] The Count suffered, constantly under attack by the French press who accused him of bringing out only the Habsburg and denying the Bonaparte in the raising of his charge.

Marie-Louise was loving, but also firm in her letters, trying to exert discipline from afar. When she reprimanded him for failing to apply himself, he would tell her that Rome was not built in a day, that it was easier to clean a filthy stable than to eradicate bad habits. He suffered terribly, just as Marie-Louise did, from her constant postponements and cancellations of her trips to Vienna. "The Emperor often asks me when you will arrive. I always say: "at the end of July: would that you would only come earlier and punish my lies!"[3] In anticipation of his mother's arrival, the Duke was always overjoyed, his dearest wish seemingly on the brink of fulfilment. He would reward her visit by his good behaviour in future. In 1826, mother and son had spent almost five months together. It was a halcyon period for both of them, though Marie-Louise ached constantly for her nine- and seven-year-old in Parma. The Duke relived every moment: "Here you were in Vienna and I saw you so often. I remember everything about you. Wherever I am or go is a sad reminder of happier times past. Would that there will be augurs of a happy future together,"[4] he wrote a month after they had parted. Count Dietrichstein reported that the Duke cried frequently. He threw himself into the translation of Julius Caesar's commentaries on the Gauls and Tacitus's writings on Germany. As the Duke grew older, his grandfather talked to him at length about Marie-Louise, sharing his deep affection for his daughter. After expounding on his passion for boar-hunting, the Duke sent her birthday greetings: "I love you more than can be expressed and wish you the most perfect happiness. May I one day be like you though I doubt I can, however hard I try."[5]

"How can I describe my joy receiving your gifts, your good letter and news of your travels! Only two more months and my most ardent wish will be fulfilled, I will be in your arms after two years of painful separation! I love you so much, my dear Mama." He was ecstatic at the prospect of seeing her. He was not the only one. "Gustav shared my transports. He loves you for life. Archduchess Sophie looks forward to being reunited with her very good friend, as do all your uncles. Archduke Jean will come to meet you."[6]

The Duke, always lamenting the pain of extended absence, relayed the details of his life, his attendance at the coronation of her father's Empress, Karoline Auguste, as Queen of Hungary where he marvelled at the splendour, luxury and magnificence, the diamonds, pearls and emeralds which no longer held any thrall for Marie-Louise. Like his father, he had neither ear nor talent for music and had a grating voice. His discordant whistling irritated Count Dietrichstein immensely. He derived no pleasure from listening to classical concerts, unmoved by the finest compositions and performers by which even Vienna's connoisseurs were astounded. Piano lessons had to be abandoned. He was electrified by modern music, the sound of military bands, easily accessible tunes, the thrill of tambourines, of trumpets and cymbals, the sense of occasion, the drama of ceremonial uniforms and the gleaming metal of weaponry and helmets. He loved drama, acting, the opera and, despite his protestations to the contrary, dancing the waltz, quadrilles and the *galope*. He hated ballet. Aged sixteen, he wrote to Marie-Louise during the carnival period and endless balls in Vienna,

> I am indifferent to the Carnival because I am not fond of dancing and the halls are always overcrowded and overheated. I am content when a bereavement occurs which causes their

suspension. Balls always rob me of sleep, leaving me the worse for wear the next day, unable to give myself over to study with that passion with which I have applied myself over the past couple of months and which has pleased you greatly... I hope the time will come when I will be of some consolation to you.[7]

Generally erratic in writing to his mother, the Duke sent the sweetest letters of condolence on her bereavements, showing astonishing empathy for his age. Marie-Louise was heartened by his sensitivity on the death of, among others, her grandfather, her sister Leopoldine, her aunt and great friend the Queen of Saxony, and Neipperg.

The Duke had grown to love Neipperg. His stepfather had shown him the greatest consideration and affection whenever he had come to Austria, whether accompanying Marie-Louise or sent by her on some commission. The couple had fostered friendship between the Duke and Neipperg's sons by his first marriage, Alfred, Erwin and Gustav, and mutual affection had flourished. The letters they brought from Parma were a soothing balm, consoling him for his mother's absence. When Neipperg died, the Duke shared their grief for a loving father. Alfred sent him a lock of his father's hair, a dear souvenir which he would always treasure. Apprised of his mother's remarriage, he wrote assuring her that he shared the full extent of her pain. He would try to emulate Neipperg and hoped one day that his actions might recall his mother's devoted friend. He could think of no better career model.

Books on Napoleon were constantly being published. Emperor Francis had instructed the Duke's tutors that the truth must be the basis of his education Responding frankly to his questions would be the best means of soothing his imagination. In 1824, Victoria de Crenneville, whilst recommending a new publication by Stendhal on the life of Rossini, asked Marie-Louise if she had read the book *'The Emperor Napoleon judged by his friends and enemies*': "There are fair refutations in this book which is also very interesting."[8] Whether positive or negative, fair or unfair, Marie-Louise insisted her son must have unfettered access to everything about his father. Count Dietrichstein presented everything dispassionately to Marie-Louise's satisfaction, with careful analysis of the available evidence.

By the age of eighteen, all the Duke wanted was freedom and, according to Count Dietrichstein, he acted as if he knew everything. Everyday, he would smile, demonstrating his indifference to his tutors. Despite his perverse nature, the Duke adored Count Dietrichstein, sporadically surprising him with little gifts and doing favours for the Dietrichstein family.

Marie-Louise had initially intended to come to Vienna in the month of July 1829 and, as usual, the Duke had been excited, preparing for her arrival. The Emperor, Empress, Neipperg's sons and various members of the imperial household were all anxious to see her. No-one would revoke with greater eager alacrity than he any premature judgment. Unable to bear the thought of her being in discomfort, he urged her to take care of herself and to nurse her painful rheumatism. It made him laugh, he wrote, to think he was giving her advice about how to look after herself, but he was worried about her, wishing she would consult younger doctors rather than her geriatrics. Hearing that his grandfather was beginning to doubt her arrival, he begged her to convince him otherwise and assured her, once again, that he and all the family ardently wanted to see her.

When Marie-Louise revealed that she planned instead to take the waters in Switzerland, he thought she had made a mistake. When she corrected him, he could not help remarking upon the fact that the society of her father and so many of those whom she cherished would have been of greater benefit to her health than the sight of the peaks of Mont Blanc. He would have liked to accompany her to Switzerland. "But you have set your heart upon this journey and that must be sufficient for me to willingly forgo the happiness which I would have felt on seeing you."[9]

He begged her not to ride in the mountains, her chest still too weak following her recent dangerous bout of illness. He thanked her for the walking sticks she had sent to add to his collection, and an array of latest fashionable ties from Paris.

Marie-Louise's father would not agree to recognise Albertina and Wilhelm, and would not allow no contact between the three children. To distract the Duke from his mother's absence, he arranged for him to take part in military exercises. The Duke had often said that he wanted nothing more than to acquire the self-discipline and skills of a consummate soldier and to distinguish himself in battle so as to earn the recognition of imperial troops. In August, for his mother's saint's day, he sent sincerest wishes with all the filial affection and deepest gratitude which his heart bore her, telling her that her family were in anguish, knowing her to be in pain. The Palace of Schönbrunn was resplendent, suffering only from her absence.

As time advanced, the Duke railed against his lack of freedom. Count Dietrichstein, expressed his exasperation to Marie-Louise that Metternich had not yet come to consult him about the Duke's emancipation, despite his fifteen years of dedication to the Duke's education. Time was running short and funds were necessary for the preparation of his household, horses, carriages, crockery, linen and staff if it was to take place in September, as the Duke hoped. While the Count tried to pin down Metternich, the Duke buried himself in books. By the summer of 1830, he had already accrued, read and annotated a library of over one thousand one hundred volumes, all on the wars of the previous thirty years and about his father. He knew more about this period than virtually anyone who had lived through it. Self-confident, modest and self-deprecating, he was a credit to the illustrious name he was not permitted to use.

The following spring, the Duke begged his mother to let him embark upon his military career in Prague with Gustav, from whom he feared to be separated forever. "Would you not be thrilled, dear Mama, to tighten the ties which bind us?...We will look after each other and restrain each other from taking any step which might lead to a precipice."[10] Desirous of accommodating his grandson's wishes, the Emperor arranged for a house to be prepared for him in barracks on the Neustadt in Prague.

The Count raised two objections. Gustav, though much loved, frequented a crowd given over to levity and extravagance which might corrupt the Duke. More importantly, it seemed contrary to good sense to send him away from the safety and international social environment of the Austrian capital. In these turbulent times, the security arrangements demanded by the Duke's slightest movement would make the boys' lives a misery. The Duke should remain in Vienna. Metternich's lack of objection to the plan only increased Count Dietrichstein's suspicions that he wanted to see the Duke diminished, consigned to a political backwater. The Count made lengthy representations to the Emperor to this effect. Reluctantly, Marie-Louise withheld her consent to her son's request.

Gustav ignored Count Dietrichstein's instructions not to speak of Albertina and Wilhelm to the Duke. Marie-Louise could have hoped for no better intermediary on this subject. Albertina and Wilhelm loved their four Neipperg half-brothers. All six children regarded each other as siblings, holding each other in great affection, sharing a wonderful sense of humour and fun, and exchanging amusing anecdotes. Mature beyond his years, the Duke reassured his mother that he adored her still.

Marie-Louise was reunited with her son for the first time after in the city of Graz the painful revelations in the summer of 1830.

"Mama, my blood craves war: only arms can make me happy. You can launch me into the world. It is true that I am not Socrates, but I have reflected maturely on my situation. I believe I have taken stock and seeing things for what they are, have taken the firm decision to exert myself to be a great statesman."[11] He knew what skills he lacked and wanted his mother to select an officer, superior to him in every respect, who could invest him with them. He wanted this individual to introduce him into society.

Fortuitously, Count Anton Prokesch von Osten had just returned to Graz, the theatre of his earliest youth as he described it, after six years. Having spent over a decade fighting the French, he had derided the abominable behaviour and mediocrity of Napoleon's conquerors and had published a paper in 1818 condemning the degrading treatment of him. Finding plenty to admire in the fallen emperor, he lamented the regression of restoration. Over the previous six years, he had assisted in the struggle for Greek independence. The western powers had given official recognition to the new nation four months earlier and had resolved to provide it with a ruler.

Marie-Louise and her father summoned Prokesch to lunch, hopeful that this known admirer of Napoleon could become the Duke's mentor. They and Archduke Johann, the Duke of Reichstadt, Count Dietrichstein and Werklein were excited to meet this major celebrity. Marie-Louise seated herself opposite Prokesch and her son next to him.

Since boarding ship at Trieste in 1824, Prokesch had crossed the seas of the Levant to the Balkans, to Greece, to Constantinople, Syria, Egypt and Nubia and had become a leading authority on the Hellenic question, on Middle Eastern languages, cultures and orientalism. The imperial company at lunch was enraptured. He had recently conducted negotiations between the Viceroy of Egypt and the Sultan of the Ottoman Empire, had arranged an exchange of prisoners between Egypt and Greece, and had implemented in Palestine a project to rid the sea of pirates enabling the resumption of maritime trade. A brilliant soldier, he was also a solid scholar who had absorbed the spiritual and intellectual life of the Middle East. An erudite luminary, his social circle included Schiller, Goethe, Beethoven, Grillparzer and Schubert. Marie-Louise sat quietly observing her son's intelligent demeanour. Self-possessed, he kept a calm, guarded silence.

Lunch lasted a lot longer than usual, no-one more reluctant to let their guest go than the Duke of Reichstadt, who had already translated Prokesch's paper of 1818 into French and Italian.

Prokesch was equally taken with the Duke, whom he believed possessed the qualities to be the leader of a nation in the tradition of religious enlightened autocracy set by Marie-Louise's great-uncle Joseph II. The boy had many of his father's talents, strategic judgment, accuracy in his assessments, extraordinary technical academic knowledge of recent military history, largely self-taught from the books Marie-Louise had insisted he be permitted. All he lacked was experience.

Marie-Louise was relaxing with her father some days later between the merry-go-round of religious ceremonies, reviews and parades, when Prokesch, whose time was now monopolized by her son, came to her with a proposal that the Duke's name be put forward for the Greek throne. "I have cast about for other candidates, but I confess that there is no-one more worthy than the son of Napoleon and your Imperial Highness to fill it."

Traditionally supporters of the Turks as important counterweight to the Russians, Marie-Louise and the Emperor favoured this idea and allowed his name to be put forward. They were too late; a Bavarian had already been selected. The Duke would have to set his sights on another vacant seat. Never forgetting his father, he coveted most of all the French throne. Prokesch obtained the French newspapers which the Duke read avidly in the privacy of his own room. He was encouraged by the call in the French Chamber of Deputies for his father's remains to be returned from St Helena to France, for the reinstatement of his father's statue at the top of the column in the Place Vendôme, and for abrogation of the law barring all Bonapartes from France. Even his grandfather was not against the project. Marie-Louise, her father and the Duke went out to watch a fireworks display. Suddenly a cry went up followed by an immense chorus: "Long live the young Napoleon!"

Marie-Louise was with the Duke when Vienna learnt that King Charles X, who had succeeded Louis XVIII five years earlier, had been forced off the French throne by revolutionaries in Paris. He ordered an immediate suspension of freedom of the press, severely limited voting rights and prorogued the government indefinitely. The public ignored him. French newspapers flouted the King's edicts, confounding him and sowing the seeds of republican political unity in his former subjects. The successful struggle for Greek independence had taught the ordinary man that the ancient concept and dream of democracy was still achievable. There was no doubt as riots spread throughout France and beyond its borders to other European countries that Bourbons, Habsburgs, Romanovs and lesser regal dynasties were all sitting on an erupting volcano. Marie-Louise received an anonymous letter purporting to speak on behalf of two million similarly minded Frenchmen seeking the reestablishment of the Empire addressing her as Empress of the French, the mother of her legitimate son Napoleon II.

"I beg you to intercede with Your August Son to get him to come with His great Sword, to vanquish tyranny."[12] The writer apologized for hiding his identity, revelation of which would mean certain death.

"All you have to do is to appear on the bridge at Strasbourg and it will all be over for the Orléans: but be cautious, there is no hurry," the Emperor told his adoring grandson. From the age of three, Emperor Francis had spent more time with him than with anyone else. The Duke had played with his toys in a corner of his grandfather's study, while the Emperor attended to the business of the day and often lunched with him. From time to time, the Duke accompanied him in his open carriage around the city, and throughout the years on trips within his Bohemian territories. Nonetheless, every moment of the day the Duke's thoughts were with his father.

Prokesch's chance meeting in Egypt with one of Napoleon's former colonels who had accompanied Marie-Louise and the King of Rome from Paris to Blois prompted memories, which the Duke longed to revisit. The Duke listened, spellbound, to Prokesch's retelling of the flight from France. Every person with whom his father had ever had contact was a rich seam of anecdotes about the legend he longed to mine. Prokesch thought it high time Napoleon's son be given access to men of distinction and to diplomatic circles and other salons of consequence frequented by international society.

Napoleon's assessment that the only party his son should fear was that of the Duke of Orléans proved correct. When rebels in Paris had tried to raise the tricolor flag at the Hôtel de Ville in July 1830, royal troops meted out fierce reprisals. Within hours, over two hundred people were dead, their bodies strewn over the cobblestones. By the time the uprising was over, a thousand Frenchmen had been killed by the Bourbon army, and over four thousand five hundred had been wounded. Following the ejection of Bourbon Charles X, Louis-Philippe, the Duke of Orléans, was appointed the constitutional Citizen King of France. Marie-Louise's maternal aunt Maria Amalia, wife of the new king of the French, wrote to her niece, "My beloved husband has sacrificed himself to save France and Europe and all his efforts are aimed at maintaining order and peace."[13] France was not yet ripe for a Bonaparte.

NINETEEN

Challenge to sovereignty in the Central Italian States, 1831

Always appreciative of cultural developments, Marie-Louise tried to keep abreast of new compositions and productions of opera and theatre staged abroad, and particularly those originating in Paris. She lavished money and time on productions, and arranged for her opera company and orchestra to go on tour throughout the Italian peninsula when she was away from her ducal seat. She was proud of the fact that her theatre was on the circuit of Europe's most illustrious composers and performers.

On her journeys to and from Austria, she attended the theatres and opera houses that lay along her route, and once in Austria, took full advantage of the cultural offering. In the summer of 1830, it was a great joy to have her firstborn accompany her to see Bellini's *La Straniera* and Daniel Auber's *La Muette dei Portici* at Graz's intimate, gracious Italianate theatre.

The demand for change promised by revolution, and which might present an opening for her son, found itself reflected in the compositions of the day. A performance in Brussels of Auber's opera, set in an uprising of commoners against tyrannical Bourbons in Naples in 1647, so incited its spectators that, by way of applause, they stormed the government buildings. In the public gardens of Venice, Marie-Louise attended a play entitled the *Siege of Missolonghi* portraying the Greek fight against Ottoman oppression: the parallels with her own society were not hard to find.

Marie-Louise found the music of Gioacchino Rossini, Neipperg's good friend ever since the Verona Congress in 1822, fresh, touching and evocative. She was particularly fond of Rossini's *Maometto*

Secondo (later revised to form the *Siège de Corinthe*, celebrating the courage of Greek patriots), which resonated with her: the tale of a woman who courageously puts self-sacrifice and patriotic duty before her love for a foreigner and enemy. The allegorical tale of struggle for freedom was also played out in *Moses in Egypt*, extremely well received at her ducal theatre in Piacenza. Having corresponded at length with Neipperg about its formulation, Gioacchino Rossini had wanted in 1823 to bring *William Tell*, his provocative tale of triumph over brutal Austrian authority, to Parma as homage to the merciful Duchess, but had dropped the idea after its poor reception in Paris. With refrains such as "Independence or death!", it was celebrated by the public in the new political climate as a masterpiece.

In Modena and Bologna, public performances were interrupted frequently by cries of "Long live Italian Independence" or "Death to spies!" or "Send the Jesuits home!" and by demands to play the March from the third act of Donizetti's *Esiliati in Siberia* or part of the chorus from Mercadante's *Donna Caritea*, both of which had become recognized though unofficial national anthems.

But it was what was happening off-stage in Paris that was creating the real drama in the Italian peninsula. Italians in exile hoped that King Louis-Philippe would be prepared to support insurrection of the entire Italian peninsula. Potential candidates for constitutional sovereign of a unified Italy were Charles Albert of the Kingdom of Piedmont-Sardinia, the son of Eugène de Beauharnais, and Marie-Louise's son, the Duke of Reichstadt. Unbeknown to her, her cousin, the Duke of Modena, who less than ten years earlier had been terrorizing and executing liberals on the remotest pretexts, had changed his tune. Whilst fawning over Metternich, who refused to allow him to recognise the new French king, he had decided to try to exploit international sympathy for the Greek struggle to expand his small territory across the central part of the peninsula.

The tidal wave of revolution was unstoppable. Across Europe,

CHALLENGE TO SOVEREIGNTY

from Belgium to Poland, to Switzerland, to various states in Germany, the pandemic spread. Within two months of the Belgian rising, the country declared independence. William of Orange's heavy-handed attempts at suppression had achieved nothing. The *Allgemeine Zeitung* reported that several towns in Belgium had nominated potential sovereigns, including the Duke of Reichstadt, referred to as Napoleon II. In November at the London Conference, England and France gave their unqualified support for the new state, making a stand against Austria, Russia and Prussia for the first time since the end of the Napoleonic wars. Rumours were rife that Metternich himself, mastermind of post-Napoleonic Europe, would be sent to live out his days in retirement, so out of touch was he with public sentiment.

Symbols of patriotism and foreign oppression were everywhere and unmistakeable. Poetry and novels stirred international sympathies. As ten years earlier, the Duchess of Parma denied the existence of sects and internal strife, emphasising to the outside world the harmony within her duchies. This time, she would not be able to keep up the front. When she returned to Parma, the tension was palpable.

Unpleasant rumours began to circulate following physics Professor Melloni's lecture at the University of Parma in November. His praise of the courage of those who had barricaded Paris and exhortation to his students to subordinate their love of life to love of their homeland had started a riot. Forced to resign, he and his student followers were briefly imprisoned. Dr. Giacomo Tommasini, well-known clinical doctor much admired by the Duchess, had opened his lecture in similar vein. The professor of theology had refused to give his inaugural lecture for the academic year in Latin, pronouncing in Italian, an act of disobedience earning him two months' suspension and forfeit of salary. Dictates from Vienna demanded the closure of Parma's university. Count Dietrichstein wrote to congratulate her: "I am pleased that Your Majesty has contained the mutinies at the university – justice and firmness – that is what is needed.... It is pitiable for, at bottom, everything is reduced to a heap of rogues in Paris and Brussels who should be hung."[1]

By December 1830, fuelled by the rapid results achieved by Belgium, nuclei of revolutionary activity had been established in Bologna, Parma, Mantua and Romagna. The mantra "independence, union and liberty" worked its way across the central states. The preponderant faction, proclaiming the compatibility of revolutionary ideals with Catholicism, aimed to achieve by insurrection representative constitutional monarchy, the sovereign to be selected by a national congress to be convened in the peninsula's true capital, Rome.

Seizing what he perceived to be his opportunity, the Duke of Modena presented his candidacy, through discreet channels, as representative monarch of a united. His offer was accepted by the leaders of the movement, working out of London.

Revolt started in Rome, led by Marie-Louise's Bonaparte nephews, Hortense's sons, who headed patriotic battalions marching through the Romagna, Ferrara and Modena waving the red, green and white flag of Italian unity which Napoleon had created, invoked his name to rouse the people to insurgency. The governments of Modena, Reggio and Bologna, without any Austrian military support, instantly collapsed. Revolution spread quickly from the central states to the Marches and Umbria, reflecting the general political discontent beyond Marie-Louise's borders. These states amalgamated and declared themselves a government of the United Provinces, their provisional governments supported by troops led by the well-known Napoleonic General Zucchi. Repression in the Papal States was so swift, brutal and merciless that Austria, this time in concert with England, France, Russia, Prussia and Piedmont-Sardinia clamoured by means of a stiff memorandum to the Pope proposing moderate administrative reforms which was immediately refused. Only Tuscany, a state governed by Marie-Louise's cousin in the spirit of enlightenment, seemed to be spared any political turmoil.

The atmosphere at the Parman court was tense. Marie-Louise

and her close advisers were well aware that officials, employees, even the government could not be counted on for their loyalty. Whistles and booing at her theatre made her feel dejected and unwelcome but she would not be cowed.

In early February, news arrived in Parma from Modena's provisional government: "Italians! The people are the masters, and the King of Italy exists. The blood of the immortal Napoleon, a beacon to the majority of the population inspires us to pursue his cause. At the first report of cannon, crush Austrian tyranny, and deliver us from the barbarians!"

The rebels seemed conveniently to have forgotten the misery the former French Emperor had visited upon them. The legend cooked up by the late Prisoner of St Helena was beginning to take hold. Outside the gates of Marie-Louise's ducal palace, there was general euphoria, heightened by the festivities preceding Lent, at the recent developments in Modena and Bologna. It seemed only a matter of time before the rebels' military leader, the Napoleonic General Zucchi, came marching through Parma with his revolutionary troops.

Breaching the barricades blocking the road from Modena, a courier brought an announcement demanding that citizens rise up against their vile oppressor and against moderate liberals. Scuffles broke out in the squares around the palace walls between moderates and extremists. Word was out that an immense revolt backed by the French was scheduled for 10 February 1831, the last Thursday before Lent, to start at the Ducal Theatre. That evening, the Duchess and her courtiers tried to maintain a light-hearted exterior as they rehearsed a play. Marie-Louise participated in these little dramas which, she confessed to Victoria de Crenneville, she found tiresome, having to stick things out to the end and then give insincere, undeserved compliments.

The following day, more people than usual could be seen congregating in the streets. Towards evening, members of the public were heard to be hurling insults against Austrian government officials.

Shots had been fired and a court chamberlain injured. Marie-Louise had no intention of abandoning her duchies – this, she knew, might be fatal. But she could move closer to the Austrian garrison at her other ducal seat who would protect her and her family. She sent an emissary to Piacenza, which remained quiet, to have the few remaining Austrian troops ready to intervene. Far too dangerous to risk making directly for Piacenza along the Via Emilia, four hours' carriage ride from Parma, Marie-Louise made secret preparations to withdraw from the capital to Casalmaggiore on the southern bank of the River Po.

From the courtyard of the Palazzo della Pilotta, directly outside her palace, Marie-Louise could hear angry shrieks. She asked Baron Werklein, her chief administrator since Neipperg's death, to go on to the balcony and to tell her what was being said. He returned a few moments later white as a sheet. He tried to act dismissively, immediately issuing orders that shops shut at seven in the evening and that the gates to the city be closed. He also issued a decree making it illegal to circulate in groups of more than four at any one time.

"Death to Werklein, death to Amelin!" A pistol- or rifle-shot rang out aimed at one of the Ducal dragoons, terrifying everyone. Then nothing. No-one could sleep though the night passed peacefully. Some time before Neipperg's death, Marie-Louise had received a death threat which upon investigation had revealed a plot to assassinate her, allegedly on behalf of leading citizens. Marie-Louise was taking no chances. At around four or five in the morning, the Duchess roused her children to prepare for imminent departure. Keeping her plans from her household staff, she had the children smuggled out of their rooms through the windows and down a rope into the little garden below, from where they could tiptoe to carriages in the courtyard of the Pilotta. There, the children waited patiently from the small hours until late in the day.

Midday on Sunday, word got out of the Duchess's plans. A citizen's delegation came to beg her to stay and to agree to a constitution. Convening an emergency Council of State, Marie-Louise entrusted her government to her ministers and made formal protest. She called for the issue of a decree reasserting her rule, but confusion impeded its publication. Then she made for her carriage in the courtyard of her Ducal Palace. Throngs of Parmans tried to get in her way, clamouring for her to stay.

"Long live our Sovereign, Duchess Marie-Louise!" Cries for Werklein's death, and the sea of tricornered hats like the one her first husband had worn, were not encouraging. Someone stepped forward: "Some of the members of the provisional government are in favour of Her Majesty's departure and will ensure that her passage out of Parma will be untroubled."

Marie-Louise announced that she would regard herself as imprisoned for as long as people sought to impose conditions upon her tenure. She regarded herself, as did her father and grandfather, as guardian of solid structures and traditions, the only change permissible that for the improvement of the lives of her subjects. The ability and opportunity to rule was a gift which had been handed down to her over the centuries. Her duty as ruler overrode all others, taking precedence over the births and deaths even of her own loved ones. This precision tool was something which could only be used by those who understood its worth, and the importance of dedication and continuity. To place the tool, either by design or under duress, in the hands of inexperience was to invite disaster, and accordingly the height of irresponsibility. In one of her green notebooks, Marie-Louise noted,

"It is essential that the people do not direct anything, but it is also essential that the people are persuaded that great account has been taken of them and that whilst their concurrence is not needed, their suffrage is always keenly desired."

As the winter sun waned, Marie-Louise mounted her carriage, her post-horses harnessed, ready along with her regiment, two cannons at their head. Her loyal ministers and household were to follow in convoy. Somebody came running in, breathlessly reporting that one of the main gates of the city had been barricaded. A loud hubbub began and members of the public tried to unharness the horses. The great square outside the palace was thronged with crowds shouting incessantly at the top of their voices, "Long live Marie-Louise!" More cries of "Death to Werklein", no less insistent, were also clearly audible. Baron Cornacchia, Marie-Louise's minister of the interior, appeared on the ducal balcony to try and calm people down, saying that the Duchess would stay, but his voice was stifled by the crowd as they demanded that she also appear at the balcony. A few minutes later, Marie-Louise, came forward, erect and resolute. The crowds went wild, shedding tears of joy and embracing each other. Albertina and Wilhelm were told to return home.

Within minutes, the crowd had relieved the soldiers of the arms to which they had been clinging for the past forty-eight hours. Marie-Louise watched in dismay as leading members of her guard yielded ostentatiously to the people who declared their own national guard, and made to seize control of the gates of the city. As arms were transferred, a gradual shift was perceptible. Marie-Louise realized that a few grenadiers who were guarding the entrance to her private apartments within the palace were all that remained to her. Suddenly, she heard angry voices getting louder. Members of the public were mounting her staircase, intent on gaining entry into her private rooms. Cornacchia and the grenadiers ran to the landing and, barring their entry, masterfully persuaded the crowd to return down the staircase and out into the street. Marie-Louise was shaking, the events reminiscent of the early days of the French Revolution. She flung her arms around Albertina and Wilhelm, who watched wide-eyed as Werklein sputtered fitfully that the crowd were out to get him, baying for his blood. It seemed that the crowd intended to re-enact the story of William Tell: the murder of an Austrian governor heralding liberation.

Marie-Louise orchestrated Werklein's escape, taking charge of his little daughter, Marie, until she could be reunited with her father. He slipped out through the public library, down to the court stables bordering the Parma Torrent. Disguised in a footman's habit, he and Lieutenant Colonel Rossi, also disliked by the Parmans, mounted hastily tacked horses, galloping hell-for-leather towards Colorno. Rebels caught sight of them and set out in pursuit. Werklein and Rossi risked their necks, ducking and diving over hedges and stone walls to avoid the rifle shots.

Marie-Louise decided to delay her departure, hoping for a gesture of *rapprochement*, not daring to venture out beyond the palace walls. Throughout the night, she discussed her next steps with her courtiers. Through her windows floated the tunes of French marches. Peeping through the shutters, she could see the tricolour flag floating in the breeze, her subjects sporting with pride the cockade retrieved from the cupboard in which it had languished these past fifteen years, against the backdrop of buildings usually dark at night, but now flooded with light. Rebels were abroad, kicking in doors of homes that did not signal their support by burning midnight oil. Unaware of Werklein's escape, the rabble had laid siege to his apartments. A lone drunkard shouting "To arms!" from the courtyard startled the few gathered together in the ducal palace.

The following morning, the Duchess of Parma was informed that her subjects, including her own dignitaries, mistakenly believed that it was she who had authorized everyone to wear the tricolour cockade. Parman survivors of the French Emperor's campaigns remembered their days of youthful stamina and passion through a rose-tinted haze. Others took immense pride in the fact that they had been prefects, or sub-prefects or counsellors to prefects, when Parma had been the French *Département of the Taro*. Marie-Louise received anonymous notes warning her that she would have been chased away had she not been the mother of the heir whom the authors wished to see king of their new kingdom. It was agreed that her courtier, the Prince Meli Lupi di Soragna, a former known loyal supporter of Napoleon, would take responsibility for having ordered the wearing of the highly symbolic tricornered hat. To avoid complicating her situation, she declared that she would neither positively prohibit its wear of the tricornered hat, nor authorize its introduction. Nor would she censure members of her household who wore it for their own safety.

Marie-Louise could not ignore the fact that her government had vanished, its place taken by a provisional facsimile not conforming to the orders she had given for administration in her government's absence. However, she could not deny that its members were not self-interested, power-crazed warmongers but eminent public-spirited men of considerable experience, committed to the general welfare, many of whom she had stoutly defended to Vienna a decade earlier. She had been on excellent terms with them.

Count Jacopo Sanvitale, elected to be a member of the provisional government, set to work issuing liberal edicts, including those relating to freedom of the press and of expression. He had already circulated widely the *Eccletico* newspaper which he had launched two years earlier to keep Parmans abreast of recent revolutions elsewhere and to prepare Parmans for a war he thought inevitable to secure the liberties being currently implemented. The newspaper, printed on blue paper, was based on eponymous patriotic precursors in other cities and formatted along the same lines. The provisional Parman government invited General Zucchi to take charge of the military. Jacopo and his wife hoisted the flag of revolution over the Ducal Theatre after nailing to the walls around Parma a notice inviting the youth to join the new battalions of *bersaglieri* and infantry under General Zucchi's command.

Well aware that Austrian and Bourbon troops were waiting to pounce, Marie-Louise had to act with caution to try and bring her subjects to heel herself. She wanted none of the carnage in her duchies which had occurred in Paris barely seven months earlier. She hoped that the Parmans would soon realize that they had little in common with the revolutionaries whose rulers persisted in unenlightened absolutism.

Marie-Louise woke on the Monday to find the situation unchanged. With no government and no army, she was powerless. That night, at one o'clock, Marie-Louise gathered Albertina and Wilhelm and the few remaining members of her court. The party set out like fugitives across spectral fields in the dead of night under escort led by Michele Varron, the Piedmontese general who had served under Napoleon and lent Marie-Louise the Rocca di Sala, where she had received news of Napoleon's death. A company of her loyal grenadiers, accompanied by wives and children, had preceded her to give her safe passage. They were only on loan this time. Marie-Louise had given her word of honour that she would send them back to Parma once she had reached the river crossing. When the grenadiers received the order to turn back, they stood wiping tears from their eyes on the Po riverbank, shouting in hoarse voices, "Long live Marie-Louise!" Rifle shots shook everyone to the core.

In addition to five of Marie-Louise's ministers, her chamberlain, Count Luigi Sanvitale, cousin of Jacopo and son of the Count Stefano who had received and served Napoleon before her, remained too. Affection had blossomed between this cultured, level-headed young man and Marie-Louise's fourteen-year-old daughter, who was fast becoming ripe for coupling. At Colorno, Marie-Louise's escort Josèphe Ugolotti, head of the National Guard, transferred the Duchess and her party into the care of an Austrian battalion which would accompany them to Cremona and on to Piacenza. Marie-Louise arrived once more at the river Po, this time to warm acclamations. She found that the locals, following the example in Parma and in Guastalla, had set up a provisional government but, anticipating her imminent arrival, had inaugurated it in her name.

From the Mandelli Palace, Marie-Louise announced that her government seat would be located, for the time being, in Piacenza, an ideal vantage point from which to communicate with Parma and sit out events until return there was possible. She was not prepared either to leave, to wait while the Parman provisional government made preparations for war or to invite in foreign troops, as her late grandfather had done before her from his seat in Naples. She missed her beloved consort more than ever in these trying times, sure that matters would never have deteriorated to this point were he still alive.

Vienna, at least, was pleased with her conduct. Metternich congratulated her, adding, "The world is sick indeed! The crisis is frightening ... the source [of the evil] is on both sides of the Channel; it would be hard for me to decide whether it is in Paris or London that the Revolution is served with the greatest zeal ... "[2] Count Dietrichstein also congratulated her: "As soon as we heard from Count Metternich of your arrival in Casalmaggiore, I and the Prince [the Duke of Reichstadt] were drunk with joy! Your Majesty conducted herself as a worthy daughter of Maria Theresa the Immortal!"[3] In his own letter, her firstborn wrote, "My grandfather refers to your conduct during the course of recent events with glory, and he radiates with joy talking to me of a mother whom I have certainly always adored but of whom I am even more proud."

Marie-Louise sent long letters reporting developments to her father and to Metternich. No-one could be sure whether the Revolution was served with the greatest zeal in France or across the Channel in England, where political unrest threatened to unseat government. Archduchess Sophie, nursing her child, the future Emperor Franz-Josef, pregnant with her second child, the future Emperor Maximilian of Mexico, wrote to Marie-Louise: "Shooting the perpetrators of the disturbances in Italy would be far too good for them ... I have no pity for these wicked subjects."[4]

There were calls in the French press for the Austrians and their appointees to get out of the Italian peninsula, to which it was said they had absolutely no right. Austria had been able for the past fifteen years to march into it without hindrance, but from now on it would have to be careful not to provoke France's wrath and facilitate a French entry onto the scene as liberators. According to Rothschild, Bonapartists and Lafayette's men were using French money and emissaries to support revolutions on the Italian peninsula. Heavily involved in negotiations behind the scenes to try to mitigate the destabilising impact of insurrection in the Central Italian States,

Salomon Rothschild impressed upon the French that France, despite its idealism, had to recognize that it would not be in French interests to see the whole of Europe dissolve into anarchy. All Emperor Francis wanted was a stable government in France, and his daughter back in her seat and peace in the country. Neither she nor her son could be held to ransom by Bonapartists. Revolution, like war, was a scourge which would bring about ruin for generations. No ruler Rothschild could think of had governed with such benevolence and popularity as Marie-Louise, and yet she had been chased away. He was astonished at how unappreciative people could be. Once more, war and peace depended on France.

Unprovoked, an Austrian corps had attacked members of Parma's new National Guard, one of whom had been killed at the town of Fiorenzuola, and had taken prisoners whom they led back to Piacenza. In retaliation, Parma's provisional government had taken several hostages, including Bishop Neuschel, Marie-Louise's confessor, and the youngest son of Marie-Louise's President Mistrali. These events notwithstanding, Marie-Louise felt encouraged by the stream of army personnel and officials who made their way to Piacenza pleading to be readmitted to their former positions.

As the Duchess of Parma corresponded with her ministers from afar, she was told of public grievances in her duchies. The provisional government accused her administration of having sold a considerable part of its wealth and having indebted the state well beyond its means. It was true that assets had been sold, but the state's liquidity, an on-going sore, had thereby been eased after the extensive construction projects she had completed which had dramatically increased employment and welfare within her duchies.

It emerged that, without her consent over the course of two years, Werklein had abandoned in gradual, imperceptible steps the laissez-faire policy favoured by Marie-Louise, implemented by Neipperg and highly prized by the Parmans, encouraging the police to increase surveillance and intervention, and turning a blind eye to corrupt practices. The majority in sympathy with the patriots saw immediately that he would have to be evicted.

Neipperg had first brought the maths teacher and infantry colonel to Parma, appointing him as Marie-Louise's and Neipperg's private secretary, a post he had occupied for eight years before promotion to her minister of foreign affairs. At Neipperg's death, he had proposed the continuance of a fair and reasonable administrative system which had reassured the Duchess that her second husband's good work would be continued. The crop-sharing arrangements and land division which had remained undisturbed since the middle of the sixteenth century continued to be of mutual benefit to the parties and to the state treasury. There had been no significant unjustified increase in taxation. He was a firm believer in free trade, and in the principle that hospitals should be neutral, treating all injured and sick soldiers irrespective of their race, nationality or creed. It was impossible to root out entirely abuses by petty officials, and in general, the inhabitants were far better off than elsewhere in the Italian peninsula. Marie-Louise had thought the Croatian was competent, industrious, intelligent, perhaps rather severe but fair, and cognisant of the limits of his remit. However, neither his coarse manner nor his rapid promotion, which many resented, had endeared him to her other courtiers. Having fled Parma in the hope of continuing his services from Piacenza, he found himself hounded out by its citizens. Received warmly by Emperor Francis, he continued to harangue Parman officials to complete his reforms, which comprised handing over the control of local councils to government officials to be able to keep them under closer scrutiny, and demanding the imposition of an immediate tax increase in the Parman duchies to cover the costs of the political unrest for which he blamed the Parmans themselves.

The summons he awaited from Marie-Louise never came. Marie-Louise expressed regret at having to dispense with his services and elevated Werklein's arch-enemy, Cornacchia, a liberal, to President of the Council of State. She rejected and declared inadmissible

Werklein's claim for compensation of ten years' back payment. The disgruntled functionary would finally give up pestering her eight years later, blaming the loyal Mistrali, Marie-Louise's prime minster, for his own failings.

Always taking the opposite side to Werklein in any argument, the liberal Mistrali had not been perfect either, but he had earned Marie-Louise's sympathies through his loyalty. Neipperg had had to pull up him up more than once for having been over-zealous in the performance of his duties, but Mistrali was far too able and enlightened a politician to relinquish. Mistrali had served Napoleon as secretary to the Mayor of Parma, and had occupied other responsible positions, gaining Napoleon's respect to the degree that he had written to Mistrali after his escape from Elba to say that he was counting upon him. He kept as far as possible the best aspects of French administration, and equitable division of taxes, dividing the duchies into two, Parma and Guastalla assigned to Mistrali, Piacenza assigned to Cornacchia. The stance of men like Mistrali had facilitated the pursuance by Marie-Louise of permissive, lenient policies. Accommodating his foibles seemed a small price to pay.

News from abroad did not give the Duchess of Parma any comfort. Modena's provisional government publicised its abolition of personal taxation for the poor and cancellation of pledges, measures bound to increase public support. When the new king of Belgium, Prince Leopold of Saxe-Coburg, called upon England and France for assistance as a disgruntled William II of the Netherlands demanded the return of his former territories, France, despite the policy of non-intervention in the internal affairs of other countries declared by its Citizen King, marched in as guarantor of the fledgling state's independence, ending Holland's claim on Belgium. Italian patriots exhorted each other to be daring, confident that the same French bayonets which had proved the salvation of the Belgians would protect a new birth in the Italian peninsula.

News that Austrian troops, led by General Frimont, were on their way, regrettable though the need for them was, came as a great relief to Marie-Louise. General Frimont had put down the riots of 1821 in Naples: the revolutionaries stood no chance. In the first week of March, Austrian troops reached and occupied Ferrara. Two weeks later, Bologna capitulated. In the second week of March, members of the provisional government of the recently proclaimed United Italian Provinces fled to Ancona and boarded ship in the hope of finding refuge on Greek shores. Their ship was intercepted by an Austrian vessel under the command of Admiral Bandiera, father of two idealistic, impressionable young men whose summary execution thirteen years later would attract broad international sympathy to the nationalist cause.

As, predictably, the Duke of Modena abandoned the cause of Italian unity, Parma's provisional government sent a deputation to announce to the Duchess that the city submitted itself to her orders. Marie-Louise accepted the provisional government's surrender and appointed Mistrali Extraordinary Commissioner to re-establish the working interim administration. By the time Austrian troops and Mistrali arrived in Parma, neither meeting with any resistance, the most prominent members of the provisional government had fled, making their way to the port of Genoa to board ship.

"They want me in Parma very much," the Duchess wrote to Victoria de Crenneville. "They say that the city is terribly sad and practically empty. I am sure that it will take years to recover from recent events, so many people compromised, so many families in trouble. Despite this, I shall be glad to return. The cares and worries are the price I pay willingly for my independent existence and a home, even though I miss my homeland."[5]

There was much jubilation when Marie-Louise finally made her entry into the city on a hot summer's day in the second week of August. The truth was that Parmans, who turned out in large numbers to receive her in respectful silence, had had no appetite for rebellion against Marie-Louise's administration. The civil delegation formed at Marie-Louise's departure went to visit her expressly to nominate members of the provisional government over which they wanted her to preside. The Parman public resented the confusion caused and wasted resources expended by a provisional administration which they had never sought, which had never dared to make any formal declaration of the cessation of Marie-Louise's regime and had only lasted for a short twenty-five days. The majority of Parmans worshipped Marie-Louise. And they wanted her back. The militant radicals, the small minority who had pushed her out, circulated leaflets threatening "those vile people, whether rich or poor" who dared to applaud her re-entry into the capital.

Attempts to reassure Marie-Louise that she had never really been threatened by popular rebellion were not wholly convincing. The episode had scared the living daylights out of her. The illuminations, the acclamations when she entered her theatre to hear a special cantata performing *'The Time of Clemency'*, and the continuous receptions did nothing to set her mind at rest. It was clear that some Parmans were less than pleased with the way events had turned out. She noticed a new insolence in the city as her carriage passed in the street, men no longer doffing their hats. "Beneath the ashes, a flame still glows. People's attitude of mind is poor," she wrote to Victoria de Crenneville. "Reforms only produce emigrants who return later,"[6] Count Dietrichstein wrote to Marie-Louise. When two miscreants tried to disturb performances in her theatre by directing obscenities at the royal box, security was stepped up, and content came under close scrutiny. Marie-Louise regularly requested elimination of "tedious" arias and vetoed disagreeable performers. She axed the entire production of Donizetti's *Alina Regina di Golconda*, which told the tale of a princess taken captive and married off against her will to an elderly king who leaves her a widow. A Frenchman with whom she had fallen in love previously comes to fight her other suitor and restores her on the French throne. She is moved by the love shown her by the French nation. The themes were more than tedious.

Beyond the city, Marie-Louise was met with greater bonhomie and affection. Most of the rural population had stood firm for the

Duchess throughout. It was a great relief to retire to the Palace of Sala where she could breathe more easily, far from malicious gossip. Nonetheless, it was clear that they hated the Austrians and regarded her as a special case, at least for the time being. Disgusted by men and life, she no longer felt at home in her ducal seat, she confessed sadly.

"Even the sky is horrible. Do you have every evening these dreadful zodiacal aurora, and the sun so pale and shrouded in mists that it only shows on the horizon as a globe without any rays, quite pale and exactly like a full moon?" she asked Victoria de Crenneville.

Trials of the revolutionaries were instigated in Bologna and Modena. The Duke of Modena showed no mercy, despite his covert support of the plan which had gone disastrously wrong from his perspective. Ciro Menotti, the resolute leader of the Modenese provisional government, was hanged and others executed in public following summary judgment. Thousands of Modenesi were exiled. General Zucchi was sentenced to death, the conviction later commuted to life imprisonment. Emperor Francis enjoined Marie-Louise to place her trusted ministers Mistrali, Cornacchia, Bianchi and Ferrari under investigation. She refused. She also refused to carry out an investigation into the origins of the unrest, knowing that this would only alienate her from her subjects.

The Duke of Modena's actions were only making new martyrs and reinforcing hatred of him and his reign, uniting liberals, Carbonari and exiles in their struggle. In Parma, only two members of the provisional government, Filippo Linati and Francesco Melegari, were arrested. Defending their apparent betrayal of their Duchess, they pleaded that they had had no choice but to defect to the substitute administration after Marie-Louise's departure. As unappealing as such claims were, Marie-Louise encouraged remaining members of the provisional government and her Guard of Honour to leave her duchies quietly before Vienna demanded that she purge them.

Marie-Louise was wounded after the trust she had placed in her subjects and the benevolence she had bestowed upon them. She was overworked, sick, distraught at having to dismiss people who had worked for her faithfully for years, reduced to begging former employees who wished to retire to a quiet life to resume their former duties with her. She felt disgusted with the unequalled cowardice she had witnessed and wanted to run away.

"All is changed and ruined!" With the Austrian troops came Austrian administrators to clean up the mess following the revolt. Baron Mareschall, appointed by Metternich as Werklein's replacement, seemed rather brusque and soon irritated Marie-Louise by prying more closely into her affairs than was comfortable. He redeemed himself to some degree by the fact that he had served as Austrian Ambassador to Brazil from 1826 and therefore was able to talk to Marie-Louise about her sister's last years. Richer, another Austrian, a captain in the Hussars, arrived as Marie-Louise's new private secretary to complete the supervision. Mistrali feared that these appointments might hamper him in the implementation of a new scheme of general administration which he had prepared upon Werklein's dismissal, but his charm, leniency and moderation won Mareschall over. The duchy had huge debts, largely on account of the expensive projects Marie-Louise had undertaken: the construction of bridges across the Rivers Taro and Trebbia, the opera house, renovation works at the ducal palaces. Marie-Louise had thus far lived out of the funds in her Exchequer. Henceforward she would have to live to a tight budget. Mistrali paid her her civil list and appropriated the remaining revenue to the public exchequer. He reorganized taxation, and reduced the public debt by two thirds, arranging with Marie-Louise that works of public utility would be funded out of her own personal resources.

One of the greatest drains on the Parman treasury was expenditure on ducal travel. It was abundantly clear that by axing her foreign trips, Marie-Louise could make significant savings which could be redirected to the needs of the impoverished, alleviating the deficit. If Marie-Louise wished to avert a state of anarchy, she would have to show solidarity with her subjects by demonstrating that she was not above making sacrifices. For the time being, she must forgo summer trips to Austria and elsewhere and live a frugal life devoted to the Parmans.

TWENTY

Impotent against Metternich's vengeance 1831

The Duke begged his grandfather to let him go to his mother's aid when he heard of the uprising in Parma. It was out of the question. "It is the first time that it has been difficult for me to obey the Emperor's orders," the Duke wrote to his mother, feeling impotent and miserable. Marie-Louise was deeply touched. In the sixteen years since her departure for Parma, she had visited Vienna only six times. Pregnancies, not all brought to term, political troubles and sovereign duties had frustrated many of her planned annual visits. In aggregate, Marie-Louise had spent barely five hundred days with her firstborn. The reality of their separation was stark and cruel.

The adult Duke was irritated that his letters always had to be written anticipating strict censorship and possible interception. He was mortified by the idea that a spy might read his deepest feelings, which he intended to share with his mother. He had plenty of friends, but their friendship was always tainted. Some gave themselves airs and graces associating with him, others expected favours or indulged him allowing him to do whatever he wanted. None of them saw him for the human being he was.

"They only like the conception of their own imagination, of their own illusions," he wrote to his mother.

> The slightest departure from the image they have made of me strips me of their affection. I have many other more mercurial friends, who having sacrificed a good many years to my upbringing, have your ear and have acquired a right to my gratitude and tender esteem. But differences in character and

the habit of such people of treating me like a child prevent me from conferring upon them the unlimited trust, the unburdening of one's heart which does as much good to the recipient as to the giver.

He felt deeply ashamed of the spelling and grammatical mistakes which still hampered his self-expression. A few days after his nineteenth birthday, he wrote,

"I already had my feather in my hand to dedicate to you the first moments of my twentieth year. My heart wants to converse with you all day but I tremble to incur your displeasure by my inveterate mistakes. It is for this reason that I have already torn up five letters which I have written to you."[1]

There were times when he was fed up with his tutors, particularly Count Dietrichstein, who, he seemed to suggest, had gained excessive empire over his mother. She should take his constant maternal concerns with a pinch of salt.

> Thus, it is you only, my dear Mama, to whom I can, I must and I wish to give my entire trust. You, to whom I owe everything since I came into this world, and who has always shown me so much love, even at such moments when my coldness and insensitivity must have hurt a heart as sensitive as yours. Believe that I frequently curse these dreadful errors.

He had often said such things to her before, but wanted to repeat them again. He wanted, once emancipated, to devote a little time each day to speak the language of his heart to her, to she who had only ever asked that he speak frankly with her. He begged her to write to him from time to time, to give him her orders, her counsel. There were times when he had behaved badly and upset her deeply, and she had expressed her hurt by silence. This had hurt him, and he did not want this to happen again. He was confident that she would accede to his request. After all, what greater joy could there be for a mother like his than to be the guardian angel of her son through the channel of love? He begged her to take care of her health after her recent spate of illness. Alfred Neipperg's reports of his lengthy conversations with Marie-Louise reassured the Duke of his mother's deep affection when there were long gaps between her letters.

The Duke wrote again to Marie-Louise from his barracks as soon as he could, following the start of his military career. At long last, he could serve the state, and lead the active life of a soldier. He was pleased with the battalion to which the Emperor had assigned him, over half of which comprised new recruits, with lots of young officers all motivated by the best will in the world. On only his third day, he was invited to command his first parade. The stifling heat and running sweat in spring uniforms could not dent his joy. He was brimming with good health, rising at four in the morning to go out on long exercises on horseback. "If Italy awakens, the Austrians already possess the means to send her back to sleep." he wrote to his mother, looking forward to the wonderful day when he could stand at the head of his own battalion. He still had much to learn: the situation was far more complex.

Marie-Louise asked her son whether he placed his hopes in war. He said he feared nothing more. "In truth, I have the sad presentiment of dying without having received the baptism of fire. I have already made my decision in this terrible event. I will declare in my will that my coffin be brought in the first clash that occurs, so that my soul shall have the consolation of hearing whistling around my bones the projectiles that I have so often desired."

Spirit, heart, duty and honour determined that he never act against the interests of France. In his will, his father had told him that he must never take up arms against France or harm her in any way, that he must adopt his father's motto: "Everything for the French people." He told his mother that in a conflict between Austria and France, his sword would be condemned to rust beside the chimney breast, worn only in squares on parades. "But, thank

God, all that is for now only a chimera and we tremble before another much more terrible peril – before cholera."

The very word "cholera" was terrifying, stirring up visions of the frequent spectacle of death occurring sometimes within hours of infection, of overpopulated isolation hospitals unable to absorb the demand, streets strewn with ravaged bodies and rotting corpses, the latter collected by carts doing daily rounds, the burning and purifying of infected or suspect belongings and correspondence, children dying of neglect when their parents and carers had been carried off. In their neurosis, many jumped to diagnosing it, frightening everyone, the relief immense when they were found to have been mistaken. All known precautions were taken by the Austrian government. Chloride of lime and vinegar were stock-piled, as were pitch, coal-tar, linen and cotton for treatment and burial of the dead. The triple cordon, to the north bordering on Prussia, to the South skirting the Adriatic Sea, established to protect Austria and countries further to the west from Hungary and Poland, which had already been devastated, had proved ineffective. Everyone prayed that the disease was spread by human contact, which could be controlled to a large extent, and not by birds of flight.

Marie-Louise dared not think of the consequences of an outbreak of cholera in her duchies. She awaited the post from Vienna with terrible impatience, terrified for her family, and then barely had the strength to read the contents. Dr. Malfatti advised Emperor Francis and Marie-Louise that the Duke was particularly vulnerable to cholera in the prevailing heat. Her father insisted that he withdraw to the Hofburg.

As riots assailed the Parman duchies, Marie-Louise received letters from the Duke and from Count Dietrichstein about the visits to Vienna of Napoleon's former marshals Marmont and Maison as representatives of the new French administration. Marmont was accused by Bonaparte sympathisers of having betrayed Napoleon by defecting to Austria as the allies laid siege to Paris in 1814.

Metternich had hoped to use Marmont to undermine Napoleon in the eyes of his son. He was disappointed. The Duke met Marmont seventeen times over the course of three months. Marmont had known Napoleon since 1790 and his days at the Dijon military academy. He, more than anyone else, could describe the boy's father in his domestic sphere, on the battlefield, at court and in his administration. The Marshal's reputation went before him, his passage of the Saint Bernard legendary. Cautious on account of Metternich's agenda, the Duke listened avidly, soaking up every detail, pulling up the Marshal when his report clashed with the Duke's own extensive knowledge, though not experience of the facts. Marmont, it seemed, was in awe of the Duke, and asked several times to become his mentor in warfare.

Fired by the advances he had made with Marmont, the Duke was keen to be introduced to another of his father's officers. Marshal Maison held a grand dinner in the Prater where everyone drank to the health of King Louis-Philippe and played *"la Parisienne"* before raising a toast and singing Haydn's *"God Save Emperor Franz"*. Maison quite forgot himself and expressed his regret that Austria had not returned Marie-Louise and her son back to Paris after Napoleon's second abdication, which would have avoided a second Bourbon restoration. The Duke was suspicious of such overtures, Maison having failed to protest against the maintenance by Louis-Philippe's government of the banishment and proscriptions against the Bonapartes.

The Duke still had much to learn about his father's country before he could countenance standing at its head. If his grandfather, the Austrian Emperor, were to die, Prokesch counselled, Austria would have to weather difficult times, providing no lack of opportunity for the Duke to distinguish himself while keeping an eye out for other vacant thrones. One such was that of Poland, "the Boulevard of Europe", as it was known.

It was the Hungarian Ignace Giulay's regiment, quartered in Vienna and to which the Duke was later assigned, which marched into Poland. Absolutist monarchs noted nervously that the leaders of the insurgents were the country's high aristocracy. Alexandre, Napoleon's illegitimate son by Countess Walewska, the Duke's half-brother, was canvassing the French and British governments for support for an independent Poland, the French government having sent him to Warsaw on a secret mission to open discussions with the provisional government there headed by Prince Adam Czartoryski, a well known friend of the Habsburgs. It was known, too, that Hortense, Marie-Louise's former sister-in-law and close friend, had also passed through Paris to London with her second child, Louis-Napoleon, her first having died, and that together they were garnering support for a return to France of Napoleon II, Marie-Louise's son. Newspapers reported that Corsica proclaimed Napoleon II their King. The Duke, raring to step up to what appeared to be an imminent call to power, was crestfallen when Poland fell to Russia. He wanted to give the Russians a good hiding, and send them back into their snows, not by burning powder magazines and stocks of food, relying for triumph not on weather conditions, but on raw courage. He wrote to Marie-Louise,

"No-one talks about Poland any more and of this calm revolution," he wrote. 'What a singular and interesting age! Events which fill centuries have taken place in six months! They want men. I will make it my task to become one."[2] He continued to study to the point of exhaustion late into the night, eating and sleeping little, like his father before him. In idle hours, he abandoned himself to the poetry of Byron and the meditations of Lamartine. The more he studied, the more he was convinced that the repose of true order was safety of property and commerce, a goal worth great sacrifice. He believed in God but not in religion, finding no support or consolation in the Catholic doctrine to which he was born. He told his mother that he would often hear applause while out on the white Arabian mare his mother had bought him, the sabre which his father had used at the Battle of the Pyramids by his side. Zealous of his rank and concomitant privileges, with an overriding sense of honour, he was nonetheless mortified by his title "His Most Serene Highness." His mother was immensely proud of him, the very son of which his father had always dreamed.

Reluctantly, the Duke had retired at his grandfather's request to Schönbrunn as soon as cholera was declared in the city. He felt ashamed at abandoning his regiment at a time of mortal danger. He yearned to return to his military career and wanted to take part in manoeuvres on the Schmelz. Uncharacteristically, Dr. Malfatti forbade it, engaging in a fierce argument with the Duke.

Cholera's first victims seemed to be of the lower classes. But it soon made rapid advances into the leisured classes, devastating countless members of the court, paralyzing government and army. By the middle of September, the Duke's household had joined him in Schönbrunn, cholera having broken out in the barracks. Count Dietrichstein wrote to Marie-Louise expressing concern at the parlous state of the Duke's finances, severely depleted by his selfless generosity in making substantial donations to help cholera's victims and the poor survive the winter.

"The air must be infested by this miasma which appears for no good reason and spares no-one. I cannot list all those who have already fallen victim," wrote Count Dietrichstein. The Duke advised his mother to avoid risk of infection by leading a life of temperance and routine, avoiding fog and receiving few. Having experienced the heavy humidity of the infested, seemingly plague-stricken air of Schönbrunn following floods, Marie-Louise dreaded what cholera might bring.

"We are all overloaded with prophylactics as Muslims with amulets," the Duke of Reichstadt wrote to his mother.

> We have large plasters on our stomachs – mine tickles unbearably. Copper plates are suspended on a silk cord attached to flasks of vinegar on our little finger which we keep on our noses all the time [. . .] The indispensable precaution which I recommend you, my dear Mama, is to have the waters of your

springs and your pits in Parma analysed and to choose the purest. Several physicians in Vienna who have performed the same exercise have found the water filled with lime and other unhealthy elements; and one group of doctors attribute to this corruption the main germ of the illness.

The Duke was convinced by this hypothesis and not by the homeo-paths who maintained that there had been an excess of copper in the earth, which, borne along rivers, was poisoning the whole of Europe.

This disease is terrible in countries where large populations are heaped one on top of the other. In Vienna, it is completely the opposite. People are fearful and rush to hospital at the slightest colic, and mortality is much less than in St Petersburg or Galicia. Much has been said about fear, but I have found a general lack of concern in many cases. In the early days of the crisis, I spent time at the hospital opposite my windows. Believe me, there were always hundreds of people thronging the hospital smoking their pipes laughing, and scoffing at the jolts which the peddlers gave them as they carried the dying into hospital. Leaving aside this pusillanimity, there has been bravery exemplified by the Emperor who has refused to isolate himself and has instead continued to visit Vienna to see public works three times a week in his brown riding habit without for a moment any thought for himself or any self-congratulation.

A story ran that the Emperor had gone for his usual walk in the hills above Schönbrunn and had accompanieed porters bearing a coffin unattended by mourners to the grave, reciting out loud the *Pater* and a hymn for the poor deceased. Such gestures were characteristic of this all-powerful self-effacing sovereign. Marie-Louise admired her father and knew she would have to follow his example, though she did not look forward to it.

Metternich had five metaphors for life: volcanoes, plagues, floods, fire and cancerous growths. He had always hated the Duke, a cancer in his grand scheme, though he had engineered his birth. The Austrian Chancellor had never recovered from the public humiliation Napoleon had inflicted by dismissing him and his family from the French court, sending them back to Vienna for alleged political intriguing. Metternich had laughed mockingly when others had been appointed to the thrones to which the Duke had aspired: "He is finally excluded from all thrones once and for all – he will never be anything more than a mere Austrian prince!"[3]

Metternich rejected any proposal relating to the Duke's advancement. Marie-Louise tried her best to circumvent him, as she had done in getting her father to grant her son a commission in the army, but absent in Parma, her father often away on business, the Chancellor's repression went unchecked. According to Count Dietrichstein, Metternich physically trembled just listening to the Duke. The Count shared many of his concerns with Marie-Louise, begging her to burn his letters after reading them, but spared her details which might upset her. The Duke complained that Metternich had selected a band of irksome poodles for his new military household, men of faint stamp for whom he had no other use. Prokesch, for whom Marie-Louise had issued a strong personal petition, was not selected. Marie-Louise learnt through Gentz that Metternich, who had never addressed his concerns to her directly, accused Prokesch of putting ridiculous ideas into an impressionable boy's head. He decided to take a last swipe at his old enemy and summoned the Duke to him. Once the interview was finished, he made a full note of it. He started by telling him that Prokesch was not for him, that the military appointments made to his household had been selected from Austria's most illustrious soldiers. Metternich trusted that the Duke had no complaints. The statement did not invite answer.

You appreciate that the world beyond our small *gemütliche*

Vienna does not perceive you to be anything more than the grandson of Emperor Francis. As yet, your knowledge is very limited, your education gleaned from books. You have known only leisure and entertainment. There is a very different world outside from which you have been shielded. Thankfully, the fires that fed the wars which devastated the first twenty-five years of your mother's life have been quenched. The architects of the peace achieved at the Vienna Congress when you first arrived in Vienna were men of extraordinary political vision who have set Europe on a course of peace which has spared the lives of many millions of men, women and children.

The world was erupting in revolution, so successful were these "men of extraordinary vision". The Duke wanted to emerge from this interview with dignity and kept silent as Metternich continued. "You are a young man full of promise. Do not be seduced by elements who have their heads in the clouds and would be reckless as to your personal safety [. . .] I personally expect your Imperial Highness to dedicate himself to duty and service of Austria, just as your mother and grandfather have so selflessly done before you and continue to do." Metternich's determination was final. He refused the Duke further introductions to his father's former generals.

For the next two months, the Duke and Prokesch read together leading publications and extracts Prokesch had culled from tractates published in German, French, Italian and English. All were on military strategy and history relating to Napoleon I, both favourable and unfavourable. Together Franz and Prokesch analyzed the causes, methods, pitfalls, consequences and repercussions of war. By the time the Duke had reached his twenty-first birthday, he had written in his own hand authoritative biographies of several of the famous generals of the eighteenth and nineteenth centuries and essays on an extensive range of topics relating to warfare. After a long day on exercises, he worked assiduously, often long into the night, returning magnetically to his father's will and the injunction never to forget his French identity. Indebted to Prokesch for his support, he asked Marie-Louise to confer the order of the Cross of the Commander upon his friend as proof of her love for her firstborn. He treasured the gold medallion of Alexander the Great which Prokesch gave him before leaving in the summer of 1831 to accompany his grandfather on his travels. By the end of the year, the Duke had been promoted to lieutenant colonel in the Nassau infantry.

Without reference to the Emperor or anyone else, Metternich prevented any further intercourse between the Duke and Prokesch by appointing the latter commissioner attached to the Papal Legate at Bologna, allegedly to reinforce the Austrian presence on the Italian peninsula. Marie-Louise bemoaned her son's frustration and her powerlessness to assist him.

TWENTY-ONE

The Tragedy of Competing Loyalties, 1832

In the autumn of 1831, Marie-Louise decided to put all her affairs in order and issued a general amnesty so as to be ready if God were to decide to dispose of her by means of cholera. The public mood was still rather poor, but at least there was no evidence of a burning desire to demonstrate.

Dr. Steer, Professor of Pathology and Pharmacology at the University of Padua, a leading authority on the disease, sent Marie-Louise a full report with recommendations for its prevention and management, and kept in regular touch with her. Should cholera arrive, a *cordon sanitaire* would have to be imposed around the areas infected. All travellers, goods and animals from infected areas, even if they showed no signs of ill health, would have to be subjected to a process of disinfection and quarantine. Travellers showing signs of sickness would be sent back whence they had come. Only if they could produce a prescribed bill of health issued from the authorities of the infected area could they expect to cross the entry point, though a twenty-four hour stop would be mandatory to monitor them. Those undergoing quarantine would have to be confined in allocated isolated lodgings. During this period, travellers would have to be carefully cleaned, taking repeated baths in soapy water with chlorine-lime solution and nitric acid, potentially noxious to the lungs. The travellers' clothes would have to be washed with water and soap or with an ash solution. All non-washable clothes would have to be fumigated in a specially designed fumigation cabinet filled with chlorine steam, and thoroughly beaten through and aired. All the travellers' other chattels and their carriages would have to be cleaned, wood, glass, porcelain, metal washed with water or vinegar or lime-chloride solution. Money, paper, books and other documents would have to be fumigated with vinegar before being punched with holes to air them. Once letters had undergone this process they would be stamped and then transferred on by post and couriers who would only be permitted to travel onward having first observed the requisite period of quarantine. Should anyone die in quarantine, his or her body should not be touched but covered in lime and buried in an isolated spot. Military, medical and ancillary staff would have to be recruited and stationed at designated entry points, and buildings erected or allocated for the use of quarantine facilities. Camphor, believed to prevent contagion, and impregnated flannel believed to cure the first signs of diarrhoea, would have to be stockpiled. The administrative and financial burden entailed by such measures would be a severe strain on the resources of the small duchy.

Meanwhile, the Duke reported that Schönbrunn had never before been more crowded, like an immense monastery. Everyone, on the slightest pretext – the very slimmest of connections to the imperial court or any member of it – flooded in through its gates to take refuge from the spread of disease. By September, the community at Schönbrunn had swelled to two thousand souls with government ministers and court members and their families, as foreign ambassadors fought over property available for rent in its suburbs, around which had been created a *cordon sanitaire*, heavily guarded by the bullets of quarantine sentinels. The Duke promised to write to Marie-Louise twice a week to keep her updated as to his health and the situation in Vienna. He assured her he was following to the letter the régime prescribed by Dr. Malfatti, which had totally cured his catarrhal cough, aching chest and high temperature. She should not worry about him contracting cholera. Dr Malfatti confirmed that she could rest completely at ease with regard to her son's health. Perhaps this new young doctor was more up-to-date with the latest cures than his predecessor, Dr. Staudenheim – "the old woman", as the Duke of Reichstadt dubbed him, who had prescribed blanket prohibitions of all forms of exercise for extended periods.

In the first few days of December, the Duke of Reichstadt wrote to Marie-Louise,

"If you could understand all the empire you exert over me, you surely would not have deprived me of your news over the past eight months," during which he had had to rely on reports from Countess Lazansky, "I really feel the heavy weight of our separation." He longed to see his mother again, making her happy being his sole *raison d'être*. "These damned circumstances! Why must they always override the wishes of our hearts!"

Marie-Louise had not written to him between taking flight to Casalmaggiore in late February and November when she had reasserted her authority in Parma. His letters to her and news of him from Count Dietrichstein had brought her immense comfort. Once more, politics had insinuated itself between the Habsburg mother and her Bonaparte son. "I kiss you so tenderly, my dear Mama, with the eager prayer not to efface me from your heart, Your most obedient son, Francis."

1832 started badly. Cholera had spread to Sweden and to England. Marie-Louise selected items from her palaces, including the valuable lacquer and lapis washstand and accessories given to her by the City of Paris on her wedding day, to melt down and convert into cash to provide funds to relieve anticipated victims and orphans of cholera.

The French landed at and occupied the port-city of Ancona following Austria's military intervention following protests at the brutality of Pope Gregory XVI's pontifical forces in the Papal Legations. The Pope had been intimidating his subjects by intrusive policing of strict religious observance through the confessional and by other repressive measures. Again, Marie-Louise saw her father as liberator and protector. She felt nervous at the presence of French troops on the Italian soil and hoped they would soon be despatched by an international congress.

In March, Marie-Louise's duchies were shaken by another eruption. A devastating earthquake forced many of her subjects to flee from their homes after midnight to sleep out in streets and gardens. Wilhelm escaped the collapse of brickwork in his bedroom. As ever, fear of a recurrence terrorized everyone. In the following weeks, demand for masons vastly outstripped supply to repair extensive damage in cities and villages.

Thankfully, the Duke's health seemed to be much improved, but not yet sufficiently to resume his career. He was morose, having lost Alfred to Bohemia and Gustav to Milan. He feared transmitting sadness and disgust to his mother, she from whom had come only happiness and contentment. Considered called to a higher destiny, he regarded it as his sacred duty to recover. Over-exertion must be abandoned in favour of complete rest, a gentle climate, milk drinks and Selz waters, and the baths at Ischl. Dr Malfatti, who had diagnosed congestion of the liver for which he prescribed rhubarb with sugar, vouched for the Duke's recovery if these prescriptions were followed.

Marie-Louise was constantly troubled by the absolute impossibility of going to Vienna in the summer. Baron Mareschall, administering Marie-Louise's duchies temporarily following Werklein's disgrace, made it quite clear that there was no question of Marie-Louise burning a hole in ducal finances for the sake of a sentimental journey. She wrote to Victoria de Crenneville, "If the Duke's condition were to deteriorate and cholera were to reach Parma, it would be impossible for me to go to Vienna. The hardships, the calamities, never mind the expenses of cholera will be incalculable. I am sure that spring will not pass without us having cholera in Italy. All the measures which have to be taken cause me terrible distress."

Besides, Marie-Louise was sick again. Preparations for cholera and four or five hours a day spent on reorganisation of schools were exhausting her. The symptoms she had suffered two years earlier had returned, her head numb and gait unsteady. Her firstborn begged her to follow Dr. Malfatti's recommendations: "Do it for love of me: just imagine my alarm when you are not well." He was sure she would recover so much faster in Vienna, far from the monotony of Parma.

At least, thank goodness, the news was improving. In Vienna, cholera, having claimed over two thousand lives, seemed to be abating. She longed for the Duke of Reichstadt to come to Parma, but order and political tranquillity militated against it. Too sick to travel herself, she thanked heaven that his chest was cured, he was no longer coughing and his lungs were free. This was a blessing. The spread of the disease to the Duke's liver did not cause her undue concern, "for the liver nearly always heals when one combats the illness," she wrote to Count Dietrichstein.

"The Duke is dreadfully melancholic and wants always to be alone." Count Dietrichstein replied. Additionally, Metternich's ambiguity gnawed at her: "Your Majesty is fully informed about the Duke of Reichstadt's state of health. This state generates concern. The doctors are still searching the source of sickness in his liver ... Let us hope for the best and rest assured that no care will be neglected."[1]

"God be praised! The news is constantly getting better!" Victoria de Crenneville reported towards the end of April. The Duke's appetite had returned, and he had resumed his walks and carriage rides. Doctors now recommended he take the waters, not of Ischl but of the island of Ischia in the Bay of Naples. Though puzzled that her son, mascot of patriotism, was to be permitted to travel across the Italian continent, Marie-Louise wanted to believe that at long last she would see her son in Parma.

Since the Duke's transfer to his regiment towards the end of 1831, Count Dietrichstein had been relegated to minor housekeeping duties. Far too fond of his charge, whom he still saw daily, to cease to be a proxy parent, the Count wrote desperate letters, in French and, when words failed him, in German. He claimed that he had never had any confidence in Dr. Malfatti from the moment cholera had been declared in Vienna, and had foreseen calamity on the horizon. He reported that the Duke had taken up smoking Spanish tobacco and ignored repeated warnings of the danger to his health, heaping imprudence on imprudence, pushing himself to commit suicide. "He promised Malfatti he would give up his pipe, but I don't believe it." The Count hated the miserable tobacco and two enormous pipes on the Duke of Reichstadt's table. "He is his own worst enemy!"[2] By the end of January, the Count claimed he could see the writing on the wall, the Duke unable to conceal the shivers which forced him back to his bed. He hid his expectorant from doctors standing in for Dr. Malfatti, who had been seized by an attack of gout. He preferred to do irreparable damage to his health for the sake of the glory of a couple of hours on parade. Even holding up his father produced no effect: "People will soon say here and everywhere that the sons of great men never equal their fathers. And once this conviction has been established, the future is nil!"[3]

Particularly disturbing was the Count's use of the past tense: "All reasoning, all precautions have failed in the face of a fatality which led him on. It was barbarous to remove Prokesch, whose very presence was a great source of comfort and a potential aid in recovery. The young man is to be pitied, for he is without support, without counsel, without friends – and Prokesch provided everything together!"

The Duke's coughing had caused his voice to become so high-pitched that members of his grandfather's Court were alarmed. "Why has everyone always rejected my advice, why have people poured scorn on me for my fears? Does one have to be a Hercules or an Achilles at the age of twenty? But I have preached in the desert!" wailed Dietrichstein impotently. Even though the Duke's illness was plain to see, the Count was mocked for wanting to pamper him. By February, he was sure that the Duke was beyond hope, and yet Marie-Louise was constantly given reason to believe that he was on the brink of certain recovery. Along with the Count's litanies came reassuring letters from Dr. Malfatti.

General Hartmann-Klarstein, the Duke of Reichstadt's new companion, wrote to inform Marie-Louise that the Duke's infection had not prevented him from going to the theatre, for walks, riding or attending court balls – though he had refrained from dancing. He loved masked balls, where he liked to dupe friends and acquaintances. His dancing on one previous occasion with a wealthy wife of a jealous husband, Naudine Karolyi, provoked much gossip. Unfounded rumours of his impending marriage to a princess of the House of Orléans still persisted.

Dr. Malfatti reported that his fears as to the dangers of the equinox had not materialised. The Duke was virtually back to normal. But all was not well. Despite the Duke's ruses to hide the symptoms of his illness so as to mislead his family, his household and, most of all, his doctors, it was clear that his cough was far worse. His personal valet confirmed that his shivers were more or less permanent and the slightest movement caused him discomfort.

Count Dietrichstein had first expressed his concern to Marie-Louise in late August 1827 as to the Duke's persistent and sporadic bouts of phlegmy coughing. Rising four times a week at four in the morning to go on manoeuvres until seven-thirty, the Duke would then go riding three or four times a week, always energetically. Thereafter, he would study until his eyes would no longer cooperate. In the spring of 1830, a cold, swollen glands and weak chest had persuaded Staudenheim that the Duke should not ride for some time. Dr. Staudenheim's death a month later and replacement by Dr. Malfatti caused the Count to despair. When Malfatti did not demand Staudenheim's prohibitions, the Count tried to exact them, determined to defeat those who would hasten the boy's demise. He wrote,

"I cannot hide it from Your Majesty, which You will have gathered from my last three letters: the prince runs the greatest dangers! The illness is making rapid advances. There can be no illusions, and if God does not protect him, medical science will uselessly employ its resources, but your presence would without doubt be preferable and necessary *in so many ways!*"[4]

All the misleading letters, "the colour pink or half pink"[5], sent by Dr. Malfatti and General Hartmann, were full of pointless euphemistic phrases designed to sew doubt and distrust or to facilitate sleep, according to Dietrichstein. "I went to the Prince's rooms last night to find him lying on his divan covered with a coat up to his teeth. I asked him gently how he was! He replied: "Very well, I am three days without a temperature!" Alas! Why this dissimulation, when he has a temperature every day, and it is a slow fever which is consuming him!"

On one occasion, he exploded, "Malfatti's behaviour is unbelievable! It is criminal to mislead you the way he does!" So weak that he was receiving breast milk, his melancholic face, a yellow pallor, inspired sadness beyond description. The Count had already begun to write of him in the past tense.

"The throne reserved for him was beyond the grave, a throne much more surely than Marshal Bernadotte, Crown Prince of Sweden, has his!" Count Dietrichstein lamented. "God only knows what his genius might have mastered! He carries off universal regrets and no prince has excited interest as he has so generally and markedly in all classes of society. How much I regret being far from Your Majesty at such a moment!"

When Marie-Louise showed Ferrari the letters received from Vienna, he told her she was behaving like a fool, wanting to dash off there. Baron Mareschall berated Marie-Louise for being overly sentimental.

Malfatti's letter arrived contemporaneously asserting that the Duke's convalescence was far advanced and his weakness diminishing noticeably. In early May, he advised her to disregard exaggeration of her son's condition in the newspapers.

"I have the honour of reassuring Your Majesty that since my last report the Prince is without fever, his stomach settled, his appetite (never hearty at the best of times) restored, and his cough and expectoration as usual. If it were to have been tuberculosis or abscesses, things would have gone in quite another direction."[6]

General Hartmann on several occasions reported more improvements in the Duke of Reichstadt's health, and his faith in the waters of Ischl. His letters were wildly misleading. In the first week of May, Metternich should have summoned the Duke's mother urgently to Vienna. Instead, he advised her that the Emperor and Empress were expecting to see her in late May, early June in Trieste, at the end of their three month tour of inspection of their dominions. At least the Adriatic port was part way to the Austrian capital. Baron Mareschall was dead against her departure. To her alarm, there had been further uprisings in France, Germany and Poland. Politics, finances and cholera demanded that she forgo the trip. Despite admonitions of her sluggish employees, precautions against cholera had been taken only on paper. No-one but she was taking cholera seriously: she would have to do everything herself. Werklein from Vienna also weighed in to urge her to listen to the voice of the inhabitants of Parma. He knew all too well how ready her citizens were to exploit her absence were she to leave her seat unattended.

Werklein wrote again from Vienna in the second week of May, sending a memorandum of his claims which he asked her to lay before her father. Forced to sell his wife's jewellery to make ends meet, he directed her attention to the "horrible lot of the man and his family" who had served her with loyalty, selflessness and great success. Werklein, of all people, knew how overstretched her own resources were. Totally self-absorbed, he said nothing about the Duke of Reichstadt's condition, with which he too must have been fully conversant.

Unbeknown to Marie-Louise, Baron Mareschall had received instructions from Metternich not to allow Marie-Louise to go to Vienna. Not unsympathetic to Marie-Louise's plight, he wrestled with the Chancellor:

> Your Highness can well imagine that for reasons of economy and order as well as for the tranquillity of the country, I certainly do not advise Her Majesty to leave and to go to Vienna

THE TRAGEDY OF COMPETING LOYALTIES, 1832

without cause, but you will imagine equally my anxiety not to contribute involuntarily to the accusation of indifference to her son (to which appearances only might give rise) which might one day be levelled against this august princess.[7]

The forces keeping Marie-Louise from departure seemed to relent. She brought forward ducal business in Piacenza, and tried to hasten preventative measures for cholera. She must travel incognito, without retinue with one or two companions only, keeping her expenditure to an absolute minimum.

> I can only propose to Your Majesty to leave on the 16th of this month for Mantua, the 17th from Mantua to Padua, and the 18th from Padua to Venice, where she will take the steamboat on the 19th to Trieste. Your Majesty will have the goodness to write to the Emperor at Trieste, let him know in advance of her arrival on the 19th and the 20th. I would ask you to establish the cost, but without purchasing the ticket."[8] When Marie-Louise's departure was deferred by five days following news of her father's delay, Baron Mareschall made a last bid to prevent her departure,
>
> I beg Your Majesty to attend as a matter of urgency to measures to be taken for cholera, an issue where one would reproach oneself seriously for any negligence. It is the duty of every government to anticipate the future when the well-being of one's subjects are at stake.[9]

Marie-Louise finally set out for Venice towards the end of May. It was over eight weeks since she had received a letter, to be his last, from her son:

> The day before yesterday, I dreamt of you, you had arrived in Schönbrunn wearing a white petticoat. You were shaking my hand and I was crying. You were kissing me and I cried again. Finally a torrent of tears awoke me with a start and since that moment I cannot get rid of the thought that something untoward

has happened to you. I cannot wait to receive news which will dispel my superstitions. But what good does it do, talking to you about my illness when all the Counts in the universe, and Mons. Malfatti send you regular reports with each post?

He had been in bed for six weeks, reading daily a huge parcel of newspapers, journals and novels. With trembling hand, he talked of Vienna's carnival, the balls and dances at which the Queen of Hungary had appeared in fashions three centuries old. He begged her to write just two words on an old piece of rag.

Marie-Louise made her way in her solitary carriage, the horses galloping at breakneck speed towards Venice. At various stages of her journey, she corresponded with her surprisingly mature fifteen-year-old, Albertina. Unable to leave the Italian peninsula without her father's authorisation, she wrote, "The journey does me immense good though I long for you. The thought that I am far from [my firstborn], fixed, so to say, at this present time to the soil of Italy, gives me cruel anxieties, and I know that you share in these with me."[10] In ordinary circumstances she would enjoy the journey, but that was impossible as each day she received bad news from her son who was wasting away fast.

Lodged in Venice at *The White Lion* overlooking the Grand Canal, Marie-Louise saw only closest acquaintances, dragging herself to the Piazza San Marco and along the Riva degli Schiavoni, going to the theatre and opera without being recognized. After several days waiting in vain to know her father's expected date of arrival in Trieste she set out. By the time she arrived, her energy had completely evaporated. Hearing that her father was expected in Pola, she boarded the packet-boat, the *Archduchess Sofia*. He was not there. She was struck by the poverty of Istria, by the ragged, miserable peasants, by the ugliness of the Cathedral which she visited having secured help from a priest to force the doors, and by the decay of the abandoned Roman amphitheatre. She returned to Trieste the same evening, preceding her father by a few hours.

"Returning from Pola, I received very bad news regarding my son," she wrote to Albertina.

There is no doubt that his chest is seized, and that he has all the symptoms of terminal illness [which] is progressing rapidly . . . Modern medicine can do nothing. All this news obliges me to do as I feared, to distance myself from you, but my maternal love bids me travel beyond the Alps and it is right that I dedicate my cares to my suffering, unhappy child. Within eight days I shall be on the road to Vienna. I do not know how I will survive I am so sick, but Providence will assist.[11]

In the next few days, still restrained from travelling northward but no longer incognito, Marie-Louise did as was required of her, visiting more churches, the stock exchange, the Mauroner theatre, orchestras serenading her with military tunes.

"I am doubly afflicted by the cruel circumstances which force me to remain still absent beyond six weeks. My thoughts are divided between you and my dear invalid whom I must go and care for."[12] The doctor informed her that her son was coughing up large amounts of expectorant. Asses milk not having done any good, leeches had been applied to let blood from his head. In desperation, three more doctors had been consulted. The early passing of her imbecile sister into the hands of the Almighty, news of which reached her from Dresden, might be the best end for the poor thing, but not for her firstborn.

In Trieste, run down, she succumbed to the fever of latent consumption which regularly plagued her, preventing her from prosecuting her journey. She cried in exasperation. Three weeks later, she was sufficiently recovered to be able to resume her journey. Passing through Klagenfurt, a letter from the Empress reported that the Duke of Reichstadt had taken communion with Archduchess Sophie, ostensibly to pray for her happy delivery, but in reality for him, without his knowledge, to receive Extreme Unction.

"My heart suffers seeing the Prince who I left so handsome, so fresh, and now – what a difference!!!" Victoria de Crenneville wrote helplessly. "It is painful to see this beautiful young plant fading and destroying itself."[13] Marie-Louise was distraught. "The French embassy is extremely occupied by the sick Duke, from whom great care is taken to hide all the newspapers which talk about him at this moment. My pain is deep!" wrote Count Dietrichstein through his tears.

At last in Vienna, Marie-Louise sat with her son, who lay motionless. Hartmann's letter had been grossly misleading, as had many of Malfatti's letters, his diagnoses mistaken. The dashing figure in ceremonial uniform, who had pushed vanity beyond tolerance, who had sparkled with wit, ladies falling at his feet was gone. Only weeks earlier, Prokesch, Count Dietrichstein and her father had been chastising the Duke for persisting in indecent liaisons and enjoying ladies of the night or "unbearable incognitos", as the Count called them, reminding him of his rank during angry scenes, Incorrigible, he insisted that he had never actually touched a woman. "He listens to me, admits the error of his ways, promises to behave better, and a quarter of an hour later has put it out of his mind!" The press had continued as ever, without any foundation, to marry him off in different directions. Now it was clear to Marie-Louise that the Duke had been dying for some time and was close to the end.

Marie-Louise could not believe the spectre her son had become. Even the deep red strips on his cheeks, a manifestation of lung disease, had vanished in the bloodless pastiness which now masked his fever-riddled skeleton. His sunken eyes were already lifeless, the keen, penetrating look which reminded everyone and particularly Marie-Louise of Napoleon was absent. Emaciated, his voice croaking with difficulty, he took his mother in his decaying arms and hugged her close to him. His suffering, bravely borne, was intolerable to watch.

With his mother's arrival, hope returned. Despite his feeble state, the Duke began to dream of travelling to Naples with her. Naples was to be the last of the many dreams denied him. Death would be the only exit from the gilded cage to which he had been confined since his father's fall.

Despite all the setbacks and revelations, the Duke had always continued to love his mother devotedly, constantly longing for her approval, anxious to satisfy her high standards, treasuring every word that issued from her mouth and hand. Just being with his mother was enough to guarantee perfect happiness, he had written after a month spent in Baden with her and the Neippergs seven years earlier, which he remembered as the happiest time of his childhood. He had burned with impatience, cursing the slow passing of time. "I cannot wait for the moment when, with all confidence which you are entitled to expect from me both by right of having given birth to me and by right of conquest, I can tell you over and over again how much I love you."[14] He could not wait to put an end to separation marked by so much pain and to prepare for a future which dawned so full of promise.

Marie-Louise sat by the Duke's bedside, the days passing slowly in quiet foreboding. She wrote to Albertina, "Malfatti talks to everyone as if he is the oracle at Delphi. He terrifies me so much that I no longer listen to him, preferring to rely on my eyes and my experience of the sick."[15] Her cough persisted – she feared she would probably have to put up with it for the rest of her life, she told Albertina. Over the Duke's bed presided the portrait of his father painted by Gérard,* which had been stored in the Belvedere at Schönbrunn until the Duke's emancipation. Propped up in his bed, he could gaze through the long windows and across the large balcony to the trim hedges and statuary of Schönbrunn's gardens and the Gloriette in the distance. A new chair graced his room which the Archduchess Sophie, "this angel of goodness" as Count Dietrichstein called her, had had made for him. Much would be made in days to come of the fact that this elegant gilt and lacquered apartment

---

* Count Dietrichstein had feared that the Duke's preferred portrait of Napoleon in his imperial cloak, left to him by his aunt, Mme Baciocchi, was rather too suggestive.

was the same in which his father had signed the peace with Austria after their defeat at Wagram, the moment in history which had sealed his mother's fate, and foretold his birth.

In the second week of July, Marie-Louise described to Albertina how she was spending her days. She would wake at eight o'clock to take her first cup of milk, and then doze until half past nine, take a little soup, get up, get dressed and go for a stroll in the garden, to seek comfort in the numerous wild birds, verdant meadows, little clumps of flowers and wide avenues of fir trees which had adorned the days of her great-grandmother, Empress Maria Theresa, evoking poignant memories.

> ... I go and sit with my son, he seated in an armchair until midday when I drink my second and third cups of medicine, the first with, the second without milk. At half past midday, I go back, half sunburnt, to the house, perform my toilette, receive a few people who want to see me or I go and find my lovely sister and her children. At half past one, we take lunch with the family and my brother, the King of Hungary. At three, I go to my son where I spend the whole afternoon either in his room or in a study next to it, where I attend to business as quickly as I can. From five-thirty to six-thirty, I go out in a carriage or on foot and return to him at nine-o'clock, when I eat with my brother Francis, the Queen of Bavaria and her daughter Maria and my relations. At ten o'clock, I go back to my son's antechamber to see how he is, and my uncle Louis stays until eleven, by which time I am fast asleep.[16]

Two days later, her son had got a lot worse, his lack of appetite and the swelling of his feet terrifying her. "God tell me I deceive myself. He needs now to be carried to the garden, which, naturally at his age, he finds extremely humiliating. I and my brother, who is an absolute angel, do our best to distract him."

Marie-Louise refused to relinquish hope in the face of the unmistakeable signs of fast deterioration. "I await my father's return for the 26th July when I hope my son will not be too bad and I will be able to entrust him to his care. Then I hope to leave four or five days after the arrival of my father. These are my plans in this base world,"[17] she ended her letter to Albertina. Briefly, the Duke rallied, planning to set out for Naples, worrying that his coach would not be ready in time. He gave instructions as to how he would like distributed his few personal effects, the collections of walking sticks, elegant bronze clock given him by his grandfather, plumes, rings, trinkets and other gifts, weaponry, rifles, pistols and swords. He bequeathed his father's Egyptian sword, which Marie-Louise had given him the day he had been promoted to Captain of Light Infantry in the summer of 1828, to his best friend Prokesch, along with the books they had read together.

Freak weather conditions, frightening horrible storms, days of blistering heat followed by icy cold blasts wrecked havoc. Marie-Louise dared no longer go for a short walk in the garden, once having returned to find her son had taken a turn for the worse in her absence. The Duke's fevers had returned with greater force, his frailty increased to such a degree that his coughs could no longer be heard. Ten days later, she told Albertina that she was living from one day to the next.

"The expectoration and suppuration have increased so much that the air in the room is infected and there is no way of getting him to swallow broth or cream of barley. He is at least happy, because he preserves the illusion until the very last that he will go to Ischl and from there to Naples where he hopes to cure all his ills."[18]

Marie-Louise did not have long to wait. A bolt of lightning felling one of the imperial eagles attached to the pediment of the Palace of Schönbrunn heralded the end. At around three thirty in the morning on 22nd July 1832, the Duke felt a violent pain and sat up abruptly, shouting: "I am drowning, I am drowning! Call my mother! My mother!" Marie-Louise had gone to the adjacent room to take a brief nap, leaving her son with the ever-present Tyrolean Captain Moll, the Duke's commanding officer. "Get my mother!

Take away the table ... I no longer need anything!" He seized Moll's arm, squeezing it convulsively. "Cataplasm! Vesicatory!"

Roused, Marie-Louise entered her son's room, shaking uncontrollably. She faltered, reached out for support. Choked, tears flooded over her. The Duke recognized her, his lips breaking momentarily into a pathetic smile. He caught her eye and signalled to her by nodding his head twice, trying vainly to say a final farewell; but his voice and lips failed him. Members of the Duke's military household, Dr Malfatti, Baron Mareschall and several servants knelt in silence as benedictions were recited discreetly by a young novice chaplain, mindful not to frighten the dying man. Marie-Louise knelt, numb, propped up against an armchair. The Duke wanted no reading, just a prayer. As the prayer was recited, the Duke flung his head from side to side and expired. Marie-Louise lay slumped by his bed, having lost consciousness.

TWENTY-TWO
Manuscripts and pariahs

Just as the Duke of Reichstadt had always hated letting his mother go, Albertina, the half-sister he had never met, felt likewise. Just as Marie-Louise had feared being spurned or even forgotten by the Duke, she worried, despite the lack of evidence, that Albertina and Wilhelm would also reject her. Albertina reassured her. She longed for her mother and wanted the person she loved most of all in the world. The children were keeping themselves occupied by making various handicraft items for a lottery to raise funds for a poor local family. Albertina hoped her mother and courtiers would buy all the, admittedly, exorbitantly priced tickets.

Initially, Marie-Louise had tried to underplay the Duke's condition to her daughter, ever hoping for his recovery and not to frighten a young impressionable mind. Soon it was Albertina who was trying to persuade her mother not to fear the worst. She told her mother that she should try and suppress morbid feelings – once the summer and spa waters had worked their cure, the Duke was bound to go from strength to strength. Even though she had never met her half-brother, she felt a love and concern for him, her parents having reared her to regard the four Neipperg boys as siblings and to feel love and loyalty that would endure for the rest of their lives. She consoled her mother on the death of her sister Carolina. A sister herself, she would be inconsolable at the loss of a sibling.

"How could we not be concerned for a human being who touches you so closely and who loves you so tenderly?"[1]

As the Duke's condition deteriorated, Albertina told her mother not to worry on her and her brother's account.

"Everything pales into insignificance when we think how much you would have suffered staying in Parma . . . I like to think that you will be in the bosom of your family, among all those who cherish you and share in your misfortune. Their sincere concern will console us . . . Don't worry about writing so often, devote time to rest . . . I . . . beg you never to doubt my respect and love."[2]

Knowing Marie-Louise to have arrived in Vienna, she wrote, "It must have been good to see the Duke of Reichstadt again."[3] She advised her not to give in to, in her usual generous-hearted way, but to close the door on the crowds besieging her in Vienna.

Dated later than those sent by Marie-Louise, letters continued to arrive in Parma from the Austrian court, announcing that both Duke and his mother were looking well and feeling better. Such false tidings prompted Albertina to presage Marie-Louise's early return and a happy future which was a far cry from reality. When Marie-Louise was silent for a fortnight, Albertina became extremely anxious. She and her brother wanted to be with their mother to offer words of comfort. "Keep taking Malfatti's prescriptions. Take precautions for cholera, we will worry less about you. We are touched by the interest Metternich takes in us."[4]

Fearing her mother's prolonged absence, she wrote,

> I feel this terrible emptiness when you are far . . . I have tried but failed to be happy in Sala without you . . . I see that it is not to places which one becomes attached, and that we are only happy in places where there are our loved ones. I am full of your memory. I [tell] myself that perhaps your eyes are looking at the same moon, the same stars as me. Some might find my thoughts exaggerated, but not you who know so well what it is to love.[5]

A week before the Duke's death, Marie-Louise tried to exploit a vaguely perceptible improvement, telling her daughter that she would fix her date of departure once her father had returned to Vienna from his travels. When it became clear that the Duke's end was approaching, Albertina told her mother that she prayed daily to God with all her soul that the Duke, so young and so suffering, would be spared. When Marie-Louise expressed her fear that she would not be able to go on without her son, Albertina told her,

"I feel without you I could not live, that the world would seem . . . a desert without the object which lends life charm in my eyes."[6]

Marie-Louise's letter to Albertina, a week after the Duke's death, was sent from the castle of Persenbeug on the Danube, far from the crowds filing past her son's coffin which lay in state before burial in the family crypt. In Persenbeug, where she had spent many happy hours during her own and her firstborn's childhood, she mourned together with her father who had finally arrived back in Austria. The words from *Emile, or On Education*, the current bible of a child's upbringing by Jean-Jacques Rousseau, the author of dubious parenting record, found ready application:

> One dreams only of keeping one's child. That is not enough. One must teach him to keep himself in adulthood, to bear the blows of misfortune, to weather opulence and poverty; to live, if necessary, in the ice of Iceland or on the burning rock of Malta. In vain, do you take precautions to shield him from death – after all, he will die. And, when his death is unrelated to your care of him, still more will you struggle to comprehend it. You must make him live more than prevent him dying. Living is not about breathing, it is about doing. It is making use of our organs, our senses, our faculties, of every part of ourselves which gives us the feeling of existing. The man who has lived most is not the one who can count the greatest number of years, but who has experienced life the most.

There still remained to Marie-Louise two children whom she must make live, for whom she must create opportunities to experience life. Albertina responded to her letter:

> I was penetrated by your assertion that you no longer wanted to live but for us and that you expect your happiness from us

alone . . . .Our task now is to make the woman who has loved us already so much feel cherished, and to employ all our efforts in bringing her pleasure. What inexpressible joy it would be for us if we were able to say to ourselves that we are not unworthy of being your children and that we have rendered your burden less hard to bear.[7]

This poor child, who barely three years earlier had lost her father, cleaved ever closer to the mother in whose heart she wished to be pre-eminent. With the Duke's death, it appeared to her that she and her brother assumed a legitimate place in Marie-Louise's life to which society had made them believe they had no right to aspire.

As Marie-Louise wept, letters reached her from those who had not yet heard the terrible news. One such was from Gustav, who had asked his Commander General Radetzky to send him temporarily to Vienna as an envoy, his current work being of little importance. He only wished he were already with her at the sick-bed in this hour of need, and offering his heartfelt loyal support. He could not find words to describe his pain at the Duke's condition. Ever since Marie-Louise had set out for Vienna, he had waited for the post each day with indescribable anxiety, unable to concede hope as long as his beloved friend could still draw breath. He could hardly bear to think of Marie-Louise's suffering, praying fervently that Heaven bless her with the considerable and rare strength which it had already granted her in abundance on repeated occasions.

> I feel a deep, true yearning to *see* the Duke, as I sometimes think that perhaps the closeness of one who is undoubtedly his *truest* friend on this earth might help his condition. As for *me* on whom he has lavished grace and benevolence for nine whole years of his young and beautiful life, whom he attracted through his affectionate nature, and has made so happy and proud through his friendship, I very much wish to be allowed to be close to him in these grave times, as I was in happier times, and an inner voice seems to tell me that the presence of

a true soul could better give him a little more strength and courage to bear his pain and to accept the decisions of the Almighty."[8] Gustav's fine sentiments arrived too late.

Albertina counted down every hour and every minute of the mortal days to her mother's arrival scheduled for 4th August. "How many conflicting feelings will our hearts share in the happy and terrible instant that we see each other again!"[9] As much as Marie-Louise longed to embrace Albertina and Wilhelm, she already knew that they could never compensate for the vacuum now opening up before her.

Marie-Louise wrote to inform close members of the family of her son's death before leaving Vienna. A particularly difficult letter was that addressed to her first mother-in-law, with whom she had had no contact for over seventeen years.

> Madame, I did not wish to let anyone else impart this sad news which I have unfortunately to tell you, and hope by writing to you personally to alleviate your pain.
>
> "On Sunday 22nd at five o'clock in the morning my dear son, the Duke of Reichstadt, succumbed to his long and cruel sufferings. I had the consolation of being with him in his last moments, and of being able to convince myself that every possible step had been taken to preserve his life. The assistance of science was powerless against a chest illness which the doctors unanimously judged from the outset to be of a kind so dangerous that it had inevitably to lead my unfortunate son to the tomb at an age when he offered the greatest of expectations. God has ordained it! It only remains for us to submit to His supreme will and to mingle our regrets with our tears.
>
> Accept, Mme, in this painful circumstance, the expression of my feelings of affection and consideration which I have vowed to you.
>
> Your very affectionate Marie-Louise"[10]

Napoleon's hope, expressed in his last will, that his son might be permitted, on reaching the age of reason, to have relationships with his grandmother, uncles and aunts, access to whom was prohibited by the Imperial House of Austria, had been ignored. If there was one thing the old lady deserved to be spared, it was learning of her grandson's death in the newspapers. Marie-Louise received a short response from the matriarch, who had assumed mourning together with her brother Cardinal Fesch. The news did not come as a surprise, the Bonaparte family having followed closely published reports of his illness which had been kept from Marie-Louise. Already frail, she was unable to write and dictated:

> Madame,
>
> Despite the political blindness which has always deprived me of receiving news of the dear child of whose loss you have just told me, I have never ceased to have a mother's affection for him. He was still the source of some consolation for me. To my daily painful infirmities, God has wanted to add this blow, at my great age, which I accept as fresh proof of his mercy, persuaded that He will more than compensate my grandson for the loss of earthly glory with the glory of His kingdom.
>
> Please accept, Madame, the expression of my gratitude for having taken the trouble, in such painful circumstances, to relieve the grief of my soul. Rest assured that it will last for the rest of my life.

There was plenty here to turn the knife in Marie-Louise's heart, possibly an insinuation that her former daughter-in-law had never had a mother's affection for the deceased. No doubt, news had reached her of the existence of Albertina and Wilhelm, which, despite the various illegitimate children sired by her children, would not have pleased her. "This fresh proof of God's mercy" might refer not to her grandson's release from disease, but from Austrian chains. Mme Mère's expression of gratitude for having taken the trouble to relieve the grief of her soul which would afflict her for the rest of her life might be regarded as an expression of contempt, suggesting that Marie-Louise's affliction would be fleeting. There were certainly no words suggesting any sympathy for Marie-Louise's painful situation from a mother who, some might say, had singularly failed to exert moral influence over her son, or her other children for that matter. It was said that the old lady had decided to have nothing to do with Marie-Louise when she heard that she had accepted that her son be called by his second and not his first Christian name, the name of his father. Marie-Louise was not aware of her mother-in-law's numerous attempts to make contact, to seek her support for the petition to the allies to alleviate his situation in exile, to appraise her of Napoleon's condition and of the people and medicines she had sent out to her son, of the lovely things he had said about her and his son in his last hours. These were, no doubt, intercepted and kept from the former French Empress.

Marie-Louise was bitter and angry. The international powers had connived to obstruct any chance of her son's recovery by opposing his sojourn in the warmer climate of the Italian peninsula recommended by the doctors. The Austrian cabinet had treated her son as undeserving of the interruption to her and her father's sovereign duties. The prospect of Mme Mère's immortal crown was powerless to diminish her grief. Gentz, who had succumbed to cholera days before her arrival in Vienna, had said one had to have attended a cabinet meeting to know just how much the ministers of the monarchy were worried about the existence and future of the Duke of Reichstadt. Malfatti's mistaken diagnoses and useless prescriptions, and the Duke's ruinous behaviour had suited the Great Powers. It was all the Coalition sought once the boy demonstrated how intent he was upon following in his father's footsteps and revolutionaries clamoured for him to lead them. It had suited Metternich, the triumphant diplomat, to have the child, whose conception had provided the necessary interval for the allies to mount a coalition fatal to his father, out of the way, a short existence soon to be forgotten. It had also suited him to distance the Duke's grandfather at a time when the end was anticipated and to admit Marie-Louise's arrival when the end was actually in sight. God keep men from the fate of kings! His justice was certainly impenetrable.

In Marie-Louise's duchies, the passing of the spurious Prince of Parma was marked by the performance of a Mozart mass in the Church of San Lodovico. The fears of the Chief of Police that the event would provoke a public disturbance proved unfounded. The Duchess was soon deluged by eulogies and letters of condolence.

Ménéval, Napoleon's loyal secretary, was one of the first: "Of what painful news do the newspapers echo! Should one really believe it? Ah, Madame, forgive me for coming to trouble you in your affliction!"[11] Sophie Durand, Marie-Louise"s former lady-in-waiting, wrote, "All French hearts groaned at this misfortune!"[12] Baron Mareschall screened the foreign newspapers, keeping away from her the excoriating obituaries which condemned the behaviour of her father and his cabinet. The Duke had treated with contempt the caricature the mendacious press so often painted of him – dulled and intellectually crippled by an upbringing designed to pervert him. Like much nonsense, many believed it to be true.

Marie-Louise complained to Victoria de Crenneville of the sadness – nowhere in Parma could she say that her firstborn had been here, he had done this or that there. The memories were all elsewhere, in France, Austria and Hungary. The unqualified happy time Marie-Louise could remember with her firstborn had been in Paris with Napoleon. Those were days before Marie-Louise and her son had been political hazards, before separation and her new family, when guilty secrets had besmirched the reunions in Austria. She had wished that the Duke of Reichstadt would take an interest in entomological collections, in butterflies and other insects in glass cases and green gauze rather than weaponry. What wasted energy! Her life seemed to be spent in nothing but sorrow and surrender. Victoria de Crenneville knew that words were powerless to ease pain,

"I will not try to find reasons or words of consolation. None exist. I feel that deeply, and pray God to preserve the health of Your Majesty, and to think that her existence is necessary to Albertine and Guillaume, whose destiny is as yet undetermined and who have need of you for entering into society . . . "[13]

Baron Mareschall lost no time giving instructions for the collation and disposal of the various papers left by the deceased. Even in death, the Duke, like his late father, seemed to represent an international threat. Mareschall asked Hartmann, a member of the Duke's military household, to gather up all the documents and to hand everything over against his receipt. Thus, they would be performing their duty and complying with propriety, he told Hartmann. Mareschall then marked them: "Papers to be restored to Mme the Archduchess by her Grand Master." Foresti, the Duke's former tutor, wrote to Count Dietrichstein, "Travelling towards Parma is a cargo of military reports and a medley of scribbles which we know and over which many eyes will be opened wide in Parma!"[14]

Before leaving Schönbrunn for Persenbeug, Marie-Louise had taken a large bundle of manuscripts she intended to burn, believing that it was the best she could do for the memory of her poor deceased, as she would call him from now on. She wrote to members of her family to ask if they would do similarly.

Reinstalled in Sala, Marie-Louise pored over her son's words, her heart breaking. Manna and tamarind did little to alleviate her headaches and rheumatism. She was a nervous wreck. Carrying out her son's last wishes, she read each piece of scrawl, each note, before watching the flames devour them. "I have finally looked through and burnt all my son's papers, holding back for you all those things which can be kept intact," she wrote to Count Dietrichstein in the middle of September. This was not altogether true. Baron Mareschall, who had assisted in the examination of documents with Marie-Louise, reported to Metternich that "the exercise was not yet finished". To his letter, he attached the Duke's own note of his conversation with Metternich in 1831, an unnecessary, unkind act given the lack of affection between the Duke and the Austrian Chancellor.

Albertina persuaded her mother not to destroy everything. Much of the voluminous correspondence attesting to the boy's love and appreciation of his mother would, with his half-sister's assistance, survive.

Many of the Duke's manuscripts, records of conversations and notes of a personal nature evidencing the trajectory of his inner, most private emotions distressed Marie-Louise. There were depths to his soul previously closed to her. "Alas! Dear Count, I would have preferred not to have seen those writings, because I learnt in them things which I would have preferred not to have known – and I am glad that you have not seen them. It was a painful exercise, and extremely difficult for me."[15]

The Count, who had been ill over the course of the few weeks preceding the Duke's death, commiserated, as distraught as Marie-Louise: "Alas! He loved scribbling, filling exercise books with incoherent and often foolish thoughts. The best thing is to burn them! If he had wanted to put some order in his thoughts, he would have written some great things!" Only in the second week of August, after a long recovery, had he felt sufficiently strong to put pen to paper to Marie-Louise: "It is only now that my memory retraces all the times devoted to the service of Your Majesty and Her son in all their purity." The arrival of the last portrait of the Duke had increased his pain. "Judge, Madame, what I must suffer on reading these eternal lies, these absurdities in the newspapers to which I cannot and do not wish to reply, save to the extent that honour obliges me to!"[16] He was touched to receive the Duke's watch-chain from Marie-Louise and would cherish it forever.

It had been not long after Count Dietrichstein's appointment to the Duke that Schubert had dedicated to him his arrangement of Goethe's famous poem, *Der Erlkönig*. One could hardly imagine the thoughts which would now torment him as the piano stopped abruptly before the dramatic cadence sounding the death-knell with the terrifying final words "in his arms the child was dead!" The last thing he wanted was for his former charge's life to be rewritten by those who celebrated his death.

"I am told that M.de Montbel has taken it upon himself to write a memoir with Count Metternich's approval. I do hope he will await my return to Vienna, for I am the only person who may furnish him with numerous interesting details." The Count heard nothing from Montbel. Five months after the Duke's death, Metternich wrote to Marie-Louise on Christmas Eve:

Perhaps you are already in possession of The History of the Duke of Reichstadt published by Count Montbel which has just come out in Paris. I followed the editing of this work in order to ensure that it corresponds to that which well-intentioned men would desire to find in it. I hope it will satisfy Your Majesty. Since it contains many curious facts, it will attract public attention, and since the facts are derived from primary sources, they will serve as a victorious denial of the earlier essays and those which will surely follow, to pervert the truth.[17]

When Metternich did not receive a response to his letter, he wrote again six weeks later:

I was very much convinced that the work of M. de Montbel would obtain Your Majesty's vote. It covers fully the subject matter which suggested itself to the author, and which, I dare admit, I suggested to him. My aim was to avenge Your Majesty, the Emperor, the Duke of Reichstadt and the Austrian government from the absurd calumnies spread intentionally by the anarchists and the revolutionary Bonapartists. The aim could only be attained by a story replete with truth, but artistically devised. With M. de Montbel's arrival, I had a bird in the hand. Proof of the weight of his work is demonstrated by the fact that the newspapers representing the various factions dare not speak either for or against it. The moment the factions keep quiet, it is because they feel beaten or that the terrain is too unpredictable to engage in battle.[18]

Metternich ended his promotion of Montbel's work by saying that the author intended to send copies to Marie-Louise and to the Emperor. Remarking disparagingly upon Count Dietrichstein's negative stand against the book, he urged Marie-Louise to send the author a token of her appreciation.

Montbel's authority to speak was dubious, reliant for his information on the man who had avenged himself by damning the child of his subdued enemy. In Count Dietrichstein's view, it was only Prokesch who was sufficiently possessed of all the facts to write about the life of the Duke of Reichstadt in a manner Marie-Louise could fully endorse. Prokesch, intending to publish anonymously, had already begun his work. Count Dietrichstein had no doubt the finished product would be a masterpiece.

Montbel's book was to be the first of many biographies, plays and novels based on the life and death of her son. Most of these, unlike Montbel's book, were typically by Bonaparte sympathizers who vilified Marie-Louise and those portrayed as his Austrian captors, the most prominent of which was Edmond Rostand's *L'Aiglon*. Marie-Louise kept a discreet silence.

TWENTY-THREE

Realising a daughter's happiness, 1833

Marie-Louise had long noticed the bond which had formed between one of her favourite courtiers, Count Luigi Sanvitale, and her level-headed daughter. Luigi, who had frequently accompanied Marie-Louise on her travels, had proved his loyalty on countless occasions, always sensitive to her with regard to her double life, traumas and bereavements. Foreign visitors loved to suppose a fantasy life that she had never had. Spreading rumours that she had made Neipperg so miserable that he had resorted to beating her, evil tongues had it that, despite her increasing purported ugliness, she was a sex fiend with a large circle of lovers. A tenor, Jules Lecomte, who allegedly visited Parma but of whom nobody had ever heard, nor had the meticulous registers of the Teatro Regio recorded his attendance, published an account of his stay at the Duchess's court. According to this, Marie-Louise was so pleased with his performance that she gratified him by her own performance in her apartment after dinner, such that he woke up the following morning thinking he was the Emperor Napoleon. Some circulated rumours that she had seduced Wilhelm's tutor, Zode, and Rousseau, her cook. Others claimed that they themselves had had a liaison with the sexually depraved Duchess who had given birth to their children. Such figments of others' shameless imagination plagued Marie-Louise throughout her life. There was no lack of prurient to adopt these lies and drag them into posterity. Just as malicious tongues had imputed sexual relations between the Duchess and her staff, they exploited the close relationship between her and her courtier, the younger Count Sanvitale, alleging that they were lovers and that an abortion accounted for Marie-Louise's delay in Venice on the way to Vienna to her dying son. In fact, Marie-Louise regarded the young Count as another of her children.

Metternich was not quite as keen as Marie-Louise to affirm the coupling. Luigi's credentials were far from ideal. The Sanvitales were a distinguished family of the high nobility, having been courtiers to the Bourbons and to the Farneses before them, and had amassed substantial properties in the duchy. However, the family had fallen into debt and their houses were crumbling. Their financial demise was due in no small measure to Napoleon. Luigi had been six years old when his father received Napoleon in the late spring of 1805. Count Stefano had incurred vast expense to house and feed Napoleon's guests and staff, and had been promised reimbursement and compensation for the reinstatement of his home to its former glory. The various changes to the house ordered by Napoleon's security personnel to accommodate him and Josephine and his entourage for their one-night stay had never been reversed. Doors and windows bricked up and walls taken down had not been restored. Napoleon's promises were never honoured, nor was the salary Count Stefano should have received for his services throughout the period of Napoleonic occupation ever paid. Like others, the Sanvitale family were bled dry by Napoleonic taxes, produce from land and livestock sequestered over the course of nine years. Luigi had recovered many of the works of art Napoleon had plundered from Parman sources, but his family still teetered on the brink of bankruptcy.

Wishing, more than anything, to give her daughter the gift of being able to marry for love which she had been denied, Marie-Louise worked with her minister Mistrali to provide Vienna with assurances as to Luigi's satisfactory financial standing. Vienna was well-acquainted with Luigi's older cousin, Jacopo, who had formed part of Napoleon's guard in 1805, and who had caused trouble in Parma ever since. Marie-Louise and Neipperg had had much respect for the university professor, philosopher and satirist, but Vienna saw

REALISING A DAUGHTER'S HAPPINESS, 1833

in him only the troublemaker, the instigator of secret societies, uprisings and provisional governments. Though Jacopo had escaped into self-imposed exile in 1831 before Austrian secret services could get to him, they were still fearful of his impact. Marie-Louise reassured Vienna that Luigi's loyalty to her was beyond question. Unlike his cousin Jacopo, he had never been implicated in any dissident designs. Instead, Luigi had been particularly active in the many local philanthropic initiatives of the Sanvitale family. Despatches ricocheted between Parma and Vienna through the officious hands of Baron Mareschall.

Luigi had come to ask Marie-Louise for her daughter's hand a respectable time after her return from Vienna. He had been embarrassed revealing his affections. To Marie-Louise, it was no revelation. Their mutual adoration had not passed unnoticed. When Marie-Louise gave her approval, subject to that of Vienna, he was overjoyed. Marie-Louise was also exultant. 'Il Grande Griffon', as Marie-Louise and her family had nicknamed Luigi, was head-over-heels in love. Whenever he attended upon Marie-Louise in the performance of his courtly duties, he could not help himself from talking about his fiancée. Even when he was not talking about her, it was clear he was thinking of her. He said that he wrote to her everyday. "Happy mortal!" Marie-Louise rejoiced. "He will come to see you this week – I do not allow myself to envy his happiness. I wish only that he derives joy from it, and you too, my good child, because I know it will give you so much pleasure!"[1]

Marie-Louise summoned her confessor. Appointed to serve Marie-Louise as court chaplain in 1818, Bishop Neuschel had at first delighted in his elevation to his young sovereign, but he soon found that he had taken on very much more than he had bargained for. He was deeply unhappy, with many enemies in positions of power, and frequently begged Marie-Louise to be released from his duties. She could not afford to risk letting him go. As the years wore on, he knew too many of her secrets, about her pregnancies, births, marriage and living arrangements which fell outside Catholic doctrine.

Reluctantly, he plodded on stoically, constantly finding creative means of acceding to Marie-Louise's wishes, listening patiently to her revelatory confessions and granting her absolution. As a man of the cloth, he had to tolerate many irregularities which went against his grain.

In the autumn of 1816, Marie-Louise had returned to Parma from her extended trip with Neipperg to Florence and the baths of Livorno to find she was pregnant. She had intended to go to Lucca but had received news that Napoleon's mother, uncle and sister were planning a visit at the same time. To avoid them, she diverted to Livorno. Still married to a living husband, albeit out of range on St Helena, Marie-Louise took immediate steps to forestall any whiff of scandal by issuing a decree suppressing the bureaucratic civil system of registration of births, marriages and deaths. For the time being, the register would no longer be available for general public inspection. The fact that the status of Marie-Louise's marriage to Napoleon was questionable in the eyes of the Catholic Church, which had never recognized his divorce from Josephine, was of no assistance or relief in the present situation. With effect from 1 January 1817, Marie-Louise decreed that all births, marriages and deaths were to be kept by the parishes as regards Catholics, by rabbis as regards Jews and by pastors as regards Protestants. The registration was to be on unstamped plain paper. Copies were to be admissible in law only if on stamped paper. Two copies of the registration were to be held, one at the place of worship, the other in the local town council who would authenticate and stamp if a copy were required.

Arrangements for Albertina's and subsequently Wilhelm's baptism were made, after extensive negotiations, with Bishop Neuschel and with the ultimate authority in the duchies, Cardinal Caselli, Bishop of Parma. Caselli owed his post, occupied since 1804, to Napoleon, having concluded the Concordat between him and the Holy See. At Napoleon's fall, he had assumed the role of protector of the duchies' citizens. In 1815, in anticipation of the final defeat of

French troops, as Neipperg in his capacity as Commander of Marie-Louise's Regiment knelt before him in Parma's Cathedral, Caselli blessed the flags for which Marie-Louise had personally embroidered bands. Sympathetic to Marie-Louise's plight and a master of diplomacy, Caselli soon became Marie-Louise's personal adviser, blessing her morganatic union with Neipperg. Caselli had since died. Neuschel would have to work the magic on his own. The certificate of Albertina's baptism, held in private, read,

"I, the undersigned, have baptised a baby girl born on 1st May at 4 o'clock in the morning, of unknown and illegitimate parents, and to whom has been given the name of Albertina, Maria, Countess of Montenuovo. Godparents are Giuseppe Rossi, physician and teacher of obstetrics, and Melania Campari Contini."

A similar birth certificate was produced for Wilhelm, and for a third child in January 1822, Enrico Augusto Giuseppe, who had died shortly after birth, save that in the case of Enrico neither the word "illegitimate" nor the surname appeared.

Marie-Louise required the Bishop to arrange for Albertina and Wilhelm, who as illegitimate children were barred from celebration of church festivities, to take communion. Bishop Neuschel agreed to do so as long as no-one knew. He ordered her to lock the doors to the dining room, which gave access to the antechamber to the Sacristy, once the children had arrived. Hearing that Albertina was to be married, Bishop Neuschel feared that the submission of Albertina's birth certificate which Bishop Sanvitale of Borgo San Donnino, the bridegroom's uncle who was to marry the happy couple, was bound to request, would put her, him and Albertina in a very embarrassing situation. Its disclosure would confirm not only Albertina's illegitimacy but also the fact that she was the offspring of an adulterous union, which no subsequent morganatic marriage could remedy. Nor had there been any ecclesiastical legitimization at the time of Marie-Louise's and Neipperg's secret marriage. Marie-Louise had had to and would have, once again, to place herself above the laws of her duchy. Bishop Neuschel was expected to find a formula to overcome the strictures of his faith.

While Marie-Louise was deploying her charm to persuade her confessor to assist her in papering over the procedural cracks, Albertina was beginning to wonder if she had done the right thing in accepting Luigi's suit. She was, after all, not yet sixteen. Marie-Louise tried to allay her concerns:

> You must be in great turmoil and it would be a bad thing were it to be otherwise, considering the decision you have taken regarding your whole future and happiness and that of another. Yesterday before lunch I gave the Count your reply, and I can assure you that, in all the time I have known him, I have never seen his face so radiant, beaming with happiness ... Every drop of his conversation proved to me to what an excellent man I was entrusting the happiness of my dear child.

Marie-Louise was impressed by the fact that Luigi intended to go as soon as he had a free moment to visit his mother's tomb in Fontanellato and give thanks to the Madonna for her protection. "I am sure that the Count's presence will make you feel awkward the first moment you see him, but if this causes you to lose heart, I will tell you that he feels exactly the same and that once you are married you will both feel as happy as you were before."[2]

Marie-Louise reassured her daughter that the marriage would not weaken the bond between mother and daughter. "He told me once again that he would never separate you from me." She loved the Grand Griffon more and more each day knowing he was destined to make Albertina's happiness. Nonetheless, she warned her daughter, "Your future happiness can only be found from inside you."[3]

As wedding plans advanced, earthquakes shook Parman duchies yet again. Thousands of chimney stacks and humble homes came crashing to the ground, leaving many sleeping in fields under the night sky. Marie-Louise gave instructions for housing to be built.

She would have to use all her ingenuity to try to replenish her coffers, fast running dry, while continuing the many projects she had started to try and improve conditions for her subjects. However, the scourge which had abated in Vienna loomed over Parma, waiting to reap its victims. In an effort to avoid having to raise taxes to fund precautionary measures for the advent of cholera, she ordered the melting down of her silver toilette which Napoleon had sent as part of her dowry, and tore into pieces Leroy's wedding dress, carefully removing the heavy gold thread from the silk on which it was embroidered. These obsolete symbols were extremely valuable in present circumstances.

In the first week of April 1833, Metternich wrote to report that the requisite approvals obtained, the marriage of Albertina Marie Countess of Montenuovo could now proceed. He also notified Marie-Louise that he had presented Montbel with a token of her gratitude for the author's excellent work.

Albertina rejoiced in the removal of any impediment to her union with Luigi. She had been deeply upset aged nine when she had first received a seal from her father for her use, saying that she loved Marie-Louise and the Signore so much that she was upset not to be able to bear the name of Neipperg. Marianne de Pury de Neuchâtel's explanation had calmed her down. At her marriage, she would be able to use the name created for her by her father, an Italian translation of Neipperg, coupled with her new married name. Marie-Louise begged Mlle Marianne, who loved Albertina as if she were her mother, to remain in Parma. "You are right to love her very much," she wrote to Albertina, "because it is to her that you owe everything that you are."

In June, Luigi set about organizing new quarters for him and his bride. Marie-Louise was pleased to see how well the next generation was getting on. Luigi adored Albertina's brother Wilhelm and her half-brothers Alfred, Erwin, Gustav and Ferdinand, who would soon receive invitations to Albertina's new home. "In the afternoon, they all smoke, perfuming my little drawing room in the most delightful manner. Remember when you told me how much you like the smell of tobacco and the pipe?"[4]

Two days before Albertina's wedding, a diocesan decree declared her existing birth certificate null and void. The fresh certificate was identical in every respect, save for the omission of the words "Countess of Montenovo". In Wilhelm's new certificate, the words "born of illegitimate parents" had been removed. It seemed the amendments, incongruous though they appeared, would ensure that both children would be able to wed their chosen partners.

Marie-Louise was convinced that Luigi was the only man in Parma who could have made her daughter happy, having observed the lack of family affection in the wider community in her duchies. In one of her green notebooks to which she committed her own thoughts and excerpts of books having particular resonance for her, she wrote,

> In the sixteen years I have been in Italy, I have seen an infinite number of marriages which end one worse than another. Thinking about them and analysing them, I believe I have finally found the reason why. The parents of a betrothed son are driven only by two motives which override all others, that of continuing the family line and of obtaining a daughter-in-law whose dowry will increase the splendour of their house and their fortune if this is considerable, or to save it from financial embarrassment. The girls' parents, if they have many daughters, are overjoyed to offload one of them, the mother no longer tied to a child she must supervise and prevent from going about in public and for whom she must stay at home.
>
> It is rare that a betrothed couple see each other before their betrothal is settled. I think that parents are too scared that the couple might not like each other. Only once the terms are settled are the couple permitted to meet and something which I have never seen anywhere else, they become, so to speak, almost enamoured of each other. The girl is fascinated because

everything seems a paradise after the severe constraints she has been used to at home, and both go to the altar without either having reflected enough on the future and without having thought of the consequences of that "I do" which ties one to the other for the rest of his or her life.

The first months of their marriage are full of love and pleasures. Everything is new for the young woman: balls, parties, theatre, a social life; she has had access to none of these things in her father's home. Her husband spends every day with her, he does not think about anything but gradually, as this first rush of feeling dies down, they begin to feel a terrible emptiness. The husband resumes his former idle life, his days passing between visits and taking coffee. The young woman, alone, abandoned at home, not having learnt to occupy herself because the general education of young women in Italy is extremely superficial, gets bored and seeks distraction in visits which she receives for much of the day. She believes everything her admirers tell her and begins to enjoy herself and gradually someone else takes the place in her heart which should have been nurtured by her husband. Initially, her husband is a little irritated, but soon he finds that the situation allows him to pursue his former habits, and when she becomes a mother, this sweet connection no longer ties them to each other.

It is not the mother who breastfeeds the newborn, it is not the mother who takes care of it. Children's first years are spent in the countryside with a wet-nurse. Later the children will be relegated to the nursery and to servants. Once they are older, they will be sent to boarding school, usually outside the city. They only return when it is time for them to make their own home.

Even in love, probity is necessary. It is not permissible to determine a woman's destiny if one does not have the hope of making her happy. When there is no such hope, one can make no objection when someone else takes it upon himself to make her happy. Very few people think thus. I only know Albert Neipperg who is capable of making such a sacrifice!

So many things on the Italian peninsula seemed upside-down to Marie-Louise. She had been nursed and brought up with the aid of servants, but she had never been anything other than fully integrated in Habsburg family life. She had tried to do the same with her own families. Certainly, her children were not the strangers to her that Italian children and parents generally were to each other.

Marie-Louise was overcome watching Albertina and Luigi applying the feather to the deed which determined their destinies. Their marriage was celebrated on Monday 28th October 1833 in the small chapel of Villa Fedolfi in Ferlaro, the house in which Albertina had been raised near Marie-Louise's Sala residence of Casino dei Boschi. Three hours later, which seemed like three centuries later that night, Marie-Louise took immense pride addressing her letter for the very first time to "Madame La Contessa Sanvitale". She implored the good Lord to pour out all his blessings upon her and to make her very happy. Sala seemed horrendous and deserted – she could not bear to look at the vacated Villa Fedolfi. "Tell me how you are, tell me the details of what you have done, my heart needs to know everything." She was envious of Mlle Marianne who had accompanied the newly-weds home invited to dine with them in celebration, acting the public role of mother, which Marie-Louise was denied. "I have never known jealousy, but today my heart feels it to the very highest degree."

Gil, as she affectionately called Wilhelm, spent much of the evening with her, both very sad. "I am annihilated morally and physically, I hope to write tomorrow that I feel much better. A thousand loving greetings to your excellent husband. Adieu, my dear Albertina, I love you and kiss you with all my heart with a feeling that the bonds between us will never weaken." [5]

Without news for little over twenty-four hours, she was beside herself with worry. She despatched Wilhelm to see her. When Albertina's letter finally arrived, she was in seventh heaven. Mlle Marianne's accompanying letter and Wilhelm's reports on his return were glowing. Marie-Louise thanked Divine Providence for the gift it had bestowed on her in allowing her to live to see her daughter happy.

Marie-Louise began to frequent her theatre, the season starting with Donizetti's *Anna Bolena*, followed by Rossini's *Bianca e Faliero*, drama once more offering her the escapism for her mind and emotions. From the royal box, she would sometimes espy her daughter and son-in-law, envious that he could enjoy the pleasure of which she had always been deprived, of being seen in public with her tender Albertina.

Marie-Louise's prayers were answered the following July. With great excitement, she planned a layette for the grandchild whom she knew she would love instantly. She set about making a beautiful little hat, suit and blanket. Albertina's was not an easy pregnancy. She wrote frequently to Marie-Louise, in Baden with her family, complaining of her trials. Marie-Louise impatiently awaited her father's departure so that she could run to her daughter.

> You will see, my poor child, that you will suffer these pains until the moment you consign your parcel and then they will disappear on their own. I had the pleasure of having them all the evenings of my pregnancy from the beginning to the end. Try and force yourself to walk about until the last moment, this will spare you pains and being bled. I beg you not to have your teeth pulled and to await delivery when I am sure your toothache will disappear. And don't get it into your head that it has to be a boy – you could be disillusioned.[6]

Albertina felt as if her legs were paralysed. Marie-Louise thought it was probably because the baby had moved and was resting on a nerve. She worried that she had been rash in allowing Albertina to marry too early, while still growing. Horrified to hear that Mlle Marianne had chosen this delicate moment to run off to marry her paramour, Marie-Louise begged Albertina not to take any medicines or cures pending the birth, however ill she felt. Marie-Louise told her that she must suffer with courage. She cried to think she could not be there lavish attention on Albertina and that there would be no close female relative by her beloved daughter's side. She wished that her precious Dr. Lang or midwife was there to give Albertina counsel for her own care and that of the "Contino", as she dubbed the child in the womb.

> When you give birth, tell Sofia to place a sheet folded into eight or twelve over your stomach or, if you do not like this idea, a napkin folded in four, and held in place by another which passes around your hips and kidneys and which stretches over your stomach with two pins. This practice is not known in Italy. You see even large tummies and large fractures which women have after a couple of children and if you place value on your figure and are concerned to maintain it, leave this to your old mother." She had no experience of breast-feeding, but told her daughter to stick to the diet prescribed by the doctor and then proceeded to specify her own prescription. "I beg you, eat during the first six days only three soups a day, and not Italian soups, but French where there is much more broth than ingredients, and light foods, like semolina, grated bread and so on. After six days eat a little chicken (not eggs, because they get hot) and gradually but slowly increase what you eat, but throughout the time of your delivery stay on soup and have a compote in the evening, you will see how well you feel on it, for the majority of illnesses from which women suffer in pregnancy come from indigestion. If you cannot eat, drink a lot of tea and tepid water. . . . Keep away from draughts and never go out without a hat for the first five or six weeks after delivery, failing which you will suffer the most terrible headaches."[7]

Marie-Louise was in Schönbrunn, preparing her departure for Parma, when she learnt that Albertina had given birth to a healthy boy. The news came with a charming portrait of the newborn by Mr. Lamprecht, one of Marie-Louise's courtiers. Albertina asked her mother to choose a name for the child. Naturally, there could be no name more appropriate than that of the child's departed grandfather. Marie-Louise could barely contain her joy.

From Sala, she dispensed plenty of advice, asking Albertina to forgive a well-intentioned grandmother. Six weeks after the birth she urged Albertina to take exercise whenever the weather permitted. Fresh air every day would strengthen both mother and baby. Albertina must always wrap little Alberto's head in a handkerchief to avoid him catching cold, and must not allow him to be exposed to direct sunlight.

"Take Alberto out for a walk between five and seven in the afternoon, a lovely time of the day, and spend the evenings with Guglielmo [Wilhelm in Italian]. Don't allow Alberto to eat bread all day, which children are allowed to do in Italy (I think to keep them quiet), but this bloats them, gives them worms and ruins their stomachs."[8] Back in Parma, Marie-Louise upbraided those who took the liberty of giving pieces of cake to little Alberto – she wanted to strike Major Pannholzer for this transgression. She stood by her German ideas of raising children and would laugh at Albertina's new-fangled Italian notions.

TWENTY-FOUR

The world destabilised by a change of emperors, 1835

In the summer of 1838, Marie-Louise formed part of her brother's retinue journeying from Vienna to Milan to attend his coronation as King of Lombardy-Venetia in Milan. She sent Albertina a vivid description of the festivities. The heartfelt enthusiasm of seven thousand peasants who filed past the Emperor, each in his valley's traditional costume, furnished a sight no other country could offer.

Marie-Louise stood throughout the five hours of the magnificent coronation ceremony in Milan's cathedral. The sun's rays shone through the rainclouds and stained glass windows upon the crown just as it was being placed upon Ferdinand's head, a sure omen, she surmised, that the Almighty would cast his protection over her brother's reign. No expense had been spared on the festivities, a fact of which Marie-Louise did not approve. It was as good as throwing money out of the window. Ferdinand left Milan convinced of the devotion of the Milanese, moving on with his sister for his first official visit to Venice, where he would draw the mistaken conclusion that he was beloved there too.

In April 1835, Marie-Louise had been devastated to hear of her father's death. He had fallen ill four months earlier, and had died, aged sixty-seven, one day after the anniversary of his own father's death, unable to withstand a seventh bleed. The Viennese were in consternation, finding it hard to believe that the world could and did continue without their emperor of forty-three years. People stopped to lament his passing outside shop-windows, peering in at his portrait, tears streaming down their faces. He was a Christian hero, a saint.

THE WORLD DESTABILISED BY A CHANGE OF EMPERORS, 1835

"We have all become orphans!" Victoria de Crenneville wrote to Marie-Louise, "Dr. Stifft is now the most hated man in Vienna! He should have found means to cure the Emperor!"[1]

Such was Marie-Louise's affection for her father that whenever she heard Haydn's *Gott Erhalte Franz den Kaiser,* she would burst into floods of tears. She had been so moved by the rendition of the anthem by the rising star Paganini that she instantly unpinned the diamond brooch she was wearing and handed it to him. It seemed to her that her father had been respected and held in affection across Europe. Emperor Francis had managed, despite disagreements, to maintain cordial relations with virtually all the monarchs of his era with the notable exception of Napoleon. No-one blamed him for the catalogue of defeats he had suffered at Napoleon's hands. He had been a victim of the tornado just like everyone else. Courageous and determined, he expressed himself ready at all times to go to war, but never committed his subjects to war without deep thought and regret that there was no other realistic option. Unforgiving as regards abusive treatment by his military, he was lenient with deserters. Like Napoleon, he took particular care to provide for widows, orphans and the wounded of war. The value he placed on human life, for which he had sacrificed his daughter, was such that he had far fewer to provide for. Marie-Louise always delighted in her father's wisdom. This had been honed from over forty years in government, from an astonishing memory for the lessons he had received from his tutor Count Colloredo in compliance with the punishing nine hour daily study schedule his father Leopold had set him, and from reading the contents of his library of forty thousand fascinating, valuable volumes, the precise location of each of which he knew by heart. His knowledge and experience of human nature, and of the conditions of his subjects' lives, were profound.

For forty-three years, Emperor Francis had governed as conscientiously and as wisely as he was able. His mild regime required strictness. He insisted on hard and fast rules of conduct in civil and military officials, tolerating no-one who might derogate from them.

Only thus would servants respect their masters. He recommended a few warning examples to forestall any need for punishment in future.

He had inherited an enlightened system of government that had proven impervious to the excesses of the French Revolution and a model of good governance. He constantly sought the improvement of the economic and social state of his extensive dominions. His capital was a cosmopolitan hub where Christian, Jew and Moslem mixed freely without fear or oppression, and he liked to think that this freedom found expression throughout his empire. When he found Jewish villages sacked and torched by ruffians, he was deeply distressed and gave immediate orders for help to be provided and for the culprits to be hunted down and punished. He believed that the ordinary man had no interest in change, which, to his way of thinking, could only be harmful. He had observed as a young man how his uncle, Emperor Joseph II, had alienated large sections of the people by seeking to introduce reforms he had sincerely intended to be for the common good.

Napoleon had always believed that men were governed and led by motives of fear. Emperor Francis made no such rash assumptions, nor did Marie-Louise. He regarded one of his highest duties to his subjects to ensure the thorough and proper administration of justice, a value transmitted to his daughter. "Justice is the foundation of kingdoms," ran his motto. By his own lights, he exacted the same strict observance of the law as rigorously from himself as from his people. Men wanted honesty and directness, and above all respect. Despite his forgiving nature and belief that kindness and leniency could be more effective than harshness, despite often intervening to reduce sentences, he rarely intervened in political crimes. He believed subversives to be cloaked in mystery and deceit whereas his administration was frank, open, transparent and public. He was sure that one day the whole of Europe would recognize the debt it owed to Austria for the preservation of its ideals.

Triumph over his son-in-law and his subsequent hosting of the stellar Vienna Congress had earned Emperor Francis a place in legitimist hearts and reinforced the indispensability of monarchy everywhere. He had lived since his coronation for most of his rule as the most popular, most beloved monarch, his kindliness legendary, respected and humbly obeyed by the aristocracy, the middle classes, the poor, town-dwellers, mountain-dwellers, farmers and peasants. All attributed the return of peace to his tenacity. Unimpressed by show, he was a man of simple tastes who treated others equally, whatever their station. Marie-Louise followed his example. He believed that man's true calling was to make others and himself happy, that the individual's happiness is completely enmeshed with that of his fellows, that virtues must be cultivated and vices shunned, and that the paternalistic monarchy was the most successful and beneficent form of social organization.

Marie-Louise believed him to be the best of all fathers. She had been frustrated at times, and disagreed with her father on some matters. The positions she had been forced to adopt towards the Bonapartes and her French retainers had caused her immense pain as had the pressure applied to root out dissension, but she was always forced back to the principle that her father was unscrupulous in his dedication to duty and to the well-being of the nation which he regarded as an extension of his family. His surrender of her to prevent a Romanov-Bonaparte union which would, in all probability, have resulted in a carve-up of Central Europe between the two dynasties had been nothing short of heroic. She would have been a fool to risk loss of his support. As she saw it, he had never abandoned her; he had always stood by her. She had never regarded his conduct in sacrificing her as cowardly or his dethronement of his son-in-law and separation of him from her and their child as reprehensible. She lamented her sufferings and the circumstances which had contrived them, but never went so far as to allow herself to think that her father had done anything other than respond to political realities. She cursed the stupid governments who continued to hate her for a marriage imposed upon her and her father under duress. The English diplomat Lord Holland accused Emperor Francis of having wanted to surrender her to the Corsican imposture, to having "approved" and "seriously sought" the betrothal. Marie-Louise could never have accepted this, nor that her father had ever wanted to disinherit the grandson whose portrait by Isabey – representing the sleeping King of Rome on a cloud, his chest swathed with the Légion d'Honneur, three days after his birth – had always occupied pride of place on the desk of his wood-panelled study. The Emperor had always adored the Duke, and mourned his untimely death. She was infinitely grateful for the paternal love extended to him.

Marie-Louise had always known that her father adored her, perhaps more than any other of his children. Her birth occurred after two years of unparalleled misery. Two days after giving birth to a daughter, Francis's first wife died, and within twenty-four hours, so too had his uncle, Emperor Joseph II, who had been as good as a second father to him. Four months later, his severely mentally impaired daughter also died. Francis's father, Emperor Leopold, selected his double-cousin, Marie-Thérèse, as his second wife. Marie-Louise's arrival was a miracle, casting a halo over his very special relationship with her. The bond of unconditional love between them became ever tighter with the death of his father Leopold within three months of her birth, of his mother shortly thereafter, and of Marie-Louise's mother fifteen years later after giving birth to her thirteenth child. Inconsolable at her death, Emperor Francis shed rivers of tears over her lifeless body, the child who lay in the nearby crib following her into the grave a few days later. Too grief-stricken to attend his wife's burial, Emperor Francis sought succour in the company of his eldest daughter and son Ferdinand, journeying together to Hungary and Transylvania. This was the first time Marie-Louise had appeared publicly in an official capacity, officiating with her father at the inauguration of public buildings and a canal linking the Danube and Tisza rivers.

On the few occasions Emperor and Empress had been parted,

barely a day had passed without an exchange of loving correspondence. Empress Marie-Thérèse had been the Emperor's closest confidante, not only in sentimental matters, but also in political and military affairs. She had accompanied her husband everywhere, even onto the corpse-strewn battlefields that had littered his monarchy since its inception. Emperor Francis, first and foremost a private, family man, who had no appetite for lovers or casual affairs, had adored his exuberant Neapolitan wife. This example of devoted matrimony provided a powerful precedent for Marie-Louise. The sanctity of faithful love hallowed by the indissoluble bonds of the church, had been central to her self-image and expectation of the future. She was never to know the peace of mind deriving from such sanctity.

The widowed Empress Karoline-Auguste sent Marie-Louise a marble bust and a portrait of her late husband at his death. Letters of condolence on her father's death came from Marie-Louise's imperial relatives, the Austrian court, foreign sovereigns and former French retainers.

"He was the person I cherished most in this world," Marie-Louise declared to Victoria de Crenneville. "To him, I could confide all my thoughts. He was everything to me, a father, friend and counsellor in all the difficulties of my life." Marie-Louise wrote to her daughter,

> The death of my father has so annihilated and lacerated all the feelings of my heart, of which I had proof yesterday when I was reminded of that which my father said to me when he saw me in 1817, the first time after my departure for Italy, tears of joy rose to his eyes and he said: 'These tears do me good – for a long time I have been unable to cry!' How I feel now, my dear daughter, the value of his words![2]

Albertina, never acknowledged by her grandfather, understood her mother's desolation.

Marie-Louise had received her father (though he visited his Italian dominions annually) only twice in Parma. He had come for a few days, first in 1819, when he was on his way to visit family in Naples after diplomatic discussions with the Pope in Rome, a city from which Marie-Louise as a Bonaparte was barred, and again in 1825. The Emperor was pleased with what he saw. At the theatre and the opera Marie-Louise was consistently received with applause, cheers and endless handclapping. Everyone seemed to speak to her with genuine affection. Standards of health and living conditions had dramatically improved since her arrival and the harvests had yielded abundantly. However, the seeds of change which had taken root during Napoleon's administration had begun to sprout. The difficult times, predicted by Prokesch four years earlier, had arrived and would have to be weathered. With Emperor Francis's death, Metternich feared Armageddon.

In Austria, Marie-Louise saw smiling faces and smiling landscapes. Peasants and townsfolk treated her kindly and with deference. She did not see what the celebrated dramatist Franz Grillparzer condemned in his plays, that her father's resistance to change had caused Austria to fall irreversibly behind France, Britain and the new United States of America. Marie-Louise did not see how oppressive the Magyars, Southern Slavs and Italians found what the Habsburgs considered to be a magnificent central administration and practically infallible code of laws. It had, after all, been her father who had been instrumental in restoring a constitution to Hungary. She knew and loved the man who had protected those whom Providence had placed in his care by refusing to remove Joseph's prohibition on mendicant orders which would have imposed demands on the financially burdened populace, by refusing to adopt artificial measures of inflation or forced loans, actively implementing tight budgetary controls. Similarly, he had imposed maximum prices on bread and wheat to check the rise in cost of living, never intending to promote a black market. He had detested poor accounting and consequent extravagance, and anything that increased human misery. Metternich's policies had not been so considerate. He knew that many were not smiling. His sympathy following the

Emperor's death came accompanied by a declaration that he would continue to pursue the same political agenda under the son as he had with the father.

> There are no miracles in the advance of affairs in this low world. Well, Madame, one might be tempted to admit of their existence casting an impartial glance at the monarchy. It is the spirit of the deceased monarch which still prevails and, the salvation of the empire, it is the firm decision of the new monarch to make no changes. Do me the honour of continuing to repose your trust in me and I will show myself worthy of it in the future just as I have shown in the past. The world's well-being rests on the fact *that nothing here moves.* Such is the will of the Nation and the general cry of Europe! It is hard to calculate the value of the principle of order maintained in the great central empire of Europe and the impact it has had, without all its beneficial ramifications.[3]

Shortly thereafter, he wrote to Marie-Louise in more exultant vein,

"The Emperor Ferdinand surpasses not only my expectations, but all those of everyone called to work with him. Accustomed always to speak with an open heart to Your Majesty, I have no need to assure you that this is the exact truth."[4]

People respected Ferdinand for the religious and moral conviction he had inherited from his father, and for his deep veneration of him. His father had written his heir two long letters shortly before his death which the Empress handed him in a quiet moment. Although only a very few were privy to their contents, it is said that they were masterpieces. In them, he urged his son to honour the rights of all men – only in so doing would the rights of the throne be honoured. Not quite the half-wit some tried to portray him, Ferdinand was simple, earnest and well-intentioned, but with none of the ingenuity, guile and wisdom of his father. Metternich dissembled. He, as much as everyone else, was aware of Marie-Louise's younger brother's mental limitations, but he was not yet ready to relinquish his position to a younger man who might introduce less reactionary policies than those he had always espoused. Ferdinand's accession was a disaster. Upon Emperor Francis's death, there had been a panic on the Viennese stock exchange and the price of Austrian government bonds had fallen sharply, such was the general lack of confidence. The Rothschilds intervened to prop up the market.

Courtiers observed that it was a sad irony that his accession to the throne occurred on the day of Saint Simplicien. Archduchess Sophie, wife of Marie-Louise's nephew and mother of the little Franz-Josef, and many others regarded Austria as being without an Emperor. Sophie was already hatching plans to create in her son, Franz-Josef, a viable, pragmatic substitute to take over when the time was right. She would take as long as politics and dissent needed to give her an opening. Times had changed. Nothing might appear to Metternich to be moving in Vienna, but seismic shifts were occurring there and elsewhere. Sophie found many supporters for her cause.

Marie-Louise had said after the death of the Duke of Reichstadt that the only reason she continued to travel to Austria was to be with her father. "At my age, one no longer seeks entertainment, but a tranquil sweet life which I enjoy seeing my father, the sole purpose of my journey."[5] Ever since the hateful day of his death, she dreaded the thought of returning to Vienna, everyone watching how she behaved, gauging her reactions, the petty gossip which would form the conversation of Viennese courtiers. She planned to stay a few days and then repair to Baden. Upon her first return, the delights of her childhood playground, the colonnade, the ruins, the obelisk, the orangerie, the palace apartments and gardens were forever places of mourning. Schönbrunn seemed deserted. She ate lunch with her brother, Emperor Ferdinand, and dined alone with Archduchess Sophie. She sat quietly in sorrow beside the recent tombs in the imperial Capucin vault. She told Albertina that, though accustomed to disappointments and pain having suffered so much in her life, these visits made her feel calmer. Her brother Francis and sister Marianne tried desperately hard to distract her. She occupied her father's apartments, and took comfort sleeping in the vast bedroom in which he had slept, entertaining visitors in the large drawing room where he had received her, playing her harpsichord in the smaller drawing room where he had accompanied her on his viola as he looked out of the window, going through her papers at the desk in the small antechamber where he had worked. The vases of flowers, and four little American birds chirping all day like nightingales, softened painful memories.

Emperor Francis's death notwithstanding, Marie-Louise's homeland remained the magnet it had always been. Imperial family ties and duty to her brother prevailed. Besides, it was now more important than ever for her to be seen on the international circuit and to maintain links with the sovereigns and their diplomats who frequented Vienna. Only by keeping her profile constantly before these people could she remind them of her existence, the sacrifices she had made for the peace of Europe and the fine job she was doing as Austrian counterweight to the French and Spanish interests which coveted control of her duchies. If she stayed in Parma, with Albertina and Wilhelm and the grandchildren, she would be forgotten, and decisions against her interests taken without the slightest prick of conscience.

In Vienna, Marie-Louise saw ambassadors and ministers who had frequented her father's court, and sovereigns and their ambassadors of the foreign courts who had been her father's and were now her brother's allies. There, she bumped into her Bourbon cousins, the Duchess de Berry, whose husband had been assassinated in Paris, and the Duke of Modena and his family. The Bourbon Duke of Lucca, heir to Marie-Louise's duchies, seemed never to give up hope of supplanting her. He even attempted to buy Parma with the aid of Spanish coin in exchange for his continued loyalty to France. Marie-Louise demanded a ridiculously high down-payment of four million francs before she would come to the negotiating table. As she had predicted, the King of Spain immediately withdrew his support. Neither Marie-Louise nor her subjects' loyalty was to be bought. When Metternich learnt of this indecent manoeuvre, he warned the Bourbon couple that if they were to take the matter any further he would arrange immediate cancellation of Maria Luisa's revenues from her Bohemian territories. From then on, the French tried to gain a footing on the west coast of the Italian peninsula by trying to convince the Duke to extend the port of Viareggio so that they would be able to land troops to take Parma by force.

Marie-Louise had little idea of the ferocity of public dissatisfaction which had simmered before her father's death but which surfaced in Habsburg dominions. Anticipating that his enthroned epileptic son would be too feeble to assume any leadership role, Emperor Francis had created a support structure so that Ferdinand was no more than a puppet propped up by the triumvirate of the State Conference, her uncle Archduke Ludwig, Prince Metternich and Count Kolowrat, her late father's former home affairs minister. It was a regency in all but name. Many had tried to prevent Ferdinand's accession. Less than a month after the Duke of Reichstadt's death, Count Dietrichstein informed Marie-Louise of an attempt on Ferdinand's life in Baden bei Wien. She feared the problems which could ensue for the monarchy if her brother were assassinated, or succumbed to an illness, such as the virulent bout of measles which hit him shortly after assuming the throne. Hungary was in political foment, contained only by her uncle Archduke Ludwig, whose efforts would be seriously undermined by her brother's premature demise. From Venice, Marie-Louise wrote to Albertina,

> The entry of the Emperor was absolutely stunning! Even the weather favoured his entry, and there were boats of every colour, the boatmen dressed in all their finery. In the evening there were illuminations in the city, at the churches of Il Redentore, of La Salute, of San Giorgio Maggiore, the Arsenale, the Accademia delle Belle Arti, and Casa Treves.[6]

Across the Venetian Lagoon, there were a series of military parades and regattas, a plethora of boats and gondolas and crowds. The party ended as the entire retinue were treated to a delightful trip down the Grand Canal. The applause of the crowds and the triumphal arch in glass threads and rare pearls erected by Murano's glass-blowers seemed an indicator that the goodwill towards her father had passed to his son. Marie-Louise was unaware that there had been considerable difficulties in marshaling crowds to salute the new Emperor. The Venetian police had had to buy the applause of the gondoliers at an exorbitant tariff of three *paoli* per head, but the ferrymen had refused to salute the new emperor at any cost. If Marie-Louise had not seen the welter of pamphlets which issued from German printing presses urging her brother's removal, she was far from ignorant of Austria's increasingly precarious position on the Italian peninsula, always destabilised by movement in France, where dissident printing presses worked unrelentingly.

As in Vienna, Marie-Louise bumped into the diplomatic throng, and consorted with the Turkish ambassador and his ugly sons, the Canning family who were travelling in their own boat, and her Bourbon cousin, the Duchess of Berry. The duchess lived in exile in Austria after a disastrous attempt from the Vendée to place her son, the Duke de Bordeaux, on the French throne.

Marie-Louise loved her trips to Venice. She felt like a true Venetian as she journeyed by gondola in the bosom of the ocean, enveloped in a shawl. She relished the sculpture and architecture, St Mark's Square and the Basilica, walking along the Riva degli Schiavoni, and on the Venice Lido where she loved to contemplate the Adriatic and collect seashells along its sands. Everything in Venice was fantastical, particularly the prices. She marvelled at the stupendous merchandise on sale – haberdashery, textiles, glass, gold, mirrors and pearls. She took a cookery course at the Leon Bianco to help her identify the ingredients of seafood dishes which she was sure were poisoning her. She attended Donizetti's *Lucrezia Borgia* at La Fenice, the opera house which had recently been refurbished, having burnt down two years earlier, a dreadful fire attributed to the installation of an uncertified heating system – though it might easily have been caused, as many fires were, by the privilege granted by the government to the nobility of holding candles in the boxes. And there were charming excursions on board the imperial steamboat from Venice to the many islands within the Lagoon, and to Chioggia.

A city unlike any other, Venice offered illusory escape, a digression from the uncomfortable, sinister, reality.

TWENTY-FIVE

Cholera, 1836 and its aftermath

Cholera finally arrived in Parma a year after Emperor Francis's death, during the month of June. By mid July, seventy-four cases of infection had been reported, all of which were in the country around the ducal capital but not in the city itself. Marie-Louise was in Vienna again, with her much depleted family, many of whom had had a touch of choleric influenza.

"I am concerned that the authorities in Parma are not doing as I asked or are taking the wrong measures and feel I must return though I hate to leave my family who have received me with more tender affection than ever, the loss which we have suffered binding us ever more closely together."[1] It seemed to Marie-Louise, from afar, that the doctors and dignitaries were scaremongers, getting everyone exercised about cholera, raising rather than allaying fears. "I will return if things get worse," she said, reluctant to leave her restorative natal air which was calming her nerves. The movement of troops infected by unsanitary lodgings was spreading cholera, she was sure. The Esterhazy regiment, decimated by the disease in Brescia, had brought it to Piacenza. Thankfully, Parman troops were not yet infected. "The contagion permeates the highways to Italy which are so infected that we do not know where is safe to pass. Nevertheless, the doctors should be reassuring, not talk incessantly of the risks of contagion."

In Vienna, people talk about cholera as if it were flu or a head-cold.[2] What would our dear protomedic [Dr. Rossi] say if he had to live with us in a place where eighty people a day were dying and if he were to see us fearlessly entering the city and suburbs, places of infection, and if he were to see how we remain healthy without immersing ourselves in chloride, he who does not even dare open medical reports! I can speak from experience finding myself right at the centre of a deadly case. Everyone has colics, but not diarrhoea. When diarrhoea calls, it is time to call the doctor and by adhering to a rigorous diet, one recovers quickly – in the last fifteen days I have already had three such attacks.[3]

Cucumbers and melons were to be avoided. Ices and iced water promoted health.

Alberto, barely two years old, was extremely ill with whooping cough and had worms, which Albertina suspected he had contracted from smoked soufflés. Albertina was pregnant again. Marie-Louise told her daughter to keep calm:

"Avoid the charlatans of the city. Don't fear cholera. If it comes, do as before but abstain from raw salads and anything which you have difficulty digesting. Be patient. Stay in the country for as long as you can and give birth there away from the city where you are more likely to be susceptible to cholera." Again and again, she begged Albertina not to allow herself to be afraid of cholera. Luigi might be, but she must not.

"Don't listen to stupid voices about contagion. The best doctors here agree that it is as contagious as nervous fever or typhus which only comes on if we are predisposed to it – and I fear four sad years of experience should give them more credit than the Parmans." She would travel home directly without stopping, having decided not to allow anyone to disinfect her entourage and their possessions, a procedure "proven to be absurd and noxious to both eyes and chest."[4]

Marie-Louise advised Albertina to go immediately to Villa Fedolfi if cholera were to arrive in Fontanellato. Marie-Louise could not contemplate maintaining two establishments so Albertina would have to bring her own horses and kitchen. The expecting mother was deterred from venturing to Sala by the inconvenience of having to observe a period of quarantine. In Fontanellato, there was an unbelievable obsession with fumigation of every kind. Guards were located at the city gates to prevent the transit of any possession which had not previously been disinfected with chlorine. In any event, leaving Fontanellato was soon out of the question. To go to Parma would be madness. She and Luigi calculated that there had already been seven hundred and eighty cases of cholera in the capital. Particularly morbid were the doctors and priests who went about their business melodramatically cloaked in black robes, terrifying the sick. Luigi was exasperated, tired of seeing laid-out bodies and receiving delegations of frightened people, referring them to the Parman authorities, refusing absolutely to endorse ridiculous notions. Many refused to respect common sense, gorging themselves on foods damaging to their health against doctor's orders, a measure which often contributed to their deaths. To avoid accusations that the Sanvitales were the source of infection, Albertina allowed no visitors, few as they were since the appearance of the illness, and received no callers save the post from Parma.

Bishop Neuschel kept Marie-Louise appraised of the advance of the disease and the public reaction. Marie-Louise was shocked at the lack of community spirit. "Some days ago they left one of the workers from Gambi to die in the fields in front of his tile factory without going to his assistance and then, without saying anything, buried him behind the house. What people! What a country! The same has occurred in Lombardy giving my uncle white hairs!"[5] She learnt that a woman had died of cholera during the night at the local hospital of Gaiano without either Marie-Louise's doctor or another doctor having been able to save her because the hospital had been so poorly organised that there was not one medicine, nor a sponge, nor a basin to heat water. Cocchi, the Councillor of Parma, had really covered himself and the local authority of Gaiano in glory, Marie-Louise commented sarcastically.

Marie-Louise was furious, the three hundred and fifty thousand francs she had allocated for cholera measures having disappeared into thin air. The generous offers of donations made before her departure for Vienna had also come to nothing. The precautions she had meticulously planned had not been implemented. Contrary to her specific instructions, cholera victims confined to hospital were placed alongside other sick inmates, which led to more victims. Cholera advanced in leaps and bounds. The death toll mounted.

In early September 1836, Sala suffered its first cholera victim, and by the second week four had died. Having returned from Vienna, Marie-Louise worked tirelessly to help many of the peasants, who came to her rather than reporting to the ducal authorities the moment they had symptoms of dysentery or diarrhoea. She experimented with vegetable soups to find the most economic nutritious recipe for distribution to the poor. She followed closely the progress of a mother of seven children whose husband had immediately abandoned her and thanked God for her deliverance. Marie-Louise drew comfort from her work, hoping that she had on occasion averted potential fatalities, and from the dedication of the German doctor whom she had brought from Vienna, who scoured the countryside from dawn to dusk, visiting the sick at home, bringing them food, medicines and linen which she had amassed. Long walks eased her troubles. Many of Marie-Louise's court members and ministers were sick, her chief administrator struck down with diarrhoea, leaving her to host Austrian General Radetsky who had come down from Lombardy to inspect Parman troops. As yet there seemed to be no sign that the plague had run its course in Europe – the imperial family had gone to Prague, shortly followed by cholera, which raged violently. Soon everyone was suffering from diarrhoea.

Thankfully, as winter set in and Christmas approached, cholera seemed to forsake Parma, moving south towards Rome. Towards the end of November, the road between Parma and Guastalla, closed for several months to prevent transmission of the disease, was reopened, but only those who could produce a clean bill of health could pass, and baggage still had to go through quarantine, a requirement which deterred most from undertaking the journey. But the Parman ordeal was not over. A subdued Christmas was followed by an influenza epidemic, once more brought by troops, sixty-four men of the Austrian battalion stationed at Piacenza struck down. Soon the general populace were infected. Along with her subjects, Marie-Louise had a sore head and throat and felt ghastly for days on end. Her court was struck down too, as terrible rains, storms and earthquakes pummelled her duchies.

Disease and sickness for the best part of a year had prevented movement of persons throughout her duchies. Albertina missed her mother terribly. "Why is it so rarely given to us to be able to talk, when the need to tell you how much I love you is so great?"[6] Alberto, recovered from his whooping cough, was causing great hilarity, mixing up French and Italian. Marie-Louise, stressing the need to get her little *Ninon*, as she nicknamed him, out into the fresh air, sent him a toy elephant so that he would not forget her. Mercifully, cholera had not hampered Albertina's pregnancy, which delivered without incident. Marie-Louise now had a granddaughter, whom she nicknamed *Cinderella*.

"When you ask about the name of the little girl of which her grandfather Count Stefano is the godfather, wouldn't Stefania be lovely?"[7] Thinking of little Ninon and Cenerentola lifted her spirits when she felt low. When Albertina and the newborn came to stay in Parma, Marie-Louise sent a vat of rice soup and a heap of roasted chicken. She also despatched herbal remedies of two little bags containing camomile, elderflower and ground broad beans to be used as heat patches to ease Albertina's suppurating breasts. She told her daughter to go to bed, and sent Guglielmo to look after his sister. She should wear a wide rather than the usual narrow corset. Even though Marie-Louise had not nursed her own children, she well understood the emotional and psychological benefits of breast-feeding, the unique bond which it created between mother and child. She sympathised with women who were unable to suckle and was contemptuous of selfish husbands who celebrated such failure. She was relieved when Albertina hired a wet-nurse for little Maria and subsequently for her third and fourth child, a second daughter, Luigia, and son, Stefano.

With the disappearance of cholera, Marie-Louise's regular daily routine, established on the day she set foot in her duchies, resumed. She confessed that she found life in the city of Parma often monotonous and trying, her initiatives circumscribed by financial and political constraints. Her day started early. Before rising, she would receive her post and attend to correspondence. Letters from her family she could not wait to open. There were others for which she had far less appetite. Throughout her life, Marie-Louise was constantly plagued by former retainers and those of her first husband seeking her patronage. One particularly persistent caller upon "Her Majesty's great heart", which the writer's "entire soul honours with inexpressible intimacy", was Napoleon's former Austrian mistress who had serviced his needs from his first appearance in Vienna in 1805 until his passage through Germany in 1813. According to her story, Napoleon had dressed her up in men's clothing so that she could join him as part of his retinue on all his journeys. She claimed that he had bestowed the title of Baroness upon her shortly before his downfall and had settled an income upon her which the horrible catastrophe of 1815 had in large part destroyed. She threatened to kill herself if Her Majesty did not come to her aid.

> Would the world countenance that the mistress of that extraordinarily great man who shines throughout Europe and whom half the universe worships, whose great deeds will be remembered with astonishment and admiration by every nation a thousand years hence and beyond, should be destitute? God knows my situation is undeserved! I was innocent, unspoiled and of pious disposition and whom did I give myself to? And I should be ruined, without help? Would that I could go to the good Napoleon and die by his grave, whence he calls me! For the third time, I dare ask Your Majesty's protection![8]

Such florid, over-written, obsequious pleas littered Marie-Louise's bundle of post. Ducal finances were stretched such that she supplemented much treasury expenditure from her own private resources and funds provided by Rothschilds guaranteed by her. These were not just for new carriages from London's Barkers, but roads, bridges, hospital equipment and furniture and much more. She was certainly not looking for more causes.

After breakfast, Marie-Louise spent the morning dealing with matters of state, reviewing reports with her ministers, signing documents, before walking in the gardens of the Ducal Palace with their long avenues, charming lake and statuary. She paid frequent visits to sit in sad contemplation and prayer before Neipperg's sepulchre, first at the Church of San Ludovico, later transferred to the subterranean chapel of the Church of the Steccata. Marie-Louise had redesigned and refurbished the Renaissance Church six years before Neipperg's death to bring together the reliquaries of the duchy's previous Farnese and Bourbon rulers, never thinking for one moment that she would be so shortly widowed.

Marie-Louise attended regularly upon the institutions she supported financially, the orphanages, hospitals, churches and monasteries, to which she gave the benefit of her wisdom. Marie-Louise took particular interest in the maternity hospital for pregnant women which she had set up shortly after Albertina's birth. She had staffed the hospital with experienced midwives, and a permanent teacher assisted by a student mistress who taught illiterate women how to read and write, and attended their deliveries when the teacher was absent. The maternity hospital also comprised eight permanent wet-nurses and a further eight provisional wet-nurses. This was, on any view, exceptional maternity care, ahead of most of the European continent. The schools she had created for young women, who received her with tokens of their charming handiwork, gratified her.

Fastidious in her attention to every detail of the menu and table, she oversaw preparation of her meals. After lunch and a short nap, she would receive in her drawing room in the afternoon, when she would chat, preferably with Albertina, but otherwise with one of her court ladies. They were not always agreeable company,

"My ladies have adopted a type of conduct so singular towards me, they distance themselves from me and hold such sardonic conversations with me that they treat me like a reject. I do nothing and see nothing in my conduct which deserves such censure. There are some days when I lack courage to bear them."[9] There were many times when she very much regretted not being a man.

Prefering often to be alone, she would paint or embroider, and then play the piano or harp, delving into her extensive library of music scores to exhort herself to attempt pieces which challenged her musical abilities. When she had the time, she read voraciously in many different languages and was always abreast of the English, French and German novels of the day.

In the late afternoon, she granted audiences and was often occupied for over five hours. She listened to ministers, nobles, guests and dignitaries from abroad passing through her territories. Despite objections raised by her most recent chief administrator, she also received petitioners and others from the gentry and peasantry. Many of her subjects she found difficult to understand. "What a nuisance!!!" she would complain to Albertina. People would bend her ear talking utter nonsense as she listened patiently without understanding a word.

Marie-Louise had refurbished and modernised the Ducal Palace in Parma, installing the latest plumbing and heating to try and combat the damp of winter months and the stifling heat of summer. Her second ducal seat of Piacenza she found quite unbearable. The Villa Mandelli was asphyxiating in July and August, such that she went about the city in a constant daze, her brains roasted to the point of imbecility, forcing her to rely on magnesium of Aousta to relieve her pains. She hated drinking the silly herbal infusions prescribed her. An afternoon constitutional walk was practically impossible, such was the ubiquitous coating of dust. When she could, she stayed indoors, writing out excerpts of historical works to send to Albertina. By contrast, in winter, when snow appeared on the Piacentine mountains, Marie-Louise felt displaced, the rooms glacial, draughts inescapable.

Marie-Louise felt most comfortable at her retreat of Casino dei Boschi in Sala, where she and Neipperg had recreated her childhood utopia of the Palace of Schönbrunn, introducing an extensive variety of birds, flowers and fruit trees. Here, she relived the lovely days spent with the love of her life, enjoying the gardens they had laid out and grown together, regaining such equanimity as her traumatic experiences permitted her. There was little to do in Sala, but at least she was far from crowds, errands, committees and tittle-tattle. Light moments passed swiftly, giving way to a deep feeling of emptiness. She buried herself in novels and newspapers, her own and those from outside her duchies, the latter providing little in the way of comforting reading, before passing them to Luigi and Albertina. Far from the incessant buzz of court gossip, the Duchess relaxed, enjoying the cool breeze from the Apennines in summer and in autumn the clear air free of fog and the damp of the Po, giving herself over to the pleasures of solitude, to the countryside, to wildlife, to nature in all its serenity. From Sala, she could, with the aid of a telescope, see as far as the six towers of Cremona, Bergamo and Brescia. Fearless walking alone, she would scale belfries and turrets of manorial homes for the sake of a breath-taking view at the top.

Visits from the family were the highlight of her life. She tried to lure them more frequently with treats, constantly asking if they had any special requests which she could serve when they visited. "Albertina and Luigi, there is a chunk of sausage which is begging to be eaten, won't you come and eat it?"[10] She showered gifts upon everyone, the produce of her garden and her hearth. She despatched with the diligence boxes of Easter eggs, bunches of asparagus, a fat Piacentine hen and oranges. She cooked sweets for the children, burning herself on occasion.

Marie-Louise found a new vitality for shopping. She trawled the bazaar and exorbitantly priced boutiques of Milan for beautiful Chinese *objets d'art* and paintings. In Vienna, she inspected the magnificent glazed ware at the imperial porcelain factory and bought up glassware, rugs, stationery and jewellery, gloves and lengths of fur.

Armed with measurements, she was constantly on the look-out for the latest creations for Albertina and the little ones. Dormant during her bereavements, her passion for fashion was reawakened. She was charmed by the 'Rococo', particularly popular in Salzburg, an ensemble of antique plates mounted on a ribbon worn around the neck. Frightening, exaggerated hats like overturned basins, chenille berets shaped like helmets in an assortment of colours caught her attention. Rarely did she return from one of her travels without a new straw hat or parasol to ward off the sun. She loved clothes which accentuated her waist, the same size as Alberto's aged seven. However, her notebook entries demonstrate that she was fully aware that she was no longer in her prime.

> Women must love flowers. They must cultivate them, paint them, dry them and imitate them, but they must refrain from adorning themselves with them once they have reached the age of forty. In former times, French women abandoned flowers somewhat earlier. There is dignity in contenting oneself with what one is, and there is none in trying to appear what one is no longer. Small usurpations are ignoble.

Marie-Louise brought French books for Alberto and sent Albertina various volumes to form part of the library she had promised to create for her. "Reading these books and thus cultivating your mind will make you think a little on those things which I have already given you. A cupboard will follow when it is ready."[11] She sent scripts by Shakespeare and others of plays which had impressed her. These were typically the gems of classical literature, not the modern pieces of theatre, which she found a heap of immorality and after which she only felt remorse at having wasted time. She sent books which she had found particularly entertaining, like the side-splittingly funny cruel critique of liberalism in England which she was sure Albertina would like. It was hardly surprising that the wallet easily emptied itself.

Marie-Louise revelled in the intimacy she shared at long last with her exceptional daughter. She was proud of her and Luigi's well-known philanthropy. Throughout his career with the Duchess, Luigi had given most of his free time to the organisation and administration of schools for poor children, many of whom were abandoned. Largely self-funded, but also supported by donations, his schools had been praised by many foreign diplomats for their order, discipline and breadth of curriculum. Hundreds of children, saved from the streets and a lifetime of begging, learnt elocution, arithmetic, the Catechism, to read and to orate, to keep clean and to take care of themselves. By the time they left Luigi's care, they were able to find employment and salaries, and to become useful members of society. He had always kept abreast of and incorporated into his schools advancements in education in Piedmont and Lombardy. His wife supported him in his projects.

"In this selfish city, Albertina and Luigi give a good example of Christian charity and benevolence. Parmesan idleness is terrible."[12] Albertina was so good-hearted, so open. Her heart sank whenever she left Wilhelm, but particularly Albertina, whether for Piacenza, Milan, Venice or Vienna, her most frequent destinations. She dreamt of a time when she would be able to say that not a day had passed without seeing her daughter, her son-in-law, and grandchildren.

Six months after Albertina's wedding, Marie-Louise lent Albertina memoirs by Mlle Avrillion about the Empress Josephine she had found entertaining, having known many of the individuals mentioned. Next, she recommended *Paris and the Parisians* by English Mistress Trollope* to give Albertina a flavour of the world she had

---

* Fanny, mother of author Anthony Trollope

inhabited. She talked of her time in France, of Napoleon and of festivities and celebrations she had attended quite naturally and in a manner which suggested she had had many good times. In the summer of 1836, Marie-Louise reported from Brandhof that she had received a visit from a French party. She had found the Dukes of Orléans and Nemours surprisingly charming, witty and modest. The other French faces seemed to her lurid and unpleasant.

"One feels a certain discomfort when one thinks that these two such interesting young men are the sons of a usurper."[13] If King Louis-Philippe was a usurper, the former Empress of the French could never have regarded herself as anything other than an unwilling participant in the usurpation of her relatives.

In the summer of 1841, Maria, Albertina's seven-year-old daughter, already quite a personality, died. The following April, her second daughter, Luigia, also died. Once more, Marie-Louise was devastated that this double tragedy should be visited on her daughter. "My first thought on waking is to implore the Lord by ardent prayer to grant you happiness, my dear child, and above all to preserve the children which still remain to you."[14] She cried hot tears when she read of Albertina's loss. "I would not hesitate for an instant to give my life to compensate for all your sufferings and misfortunes. You are quite right to say that childhood is the happiest time. How many losses have we had in addition to yours!"[15] She had told Albertina countless times, ever since she was ten years old, how important it was to keep oneself occupied. "In whatever life brings, being able to occupy oneself is a good habit and an invaluable consolation in hard times."[16]

Marie-Louise completely understood her daughter's pain. Albertina should talk and talk always of her dear departed children and should not fear to tell her mother of the consolation she felt staying close to her remaining children.

> Only time and resignation to the will of God will bring bittersweet consolation – believe me, as I speak from experience. You

must say that Mimina was too beautiful, too good for this world and that God has taken her to make her happy. Thanks to Him, she will avoid all the dangers and suffering she would have had in this miserable world. You will find her again one day, never to leave her. Then you will both be happy together, there where no suffering or pain exists, I know and feel for myself that the vacuum left is terrible and that those who remain only make the absence even more acute. I would that all my affection could replace that which the deceased has taken from you![17]

Marie-Louise consoled her daughter from Ischl, where she was taking the waters for her health with the Imperial family and where Albertina and her four children had joined her the previous summer. All she could do was to impart the painful lessons she had learned:

The love which one has for one's own children is virtually always a love of abnegation and sacrifices, but in exchange, children give much back from the moment they are born. You are the proof, my dear Albertina, and this is my greatest consolation in this ugly world so full of misery and unhappiness! I will certainly look after the portrait you sent, a good likeness of our dear angel, and hope that following your and my observations, an artist will be found so that we can have another of Louise. Dear little Mimina! She is always in my thoughts. The pain never leaves my heart.[18]

Though the double life Marie-Louise had led until 1829 had ended with the publication of Neipperg's will, she had still not been able to talk freely about Albertina and Wilhelm. Her firstborn and father now dead, some members of the imperial family began to recognise the tie of kinship. They cried for Albertina's loss, wishing they could lay down their lives to bring her children back to her.

There was nothing to be done, save to concentrate one's efforts and hopes on those that remained, to bind oneself more closely to the family, on whose love and support one could always rely. There could be no substitute for the affection of these loved ones or for the happiness of knowing oneself cherished by them. These are what made true happiness in life. These were the real, pure, legitimate joys that warmed the heart, a fact becoming ever more true as Marie-Louise grew older.

Marie-Louise was deeply distressed by the fact that there seemed to be very few people in her duchies who appreciated the strength of family ties and the importance of family duty. In her eyes, it might have been thus on the Italian peninsula from time immemorial, but she could never adjust to a society where sons did not honour, respect and look after their parents, nor mothers their own children. "The customs of this country are truly singular!"[19] She reprimanded Albertina for not observing mourning for her Sanvitale niece, and for complaining about having to go and see her little nephew. It might take time out of her day, but it should be a priority.

The Sanvitales received invitations to the Neipperg family seat in Schwaigern that they accepted enthusiastically. Everyone looked forward to visits from the handsome, charming young men who graced Marie-Louise's and the Sanvitale tables when on leave from their military duties. Guglielmo was particularly thrilled, anticipating opportunities to go out riding all day with kindred daredevils. Ferdinand, the youngest of the four, visited less often than the older three, Alfred, Gustav and Erwin, who tried to spend as much time as they could with Marie-Louise when she was in Austria. After his return from Morocco in 1832, Gustav, promoted to lieutenant in Radetsky's army in Northern Italy, corresponded regularly with Marie-Louise and would often pop in to see her and his half-sister. All the Neipperg boys adored and loved Marie-Louise as a parent, honouring her by sharing their confidences, particularly when it came to relationship issues. Erwin came to her for advice.

"As you know how much I love you, I will betray his secret notwithstanding, but with the express prayer that you must talk to no-one about it save Luigi, not even to your brother Guglielmo,"

Marie-Louise wrote to Albertina. "It concerns a very wealthy marriage. Since the girl is beautiful and well brought up, I gave him much encouragement in his project, there being only one obstacle which requires that he wins over the parents, who want him to leave the army and set up at Capo d'Istria to which he does not want to consent."[20] It was not to be. Marie-Louise commiserated with a heart-broken Erwin following his break from Irma, with whom he remained deeply in love. In the summer of 1843, he found love once more and wrote to ask for Marie-Louise's consent to his marriage.

"His letter shows that he is behaving consistently with being in love for the confusion of his thoughts. He talks about parents who want to drag things out for as long as possible and about their poor financial situation and says that his own is not very good without telling me why. If you know anything, dear friend," she asked Albertina, "let me know, because I would willingly help good Erwin, whom I love as a son. I fear the Waldstein parents are operating less honestly than his former prospective parents-in-law."[21]

Conscious of her position as sole surviving parent, Marie-Louise had set up a small fund in favour of the three youngest of the Neipperg brothers, to which they would be entitled after her death, a step which had tied up her resources and which prevented her from giving Erwin immediate assistance. She wanted him to be happy but feared he was foolish to marry someone without fortune though Gustav said she was lovely. This time, nothing was going to stop Erwin. But within two years of their marriage, after a distressing miscarriage, his new bride was dead. Albertina, Guglielmo and Marie-Louise wept together over Erwin's gift to Marie-Louise, a hat on which his poor wife had painted delightful butterflies. Marie-Louise travelled to Celje in Lower Styria to console her stepson from afar, from a little sloop as he served quarantine.

Gustav, no longer wayward, surprised Marie-Louise by his coyness when he visited her daily in Vienna. Gustav would not be drawn, when she told him she had bumped into his sweetheart. "He is extremely cordial and good and much better than once upon a time, but I cannot get him to tell me what is in his heart."[22] She hoped Albertina would be able to get more out of him. Following Alfred's wedding to the adoring Marie, gynaecological problems were diagnosed. It seemed to Marie-Louise that life was always full of complications and disappointments.

The many reminders of mortality impressed upon the Duchess the need to put her affairs in order. Having withdrawn her claim to Napoleon's estate, she made her first will in May 1837, and a second substituting the first seven years later. Her testament ran to over a hundred legacies. The first thirty-four related to financial bequests directed to specific legatees as beneficiaries, and to her son and Count and Countess Montenuovo as trustees to administer pensions to the many who had served her over the years in Vienna, Paris and Parma. She made bequests to her children, stepchildren and their partners and godchildren, her children's carers and tutors, valets and wardrobe staff, to her Parman household, ministers, doctors, clergy, and to lifelong friends including Prince Metternich, Count and Countess Dietrichstein, Lord and Lady Burghersh and the Duchess of Montebello with whom she had had practically no contact for over twenty years. The remaining legacies, too numerous to list, were of her personal effects, including paintings, jewellery, porcelain, furniture and various other chattels and heirlooms. The beneficiaries of her personal effects, of which there were over sixty, were, in addition to her surviving children and grandchildren, those she saw in Austria, her remaining brothers and sisters and their spouses, her uncles, aunts, nieces, nephews, first and second cousins, a roll call of the sovereigns of Europe, including the King and Queen of Piedmont-Sardinia.

Though Marie-Louise had made meticulous provision for all those who relied upon her in life, she would not be released from her earthly duties for another decade. The future still held tumult that would strike at the very heart of her stewardship.

TWENTY-SIX

Railways and derailment, 1838

The Austrian secret police in Italy reported to Metternich, now the only real power behind the Habsburg throne, that people spoke in transports of the personal character of the Duchess, of her clemency and liberality. Loyal to her dynasty, the servants of her father and, since his death, her brother's administration, she never spoke ill of Austria.

Metternich did not like Marie-Louise's behaviour. He could see that to some honest men – and sentimental women – the seemingly reasonable opinions and principles of agitators, particularly the so-called intellectual nobility, did not seem intrinsically worthy of condemnation. Metternich knew that, despite the catastrophe of 1831, the Duke of Modena still hankered after a unified state under his hegemony. Using Marie-Louise's latest chief administrator, Charles René de Bombelles, carefully selected to keep Marie-Louise under surveillance, the Austrian Chancellor decided to frighten her into submission. She should not forget her dependence, since her father's death, on his goodwill. "The Duke of Modena takes me for an obstacle to a host of fanciful utopia and dreams to which he accords a quite disproportionate value. I know this man inside-out. Him and his dreams."

Vienna's dictates became harsher, more urgent, intolerant of Marie-Louise's divergence from Metternichian policy. With her firstborn dead, there seemed no need to pander to French sensitivities. Baron Mareschall advised her that she should avoid further "embarrassment" and the risk of punishing too severely – never one of Marie-Louise's failings – or too leniently. Her interests would be best served by allying herself more overtly with her Austrian masters.

"You have not one able officer on whom you can rely to lead your troops – even your president would not know what to do. It is my personal opinion that an Austrian battalion should be maintained at Parma's expense, allowing your troops to be dissolved." Marie-Louise's troops comprised local young men who might well be attracted by patriotic propaganda. "Thus your government would have a prop on which it could count and the battalion would march more easily, financed by the country and by twenty thousand francs from your own pocket which Your Majesty would be sufficiently wealthy and generous to give. Thus, She would open a career in the Austrian army to a significant number of young men from good families."[1]

Metternich was assisted in his agenda by a very useful pawn. Marie-Louise hoped that her son would forge a career in the Austrian army, practically the only path available to him which would provide a decent stipend. Wilhelm had been six years old when he had gone with his sister to the theatre to see *The Siege of Missolonghi* and courageously withstood the rifle shots. "I will buy him a small rifle immediately, something very, very nice," Marie-Louise wrote to Albertina.

Marie-Louise had grave reservations about replacement of her regiment with an Austrian battalion. She had little say in the matter. To relieve her of the burden of a decision, as he put it, Mareschall had organised everything with Count Bombelles. He congratulated her on her fortitude. "I know, Madame, your intentions for Guillaume and can only congratulate Your Majesty for taking this position, the more painful [Her Majesty's] sacrifice to her heart, the more she will feel rewarded one day by the progress of the Child and the feeling of having done her duty." He continued,

> The affair is being settled and to the great advantage of Your Majesty, but it has to be done *without noise, without decree*, in other words, unnoticed. We have had a good start by sending

the Chief of Police, Count Ferrari into retirement. All that has to be done is to continue, and I only ask Your Majesty not to hesitate in granting a pension to those officers who have not completed ten years service and to give preference in trying to place the children of former soldiers in our service for which they will receive five hundred francs a year until they are captains, when pay will increase to twenty thousand francs a year. Your Majesty will do much thereby and place herself in the affections of many good families![2]

Baron Mareschall advised that Marie-Louise should go to Piacenza, insulated by Austrian bayonets, but Marie-Louise refused to make a move which would play into the hands of those who wanted to unseat her. After reorganising Parma's military affairs and overseeing the appointments of Austrian sympathiser Odoardo Sartorio as Chief of Police and Bombelles to head Marie-Louise's administration, Mareschall asked for permission to return to Vienna. Following Sartorio's assassination in January 1834, Marie-Louise had little choice but to close the university temporarily, and the reading rooms, and to prohibit the circulation of foreign newspapers and periodicals. She could no longer stand by the public employees compromised by the events of 1831 with whom she had been lenient. In order to accommodate Vienna, she arrested subjects found to be members of the new sect, Young Italy, but only for a brief period, treating them always with the greatest humanity. No other monarch on the Italian peninsula behaved with such leniency or grace.

By the end of the year, Metternich had exchanged correspondence with Marie-Louise regarding the enrolment and commencement of thirteen-year-old Wilhelm Albert Count von Montenuovo in the Military Academy in Wienerneustadt, but had made no firm commitment, dragging things out to keep Marie-Louise submissive. Reluctant to have her last child leave home until he was a good deal stronger, she wanted to know that he would receive a public education in the fullness of time. Albertina warned her mother not to bring up Wilhelm's health problems, for fear of alienating him.

Wilhelm was very different to his obliging sister. Headstrong, moody and true to his sex, he kept his inner feelings to himself. Without the restraining influence of his tutor Zode, who had resigned to live with his bride, Wilhelm let off his anger and frustration by running amok. When his mother scolded him for running along the Corso in Piacenza with his riding friend so recklessly that they had caused chaos among the carriages, he refused to hear reason. The only things which Wilhelm seemed to enjoy were riding, target practice, at which he excelled, and hunting, for which he would get up at five in the morning. He had adopted two little wolf-cubs and looked after them, planning to raise them until he could kill them at Sala. After a day's shooting, he would return with over twenty quails, pleased as punch, even though he had had to wade through water up to his knees for five or six hours.

"As much as I love Guglielmo, he is becoming intolerable with his spirit of contradiction, pronouncing on everything and for everything. He always thinks he is right and can be extremely impertinent. His self-righteousness is not going to take him very far in the army. His head needs a good seeing-to!"[3] She feared he might collapse into total apathy. Anxious to hear that his entry into the army had been settled, he badgered Albertina, who, he complained, did not write to him often enough, to tell her anything that Marie-Louise had let slip. Albertina feared that a refusal would be a terrible knock to his confidence.

Despite his obstinacy, Wilhelm charmed everyone. However much anxiety he caused Marie-Louise, her "terrible Nimrod" easily redeemed himself when he came home and sat smiling on her yellow settee with a wonderful large bouquet of forget-me-nots for her.

Four years after the first exchange between Marie-Louise and Metternich as to Wilhelm's future, the matter finally seemed to take a step in the right direction. One year after her father's death, after an impressive military parade, mass and march-past outside the Villa Mandelli in the asphyxiating heat of Piacenza, she received her usual annual visit from the officers of the Austrian regiment. At the grand lunch, the toast to the health of her brother, the Emperor, drove home her father's death, prompting her to burst into tears. She was not the only one. The gentle Commander Radetsky was visibly moved, and General Reczey's eyes were also wet with tears. General d'Aspre, perfumed with musk, limping and aged since falling from his horse, cried like a child when he began to talk about the late emperor. General Reczey chose this moment to tell Marie-Louise that he wished to appoint Wilhelm an officer in his regiment in the autumn, and asked her if she would release her son for the coming year. Wilhelm, overwhelmed with excitement, promised to apply himself to his studies if she would agree.

"If Metternich is not against it, I will accept this proposal because it is hard to come by a post of officer in the officer corps and the colonel of this regiment is an excellent man," Marie-Louise wrote to Albertina. Her father dead, there could be no impediment to Wilhelm's advancement in the Austrian army. Overnight, Wilhelm's attitude and mood changed. He could not wait to start.

Later that summer, while Wilhelm devoted himself conscientiously to his studies, Marie-Louise was again in Austria and reported her conversation with Metternich to Albertina. Metternich flattered Marie-Louise, taking an unusually keen interest in her daughter and her offspring, and talking at length about Wilhelm's prospects. He wanted to get to know Wilhelm when he next came to Italy, which he planned to do the following year. Only then could a final decision as to his future be taken. He wanted to examine Wilhelm's state of health and the advance of his growth, having on his conscience the death of the Duke of Reichstadt, so he said.

Marie-Louise's feelings towards Metternich had changed, his dealings as regards Albertina and Wilhelm handled with surprising sensitivity. "Both he and I have had the saddest experiences of the consequences of young men with too delicate chests and excessive growth to not have great fears in this respect."

Within two years of this conversation, Wilhelm was appointed

Lieutenant in two battalions of chasseurs at Gritschen in Bohemia. "With boys one really has to sacrifice oneself when they leave the maternal home."[4] Marie-Louise missed him but was thrilled and proud when she next saw him: "I admire everything in our young lieutenant – and he has practically abandoned his habit of contradiction!" He was full of optimism and enthusiasm for studies and for the piano, for which he had inherited his mother's talent. Marie-Louise gave him as a present some piano lessons, at which he jumped for joy. Marie-Louise was delighted to hear that he had invested heavily in an excellent piano.

Marie-Louise's accommodation of Metternich did not prevent her from pursuing her own path discreetly, and she continued to express her sympathy with political exiles by granting them effective assistance.

By the summer of 1838, Wilhelm, bashful at nineteen, made his first entry into society. For moral support, he was accompanied by Anguissola Sanvitale, Luigi's cousin. When Marie-Louise saw Wilhelm in Salzburg, where he was stationed, she was happier than she had been for a long time. "I should divide myself in three between Parma, Salzburg and Vienna. Guglielmo is very happy; he was delightful to me as I have never seen him before. Don't you find his letters much more cordial and agreeable than previously?" she asked her daughter.

Wilhelm was a success with everyone he met, including the imperial family, who took to him immediately. "The Major and everyone else are thrilled with him and our Gilles responds with such cordiality and amiability that he has conquered all hearts. He always eats with them at the guests' table and they have included him in a large number of picnics." Marie-Louise was delighted to know that her son was now circulating in the highest circles from which he had previously been barred. Not only was Wilhelm extremely happy with his new lifestyle, but his feelings for his mother had matured. Far from resisting her caresses, he was effusive and demonstrative. "I have never seen Guglielmo so cordial and lovely to me as he is now. He held me so tightly in his arms at Reichenhall that I thought I would suffocate. May God, in his mercy, see that this continues and we cannot be anything other than content."

Marie-Louise was amazed. Her little boy who had never shown any interest in furnishings or elegance was now being congratulated by everyone; they too astonished at how tastefully he had arranged his room. The day he mounted the guard for the first time, he gave, as was customary, a grand lunch and was taken aback by the expense of thirty-six bottles of excellent wine which he found himself obliged to offer. "How I rejoice at these small pleasures with him!" She brought him an English saddle horse, ten years old and well-trained, and a carriage, "but you cannot believe how hard it was, people holding a knife to your throat when they know you are in a hurry."

During his extended convalescence, Guglielmo could think of nothing other than marching with his battalion. Conflicting instructions kept him in Salzburg. Marie-Louise wanted to interfere, but refrained, conscious that she was strictly under orders to speak only to Padre Metternich, as she called him, "whom I consider to be like a second father."

The following year, Guglielmo was promoted to cavalry lieutenant and sent to Vienna to reside at the Viennese Court. Now, far from being the unspeakables, everyone wanted to meet both Wilhelm and Albertina. Finally Guglielmo was recalled to his battalion.

In the summer of 1841, four weeks elapsed without word from him. "I would repay him with the same coin if I thought it would do him some good." Marie-Louise was shocked when her son suddenly arrived in Salzburg desperately ill and the doctors told her to fear the worst. Nursed by his mother, he revived. He had kept silent because he had not wanted to distress her and his sister following the sad news of Albertina's little Maria's death.

As the years passed, Guglielmo spent more time with Marie-Louise in Ischl, where she went annually to take the waters for her impaired health, his health too in need of careful management.

Marie-Louise was touched when she spoke to him about entrusting to him the funds into which he would come on his twenty-fourth birthday. Most young men could not wait to get their hands on their entitlement, but Guglielmo begged his mother to continue to manage his funds for him. She was delighted that he was flourishing in Vienna, accepted socially by her brother, Louis, and his wife, Archduchess Sophie, and to receive him when she was in residence in Schönbrunn for at least a couple of hours every day before dining with her imperial family. She regretted that she sometimes had to forgo his company, obliged to accept invitations extended to her.

The following year, Guglielmo once more went silent, this time for three months. Marie-Louise told Albertina she did not know whether to be angry or relieved when he made contact recuperating after a life-threatening bout of gastric flu. This time, his chest was a lot worse, forcing him to retire temporarily from military life. He returned home to be nursed by his mother, constantly complaining about his misfortune at having such poor health at the age of twenty-six. Marie-Louise was extremely anguished, thrown back to her firstborn's premature end. She could not bear to leave Wilhelm alone. Going for days with no appetite, he would suddenly scream with hunger and eat four or five times a day, begging for lamb. He insisted on eating roasted mutton against Marie-Louise's advice and suffered horrible stomach upsets as a result, delaying his recovery. In moments of optimism, Wilhelm expressed his hopes for the future and busied himself with his coin collection, largely made up of medals and coins looted from various parts of the former French Empire given her by Vivant Denon, Director-General of the Musée Napoléon. In his mother's absence, Albertina looked after the invalid, to his delight. After several months' illness, his condition seemed to improve. In the summer of 1846, he begged Marie-Louise to allow him to precede her to Venice, to accompany her on the steamboat to Trieste, before setting off for Graz to see Dr. Gleichenberg, who looked after his health in Austria. Malicious tongues lamented that experience had taught him nothing and that his illness was a result of his carelessness, that he would meet the same bad end as his half-brother. Marie-Louise ignored such chatter. It was natural that a young man at the peak of his powers wanted to explore life. She was bereft when Wilhelm's cordiality suddenly evaporated. His coolness towards his mother, his apparently deliberate attempts to throw off the links uniting her to him with such maternal affection, upset her deeply.

> If he only knew how this breaks my heart, he might behave differently. You know that he has now become Chamberlain at the Austrian Court, which promotion we owe to the Emperor and to the assiduous attentions of my good Sophie (whom he says he hates), who has won over the obstinacy of Count Dietriechstein. I am glad because he has achieved what I was unable to procure for him. My Uncle Louis and Count Henri Bombelles have been his protectors on this occasion.[5]

Wilhelm's new appointment was a *coup* indeed. He blanched at the prospect of having to pay high taxes – he never seemed to have any money, which made him fear for the future. At Schönbrunn, he seemed confused and embarrassed in his mother's presence. He was pale and thin, his nose in a complete mess, mutilated by a shot from a badly loaded rifle. Marie-Louise was sure he must regret his behaviour and silence towards her, though he showed little sign of it. His innate intelligence, his sociable, outgoing personality and his meteoric career success could never compensate him for his equivocal status in the imperial world, of which his mother was part. Marie-Louise wished that her son could come to terms with his irregular situation. She was terribly proud to see him a fine upstanding Austrian, established in the motherland, and at its very centre. Wilhelm was the German citizen she had wished her firstborn to be. And his future was in Austria, she was sure. Neither the Austrian battalion, nor the recruitment of promising young Parman men into the Austrian army could stem the advancing tide that would soon engulf the coveted duchies. Albertina had married into a local family and was Parman, through and through.

Marie-Louise next saw Padre Metternich at Ischl. Emaciated and aged, he still had much fire left in him:

> Nothing can surprise me, still less, make me change direction. If I make a mistake, I do so in good faith, and no-one can divert me from my faith. Everyone is free to think what he wishes and to judge things and men as he takes them. I rely upon the resource of over a quarter of a century of experience and the memory of the conscience of him who is no longer, the best judge of human affairs I have ever known, to whose maxims I will remain forever faithful! Your Majesty knows me from another side too well not to know that nothing will succeed in derailing me and that neither criticism nor praise have any empire over me.

It was true that criticism would not divert Metternich from his purpose, and that praise rarely detained him more than temporarily. But he was wrong in thinking that nothing could derail him.

Metternich was not the only one out of touch. Marie-Clementine, Marie-Louise's sister, living since 1816 in Salerno in the Kingdom of the Two Sicilies, wrote to Marie-Louise about the project to build a railway. "I think that no advantage will accrue to the country from it – the shareholders are nothing but foreigners."[6] Marie-Clementine might be forgiven for not having recognised the arrival of the century's most important phenomenon. Everyone had hitherto been fighting over Marie-Louise's duchies because of their strategic location on the River Po, the largest arterial river cutting across the Italian peninsula. Along this waterway, men and commodities, exports and imports were transported across the country. With the advent of railway tracks and steam engines, the dependency on rivers for mobility was to diminish fast and dramatically.

Always thrilled with innovation, wanting to be ahead in scientific progress, Marie-Louise could not wait to try out the new steam carriage on the first completed stretch of the line projected to link Vienna with the coal mines of Bochnia, south-east of Cracov. Christened the Kaiser-Ferdinands-Nordbahn, the line had been inaugurated in the summer of 1838, for which event Johann Strauss had composed a waltz entitled the *Eisenbahn-Lust*, taking as its motif the movement of the train.

> I have to confess that my heart was beating very hard when I mounted by means of a kind of portable ladder, the famous vehicle into which I was locked. I do not know how to describe it to you, dear Albertina, otherwise than to say it was as if we were being dragged by a hurricane, by the devil's carriage.

> As a horrible whistle blew, a column of smoke rose from the engine, flecked with sparks of fire.

> In all, we covered three German leagues – fifteen Italian miles – in twenty minutes and returned in twenty-one. Not far from the village of Wagram two restaurants have been built where we stopped, treated ourselves to some ice-cream and watched as the engine with other wagons full of people arrived, the gentleman of the commission having had the amiability to have us set out alone with three carriages to watch this spectacle.

It was almost thirty years since the battle which had sealed her fate had taken place, and here she sat on the railway licking ice-cream. These were the advances revolutionising existence, which promised a better future, not the desecration of human life which had seen rotting corpses floating down the Danube.

"The machine travels at a speed of thirty-six feet in two seconds [and] weighs two hundred quintals of iron. The invention is so ingenious that two men can move it with ease to set it back ready for its return journey." [7]

As the years wore on, Vienna, no longer the cradle of happiness, continued to be the exciting cultural hub she had always loved. She became quite another person. Her energy returned, and with it her appetite. Her breakfast would consist of an enormous plate of soup and a *kipfel*, a large Viennese biscuit. By midday she would be hungry again. Vienna was where Marie-Louise saw the familiar faces who had lived with her through the dramas of her life. In addition to family and aristocratic friends, she consorted with Dr. Malfatti, who was so agreeable she could willingly spend hours with him. Nothing delighted her more than when they were all assembled with children and grandchildren. She loved watching her nieces and nephews swim and to giggle at their foibles. A childish sense of fun in an adult was great proof of candour when united with amiable qualities of society.

Marie-Louise went to the balls of high society, often attended by several thousand people, to enjoy the parade of sumptuous dresses and the men's elegant uniforms. She felt like a lost sheep, knowing few of the younger generation. City life required her to dress and undress as never before and she could barely keep up. From the whirl of parties, theatre, concert and opera performances, she retreated to the mountains and lakes of Wirninzel, where she could spend whole days without pain and she longed to end her days. She wished she could send Albertina a dose of sharp alpine air, and a whiff of the pervasive perfume of freshly cut wheat. There was so much variety, so much diversity in Austria. In comparison, the terrain of her duchies was monotonous, offering little incentive to outdoor exercise.

"I tell myself that so many delightful places which are so dear to my heart will never allow me to attach myself to Italy. I would willingly take my bundle and set up home in any little country cottage for the rest of my days."[8] Much as she loved to be in Parma with Albertina and Guglielmo, she was unhappy in Italy, which was trying and dull. Her borrowed duchies could never be anything more than a form of exile. She hankered after a past that had largely vanished, the remaining fragments correspondingly all the more precious.

RAILWAYS AND DERAILMENT, 1838

From Schönbrunn in the summer of 1838, Marie-Louise wrote:

I would love to be able to transport you, dear Albertina, with all your family, in what you call my Eden, and you would see for yourself what an Eden my homeland truly is. People are very good-natured, very serious-minded. You never hear people complaining, because they all want to live in peace in this Court. One meets people everywhere with full happy faces who only think about eating and enjoying themselves, who do not concern themselves with politics or with other things of which they have no understanding.[9]

She was putting on too much weight, eating like a wolf, "and I end up by worrying that once I get back to Parma everything I have gained will be lost in haste since in Italy I haven't digested for years!"[10] The days when Napoleon had told her that a woman should never be seen eating had long passed. Unlike in France, in Austria, no-one was ashamed of tucking in. So much so that when Marie-Louise and the imperial family were enjoying their lunch at the invitation of the Dowager Empress, someone suddenly remembered that it was a fast day! She revelled in her home cuisine, though she confessed she found the use of marsala, nut and saffron overpowering in Austrian cooking, and disliked truffles and mock turtle soup.

Content in her homeland, she could never escape her inner struggle. She cried as Albertina's birthday and her own saint's day approached, wishing it could be a perfect world and they could all be together. But that was an impossible dream. "Your affection and that of your brother still make me love life and when I hear your protestations of love I wish I had never set out."[11] "My heart is always in Parma," she would later claim.[12]

Marie-Clementine had had to recant. While Vesuvius threw out ash and stones, causing the local inhabitants considerable agitation, the first railway in the kingdom from Naples to Granatello dei Portici was opened. She wrote to her sister telling her that, though at

409

first reluctant to try it out, having heard of the numerous accidents and injured, she had agreed to venture as far as La Favorite and back.

"It felt like being in a hay cart with a roof – my heart was pounding. But then when it got up to speed, the rhythm was so pleasant that all fear of anything untoward evaporated. Everybody was delighted and that day the railway was open to the public."[13]

Each year, the length, destinations and speed of the railways increased, "giving passengers the opportunity to shatter their bones for a few hours less,"[14] Marie-Louise remarked. A railway from Milan was planned to pass through Piacenza southward as far as Naples. Everyone was forced onto the railways, and steamboats introduced along coastlines, on rivers and lakes, the regular staging posts for changing horses in large part done away with. Though journeys were generally faster and, notwithstanding Marie-Louise's reservations, more comfortable, they were not always predictable. To her great annoyance, she was obliged to change trains at Padua, where she often had to wait a long time for the arrival of the train to Venice. Upbraiding the authorities achieved nothing. The advance of rail was unstoppable, despite sporadic tragedies and the embryonic state of the machinery: "The last wagons of the train often derail from the platform. Thank goodness we were in the middle of the train."[15] Metternich might have been dubbed "the coachman of Europe", but he was no longer in the driving seat or even in the invulnerable centre.

TWENTY-SEVEN

Verdi and the power of opera 1846

Improvements in transportation were facilitating all kinds of communication, so that information travelled across the Italian peninsula much faster than it had ever done before. Of the Italian peninsula, the central states, the Marches and the Lombardy-Veneto regions were the areas most densely populated with theatres. Marie-Louise's new Ducal Theatre was one of many such new establishments across the region. Even small towns like Guastalla and Cortemaggiore had opened their own theatres. Across the Romagna, there were theatres practically every three to six miles.

In the evening, on days when the business of governing did not detain her, Marie-Louise would go to her theatre across the little connecting bridge linking her palace to the floor on which the ducal box was located. She would often return quite exasperated at the bickering backstage which had inevitably adversely impacted upon the quality of performances. Born into a world of musical excellence, Marie-Louise found it hard to tolerate the mediocrity of performance in Parma. She had hoped that the new opera house, the realisation of her and her beloved's dream, would usher in a new era of musical attainment.

Everything seemed possible when the great virtuoso violinist Niccolò Paganini agreed to give a benefit concert in the summer of 1834 at the Duchess's theatre. Marie-Louise and Neipperg had first heard Paganini performing at the home of Countess Dietrichstein in the summer of 1828. Since then, the violinist had scored triumph after triumph in Paris, Prague, Bratislava, Warsaw and in London, where piano duets played with Mendelssohn caused a sensation.

With his recently acquired gains, he invested in a country estate outside Parma and in the Palazzo Linati in the city itself. The benefit concert at the Teatro Reggio was so oversubscribed that the stalls and circle were stuffed to the gills, some of the audience accommodated on the stage. Paganini followed this with a concert in Piacenza and then returned to Parma to perform for the Duchess's birthday. Marie-Louise hoped that her court orchestra and choir might become one of Europe's leading orchestras when Paganini agreed to accept the new position of Superintendent of all matters relating to court music. She desperately needed someone to bring her argumentative and cantankerous court musicians and singers to heel. At the end of 1835, Paganini set exams to test each of the ducal company members and found many so incompetent that he fired them. For a time performances improved, Marie-Louise rewarding Paganini's first successes with a new violin. But the atmosphere was soon soured by callous rivalries and resentments, indifference and sluggishness frustrating the great conductor who, in his isolation, considered that there were many other matters and people worthy of his time. Away attending her brother's coronation, Marie-Louise was unable to use her powers of persuasion to stop Paganini abandoning his position in exasperation. She was upset, but she had to face competing priorities for her resources and forgo the reform of her orchestra. There were still many mouths to feed, salaries and pensions to be paid and provision to be made for cholera. She would have to make do with singers unequal to their roles and musicians unequal to their instruments. At Paganini's departure, those dismissed by him demanded reinstatement, which she had little option but to grant, strictly prohibiting beards and moustaches.

The Chief of Police, Odoardo Sartorio, watched all this with an eagle eye and, dropping in on a rehearsal of *Lucia di Lammermoor*, threatened to arrest everyone for sedition if they did not remove the green ribbon attached to their red and white costumes. The impresario Claudio Musi had inadvertently used the colours of the flag of Napoleon's Italian Legion. Such was his terror at this unintended trespass into the realm of liberal nationalism that he immediately ordered the substitution of a black ribbon at a cost of over a thousand francs, to be paid out of his own pocket. Marie-Louise tried to reverse the deterioration of her ducal orchestra by inviting students from the orphanage school to supplement it, subject to audition, but with very little improvement.

Ever since Marie-Louise's instigation of a season of spectacle, going to the opera had become a regular outing in urban centres. More than an artistic experience, the theatre was a place to be seen. Everyone looked forward to the season. The opera was now no longer attended just by the nobility, but by a much wider audience of the emerging bourgeoisie, dignitaries, academics and professionals. Rossini's output and success broadened further the opera-going public, the theatre becoming the focus of urban social life, a place to congregate every evening, to chat with friends, to smoke, discuss business or play card games. The Italian public treated the performance as if it were taking place in their living room or in a café, gossiping away, paying each other little visits, conducting love affairs, devoting very little attention to the performance, though they suddenly woke up at the strain of a well-known aria or chorus and demanded several encores. The stalls typically accommodated businessmen, civil servants, and the soldiery stationed in the town, who received discounted tickets. The craftsmen, students and small traders occupied the gallery. Every now and again, in attempts to curb the noise so that performers could be heard, rules of conduct for attendance were published and enforced by police officers who surveyed the audience. Excessively boisterous applause, foot-stamping, carrying sticks and umbrellas were forbidden. For a while, the rules were observed but then soon forgotten.

Affordable for all classes in society, opera was raising awareness of the common aspiration for nationhood. The heavily censored news-papers were powerless to hold back the sense of empowerment promoted by allegorical heroic aria and chorus. Music pierced the heart and roused pluck. The *opera lirica* brought about the consolidation and informed the opinions of the new important voice in Italy, the bourgeoisie. If the Austrians surreptitiously directed a command economy in relation to the output of their territories, save for political censorship, they allowed free market trading in matters of performance. Opera and the men and women who peopled its world enjoyed enviable freedom of movement. Composers, impresarios and cast could transport their productions across the peninsula and beyond to important foreign courts and their theatres without impediment. In no other sphere of life could a human being permeate so many different levels of society. In no other sphere could a person take messages overlaid with dangerous meaning into the hearth of his social superior to whom he would otherwise have no access. Publishers of music and of new periodicals keeping abreast of the musical scene increased the celebrity status of composers and performers and enabled them to capitalise on the power they had accrued on the stage.

In other countries, the popular novel was making a huge impact on European society. On the Italian peninsula, these had only begun to make an impact when Giuseppe Verdi adapted them to the operatic stage, from Victor Hugo's *Ernani* to Schiller's *Giovanna d'Arco*. Through his compositions, he had begun to spin a national historical memory. The young Verdi, born in the village of Busseto in the Duchy of Parma, had applied in the spring of 1834 for the position of Director of Music of the Ducal Court, but Marie-Louise had favoured a more senior, better qualified candidate. Then unknown, Verdi left the duchy to seek employment in Milan. In 1836, he wrote a pamphlet entitled 'the Philosophy of Music' in which he demanded greater civil emphasis in opera, convinced that this could and should make an important contribution to the education of the Italian people in patriotism and in their own nationality. Thus, the maestro carefully prepared the ground for his participation in stoking passions which would soon erupt.

In 1837, Marie-Louise extended a helping hand to widowed Giuditta Bellerio Sidoli. Passionate about the creation of a unified state, burning with resentment at the injustices inflicted daily upon her compatriots, Giuditta Bellerio had joined the revolutionaries as a young woman. She had participated in the riots of 1830-1, marching proudly to the town hall in Reggio Emilia wrapped in the green, white and red Italian flag, the undisputed standard under which everyone, monarchists, republicans, democrats and moderates, united in patriotism. Banished from the Duchy of Modena, she fled to Marseille creating a haven for Italian revolutionary exiles. There she met her lover and political mentor, Giuseppe Mazzini. With Sidoli's support, Mazzini had instigated a programme of continuous propagandistic education and constant insurrection through his creation, Young Italy, to cause unrest and un-glove the hateful Austrians. Sidoli lived constantly on the run, fleeing from state to state, hounded by police wherever she went. She pined for her children in Reggio Emilia, with which Parma shared a border.

Giuditta's desperate plea for asylum was received sympathetically by Marie-Louise, who understood the plight of an exiled mother. Despite Giuditta's connection with Mazzini and evident political leanings, Marie-Louise granted her the right to reside in her duchies without interference or surveillance and lent her support to Giuditta's petition to the Duke of Modena for permission to see her children. With Marie-Louise's signature appended, he could not refuse it. But his terms were severe. Giuditta would be allowed only two visits a year. It was such gestures as these which would ensure Verdi's loyalty and affection for Marie-Louise, the only sovereign on the peninsula who did not oppress his people.

First performed in March 1842 in Milan's La Scala, there was no doubting that *Nabucco* was anti-Austrian, the main theme a quest for liberation of the homeland, where the protagonists proclaimed themselves prepared to give their lives for freedom from the oppression of foreign domination. Verdi himself was said to have been terrified by the uproarious applause, the extraordinary ovations from the Milanese public which the opera prompted. When the opera was first performed at Marie-Louise's Ducal Theatre following argumentative, precarious rehearsals with her grumbling orchestra, the ovations were repeated. The message was unmistakeable. Marie-Louise was moved as she witnessed the enthusiasm of the Parmans in the presence of the composer himself, who was called over and over again to the stage to take a bow. The production drew to her capital huge numbers of foreigners who were eager to see the great new sensation. *Nabucco* was the first of Verdi's operas to articulate the common grievance of the Italian peninsula, and to marshal its inhabitants to pursue a common purpose. Its message conveyed abroad, many Italian exiles found a new sympathy in the highest most influential circles.

Marie-Louise's strong survival instinct did not preclude her from feeling the sympathy Verdi sought to elicit. In the stories, the homeland was a distant land far from the political reality of the Italian peninsula, but these were not mere stories. The romantic aspirations with which arias and choruses were infused were infectious. Marie-Louise could not remain impervious to the yearning, expressed by the Hebrew slaves in the chorus of *Nabucco* for their long lost beautiful homeland. She was moved in *Ernani*, when the Spanish armed conspirators fighting against her ancestor, Emperor Charles V, invoked the homeland to be redeemed from servitude, when Joan of Arc sang that her homeland was her only thought, when the Scottish refugees in *Macbeth* extolled the sweet name of the oppressed homeland. During the early years, the audience had made the connection with their own situation at a distance, but as time advanced and the message of freedom from oppression was reinforced over and over again, the public was roused by the political resonance of the opera and emboldened to shake free of their fetters.

Verdi followed *Nabucco* by staging a more daring allegorical opera, *I Lombardi della Prima Crociata*. This composition, based on the poem by the Milanese poet Tommaso Grossi, portrayed the Lombards trying to liberate Jerusalem from the Saracens. Verdi met with considerable resistance from the censors, who were kicking themselves that they had not foreseen the impact of *Nabucco*. They found fault at every turn. The Archbishop of Milan was furious, calling a sacrilege the portrayal on the opera stage of the holy sacrament of baptism of a Saracen by a Christian maid. The cries of the censors and the Archbishop came too late. The public immediately took to the new opera and, just as Verdi had hoped and the censors had dreaded, identified with the Lombards. When the tenor sang his rousing aria: "La Santa Terra oggi nostra sarà! [The Holy Land will be ours this day!]" the audience shouted back, "Si, si, Guerra! Guerra! [Yes yes, War! War!" Already they could see the promised land and they wanted war to purge it of their oppressors.

Marie-Louise was thrilled when Verdi dedicated the score for song and piano to her, which he expressed as an act of gratitude for the support she had given to the arts in her duchy. Everyone knew that Verdi's recognition of his sovereign was not only about art appreciation, but demonstrated his appreciation of her role as moderator between political factions, the woman who never gave up on finding and working with the common ground. She was truly the Concordia, as she been had been represented by Canova in the sculpture* which now stood in the Palatine Library of the Palazzo della Pilotta adjoining her Ducal Palace. Verdi repeated the dedication to her on the first page of the music over *The Hymn of War and of Battle,* which exhorted patriots to fight for independence, a mark of the esteem, understanding and sympathy between him and the sovereign who tried to accommodate as best she could the current which would soon win out. Marie-Louise received Verdi in audience, giving him a gold pin with his monogram set in diamonds, inviting him to supervise a new production of *Nabucco* in which his love and diva, Giuseppina Strepponi, would take the leading role.

Marie-Louise respected her home-grown composer highly, though she feared his current populist output would not bear the test of time. It was too commercially driven, pumped out to appeal

---

* This commission by Napoleon of his pregnant empress was completed after his fall and remained in Rome until purchased by Marie-Louise in 1819.

to the common man, the simplest, least sophisticated audience. He had hit upon a formula which worked and which was highly entertaining, but hardly durable, she thought. She loved Italian opera, which was at its best when composed by Italians. She loved Mozart's *Marriage of Figaro*, even though she called it arch-antiquated, but Italian had to be sung by Italians – Germans should avoid singing Italian, it was such a terrible sound!

> Bellini will always find a ready audience, whereas Verdi will pass. Don't be surprised at how Parman I have become in my feelings towards Verdi. I have written that his popularity will pass because he has much talent but precious little education and a new genius may be born who will take music along a different, more scientific route. Then it will be entertaining to see the contrast. Nonetheless, I hope that Verdi will increasingly find in the spirit of his homeland the sublime inspiration of eternal life.

In 1846, Giuseppe Verdi, firmly established as promoter of the Italian nationalist cause, decided to set to music Zacharias Werner's play of *Attila*. Thirty years earlier, Marie-Louise had seen the original play in Vienna, eight years after it first graced the stage in 1808. Then, anger had raged in her heart at her first husband. The play tells the story of an unstoppable conqueror, obeyed by all, who strikes fear into the hearts of all Asia and Europe. In *De L'Allemagne*, published in 1813, de Staël wrote:

> Attila has a kind of superstitious belief in himself, he is the object of his own cult, he believes in himself, he sees himself as the instrument of Heaven's decrees, and this conviction brings a certain equity to his crimes. He reproaches his enemies for their failings, as if he did not have more failings than anyone else. He is ferocious and a despot, a generous barbarian who is, nonetheless, faithful to his word. Surrounded by the best the world has to offer, he lives like a soldier, asking only that the

earth grant him the joy of conquest. He dispenses judgment by natural instinct without the dispassionate and consistent application of the law[...] The idea of an inflexible necessity drives him, and his own will seems to him this necessity. The vacillations of his soul have a kind of rapidity and decisiveness which exclude any nuance[...] His court is a cauldron of intrigue, his family members devoured by frivolity, insolence and general base behaviour, each man and woman protesting his and her humble submission to the good of the empire. Deep down, he is a heartless coward incapable of achieving his means through love.

Napoleon had recognised all too clearly the parallels de Staël was drawing, that Attila was himself thinly veiled, the contemporary incarnation of evil. Marie-Louise's entry in her green notebook relating to Werner's *Attila*, as Napoleon languished on St Helena, was unequivocal:

In my view, there is nothing more ridiculous than seeking to make a comparison on the basis of hearsay, rather than on the basis of a thorough knowledge of people, and this is the trap into which Werner falls trying to draw a comparison between his Attila and a conqueror of our time. Not only has he mistaken his character, making Attila an extremely interesting man, but of the two, one can find only one resemblance, that of having been the scourge of God.

In the tragedy, Attila is a man who is coarse, ferocious, insensitive to danger, but admirably just, sticking religiously to his word of honour, with absolutely no fear of death, his heart sensitive to conjugal and paternal love, whereas Napoleon's sensitivity was born of fear and his weak nerves, pardonable in a woman, not in a man. I have seen him on the verge of vomiting on seeing a wounded postilion, while at the very same moment he was quite capable of having given the order in cold blood for a man to be poisoned. He did not recognise justice, unless it came in the form of punishment, and so many times then did he want for words! Ultimately, he loved his son, but he never truly loved nor will he ever truly love a woman. And he feared death, proof that he did not know how to end with glory the drama he had started.

Werner's play opened with an image intended to demonstrate the awesome, ruthless power of the tyrant, groaning women and children fleeing from their torched homes as the scourge marched towards Rome. Marie-Louise had seen for herself these men and women from her earliest childhood until her arrival on Italian soil. She had seen Austrians, Hungarians, Germans, French and Italians bereaved and maimed, their lives and livelihoods devastated forever. Werner's play ended with the Eternal City being spared, when at the eleventh hour, Pope Leo the Great halts Attila at the gates of Rome and promises him a place in heaven if he desists from his purpose. As his final hour approaches, Christianity conquers Attila's soul. Marie-Louise had seen this too. Her husband returning to his Catholicism and the Papacy to find salvation, in the myth he had fashioned transforming himself from tyrant to hero and martyr.

In Verdi's adaptation of the Werner text, the heroine scorned the weak, passive barbarian women, extolling Italian women who, trained and dressed for warfare, fought beside their men on blood-strewn battlefields. The message was all too clear. Women, as well as men, were to fight for independence.

In France, Louis-Napoleon, Hortense's son and Marie-Louise's nephew by Napoleon, in exile in London, was busy recycling his uncle's image. In 1839, he published *Les Idées Napoléoniennes*, a document which purported to represent the policy and philosophy which Napoleon had adopted for the exercise of his power. It was a far cry from the reality. However inaccurate the nephew's distillation of his uncle's ideas, it was a masterstroke in public relations. Louis-Napoleon had laid down his marker at the very moment the

French public wanted to believe in the myth his uncle had spun on St. Helena.

On 2 December 1840, *La Belle Poule* sailed into Cherbourg harbour to the report of a thousand guns. It was carrying the body of the Emperor Napoleon, enclosed in resoldered coffin and ebony sarcophagus, itself enclosed in a heavy oak casket. Elderly soldiers and country people walked miles from their villages in the freezing cold along the riverbank to catch sight across dense fog of the ornate barge bearing Napoleon's body, covered by ermine-edged velvet pall studded with Napoleonic bees, Imperial eagle and letter 'N' in silver brocade, as it made its way down the Seine. William Makepeace Thackeray watched as many knelt down on the shore and prayed for him. Transferred to a fifty-foot high funeral carriage drawn by sixteen horses attended by footmen liveried in Napoleon's household uniform, the coffin was carried from the Seine to the Hôtel des Invalides. More than thirty-six thousand people had gathered to witness Napoleon's return. His dying wish had been to be buried among the French, whom he "had loved so much". Whether or not he had truly loved them, he had certainly killed many more of them than any other monarch in French history. The French complained that the festivities under Louis-Philippe were no match for those under the Emperor Napoleon, when all the fountains in Paris ran with wine. How readily the French remembered the days of joy and plenty, and forgot the hardships and miseries which lasted far longer! Few cared to remember his military tyranny. It was the benefits his colossal power enabled him to bestow upon France which remained, and which would remain forever imprinted on the French collective memory.

In her book *Paris and the Parisians*, Mistress Trollope made a chilling prediction as to how Napoleon's memory might be eclipsed:

> The only means by which another sovereign may rival Napoleon in popularity, is by rivalling him in power. Were some of the feverish blood which still keeps France in agitation to be

drawn from her cities to reinforce her military array, and were a hundred thousand of the sons of France marched off to restore to Italy her natural position in Europe, power, glory and popularity would sustain the throne, and tranquillity be restored to her people. If King Louis-Philippe would undertake a crusade to restore independence to Italy, he might convert every traitor into a hero. Let him address the army raised for the purpose in the same inspiring words that Napoleon used of yore: "Soldiers! Let's go! Let's re-establish the Capitole! Let us awake the Roman people benumbed by several centuries of slavery! That will be the fruit of your victories. You will return to your hearths, and your fellow citizens will say, pointing at you, "He was in the Army of Italy!"

Would a Frenchman reawaken the Italian peninsula?

Marie-Louise was in Venice with Wilhelm on his way to Graz to recuperate in the June of 1846 when she learnt of the death of the Pope. "It is a terrible calamity at this particular moment and one must pray God that it does not bring bad consequences for the tranquillity of Europe. I confess that this idea worries me so terribly that I am in a state of considerable agitation."[1]

TWENTY-EIGHT

Death of a duchess and expiry of the moratorium, 1847

Marie-Louise asked Count Dietrichstein what he knew about Count Charles René de Bombelles when, in 1831, the Viennese cabinet proposed to appoint him as her next Chief Administrator.

"He is an educated man, gentle and likeable. His company will please Your Majesty very much and I think he is also a friend of order and economy." An experienced diplomat, he inspired respect. Like Marie-Louise, he had been widowed, his wife – with whom he was said to have been very much in love – dying at the age of twenty-five, leaving him with four children. When Count Dietrichstein realised that Count Bombelles was proposed as Marie-Louise's chief administrator, he expressed reservations. "I cannot see how Charles Bombelles, who is in France and an out-and-out royalist, could have the position of Grand Master at Your Majesty's Court – it would be incongruous."[1]

Bombelles arrived in Parma towards the end of 1832, Marie-Louise's *annus horribilis*. Marie-Louise was pleasantly surprised. A year later, apologising profusely for his audacity, the Count caught her by surprise by inviting her out to lunch. Marie-Louise confided in Albertina that she had responded by saying that he could invite her to lunch every day. She wrote to her great friend, Lady Burghersh, saying how excited she was. Count Bombelles was a real saint, so agreeable in society. At ease as much in company with or bumping into her Parman subjects in the streets or country lanes as at the military galas she held for ceremonial occasions, he always wanted to be introduced to everyone and was interested in what they had to say. Extremely diligent, he rose early, prepared the work of the day, dealt with political correspondence and attended on Marie-Louise only after going to chapel to hear mass. At nine in the morning, he summoned his staff and gave them their orders. Before holding conferences on matters of state, he took Marie-Louise out in his carriage in the afternoon, and after dinner accompanied her to the theatre. Marie-Louise told Lady Burghersh that he repeatedly expressed his approval of the manner in which she governed her duchies. She was pleased to see that he filled vacant posts with those favoured by Parman public opinion and had reformed the military composition of her household. He was all she wanted, firmness combined with gentleness and virtue, a real find. In sum, she had every reason to be delighted with her new majordomo.

"Everything Your Majesty tells me about the character of M. de Bombelles gives me reason to hope that *finally* you will no longer be tormented by your inner self."[2] Lady Burghersh replied.

Spending most of his days in Parma when Marie-Louise was at her ducal seat in Piacenza, Count Bombelles kept regular contact with Albertina and Luigi. He soon held them both in great affection. He brought them little gifts upon his return from Vienna whence he travelled to see his children whom Marie-Louise found the sweetest. He also showered her with presents, sending her magnificent bunches of rare flowers.

Marie-Louise had been lonely without her daughter. She found Bombelles' warm reports as to Albertina's welfare invaluable, grateful to him for devoting so much time to her family. She assured Albertina of Bombelles' affection for her – to an extent that might alarm Luigi, she confessed.

Five years after Neipperg's death, it was propitious that Marie-Louise should have a fresh romantic interest. Three days after Valentine's Day 1834, as snow began to fall, Bishop Neuschel presided over Marie-Louise's third wedding in strictest secrecy.

In Bombelles, Marie-Louise had found a companion to share life's burdens. He remained constant in a world changing beyond recognition, and she blessed the Heavens each day for having sent him.

Empress Karoline-Auguste reassured her that Emperor Francis, to whom this time Marie-Louise had made full disclosure, respected him infinitely, and that he would receive a warm welcome in Weinzierl on the imperial family summer holiday. After Emperor Francis's death, Karoline-Auguste persuaded her to reveal her new status to her Parman Court, it seeming to her that Marie-Louise's ladies-in-waiting had already noticed something of the couple's intimacy.

Marie-Louise had no doubt Count Bombelles was guaranteed a place in Heaven for the steps he had taken and the infinite generosity he had shown when cholera had set in. The offers of beds and property for the treatment of the sick, which he had procured, assured her of her subjects' esteem for him. He helped her wage war against the elements as she tried to stem the incessant floods, prohibiting the cutting down of mountain woodland in an effort to regularise the seasons and reduce the frequency of devastation. Every year, weather conditions seemed to be becoming more extreme.

At length the honeymoon period with Count Bombelles wore off. The melancholy which memories asserted over Marie-Louise returned. She felt so miserable and ill that she was sure that her happy times were past. In 1845, she told Albertina that she had suffered too much over the past fifteen years to be agreeable company. "We spend most of our evenings in the dark talking whenever the mood takes us but most of the time we are silent." To her green notebook she confided:

> The sacrifice of life is not always the most difficult . . . How are the minds and great impressions felt in common with a loved one? With a firm will to meet half way in a manner which is acceptable to our conscience. Real happiness on earth is virtuous love, based on harmony of tastes and opinions. Conformity of principles and tastes is essential in marriage and not conformity of character. It is essential that one of the couple tempers

and excites the other. Two people who are both indolent or both aggressive cannot be happy together. The same virtues, by contrast, are the makings of true empathy. The same character defects continually disturb inner peace.

The peace Marie-Louise had found in her domestic environment was about to elude her as sovereign. She was not Italian and could not become Italian. She was Austrian and, in her way, both oppressor and exile. She tried as best she could to tread a path which allowed as much freedom as seemed commensurate with order. Her family and friends in Vienna urged her to strengthen her ties to them and to stand firm against those who might challenge her authority. When Marie-Louise expressed her weariness at the lack of moral fibre of many in her duchies and of the Parman public schools, which despite her exertions had become places of disrepute, the Court of Vienna headed by her brother's empress prevailed on her to invite the Jesuits back to Parma to take charge of moral, religious and scientific instruction of Parman youths. Marie-Louise, having long opposed the Jesuits, knew that this move would not be popular, but her efforts to improve attitudes had achieved little. She could not leave things as they stood. The secularism of Mazzini's Young Italians and of liberals was challenging the Catholic as much as the monarchical order. Marie-Louise had encouraged eminent scientists in her duchies to attend the Italian Scientific Congresses held annually since 1839, but these too seemed to challenge the moral authority of religion. It seemed to her something had to be done.

In March 1844, to the consternation of her subjects, Marie-Louise announced the ascendance of the Jesuits in her duchies and granted them the Church of San Rocco and the adjoining buildings from which to operate. The era of religious enlightenment and tolerance which Marie-Louise had nurtured over the previous thirty years began to darken, Parma's cathedral and the new reactionary Archbishop ostentatiously performing the baptism of a young Jewess, Fontanella di Colorno. Despite their success, the reported mass conversions of Protestants to Catholicism in England, and the creation of a sect in Russia called the German Catholics, the Jesuits were not appreciated everywhere. Louis-Philippe had imposed severe constraints on their *modus operandi* in France, which prohibited more than twenty of Jesuits living in any one place.

Marie-Louise waited with trepidation for the political bombshell. Over the course of the past twenty years, her bereavements and the political troubles constantly challenging her had all but destroyed her nervous system. She suffered from terrible and persistent migraines, from which she could escape only by taking opium, which sent her to sleep. The removal of a bone from her head, surgery which she demanded her reluctant doctor perform on her, did not improve her health. She was afflicted by tedious respiratory problems, finding, like most of the Parmans, the air of the Po plains oppressive in summer. Whey baths and the air at Ischl seemed to alleviate her symptoms, clearing the fog in her mind: "In Parma, I feel like I am wearing an iron helmet which crushes my head, dulling the free use of my intellectual and moral faculties." She suffered the pains of hell, she said.[3]

Chest pains plagued her, and her rheumatism grew steadily worse, preventing her from sleeping any length of time. The doctors prohibited her from walking and riding. She underwent numerous cures, to which she became addicted. Sometimes, she was ordered to bathe not in hot but only in cold and salted water. Sometimes the sulphurous waters of Baden gave her relief, at others they left her breathless and nervous. She spent so much of her life immersed in salt water, she feared she must look like a herring! When long immersions in cold water had little effect, the physicians ordered her to undergo searing burning therapy which so attacked her nerves that she nearly passed out with convulsions. Perplexed by her failure to respond to their contradictory prescriptions, the doctors argued between themselves as regards the management of her health, to her exasperation. Dr. Rossi, who had brought up Albertina and Wilhelm, called them all charlatans. Marie-Louise resorted to milk and tamarind, ipecacuana, Water of Tetreis and pomade of Lausanne to soothe her. She applied pitch plasters constantly to aching parts of her body. By the summer of 1846, she complained of having sprained her muscles in her fingers and could no longer play the harp, guitar and piano which had previously absorbed much of her emotional pain, and dared not open a door or close a window. She could only write with the greatest difficulty.

Over the course of the 1840s, Giuseppe Mazzini's liberation movement, Young Italy, which aimed for fusion under a republic of the eight governments on the Italian peninsula and their respective patriotisms, had made giant strides. As the years passed, Mazzini's young affiliates carried out numerous acts of sedition and fomented uprisings. Two such young men were the Bandiera brothers in the service of the Austro-Hungarian Navy. In correspondence with Giuseppe Mazzini himself, Emilio and Attilio Bandiera had hatched a daring exploit. Spreading propaganda among Italians in service to the Austrian Navy aboard a warship, the brothers planned, as 1844 dawned, to seize control of it and to bombard the Sicilian city of Messina. Betrayed by informants, they jumped ship in the nick of time and took refuge on Corfu. There, they received intelligence from Mazzini that the Kingdom of the Two Sicilies was in ferment. Mazzini urged them to gather together a band of men to make a raid on the Calabrian coast to free political prisoners. The mission backfired. Mistaken for Turkish pirates and betrayed once again by an insider, the whole group, along with sympathetic Calabrians, were taken prisoner. On 24th July, under a hot Neapolitan sun, Emilio and Attilio, along with nine of their companions, were executed by Bourbon firing squad, crying "Viva l'Italia!" as they fell. The case of the Bandiera brothers caused an international uproar. The mass executions were universally condemned, the barbaric response rallying support for the underdog. The Bandiera brothers instantly became martyrs, their memory tacitly invoked as men and women sat at the opera, wiping a tear with their handkerchief as they swathed themselves in Verdi's choruses decrying slavery.

Marie-Louise would not have missed the implications for her kind.

Marie-Louise had been right to fear the consequences of Pope Gregory's death. The new Pope, styled Pius IX and uncharacteristically young for a pontiff at fifty-four, seemed to offer those with liberal aspirations strength, courage and confidence to commit themselves to the eviction of the Austrians. There seemed to be a remarkable religious regeneration, reviving faith in the Papacy, previously on the wane to the point of despair. Upon his appointment, Pius granted an amnesty to all political prisoners in his states, and instituted a civic guard, allowing moderate freedom of the press and of the State Assembly. He reformed the codes and prisons, prepared plans for railways and relieved Jews of their civil disabilities. Such measures had been unthinkable under his predecessors. Intellectuals throughout the Italian peninsula and former detractors of the Papal States rallied to him. The new pontiff was hailed as the Apostle of religious truth and revolution, the long-awaited counterweight to Mazzini. Unlike Mazzini, whose message reached the literate, a small minority, the Pope could speak to every class and every type of Italian, including the illiterate peasants who formed the bulk of the peninsula's population. Enthusiasm for the man and his initiatives grew exponentially, the newspapers dubbing him the Hero of Charity.

The Pope's encouragement of lay involvement in administration was teaching Italians how to hold meetings and elections, how to run newspapers, to prepare mentally for self-government and for operating its apparatus. Young men sported a hat and haircut *alla Pio IX*, wore yellow and white, his ancestral heraldic colours, and carried handkerchiefs with his image printed upon it. His amnesty of political crimes led liberals to think that dramatic reforms would follow. Disappointed when he lunched with the Jesuits, they nonetheless still saluted his courage and magnanimity, seeing in him the liberating heroes portrayed in Verdi's operas, adapting the maestro's choruses to extol his virtues. Marie-Louise raised no objection when, at the new year, a group of Parma's intellectuals opened a new conversation club intended to be a forum for exchange of ideas.

In cities up and down the peninsula, the proliferation of secret sects had been fuelled by the operas of Giuseppe Verdi and Gaetano Donizetti, and the literature of Alessandro Manzoni which had adopted the Tuscan dialect as transnational language. The emergence of this common language prompted young men and women throughout the Italian peninsula to recognise their bond of kinship, so long submerged by Bourbon, Austrian and Papal divisions. Nationalist tracts in the new national language promoting Italian unification were all bestsellers, attracting international attention and sympathy. Vincenzo Gioberti's *Moral and Civil Primacy of the Italians*, published in Brussels, envisaging a federated Italy under the aegis of the Pope, dispensed with the premise that to be liberal was anti-Catholic. His book, articulating the human suffering and feelings of his nation, won over many inhabitants in the Italian peninsula who had thought the cause of unification ungodly. Now observant Catholics, still wary of radicals, warmed to patriotism, distrust turning into a new pride. Italian young Napoleons no longer saw their future in terms of advancement in Austrian or Bourbon institutions. Theirs was a vision of much wider possibilities facilitated by the new growing railway network.

Luigi Sanvitale, Albertina's husband and Marie-Louise's loyal courtier and beloved son-in-law, considered himself an Italian patriot, having been initiated in the Sublime Perfect Masters by his now exiled cousin, Jacopo. His studies in Siena had cemented his political affiliations and brought him into contact with many likeminded individuals from different parts of the Italian peninsula. Since then, he had travelled extensively throughout the Italian states and to Austria, service to Marie-Louise facilitating his private agenda. He regularly travelled to the Italian city of Nice, where he exchanged information regarding the Parman exiles in France, and received briefings regarding planned insurrections and the dissemination of intelligence and propaganda. Serving Marie-Louise dutifully, Luigi tutored Albertina in political realities, and it was not long before she too dreamed of a unified state free from Austria. A pious, God-fearing woman, Albertina found in Gioberti's work the good sense which Mazzini's troublemakers seemed to disdain. Cesare Balbo's *Hopes of Italy* advised military and moral fortitude to eject Austria from the peninsula, anticipating his own state of Piedmont's lead in the struggle to the Promised Land. Bestseller historical novels, *Niccolò dei Lapi* and *Ettore Fieramosca* by Massimo d'Azeglio emphasised the evils of foreign domination in Italy to spur national feeling.

January and February of 1847 were exceptionally cold. Terrible storms did not produce the rain necessary to reap a plentiful harvest later in the year. The cost of cereals increased steadily, a bushel of wheat or maize fast exceeding the peasant's pocket. In many cities throughout Europe, famine incentivised popular risings, and in Ireland, extreme hunger produced epidemics causing substantial fatalities. In Piacenza, peace had already been disturbed by riots, suppressed only with rifle-fire from the Austrian garrison. Undeterred, the rioters demanded that the granaries be opened and grain sold at slashed prices. When the authorities refused, they broke into the warehouses and sacked them. Throughout the first half of the year, Marie-Louise's pains, particularly in her right arm, were unbearable. The doctors ordered her to stay in bed for the months of February and March. Feverish, she implored the good Lord to bring rain. Others could see that there was already death in her soul. In late May 1847, warm weather set in, finally dissolving the snow but there was still no rain.

The Duchess insisted on travelling to Vienna, despite the frailty of her health. Perhaps she knew in her heart that it would be the last opportunity see loved ones there again. Some thought she had absented herself in anticipation of disturbances. Venice was flooded with foreigners, particularly and ominously royalist French escaping the troubles at home. In Vienna, she saw her beloved Wilhelm. In her presence, he seemed confused and embarrassed after another long period of silence, the reasons for which Marie-Louise did not comprehend. Deeply saddened, she confided her disappointment to Albertina, asking her to show visitors the beauties of Correggio and the other remarkable works in her duchies. "I can only repeat the old refrain, the one that I love you very much and that I will love you for all the time that my heart continues to beat."[4]

While Marie-Louise was taking the baths at Ischl to find the relief seeming always to elude her, the political temperature in Parma rose dramatically. Baron Mistrali, upon whose wisdom and insights Marie-Louise had long been able to rely, had died the previous year only a fortnight before the previous pontiff. Upon his death, Marie-Louise had assigned the administration of her duchies to four director-generals, entrusting the military to Count Bombelles.

The first anniversary of the election of the new Pope was the catalyst for popular demonstrations in cities throughout the Italian peninsula. Pope Pius had continued to endorse a press in the Papal States infinitely more liberal than elsewhere on the Italian peninsula. Riots started in Tuscany, Lucca and Vienna, the populace, now distinct from the military, demanding the same concessions. Unable to bear the pressure of demands for reform, the heir to Parma, the Duke of Lucca, fled in his carriage, pursued by angry subjects, and was lucky to get away in one piece. There were demonstrations in Piedmont, to which King Charles Albert responded by carrying out reforms to the police, transforming them from a military into a civic organisation. He introduced new legislation to support freedom of the press, and promised further reforms. The Piedmontese press printed open hostility to Austria.

Liberals among Marie-Louise's subjects decided to mark the occasion by attending a mass and benediction at the Church of San Giovanni, and by distributing to the poor three thousand five hundred loaves of bread, funded by private donations. The government raised no objection to these plans but orders were given that the demonstrators be watched so as to prevent matters going further.

Marie-Louise did, however, prohibit the holding of a patriotic luncheon planned by the professors of the university. Tickets for the loaves of bread were allocated to ministers, to the Chief of Police, to the military authorities, to doctors working for the state, to important local institutions and to many prominent families to distribute to the neediest in society.

Tension was mounting as dawn rose on 16 June. Thick columns of soldiers stood in the square behind the Cathedral before the doors of the Church of San Giovanni, ready to pounce on elements whom they suspected. In the vast interior of the church, students and their professors, the leading citizenry, the common people, believers and non-believers and the city's Jews expressed their solidarity. The distribution of bread took place with the greatest solemnity, everyone behaving in an exemplary, blameless fashion.

The liberals had declared that on the evening of the same day there should be a general illumination, every household to light their lamps to show support for the new Pope. As the sun set, ragged young men ran along the streets shouting, "Long live Pius IX! Light your lamps, light your lamps!" As dusk fell, more aggressive elements began to insult the occupiers of homes remaining unlit and to throw stones at their windows. On the prescribed orders of Count Bombelles, ducal soldiers and cavalry were despatched to patrol the streets. Soon whistling began.

Eyewitness reports each told a different story. Some maintained that troublemakers had hurled abuse and threats at the soldiery who, under orders to use force to disband the troublemakers, commanded them to withdraw. Others claimed that a few rascals with an axe to grind, wanting to ingratiate themselves with Count Bombelles, decided to ruin the party. Others said that the ducal Captain Anviti had ostentatiously led a band of urchins, screaming and shouting at the top of their voices into the main square, where the townspeople were assembled in merriment, to sew disorder and confusion. The soldiers were eager to flex their muscles, thirsting to sack the city and give the rich burghers a good hiding. Half an hour later, the Count reappeared accompanied by a patrol of troops, violently striking and shoving unsuspecting citizens with the flat of his sword as soldiers rained down blows and insults, kicking people with their boots and the butt of their rifles.

"Go home, scum! To bed, you coward!" They spat. When more troops arrived, they egged each other on, "Keep screaming boys, our superiors love it!" and "they think they are going to start a revolution! Be brave boys, shoot them, none of the townspeople are armed!"

As they went, they extinguished the torches lit in innocent celebration of the Papal anniversary and insulted the clerics whom they chanced to meet in the street. It was said that when the Parman townsfolk had dispersed and fled to their beds, Colonel Salis, who had been received often by the Duchess on whose behalf he purported to act, expressed his regret at not having gunned down a good few vile citizens. The authorities said that the revellers had become over-excited, that their applause, singing and merriment had boiled over into sedition. Those who had refrained from showing their support either through caution or aversion for the new aspirations were subjected to acts of violence and virtually all had their windows broken. The agitators urged the populace to condemn the soldiers, calling them mercenaries of an unwanted regime. By the end of the evening, there had been twenty arrests.

Count Cantelli, head of the town council, rushed to Ischl to give Marie-Louise a full account of events. But he found that minds had already been made up. His account was ignored. Marie-Louise had been led to understand that the authorities and the troops had acted responsibly and in performance of duty to protect innocent bystanders. An ungrateful minority had abused the Pontifical name and office to vent their pitiful aggression. Disgusted by the disregard for his person and for the constituency he represented, Count Cantelli returned to Parma without appetite to continue his services.

Count Bombelles arrived back in Parma to demand that all state

DEATH OF A DUCHESS AND EXPIRY OF THE MORATORIUM, 1847

employees sign a declaration of loyalty to Marie-Louise's government. He immediately discharged the Chief of Police, Count Ferrari, who had given many years of loyal service to Marie-Louise, his only crime to have been too lenient as regards celebration of the Papal anniversary. Bombelles pronounced himself forcefully against the instigators of the illumination and approved the conduct of the military authority. Victims, not perpetrators, found themselves placed under investigation. Threatening letters were addressed to the Count and to his friends, making known plans for his assassination. Bombelles stood firm, unperturbed, unshakeable in his resolve. With complete sangfroid, ignoring universal protest, he embarked on reactionary measures.

Over the next few days, there were sporadic disturbances, graffiti appearing around the city: "Long live Pius IX". The Parmans studiously avoided the military, and whenever a soldier chanced to enter a café, those present immediately fell silent and made for the door. Matters came to a head ten days later when a young Parman, the son of a prominent lawyer, insulted a sentinel as he passed a House of Correction in the city. The sentinel and two of his comrades beat up the Parman so severely that for several days he was fighting for his life. The doctor had never seen such horrific injuries, the boy's face unrecognisable. The young Parman never recovered and took refuge from his deformities in insanity. Marie-Louise's ministers determined to bring the malfeasors to account and to impose upon them the full severity of the law. The three sentinels were tried and sentenced to long terms of imprisonment.

The Parmans, who had flocked to their churches to make generous contributions to their oppressed Irish brethren, following the Pope's exhortations to all Catholics to come to their aid, noticed his distinct change of heart. Reactionary elements within the Papacy had not anticipated that patriotic expectations would fall upon the young Pope's shoulders. The cardinals who had appointed him in conclave feared that Pius's liberal vision would cost the Church dear. A unified Italy would threaten the primacy of Papal authority.

Pope Pius was prevailed upon to authorise the formation of a civic guard which had within days of its creation arrested large numbers of liberals. Many across the Italian peninsula and beyond saw Austria, their glittering bayonets poised menacingly towards Rome, as the culprit. "The Huns are on the Po. The dogs! The wolves! May they perish!" Byron wrote angrily.

In mid August, as if weather conditions were a reflection of the political volatility, Parma was shaken by an earthquake which also disturbed Livorno and Pisa, causing in all sixty deaths and a hundred and fifty wounded. King Louis-Philippe and Marie-Louise's cousins, the Princes of Salerno, were the target of assassination attempts. Sovereigns everywhere felt nervous. To warn the Pope off introducing any further reforms, Austria had its garrison stationed at Ferrara fire off cannon and explode bombs. Cries of outrage followed. Slowly, Rome and the Papal States seemed to be sinking into anarchy, the Jesuits unable to appear in public for fear of attack. In the second week of September, Austrian police claimed to have put down a rebellion in Milan. In fact, the police had shot indiscriminately at a crowd that was honouring the new liberal Archbishop of Milan, Monsignor Romilli, and singing hymns on behalf of Pope Pius IX. There had been one dead and sixty wounded.

Only when calm seemed to have been restored did Marie-Louise venture across the Alps back to her capital. She seemed the picture of health upon her arrival in the third week of November. But not two weeks later. One Thursday morning in the second week of December after a night disturbed by pain in her chest, she decided to go out for a ride. No sooner had the carriage passed out of the palace gates than one of the horses got into an altercation with a cart which crossed its path. Terrified, Marie-Louise immediately got out and wanted to return to her palace on foot. A few moments later, the crisis having passed, she got into the carriage again and continued her promenade. But by lunchtime, she was feeling much worse. She could barely eat. She insisted on presiding over a conference with her ministers and receiving her ladies later that day, despite running a very strong fever. That night, the pains in her side and fever had worsened to such a degree that she summoned the doctor, who diagnosed consumption. "You will see, I shall not get up again. Eight days from now I shall be carried out of here."

Within three days, Marie-Louise was unable to swallow or breathe, her fever extremely high. She vomited bile sporadically. Albertina and Luigi, who were by her side, decided it was time for her to receive the last sacrament. The Bishop had refused Marie-Louise's request for its administration five days earlier, on her fifty-seventh birthday, regarding her still very much in the world of the living. She seemed then to rally and prayed that she would have time to finish the embroidery for the Church at Maria-Zell to which she had gone on a pilgrimage that summer. She had looked forward to dressing the Christmas tree, her *'Christbaum'*, as she called it when talking or writing in Italian, a German custom she had brought with her to Parma.

She knew that she would not celebrate another Christmas with the family and was eager to distribute the gifts she had kept by from her last trip to Vienna. That afternoon, the dying Duchess signed the decree conferring a regency on her government and sent off letters to Vienna, including one to Wilhelm. She was tired and ready to go, though she was sorry to leave her children and grandchildren.

There being little doubt that the end was near, Albertina carried out her own censorship of her mother's letters to her, striking through sensitive material to protect her mother in death. Beyond the palace walls, Marie-Louise's subjects assembled in public processions to Parma's many churches to beg the Almighty to prolong her days. Now she nodded, no longer able to articulate save in broken words. Haggard, toothless, old before her time, this gentle, infinitely kind woman who had braved constant buffeting by destiny believing rightly or wrongly that her chances of changing it were slim and in any event likely to be detrimental to her and her loved ones, looked forward to death as a release from her earthly struggles. Having removed her stockings to receive Extreme Unction, she rallied her forces to respond to the Bishop's litanies with the corresponding couplets begging the Heavens for a peaceful death. Then she called her husband, Count Bombelles, to recite her last will prepared three years earlier, to which, with Albertina's aid, she added a few last wishes, appending with trembling hand her signature to the codicil. She thanked everyone who had been of service to her, and requested that each person present receive as a memento one of her personal possessions she had regularly used.

> I forgive all those who, under my peaceable government, have filled my heart with bitterness, and who, at different moments, have caused me pain, affliction and worry. I hope in the mercy of God that He will pardon and enlighten them and that they will show their new sovereign obedience, respect and fidelity.

Then Marie-Louise asked that her grandchildren be brought before her to receive her last blessing. Luigi led them in, she gesturing to them to kneel by her bedside. "Remember me in your prayers, honour my memory by always being pious, good and obedient to your parents, and in fulfilling your duties. I bless you, my dear children: honour my memory and remember your poor grandmother," She tried but was too frail to reach out to hold her hands out over their heads. Albertina and family wept, Wilhelm, from whom she had received a last letter two days earlier, sadly absent. "Tell him that I bless him in my thoughts and pray from above for his happiness."

Luigi kissed her hands and said his farewell. "Adieu, Luigi. Remember me too. I hope that the Parmans will not forget me, for I have loved them and I have always sought to do them good."

She wanted her funeral to be a quiet affair. "Make no fuss after I am dead, for I have lived through an age which was greater than me."

At ten minutes past five in the afternoon on 17 December 1847, Marie-Louise expired. Couriers were sent to inform Bourbon

Charles Louis, Duke of Lucca, now her heir by virtue of the Second Treaty of Paris. The Parmans had seen him twice. He had made a good impression, seven and five years earlier, on the latter occasion attending *Nabucco* to spontaneous applause and a long ovation by spectators. Then the Parmans had had high hopes of him.

Just as gossip had pursued Marie-Louise in life, so it did not forget her in death. Fantasists continued to accuse her of having an insatiable sexual appetite, a well-known Habsburg weakness if similar gossip relating to her great-aunt Marie-Antoinette was to be believed. Her premature death was said to have resulted from her over-indulgence. More credibly, some said that she had contracted typhus from her chaplain, Monsignor Lamprecht, whom she had visited shortly before her demise and his death. Some said that she had died from poisoning. This hypothesis seemed improbable unless there had been a terrible mistake, Count Bombelles a more likely target of any such attempt.

Marie-Louise had expressly requested that no autopsy be performed on her body. A waxen mask was taken of her head, her body embalmed by Dr Rossi by injecting ten litres of alcohol and a kilo of arsenical acid into her carotid artery through a simple short incision around the neck. With tears streaming down their faces, her loyal maidservants laid out her shrunken form in a black silk dress, then a white robe and a luxurious red coat embroidered with gold. They cast around her face a white veil and around her feet white slippers. Across her breast was laid the heavy necklace and decorations of the chivalric Constantine Order of Saint George the Martyr, her hands interlinked, holding a rosary and crucifix.

Thousands of Parmans and people hailing from further afield who had held the deceased in high esteem flocked to file past her over the course of the next fortnight as she lay in state in the Church of San Ludovico in Parma's Ducal Palace, on a ceremonial bed, the whiteness of her skin contrasting with the vermilion velvet edged with gold tassles. When the fortnight was over, Marie-Louise's body was transferred into a coffin of maritime wood lined with purple velvet on which lay a horse-hair mattress and pillow covered in white silk. A crucifix was placed on her chest and a row of rosary beads between her fingers; alongside her a leather-bound casket containing within a crystal box a scroll of parchment bearing her names. The lid of the coffin closed, the coffin itself was placed in another box made of lead, which in turn was placed in a third made of varnished walnut. Her body, thus thrice encased, returned to the Church of San Ludovico to stand for one last time in state under a velvet pall and golden crucifix until the funeral on 24th December, conducted by the Bishop of Parma and attended by her court, officers of State and cousin, Archduke Ferdinand of Este from Modena.

One month from Marie-Louise's death, 17th January, her bier was placed in a funeral carriage drawn by three pairs of horses, caparisoned in black, their tack embroidered with her personal coat of arms. The carriage was flanked on all sides and followed by a long cortège of mourners on horseback, in carriages and on foot. Large crowds of the people who had loved her accompanied the procession to the banks of the Po at Casalmaggiore where the river had to be crossed by barge. From Casalmaggiore, the carriage, with its Hussar escort of honour comprising a hundred and fifty soldiers on horseback, carried Marie-Louise's body to the Imperial vault of the Capucin crypt in Vienna, to be entombed alongside her Habsburg ancestors and next to the child from whom she had been long separated in life. Bishop Neuschel, her confessor, carefully placed documents relating to Marie-Louise's secret marriages and her illegitimate children, adjusted to prevent future embarrassment, in the registry in Parma's Episcopal Chancery.

Throughout her ducal territories, bells rang out in mourning. As the carriage bearing her remains sped northward towards the Austrian capital, civil disturbances and rioting erupted throughout the peninsula. Livorno had already risen, on 6 January, Palermo on 12th. The rest of the Italian peninsula, the German Confederation and Hungarian dominions followed suit shortly thereafter.

Everywhere, people clamoured for revolution and for liberation from the Habsburg yoke. Marie-Louise's brother, Emperor Ferdinand, found himself besieged on all sides, facing demands to dismiss Chancellor Metternich, who was hated by everyone. To maintain the Austrian army, police and secret services, the 'Coachman of Europe' had imposed such heavy taxes on commerce and tobacco and had refused to lower tariffs on foreign wheat in time of famine, that crime, prostitution and begging had provided many with the only means of affording a measly potato to fill their stomachs. Boycotts were organised by the common people, and attempts were made to murder tax collectors.

The Parmans, young, old, priests, magistrates, men and women, demanded the reforms granted by the magnanimous Pius IX, by the Grand Duke of Tuscany and by Charles Albert, and the ejection of the Jesuits. Revolutionary committees urged everyone not to buy tobacco or lottery tickets and not to attend public theatres, all important sources of ducal revenue, and warned that anyone doing so would be branded a ducal spy. New hair-styles were introduced in imitation of revolutionary figureheads: the *Cicervacchio*, after the charismatic Roman demagogue who championed Pius IX and urged him to further reforms; the *Calabrese*, after the feisty warriors of the south; and the *Ernani*, after the Verdian hero.

The new Duke of Parma, Charles II, called in the Austrians. He refused to be drawn into the customs union concluded between Piedmont, Florence and the Papal States, and instead concluded an offensive alliance with the Duke of Modena, cleaving closer to the Imperial Government of Austria. This was a gamble, and a poor one at that. Several hundred hussar cavalry marched into the ducal capital, their brash uniforms contrasting sharply with the draperies of mourning for the late Duchess. They were soon augmented by an Austrian battalion sequestered from Piacenza.

The Austrian soldiers brazenly ignored the boycott, prompting bloody encounters between military and citizenry previously seen across the Italian peninsula but not during Marie-Louise's tenure in

Parma. Edicts were promulgated making it a criminal offence to sport a revolutionary hat or hairstyle. As darkness fell, patriotic hymns and revolutionary songs reverberated across the city, the Austrian patrols unable to stem their tide. News arrived of Louis-Philippe's fall and the proclamation of the Republic of France, and then of the outbreak of revolution in Milan, Venice and, inconceivably, Vienna. Metternich and the Archbishop of Vienna were forced to flee their own capital. When Hungary announced its intention to break away from the Habsburg Empire and a recently constituted Polish National Committee declared its territory the Kingdom of Galicia and Lodmeria, and when Venice declared itself once again a republic, the Austrian government was powerless to challenge them. By mid March 1848, Emperor Ferdinand was forced to accede to the revolutionaries' demands and to grant a constitution to those parts of the empire which had not yet seceded.

As the Kings of Naples and of Piedmont-Sardinia, the Grand Duke of Tuscany, the Pope, and the Habsburg Emperor himself surrendered to the revolutionaries, Charles II, his daughter-in-law pregnant with his successor's baby, seemed to indicate that he would grant the concessions demanded. With dissension in the ranks and the armies upon which the Habsburg dynasty had so long relied overstretched, order rapidly collapsed. A week later, Charles Albert, King of Piedmont-Savoy, declared war on Austria in the Austrian held northern Italian provinces, consuming the attention of the entire peninsula.

From that moment on, most Italians who aspired to nationhood saw their redemption in the Piedmontese monarch. Thenceforward, he was called the Magnanimous King. Following five days of intense fighting in Milan, General Radetsky was forced to withdraw beyond the Mincio River and to vacate the fortresses of Verona, Mantova and Peschiera, the vantage points which had previously buttressed Austrian hegemony over Lombardy-Venetia and its satellite states on the Italian peninsula. Within the week, Charles Albert's army had taken control of and hoisted the tricolour flag over Milan, Brescia, Bergamo, Pavia, Cremona and Crema, and instituted provisional governments.

The Piacentine ducal subjects were already burning portraits of Parma's new duke in the city's squares, and proclaimed a provisional government pending accession to the State of Piedmont. The new Duke of Parma was terrified when he heard of the political upheavals and surrounded himself with large groups of soldiers, stationing troops at critical points in the city.

The night of 19th to 20th March passed without incident in Parma, save for a total eclipse of the moon which was surrounded by an ominous blood-red halo. No-one slept, hoping that the morning would bring an announcement of the grant of those rights which had been obtained elsewhere. But the Duke kept silent. Several adjudged it time to achieve by force what was being withheld. Just before eight o'clock in the morning, a young carpenter was the first to fire. He took aim in the main square before the Ducal Palace at an Austrian sentinel, who instantly fell dead to the ground. The struggle between Austrians and Parman citizenry began in earnest. The insurgents took control of the bell-tower of the Cathedral and rang the bells to rouse everyone to action. From rooftops, windows and loggias on the façade of the Cathedral, patriots took aim at Austrians and any members of the Ducal Regiment within range. Within four hours twelve men were dead, divided equally between oppressors and oppressed. Charles II hastily convened his Council of State, and announced that he intended to grant all the concessions made by the other sovereigns in the Italian peninsula with immediate effect in the interests of preventing further bloodshed. He announced further that he was forming a Regency comprising five highly respected men to administer his duchy, selected with assistance from intermediaries who he knew had been instrumental over the past two decades in promoting the cause of Italian unity in the Parman duchies. One of the five was Marie-Louise's loyal son-in-law, Count Luigi Sanvitale.

Immediately after the appointment of the Regency, hostilities ceased. Austrian troops were ordered to leave the duchy, and a local National Guard formed, all by the afternoon of 20th March. The Parmans demonstrated their appreciation of the new sovereign's concessions by applauding him wherever he passed. Many prevailed on him to give up his plan of temporary absence from his States, and on 25 March he was persuaded to parade the main streets of the city in an open carriage to receive the acclaim of his grateful, exultant subjects. Luigi Sanvitale and the other seven members of the provisional government sat alongside the Bourbon duke and his family as the Parmans detached the horses from their harnesses and bore the carriages forward, white handkerchiefs fluttering from balconies and effusion gushing from every mouth. As a token of the affection in which the Duke was held and as a demonstration of the absence of threat or danger, one citizen handed his four year old daughter to the Duke to accompany his party on his tour. The little girl sitting beside him, the Duke was moved to tears. For a few brief moments, it seemed as if the Duchy of Parma had finally broken free from the Austrian yoke.

It was a chimera. The Duke was playing a game with his new subjects, biding his time. It was the last they would see of him. As he lifted his faithful subject's little girl in his arms to public acclaim, the Duke had already planned his next move. In the third week of April, Marquises Paveri Fontana and Dalla Rosa Prati, both masters of diplomacy who had proved their loyalty to the late Duchess though patriots, accompanied the Duke as far as Bologna. Days later, having reached Marseille, the Duke issued a public protest against everything which had been done in Parma since 20 March. He claimed that all acts had been performed and all deeds had been signed by him under duress.

Within the week, Piedmontese troops had reached Parma. A decree was issued by the provisional government on 2 May 1848, declaring that the Ducal Court and House of the former Duke had ceased. State goods henceforward were the property of the Piedmontese-Sardinian Crown, which also appropriated over half the funds in the Parman treasury. Those ministers who had served the ducal government of Charles II were dismissed. In a new newspaper entitled *'Independenza Nazionale'*, printed in Parma, the seven members of the provisional government were acclaimed as "the Seven Kings". They, on behalf of the city, hosted the celebrated Abbott Gioberti, who had brought fervent Catholics into the patriotic fold, with full honours, immense banquet and illuminations in his honour. The provisional government decreed that a register should be opened in every parish of the duchy, inviting citizens to declare if they wanted to amalgamate with Piedmont or with Pius IX, or if they wished to remain a Duchy under Charles II. The results were announced in Parma's Cathedral, the thirty-seven thousand votes cast for fusion with Piedmont far exceeding all others, and the deed of annexation to Piedmont executed in the presence of all civil, military and ecclesiastical authorities, the National Guard and the Clergy. Luigi Sanvitale had been one of the main protagonists in the advancement of the Piedmontese cause. There was still much work to do. Piedmont was at war with Austria. If Austria should prevail, the Italian peninsula would be back to square one. The intelligence received suggested that Austria was losing men, artillery and battles as if there were no tomorrow. For once, without Marie-Louise's benign governance and wider protection, the Habsburgs were on the run.

AFTERWORD

The overwhelming vote by the Parmans to accede to the Kingdom of Piedmont-Sardinia came to nothing. Duke Charles III, his father having abdicated, returned with Habsburg backing. Luigi Sanvitale was forced to flee and joined his cousin Jacopo in exile in Turin. It would take two of history's bloodiest battles at Magenta and Solferino between Austria and France in 1859 and the intervention of the British government to change Parma's fortunes.

Sir James Hudson, Queen Victoria's ambassador to the Court of Turin, worked tirelessly to persuade Emperors Franz-Josef of Austria (nephew of Marie-Louise) and Napoleon III (nephew of Napoleon I) to come to terms without further bloodshed. The British put forward their proposals, which were to seal the fate of the peninsula at the Conference of Paris which took place, notwithstanding Austria's refusal to attend. The *Morning Post* of 3rd February 1860 announced that the English government and the nation were of one mind. The Italians must govern themselves without any foreign intervention. For the last time, the Parmans, Modenesi and Florentines cast their votes overwhelmingly in favour of annexation. In early April, Luigi and Jacopo Sanvitale and Giuseppe Verdi stood side by side in the Turin parliament to hear their new king at the inauguration of the Kingdom of Italy. Albertina, setting out for Turin, chanced to encounter Ponza de S. Martino, sent down by the Piedmontese government to report on the administrative needs of the new provinces.

Some say that this is just an excuse, that he needs an alibi for his real mission, which is to assess financial resources ... so that Turin can appropriate the respective treasuries. There are rumours afoot that the assets of the Parman state will be seized, Parma's jewels cruelly plundered. But perhaps these are only suppositions.[1]

As Parma rejoiced, the world heard about the consecration of the mausoleum of red Kostchoka quartzite imported at vast expense and logistical difficulty from a remote island on Russia's Onega Lake which Napoleon III had built for his uncle. Upon it, Napoleon I's name was etched in gold capital letters. The sarcophagus was mounted on a green pedestal in a circular crypt under the two cupolas of the magnificent dome of the Church of Saint Louis in the Invalides. The symbolism reinforced the image Napoleon had liked to convey of himself in life. In the language of the ancients, Napoleon is Hercules shattering the chains of tyranny, blessed by Minerva, the promoter of human liberty, who had endowed him with wisdom and justice. In the language of Catholicism, he is Jesus Christ's holy crusader, to whom St Louis offers his sword, as the Apostles and Evangelists look on in adoration. The splendour of the tomb and transformations of Paris effected by Baron Georges-Eugène Haussman would make people believe that the age and the city of the first Napoleonic Empire had resounded with unalloyed glory. The names of Napoleon's generals and of his triumphs, his defeats obliterated, would be used to consolidate the myth.

At the beginning of May 1860, King Victor Emmanuel II set foot on Parman soil as its sovereign. Everyone wanted to touch the hand that had unsheathed his sword and triumphed for liberty. The King processed in his carriage to deafening acclamations to the Cathedral for Mass and thence to the Royal Palace to receive tokens of admiration and gratitude. The following day, he rose early to visit the monuments and treasures of Parma. He spent several hours in the Palatine Library at the entrance of which still stands Concordia, the sculpture by Canova of Marie-Louise.

Shortly after the King's visit, Representatives of the Piedmontese Royal House gave orders for the removal of the furniture from the city's royal palaces, so that all that remained were the bare walls, doors and window frames. The rooms were stripped of the languid landscapes of Rousseau, of Daubigny, of Courbet, of Troyon and Prud'hon's sleeping King of Rome and Lawrence's Duke of Reichstadt. Gone was the Museo Storico del Ducato (the museum of history of the duchy) which Marie-Louise had created in the Palace of the Garden in imitation of that at Versailles. Also gone were all the objects purchased by the house of Bourbon-Parma. The charming apartments of the Ducal Palace were left empty, squalid and silent, later to be used as a lunatic asylum.

The Civil Code of the Kingdom of Italy by its first king, introduced in 1865, turned the clock back, undoing much of Marie-Louise's innovations. Once more, women ranked alongside those without legal capacity, minors, the disqualified and the ineligible. Men and women were recognised as equal under Italian law only in 1975.

Marie-Louise had been right in predicting the emergence of a composer who would take music to a level more scientific than that attained by Verdi. A German composer by the name of Richard Wagner astonished opera-goers in Dresden with his composition of *Tannhäuser*, and a decade later with a trilogy of operas based on Norse saga. His music was a new sound, its patriotism symbolic but more blatant and disturbing than Verdi's scores.

By 1860, Marie-Louise would no longer have said that Verdi's popularity would pass. Over the course of the decade since her death, he produced some of the most sublime music of passion ever composed, qualitatively far superior to his earlier works. Within four years, he had written the *Battaglia di Legnano, Luisa Miller, Stiffelio, Rigoletto* and *Il Trovatore. La Traviata* clinched his international reputation. At its first performance in March 1853, neither the performers nor the audience understood the spirit of the opera. The audience broke out into applause at the prelude and the *"brindisi"*, but thereafter they panned it. The conductor called the opera *"il traviatissimo"*. The public were not yet mature enough to understand the predicament of the 'fallen' woman who has no option but to live outside conventional morality. Until Violetta, the world had seen a woman's heroism in her selfless conjugal devotion, her fate inseparable from the heroic man. Verdi had seen in his benevolent monarch the shame and exclusion suffered on account of prevailing hypocritical morality. Like Violetta, Marie-Louise had been cast as a moral inferior. Like Violetta, she had proved her self-evident superiority in wisdom, sensitivity and consideration over the men who determined the rules by which her life had to be lived. A year after *La Traviata*'s première, Violetta's soprano arias conveyed the pathos and sincerity of her story, enabling the public to see her not just as victim, but also as heroine. In addition to the *Sicilian Vespers, Simon Boccanegra, Aroldo* and *Un Ballo in Maschera*, there were many more jewels Verdi had planned, ensuring his immortality. From his ancestral farm in Busseto, Verdi, the self-styled peasant who loved his fellows, helped the poor, sick, abandoned and desperate people who lived around him. He had found much common ground with Marie-Louise, for whom he had immense respect and affection.

Guido dalla Rosa Prati remarked that Marie-Louise had never possessed a fortune of any significance. All she had asked a month was a mere fifty *scudi*, which she liked to receive in shiny newly minted coins, all of which were destined for small acts of charity. Her homes had not being dripping with the gold of conquest and of self-aggrandisement. The rooms of her palaces to which courtiers and public were admitted were largely bare, completely absent of pictures, reflecting both her frugality and transparent style of government, the unadorned solemnity of the purple Throne Room in the Ducal Palace a clear signal to all of the weight and sanctity she attached to her position. Lady Blessington, visiting Parma in 1828, had pitied Marie-Louise, considering her reduced to a mimic form of regal splendour shorn of all dignity. She thought that the Promethean crag of St Helena had something of the sublimity in it and that

Marie-Louise must have less pride or more philosophy than other women to be able to tolerate her reduced state with such equanimity. She found nothing remarkable about the Ducal Palace, having no more rooms than the home of an ordinary private individual, its décor commonplace, the upholstery in tatters. Vitrolles had remarked that the only prominent items in her palace were the marble bust of Neipperg, and various portraits of her firstborn of whom mention was never made. The name most frequently on her lips was that of her father. Lady Blessington found it extraordinary that Lord and Lady Burghersh enjoyed spending time there with Marie-Louise, and that she should have consigned to a lumber-room the toilette presented to her and the cradle given to the King of Rome by the City of Paris. Lady Blessington did not have the honour of being received by the Duchess, nor the opportunity to understand the benevolence of her administration. Had she done so, she would have found, as most did, what an exceptionally unassuming, dedicated, hard-working and charming woman she was. She would have seen, too, how Marie-Louise found her dignity and pride not in outward display or the trophies of the past, but in the preservation of human life and the betterment of the human condition. She had signed death warrants only for murders committed in cold blood and with the greatest reluctance. Lady Blessington would have appreciated what a waste of her talents and a loss for humanity it would have been had Marie-Louise, in an absurdly inappropriate romantic gesture, demanded to sit out her days with her first husband on St Helena.

Marie-Louise's only ornaments which remained after her death were those things which had held special significance for her, souvenirs of her early family life, of her Parisian adventure, of Napoleon, of Neipperg, of her children and grandchildren. The sketches and watercolours which surrounded her, away from the gaze of her courtiers were scenes which were sources of wonderment and spiritual regeneration. She loved, honoured and respected utility, the touchstone of her select pieces of Biedermeier furniture of her interiors, her extensive collection of fans in tulle, mother-of-pearl, tortoiseshell, ivory and gauze, the baskets and embroidery frames, the samplers, the chenille boxes, the easels, the paints, her albums of her own watercolours from the numerous journeys she had undertaken in her life, the grand piano, the harp, the guitar, the billiard table and the extensive library of the red straight-grained morocco bound books impressed with her monogram, edged in fine gilt dentelle. She had collected and read many English, French, Italian and German classic and contemporary authors, more than a few volumes dedicated to her by writers throughout the peninsula and further abroad, so widespread was her passionate patronage of literature, arts, music and science.

Above all, she loved nature, the beauty of the countryside, flora and fauna, the gardens she had cultivated, the sky, the cycle of the seasons, the animal world but particularly horses and dogs, from Tisbé which her father had given her just before her second flight from Vienna in 1809 to Lovely, which Neipperg had given her. The piano was her passion and her escape. She kept sheet music everywhere and carried a large portion of it wherever her journeys took her. Music represented a safe haven in which she found equanimity, whatever the storm outside. She judged music as she judged people, quality more important than political leaning or message.

Marie-Louise's life-work is clearly visible in her former duchies, despite the despoilment after her death, and the destruction caused by allied bombing of the city during the Second World War. One can barely walk a few feet in Parma without seeing something of her imprint. Surviving her, there were and in some cases continue to be, thriving institutions which she created or which she extended and improved, separate schools for boys and girls, specialist schools including one for deaf-mutes, museums, libraries, academies, diverse cultural institutions, a military college, and the public works funded in large part if not wholly from her private purse – from the bridges over the rivers Ada, Taro, Trebbia, Stirone and Nure nell'Emilia, to the Teatro Regio and the modern meat market of Le Beccherie, hospitals in Parma and Piacenza, hospices for the destitute, hostel and boarding houses, almshouses and shelters, workhouses, orphanages revolutionised beyond all recognition, winter warehouses for citrus fruits, for wood and other goods, and the countless embellishment of churches and other historic buildings in Parma. Her hand is visible in the extensive restoration works to the Farnese ducal and Bourbon palaces, in the new roads across her duchies and from Parma to La Spezia on the Ligurian coast. The Palazzo della Riserva in which Marie-Louise hosted her guests now houses the Museo Glauco Lombardi, devoted to the preservation of her memory and evidencing the range and depth of her talents. Marie-Louise's city continues to flourish, one of the most prosperous in Italy.

Historians of earlier ages have made countless allegations against Marie-Louise. She is criticised as a young bride for her naivety, lack of charm, wit and charisma, and during her tenure as empress for lack of empathy and affection for the French, a poor substitute for Josephine. She is criticised for failing to run to Napoleon as the Allies closed in on him, for failing to return to him upon his return to France after escape from Elba for the hundred days, for failing to take a close interest in him in exile, for failing to speak up in his defence at the Congress of Vienna when it determined his exile to and set the terms of his isolation and imprisonment on St. Helena, and for lack of feeling upon his death. Marie-Louise is upbraided for falling for the charms of Count Neipperg, setting up home with him and bearing his children, for leaving her young son by Napoleon in her father's care in Vienna in order to take up residence in her new duchy with her new infatuation, for her infrequent visits to Vienna and lack of haste when she knew her son to be seriously ill. She is attacked for forgetting the French, who disingenuously claim how fond of her they were. She is slated for having had such a shallow affection for her second husband that she engaged a third barely three years after his death. And so the list goes on.

I have wrestled with the many truths in Marie-Louise's story and have been at pains to find other paths she might have taken. There was no purpose in, nor justification for, regrets. She did her best within the limits imposed upon her. The complexities of her position posed insurmountable challenges. Far from demonstrating weakness or passivity, the path she followed demonstrated deep thought, consideration and prudence. Archduke Rainer said of her, "they tried to fill Louise with dislike of Napoleon, but she was so sensible that it had no effect, and she surrendered herself to her fate with patience and wisdom."[2] The moderation and humanity which Napoleon lacked were hallmarks of her character. Her strength and immense capacity for love was reflected in the affection in which she was held by all her children, her family and her subjects, and many more besides. It was a mark of Marie-Louise's extraordinary qualities as a mother that she had brought up one child as French, another as Austrian and a third as Italian. To each, she gave a loving upbringing and provided for his/her future, despite formidable obstacles. She had been born and raised to govern and to promote the harmonious cohabitation of men, which she achieved with great distinction. She saw and appreciated the good in everybody, even when she might have been better advised to scepticism. The Parmans sympathised with her plight, continuing to celebrate her today over one hundred and fifty years after her death. Marie-Louise is remembered as 'La Buona Duchessa', a woman of integrity, wisdom and mercy.

Over one hundred and fifty years have passed over which men in every generation across the globe have generated debate and controversy, have fought and argued, expressing opinions across a spectrum of emotions from hatred and dishonour to unconditional love and unqualified admiration for the diminutive man who transformed reality to legend. Marie-Louise saw the best and the worst of him and of his legacy and could never endorse the legend. Their union had been unexpectedly loving, but Napoleon had not shared her devotion to the common good nor her deep love of the arts. The guilt and sadness she suffered at Napoleon's fall and death reflected her deep understanding of the duality of his nature, of his extraordinary qualities, but also of his unconscionable excesses. In Neipperg, she found someone who did share her devotions, as well as true marital happiness and fulfilment. This could not be said of her relationship with Bombelles, who provided the companionship she badly needed to shore up her insecurity. In all likelihood, her last chief administrator also provided the physical attention she craved, though the union may have been a front to conceal dalliances with courtiers, of which some Parmans accuse her, but for which not the slightest shred of evidence has been produced. She ignored ignoble attempts to trawl through her past and kept a discreet distance from suspicious elements, never undermining her origins or her husbands, to each of whom she remained loyal.

Like Marie-Louise, Jacopo Sanvitale, barred from his homeland, felt estranged from the world he knew and loved. His outlet for his pain was his poetry, copies of which he sent regularly to Luigi and Albertina, whom he adored (and which may have been directed at and come to the notice of Marie-Louise). In 1835, the year of Emperor Francis's death, Jacopo described what it was like to be an exile.

> It is a restless feverish delirium, it is the devouring wind of the desert. It is thirst in an arid, unbounded desert. Indeed, it is, as has already been said, *the* desert. Everywhere, the exile is alone. And it is the desert which always pursues you, chases after you, which seizes you, swathes and embraces you in the folds of its immense shroud even in the midst of the most boisterous festivities and celebrations. It is the monotonous desert, but it flaunts itself at the imagination of the dazzled pilgrim, its perfidious illusions, its illusory oases, its tantalising waves, while the exile suffocates and dies through lack of a drop of water. Nostalgia is the body which torments itself away from its own elements, and the spirit which is no longer the host of its body and which eddies in the emptiness exhaling in sighs which can find no echo. It is a tender, bittersweet melancholy,

an eternal yearning which cannot be satisfied by any other aspect of life.*

Alphonse de Lamartine remarked that, even by 1827 when he visited Marie-Louise in Parma, her history had been written in ignorance of truth, and with the resentment of Napoleonic courtiers. The general sorrow expressed at her death by all classes of society who had had direct experience of her humanity was testament enough of the deep affection in which she was held. Neither she nor her descendants had any need to resort to myth-making. Nonetheless, the ignorance and resentment would continue to hound her memory until today.

In one of the four round chapels around the crypt containing Napoleon's outsize sarcophagus is an idealised statue of a Roman emperor which stands over a small slab. Beneath this slab lies the coffin of the King of Rome, brought to Paris from Vienna by Hitler in a misguided effort to reconcile French patriotism with Nazism. The Duke's body is in Paris with his father. But the Duke's heart remains in Vienna with his mother. His heart and his intestines are contained in urns in the Ducal Crypt of the Augustinian Church within the Hofburg Palace, where his parents' first marriage by proxy took place. In Paris, there is no monument to the Emperor's Empress, no shrine to the consort to the phenomenon, who had been mother to his child. Everyone remembers the profligate, charming, uneducated and utterly self-absorbed Josephine. But it was Napoleon's second wife whose life was truly worthy of examination and admiration. In contrast to Napoleon's mausoleum,

---

* Jacopo's poem, "Nostalgia", translated into French by his daughter Clementine, and into English by an Italian émigré in England, was an immediate success running to six editions, finding resonance and sympathy across Europe. It was soon circulated on the Italian peninsula to wide acclaim, considered by some to be the most evocative poem of the age. Jacopo returned to Parma after nine years' absence, granted a temporary visa by Marie-Louise to visit his relatives in 1840, the year which saw the return of Napoleon's ashes to France. His poem "The Return" repeated the success of "Nostalgia".

Marie-Louise's body lies in a simple solitary coffin in the Imperial Crypt in Vienna, adorned from time to time by violets placed by the loyal of Parma.

SELECT BIBLIOGRAPHY

A selection of the extensive bibliography of the life and times of Marie-Louise which the author has consulted is provided below.

Primary sources:

Letters to and from Marie-Louise held at:
>the Wiener Haus-Hof und Staatsarchiv, the State Archive of the Austrian Court and the Habsburg Imperial Family, Vienna, Austria (VSA);
>the Museo Glauco-Lombardi, Parma, Italy (GL);
>the Archivio di Stato di Parma, Italy (ASP)
>the Central State Archives, Prague, the Czech Republic;
>the Rothschild Archive London;
>the Swedish State Archive, Stockholm, Sweden;
>the Archives Nationales, Paris, France;
>the Pierpoint Morgan Library, New York, USA.

Marie-Louise's diaries, travel journals, medical records, testaments and other sundry documentation and diaries of her household and servants, kept at the Museo Glauco-Lombardi, Parma.

Marie-Louise's official papers and those of her children and her ministers held at the Vienna State Archives and at the Archivio di Stato di Parma.

Marie-Louise's daughter's correspondence held in the Archivio Sanvitale at the Archivio di Stato in Parma.

Corréspondance de Marie-Louise, lettres intimes et inédites à la Comtesse de Colloredo et à Mlle de Poutet, depuis 1810 Comtesse de Crenneville, Vienna, Charles Gerold Fils Editeurs 1887 (G).

Marie-Louise nachgelassene Korrespondenz dabei 119 Briefe von Herzogs von Reichstadt, Napoleonica, Auktion 63 am 29-30 April 1958, München, Karl & Faber (K&F).

Lettres inédites de Napoléon Ier à Marie-Louise, écrites de 1810 a 1814 avec introduction et notes par Louis Madelin, Paris, Bibliothèque Nationales de France, 1935 (N/ML).

Palmstierna, C.F., Marie-Louise et Napoléon, 1813-1814. Lettres inédites reunites et commentées. Paris, Librairie Stock, 1955.

Palmstierna, C.F., My Dearest Louise, Marie-Louise and Napoléon, 1813-1814. Unpublished letters from the Empress with previously published replies from Napoleon. London, Methuen & Co. Ltd, 1959.

Gachot E., Lettres de Marie-Louise à la duchesse de Montebello, in Le Corréspondant, Paris, 1910.

D'Hauterive, E., Lettres de l'Impératrice Marie-Louise et de la Reine Catherine, in Revue des Deux Mondes, Paris, 1928.

Catalogue of Valuable Books from the library of Marie-Louise Archduchess of Austria, Empress of the French and later Duchess of Parma, Piacenza and Guastalla, sold by order of an archduke of Austria 26 July 1933. Sotheby & Co, 1933.

Frankfurter Allgemeine, Moniteur, Gazzetta di Piemonte e Gazetta di Parma, and other contemporary German, French and Italian newspapers.

Exhibition catalogues

Maria Luigia, Donna e Sovrana. Una Corte europea, Parma 1815-1847. Parma, Ugo Guanda Editore, 1992.

Trésors de la Fondation Napoléon, Chevallier, B., et Huguenaud, K. Paris, Nouveau Monde Éditions, 2004.

Nelson & Napoleon. Lincoln, Margarette, National Maritime Museum, Greenwich, 2005.

1810 – la politique de l'amour – Napoléon Ier et Marie-Louise à Compiègne. Paris, Réunion des Musées Nationaux, 2010.

SELECT BIBLIOGRAPHY

Books and articles

D'Abrantès (Duchesse), Laure Permon Junot. Mémoires de madame la duchesse d'Abrantès, Paris, L. Mame, 1835.

Acollas, Émile. Les Enfants Naturels. Paris, Librairie de la Bibliothéque Nationale, 1871.

Acton, Harold. The Bourbons of Naples (Prion Lost Treasures). Trafalgar Square Publishing, 1998.

Adamson, John. The Princely courts of Europe 1500-1750, London, Weidenfeld & Nicolson, 1999.

Adalbert, A. and Stifter, I. Pictures of rural life in Austria and Hungary, 1805-1868, translated from the German by Mary Norman, London, 1850.

Adorni, G. Vita del Conte Stefano Sanvitale LP. Parma, Filippo Carmignani, 1840.

Aretz G. Marie-Louise Erzherzogin von Oesterreich, Kaiserin der Franzosen, Herzogin von Parma, Piacenza und Guastalla. Wien-Leipzig, Höger, 1936.

Arblaster, Anthony. Viva la libertà, Politics in Opera. New York, Verso 1992.

Arnaud, Eugène François Auguste d', Baron de Vitrolles. Mémoires et relations politiques du baron de Vitrolles, 3 tom. Paris, Eugène Forgues, 1884.

Artz Frederick B. Reaction and Revolution 1814-1832, the Rise of Modern Europe. New York, Harper & Row 1934.

Aubry, Octave, Le Roi de Rome, 2 toms. Paris, Librairie Plon, 1937.

Babington Macaulay, Thomas. Napoleon and the restoration of the Bourbons. London, Longman, 1977.

Bainville Jacques. Napoleon. Paris, Arthème Fayard, 1931.

Bassi, Adriano e Bassi. Il Conte Federico Confalonieri. Zanetti Editore, Brescia, 1994.

De Bausset, L.F.J. Mémoires anecdotiques sur la cour et l'interieur du palais imperial de Napoléon. Paris, A. Levavasseur, 1829.

Beales, Derek and Biagini, Eugenio F. The Risorgimento and the Unification of Italy. Allen & Unwin, 1971.

Bellot de Kergorre, Alexandre. Journal d'un commissaire des guerres sous le premier Emprie (1806-1821), édition de Theirry Rouillard. Paris, La Vouivre, 1997.

Bernier, Olivier. The World in 1800. New York, John Wiley, 2000.

Bernini, Ferdinando. Storia di Parma. Parma, Battei, 1976.

Bertaut J. Marie-Louise femme de Napoléon I (1791-1847). Paris, les Editions de France, 1940.

De Bertier de Sauvigny, G. Metternich et la France après le Congrès de Vienne, 3 toms. Paris, Hachette 1968.

Bessard Raymonde. La Vie Privée de Marie-Louise. Paris, Hachette, 1953.

Bibl Victor. Napoleon II, Roi de Rome 1811-1832. Paris, Payot, 1935.

Billard, Max. Les maris de Marie-Louise. Paris, Perrin, 1909.

Blanning T.C.W. The Nineteenth Century. Oxford, Oxford University Press, 2000. The Pursuit of Glory: the Five Revolutions that made Modern Europe: 1648-1815. London, Penguin Classics, 2008.

Blécon, Jean. Le palais du roi de Rome. Paris, Editions D`Art, 2004.

Boileau de Castelnau, Dr. Ph. Des Enfants Naturels devant la famille et devant la société. L`Imprimerie Clavel-Ballivet et C. 1864.

Borghesi, Giovanna Battista. Maria Luigia, Donna e Sovrana, una corte Europea a Parma. Parma, Ugo Guanda Editore, 1992.

Boselli, Conte Antonio. Derniers moments de Sa Majesté Marie-Louise, Archiduchesse d'Autriche, Duchesse de Parme, de Plaisance et de Guastalla. Parma, 1847.

Botti, Ferruccio. Maria Luigia, Duchessa di Parma, Piacenza e Guastalla, 1816-1847. Parma Casa Editrice Luigi Battei, 1969.

Bourgoing de, Baron Jean. Journaux et confidences de Marie-Louise, in the Revue des Deux Mondes, année CVIII, Paris, 1938. Le Coeur de Marie-Louise: 1. Marie-Louise Impératrice des Français, 1810-1814. Paris, Calmann Lévy, 1938. 2. Marie-Louise, Duchesse de Parme (1814-1821); lettres et documents oubliés et inédits. Paris, Calmann Lévy, 1938. Papiers intimes et Journal du duc de Reichstadt, Paris, Calmann Lévy, 1828.

Bourrienne, L. Mémoires de M. de Bourrienne, minister d'Etat sur Napoléon, le Directoire, le Consulat, l'Empire et la Restauration. Paris, Ladvocat, 1830.

Brion, Marcel, Daily life in Vienna in the age of Mozart and Schubert, London, Weidenfeld and Nicolson, 1959.

Brooks, Richard, Solferino 1859, the Battle for Italy's Freedom, Osprey Publishing Ltd, 2009.

Bruce, Evangeline. Napoleon & Josephine an Improbable Marriage. London, Weidenfeld & Nicolson, 1995.

Buckland, C.S.B., Metternich and the British Government from 1809 to 1813. London, Macmillan 1932.

Burghersh, Lord. The correspondence of Lord Burghersh 1808-1840. London, John Murray, 1912.

Burke, Edmund. The Evils of Revolution. London, Penguin, 2009.

Campolieti, Giuseppe. Il re Lazzarone, Ferdinando IV di Borbone. Mondadori, 1998.

Capra, Marco. Pel Servigio di Sua Maestà. Parma, Tipografia Supergrafica Parma, 2000.

Carmona, Michel. Le Louvre et les Tuileries. Paris, Editions de la Martinière, 2004.

Carrà, Ettore. La prostituzione a Piacenza nell'età di Maria Luigia, 1814-1837. Piacenza, Tipolitografia Tip. Le. Company, 1982.

Casa, Emilio. La vita privata a Parma nella prima metà dell"Ottocento. Parma, PSS Editrice, 1999. Parma da Maria Luigia Imperiale a Vittorio Emanuele II, Tipografia Rossi-Ubaldi 1901. I carbonari parmigiani e guastallesi cospiratori nel 1821 e la duchessa Maria Luigia Imperiale. Parma, Tipografia Rossi-Ubaldi, 1904.

Cassone, Joseph. Custoza. Torino, In fine 1849.

Caulincourt, Armand de, Duc de Vicence. Mémoires, edited by Jean Hanoteau. 3 vols. Paris: Librairie Plon, 1933.

Cecchini, Bianca Maria. La danza delle ombre : Carlo III di Borbone Parma : un regicidio nell'Italia del Risorgimento. Lucca, Istituto storico lucchese, 2001.

Cecil, Algernon. Metternich (1773-1859). London, Eyre and Spottiswoode, 1947.

Cerny, Heimo. Die Jügend-Tägebücher Franz-Josephs 1843-1848. Wien, Boehlau Verlag, 2003.

Del Cerro, Emilio. Giuseppe Mazzini e Giuditta Sidoli. Torino, S.T.E.N. 1909.

Chambonas, Comte A. de la Garde, Souvenirs du Congrés de Vienne, Librairie Émile-Paul, 1904.

Chandler David. Napolen's Marshals. London, Weidenfeld & Nicolson, 1987.

Chastenet, Geneviève. Marie-Louise, l'Impératrice oubliée. Paris, J.C. Lattès, 1983. Marie-Louise, l'ôtage de Napoléon. Paris, Perrin, 2005.

Chateaubriand François-René. Mémoires d'Outre-tombe. Paris, N.D.F Gallimard, 1983.

Cirani, Paola. Maria-Luigia e la musica. Mantova, Edizioni Postumia, 1999.

Clary-und-Aldringen, Prince Karl Joseph von. Souvenirs du prince Charles de Clary-et-Aldringen, trois mois à Paris lors du mariage de l'empereur Napoléon Ier et de l'archiduchesse Marie-Louise. Paris, Plon Nourrit, 1915.

Cochelet, L. A. P. *Mémoires sur la reine Hortense et la famille imperial*. Paris, Hachette, 1836.

Collins, Irene. Liberalism in Nineteenth-Century Europe. Routledge and Kegan Paul, London, 1957.

Confalonieri, F., Count. Memorie e lettere, pubblicate per cura di Gabrio Casati. Milano, U. Hoepli, 1889.

Cooper, A. Duff. Talleyrand. London, Cassell, 1932.

Cordingly David, Billy Ruffian, The Bellerophon and the Downfall of Napoleon. London, Bloomsbury 2003.

Corti, E. C. G. Metternich und die Frauen, 2 vols. Vienna, Buchgemeinschaft Donauland Kremayr & Scheriau, n.d. The Rise of the House of Rothschild. London, Victor Gollancz 1928.

Coxe, William. History of the House of Austria, from the accession of Francis I to the Revolution of 1848. Henry G. Bohn, 1853.

Crankshaw, Edward. The Habsburgs. London, Weidenfeld and Nicolson 1971. Vienna: the image of a culture in decline. London, Macmillan 1938/1976.

Credali, Adelvardo e Credali. Anime del Risorgimento, il Conte Jacopo Sanvitale 1785-1867. Parma, 1951.

Cretineau-Joly, J. Mémoires du Cardinal Consalvi, 2 tom. Henri Plon, 1864.

Curti, Adele. Alta polizia, censura e spirit pubblico nei ducati parmensi 1816-1829. Rass. Stor. Del Risorg., IX (1922).

Cuthell, Edith E. Marie-Louise Archduchess of Austria, Empress of the French, Duchess of Parma. 2 Vols, Brentano's, New York, 1912.

Cognetti De Martiis, Raffaele. Il Governatore Vincenzo Mistrali e la legislazione civile parmense. Parma, F.lli Bocca, 1917.

Dallas, Gregor. 1815 The Roads to Waterloo. London, Richard Cohen Books, 1996.

Dallaturca, Francesca. Parchi e Residemze Extraurbane Dei Duchi Di Parma. Parma, Artegrafica Silva, 1987.

Dickens, Charles. Pictures from Italy. London, Penguin Classics, 1998.

Didier, Eugene L. The Life and Letters of Napoleon Bonaparte. London, Gilbert and Rivington 1879.

Drei, G. Gli ultimi anni del governo di Maria Luigia a Parma. Firenze, Miscellanea di Studi Storici inonore di Alessandro Luzio, Le Monnier, 1933.

Droz, Jacques. Europe Between Revolutions 1815-1848. London, Collins, 1967.

Dupuy, Micheline. La Duchesse de Dino. Paris, Perrin, 2002.

Durand, Madame, Veuve du Général. Mémoires sur Napoleon, l'impératrice Marie-Louise et la cour du Tuileries (1810-1814). Paris, Ladvocat Librairie 1828.

Emerson, Donald E. Metternich and the Political Police, security and subversion in the Habsburg monarchy 1815-1830. The Hague, Martinus Nijhoff, 1968.

Epton Nina. Josephine, The Empress and Her Children. London, Weidenfeld and Nicolson, 1975.

Errera, Caro. Il Confine fra l'Italia e l'Austria. Rava & C, Milano, 1915.

Fabré, Augustin et Chailan, Fortuné. Histoire du cholera-morbus asiatique depuis son depart des bords du Gange en 1817 jusques à l'invasion de l'italie en 1835. Marseille/Paris, Marius Olive/Hivert, 1836.

Fain, Baron, Agathon Jean. Manuscrit de mil huit cent douze, 2 Vols. Manuscrit de mil huit cent treize. Paris, Delaunay, 1827.

Fairweather, Maria. Madame de Staël. London, Constable, 2005.

Falcionelli Albert. Les Sociétés Secrètes Italiennes, Les Carbonari – La Camorra – La Mafia. Paris, Payot, 1936.

Fane, Priscilla. The letters of Lady Priscilla Burghersh (afterwards Countess of Westmoreland) from Germany and France during the campaign of 1813-1814. London, J Murray, 1893. Correspondence of Lady Burghersh with the Duke of Wellington edited by her daughter Lady Rose Weigall. London, John Murray 1903.

Farel Pierre. Mémoires de Vitrolles, tomes I et II. Paris, nrf 1950.

Farinelli, Leonardo. Maria-Luigia duchessa di Parma, schede a cura di Giovanni Godi e Giorgio Carrara. Rusconi Immagini, Milano, 1983.

Federico, Massimo. Le Medaglie di Maria Luigia Duchessa di Parma. Parma, La Pilotta, 1981.

Ferguson, Niall. The World's Bankers, the history of the house of Rothschild, 1798-1848. 1998.

Fierro, Alfred, A. La vie des Parisiens sous Napoléon. Saint-Cloud Napoléon 1er éditions, 2003.

Fornari Schianchi Lucia, Sandrini, Francesca, Sivieri, Patrizia (a cura di). Museo Glauco Lombardi. Maria Luigia e Napoleone, testimonianze. Milano, Touring Editore srl. 2003.

Fouché, Joseph, Duke of Otranto. Memoirs: Minister of the General Police of France. London, William W. Gibbings, 1892.

Fournier, August und Winkler, Arnold. Tägebücher von Friedrich von Gentz (1829-1831). Zurich-Leipzig-Wien, Amalthea Verlag, 1920.

Franchini, Silvia. Elites ed educazione femminile nell'Italia dell'Ottocento. Firenze, l'Istituto della SS Annunziata di Firenze, Olschki, 1993.

Fraser, Antonia. Marie-Antoinette – the journey. London, Weidenfeld and Nicolson, 2001.

Fraser, Flora. The Unruly Queen, the life of Queen Caroline. London, Picador, 1996.

Fulloni, Modesto. Il secolo delle Duchesse, Parma da capitale a provincia del Regno, 1816-1870. Parma, PPS Editore, 1994.

Gabory Emile. Un Grand Evêque Oublié. Mgr. Duvoisin, Evêque de Nantes aumônier de l'impératrice Marie-Louise, Editions du Porte au Large, 1947.

SELECT BIBLIOGRAPHY

Gachot, Edouard. Marie-Louise intime, Sa vie à coté de Napoleon, 1809-1814 et sa vie après l'abdication, 1814-1824, vols. I-II. Paris, Tallandier, 1911-1912.

Gaillard A.H. Abbé. Recherches Administratives, Statistiques et Morales sur les enfants trouvés – les enfants naturels et les orphelins en France, Poitiers 1837.

Gal, Hans. The Golden Age of Vienna, London, Max Parrish & Co., 1948.

Gallois Leonard. Histoire de Napoléon d'après lui-même, suivie de son testament original. Paris, Imprimerie de Cosson, 1829.

Ganière, Paul. Corvisart, Médecin de Napoléon, Paris, Ernest Flammarion, 1951.

Gardiner, Margaret. Countess of Blessington, The Idler in Italy. Paris, Baudry's European Library, 1841.

Garrone, A. Galante. Filippo Buonarroti e i rivoluzionari dell'Ottocento, 1828-1837, Giulio Einaudi Editore, 1972.

Gentz, F. von. Mémoire sur la paix maritime of March 1810 with an instroduction by C.S.B. Buckland. Oxford, Basil Blackwell, 1931. Tägebücher, Leipzig Brodhaus, 1873. Gesammelte Schriften, Briefe von und an Friedrich von Gentz: Schriftwechsel mit Metternich: Erster Teil, 1803-1819. Zweieter Teil 1820-1832. Olms Verlag, München und Berlin 1913.

Geyl, Pieter. Napoleon, for and against. London, Penguin Books, 1965.

Gleig, G.R. Germany, Bohemia, and Hungary, visited in 1837. London, John W. Parker, 1839.

Goethe Johann Wolfgang von. Italian Journey. London, Penguin Classics, 1992.

Goldoni, Luca. Maria Luigia, donna in carriera. Milano, Rizzoli, 1991.

De Goncourt, Edmont et Jules. La femme au dix-huitième siècle. Académie Goncourt, 1882.

Graf, Arturo. L'Anglomania e l'"influsso inglese in Italia. Torino, Casa Editrice Ermano Loescher, 1911.

Grainville, Dr. Bains d'Europe, manuel du voyageur. Paris, Librairie du Maison, 1841.

Gretton, A.L.V. The Vicissitudes of Italy. London, Woodfall and Kinder, 1859.

Gruyer, Paul. Napoleon King of Elba. London, William Heinemann, 1906.

Guarnaschelli, Francesco. I Padroni di Parma e Piacenza. Piacenza, Editor D.F.G., 1972.

Hamilton, Emma Lady. Carteggio di Maria Carolina – Regina delle due Sicilie. Napoli, Tulio Pironti, 1999.

Hearder, Harry. Italy in the Age of the Risorgimento 1790-1870. London, Longman Group, 1983.

D'Hauterive, Ernest. Lettres de l'Impératrice Marie-Louise et de la reine Catherine. Revue des deux mondes, François Buloz, 15 mai 1928.

Heer, F. The Holy Roman Empire, translated by Janet Sondheimer. London, Phoenix Giants, 1995.

Von Helfert, J. A. Maria Louisa Erzherzogin von Oesterreich, Kaiserin der Französen. Wien, Wilhelm Braumüller, 1873.

Herre, Franz. Maria-Luigia, il destino di un'asburgo da parigi a Parma. Place, Arnoldo Mondadori Editore SpA 1998.

Herold, Jean Christopher. The Mind of Napoleon: A selection from his written and spoken words. Oxford, Oxford University Press, 1955.

Hobhouse L.T. Morals in Evolution. London, Chapman & Hall, 1906.

Hobsbawm Eric. The Age of Revolution – Europe 1789-1848. London, Weidenfeld and Nicolson, 1962.

Hortense. Mémoires de la reine Hortense, Queen consort of Louis Bonaparte King of Holland, edited by Jean Hanoteau. Paris, Plon 1827.

Imbert de Saint Amand. Les beaux jours de l'Impératrice Marie-Louise; Marie-Louise et le duc de Reichstadt. Marie-Louise et la decadence de l'Empire. Marie-Louise, l'ile d'Elbe et les Cent-Jours. Marie-Louise et l'invasion de 1814. Paris, Dentu, 1901.

Jenks, William A. Francis-Joseph and the Italians. University Press of Virginia, 1978.

Johnson Paul. The Birth of the Modern – World Society 1815-1830. London, Harper Perennial, 1991.

Keates, Jonathan. Stendhal. New York, Carroll & Graf, 1994.

Kelly, Ian. Cooking for Kings, Biography with Recipes. London, Walker and Co. 2003.

Kertzer, David I. Sacrificed for Honor: Italian infant abandonment and the politics of reproductive control. Boston, Beacon Press, 1993.

Kraehe, Enno E., Holt, Rinehart & Winston. The Metternich Controversy, University of Virginia, 1971. Metternich's German Policy, The Contest with Napoleon 1799-1814. Princeton, 1963.

Laborde, Alexandre Louis Joseph de, Count. Voyage pittoresque en Autriche (Précis historique de la guerre entre la France et l'Autriche en 1809), 3 tom. Paris, P. Didot l'ainé, 1821-1822.

Laclotte Michel et Cuzin, Jean- Pierre. The Louvre. Paris, Editions Scala, 1982.

Lacour-Gayet, Georges. Talleyrand Vol II, 1799-1815 et Vol III 1815-1838. Paris, Payot, 1931.

Langsam, Walter Consuelo. Francis the Good, the education of an emperor, 1768-1792. New York, Macmillan Co., 1949. The Napoleonic Wars and German Nationalism in Austria. New York, AMS Press Inc, 1970.

Lecomte, J. Parme sous Marie-Louise. Paris, Souverain, 1845.

Lejeune, Mémoires du general. En prison et en guerre. A travers l'Europe (1809-1814). publiés par M. Germain Bapst, Paris: Firmin-Didot, 1895.

Lentz Thierry. Nouvelle Histoire du Premier Empire: Vol II. L'effondrement du systeme napoleonien 1810-1814. Paris, Fayard 2004.

Lepelletier, E. Les Trahisons de Marie-Louise. Paris, Colin, 1900.

Lucas-Dubreton, J. La Grande Peur de 1832 (le cholera et l'émeute). Librairie Gallimard 1932.

Mack-Smith, D. Italy and its Monarchy. New Haven, Yale University Press 1989. Mazzini. New Haven, Yale University Press, 1996.

Madelin, Louis. La Rome de Napoléon, la domination française à Rome, 1809-1814. Paris, s.n., 1906.

Magris, Claudio. Danube. London, Harvill, 1989.

Mahan, Alexandre. Marie-Louise, la Némésis de Napoléon, Paris, Editions Payot, 1933.

Maison, Françoise & Caude, Elisabeth "L'Aiglon et le Prince Impérial, La pourpre et l'exil" Editions de la Réunion des Musées Nationaux, 2004.

Mallet du Pan, Jacques Francois. Correspondance inédite de Mallet du Pan avec la cour de Vienne, 1794-1798, publiée d'après les manuscrits conservés aux archives de Vienne. Paris, A. Michel, 1884.

Mancuso U. Vincenzo Mistrali, ministro e poeta parmigiano. Sessantun lettere di Maria Luigi e altri documenti inediti nelle appendici. Pisa, Valenti, 1909.

Mann, Golo, The Life of Friedrich Gentz, Enemy of Napoleon. New Haven, Yale University Press, 1946.

Mansel, Philip. The court of France, 1789-1830. Cambridge, Cambridge University Press, 1988. Paris Between Empires 1814-1852, Monarchy and Revolution, John Murray 2001.

Manzoni, Alessandro. Gli Inni Sacri e il Cinque Maggio. Torino, Tipografia e Libreria Salesiana, 1880. "The Betrothed" I Promessi Sposi 1827. London, Penguin 1972.

Marchand, Louis-Joseph. In Napoleon's Shadow, the complete memoirs of, valet and friend of the emperor, 1811-1821. San Francisco, Proctor Jones Publication, 1998.

Marchesi Gustavo. Parma, history of a capital city. Parma, Battei, 1999.

Marchi, Adele Vittoria. Parma e Vienna. Cronaca di 3 secoli di rapporti fra il ducato di Parma, Piacenza, Guastalla e la corte degli Asburghi, Parma, Artegrafica Silva, 1988. Volti e figure del Ducato di Maria Luigia. Parma, Antea Edizioni, 1991.

Martineau, Gilbert. Napoleon's St. Helena, La vie quotidienne a Sainte-Helène au Temps de Napoléon. Paris, Hachette, 1966; Madame Mère, Napoleon's mother. London, John Murray 1978.

Martineau, Henri. Rome, Naples et Florence en 1817. Paris, Le Divan, 1956.

Masnovo, Omero. I moti '31 a Parma. Parma, Società editrice internazionale, 1925.

Masson, Frédéric. Joséphine repudiée 1809-1814. Paris, Société d'Editions Littéraires. Librairie Paul Ollendorff, 1901. L'Impératrice Marie-Louise, Société D'Editions Littéraires et Artistiques 1902. The Private Diaries of the Empress Marie-Louise, Wife of Napoleon I, London, John Murray, 1922. Marie-Walewska, (les maîtresses de Napoléon). Paris, Libraire Borel, 1897.

May, Gita. Stendhal and the Age of Napoleon. New York, Columbia University Press, 1977.

Maze-Sencier, A. Les Fournisseurs de Napoléon Ier et des deux impératrices. Paris, Librairie Renouard, 1893.

Mazzini, Giuseppe, the Patriot. Italy, Austria and the Pope. A letter to Sir James Graham, Bart. London, U. Albanesi, 1845.

Mazzini Joseph. The Duties of Man and Other Essays. London, J.M. Dent, 1894.

McGuigan Gies Dorothy. The Habsburgs. W.H.Allen 1966

Ménéval, Monsieur le Baron. Napoléon et Marie-Louise, Souvenirs historiques. Paris, Librairie d'Amyot 1844/45 (1844). Récit d'une excursion de l'impératrice Marie-Louise aux glaciers de Savoie en juillet 1814. Paris, Librairie d'Amyot, 1847.

Ménéval, Baron Claude François de. Marie-Louise et la Cour d'Autriche entre les deux abdications (1814-1815). *Emile Paul,* Paris, 1909. *Mémoires pour server à l'histoire de Napoléon Ier depuis 1802 jusqu'à 1815. Paris, L.E. Dentu Editeur, 1894.*

Metternich, le Prince Richard de. Mémoires Documents et Ecrits divers laissés par le Prince de Metternich. Paris, E. Plon 1880.

Mezzadri, Achille. Carlo Francesco Caselli, consigliere intimo di Maria Luigia. Parma, Battei, 1978.

Mezzadri, Angela. Tesi su Jacopo Sanvitale. Università di Parma, 2010.

Misciatelli, Piero. Lettere di Letizia Buonaparte. Milano, Ulrico Hoepli, 1936.

Mola, Aldo A. Silvio Pellico, Carbonaro, Cristiano e profeta della nuova Europa. Milano, Tascabili Bompiani, 2005.

Montale, Bianca. Parma nel Risorgimento, Istitutzioni e società (1814-1859). Milano, FrancoAngeli, 1993.

Montanari, M., Ridolfi M. & Zangheri R. Storia dell'Emilia Romagna. Editori Laterza, 1999.

Montanelli Indro. L'Italia Gicobina e Carbonara. Milano, Rizzoli 1971.

Montbel, M. de. Observations sur la choléra faites à Vienne, et adressées à l'Académie des Sciences de Toulouse. Toulouse et Paris, Julien Bonnefoi, G. A. Dentu, 1832. Le Duc de Reichstadt – notice sur la vie et la mort de ce prince. Paris, J. Ange, 1836.

Montesquiou, A. de. Souvenirs sur la Révolution, l'Empire, la Restauration et le règne de Louis-Philippe. Paris, Librairie Plon, 1961.

Du Montet, Alexandrine Prévost et René de la Boutetière de Saint-Mars. Souvenirs de la baronne du Montet, 1785-1866. Paris, Plon-Nourrit, 1904.

Mordacci, Alessandra. La Rocca di Sala Baganza. Parma, Gazetta di Parma Editore, 2009.

Musulin, Stella. Vienna in the Age of Metternich: from Napoleon to Revolution 1805-1848. London, Faber & Faber, 1975.

Myers, Jesse. Baron Ward and the Dukes of Parma, Longman, 1938.

Napoléon I. Corréspondance de Napoléon Ier, vols XXIV & XXV, Paris, H. Plon et J. Dumaine, 1866. Lettres inédites de Napoleon Ier à Marie-Louise écrites de 1810 a 1814 avec introduction et notes par Louis Madelin, Editions des Bibliothèques Nationales de France, 1935.

Naudon, Paul. Histoire Générale de la Franc-Maçonnerie. Paris, Office du Livre, 1987.

Nicolson, Harold. The Congress of Vienna. A Study in Allied Unity: 1812-1822. London, Harcourt, Brace and Company, 1946.

Onger, Sergio. L'infanzia negate: storia dell'assistenza agli abbandonati e indigenti a Brescia nell'Ottocento. Brescia, Grafo, 1985.

Palazzolo, Maria Iolanda. I salotti di cultura nell'Italia dell'Ottocento. Milano, Angeli, 1985.

Palmer, Alan. Metternich-Councillor of Europe. London, Weidenfeld & Nicolson 1972. Napoleon & Marie-Louise, the Second Empress. London, Constable, 2001.

Paltrinieri Vincenzo. I Moti contro Napoleone negli Stati di Parma e Piacenza, 1805-1806. Bologna, N. Zanichelli, 1927.

Panizzi, Anthony. Dei processi e delle sentenze contra gli imputati di lesa-maesta e di aderenza alle sette proscritte negli Stati di Modena Notizie scritte da Antonio Panizzi, pubblicate da***. Madrid, Torres, 1823.

Pasquier, Etienne-Denis. Mémoires du chancelier Pasquier, histoire de mon temps. Paris, M. le duc d'Audiffret-Pasquier, 1893-1895.

Pécout, Gilles. Naissance de l`Italie contemporaine. Paris, Armand Colin, 1993.

Pedroti, Pietro. La missione del Barone Mareschall nei ducati di Modena e di Parma. Modena, 1933.

Pelet, Général, Bonnet, Capitaine. Everts General-Major. Carnets de Journal sur la campagne de Russie. Paris, Librairie Historique Teissèdre, 1997.

Pellegri, Marco. Il Museo Glauco Lombardi. Parma, Luigi Battei, 1984.

Pentad. The Remaking of Italy. Penguin Books, Harmondsworth, Mddx, 1941.

Pescatore, Angelo. Il declino di un ducato (1831-1859). Parma, Palatina, 1974.

Pigorini Beri, Caterina. Cenni biografici del Conte Jacopo Sanvitale. Parma, Tipografia Rossi-Ubaldi, 1867.

Pillepich Alain. Napoléon et les Italiens. Paris, Nouveau Monde Editions, 2003.

Leduc, Edouard. Portalis, 1746-1807. Paris, Collection Panthéon, 1990.

Postgate Raymond. The Story of a Year 1848. London, Cassell 1955.

Potocka, Anna. Mémoires de la Comtesse Potocka. Paris, Plon, 1897.

Pozzo di Borgo, Carlo Andrea, Count. Corréspondance diplomatique du Comte Pozzo di Borgo et du Comte de Nesselrode 1814-1818, publiée avec une introduction et des notes par le Comte C Pozzo di Borgo, 3 vol. Paris, Calmann Levy, 1890-97.

Prampolini, Marianna. La Duchessa Maria Luigia. Ugo Guanda Editore, Parma, 1991.

Prantner, Johanna. Kaiserin Leopoldine von Brazilien. Wien und München, Verlag Herold, 1974.

Praz Mario. An illustrated History of Interior Decoration – from Pompeii to Art Nouveau. Thames & Hudson 1994.

Prokesch von Osten, Anton Gf. Mein Verhältniss zum Herzog von Reichstadt: zwei Sendungen nach Italien. Stuttgart, W. Spemann, 1878.

Quin, Michael Joseph. A Steam Voyage down the Danube with sketches of Hungary, Wallachia, Servia and Turkey, etc. London, Richard Motley, 1835.

Ramsey Matthew. Professional and popular medicine in France 1770-1830. Cambridge, Cambridge University Press, 1988.

Raphael, Sylvia, Madame de Staël, Corinne or Italy, Oxford University Press, Oxford, 1998.

Rath, R. John. The Fall of the Napoleonic Kingdom of Italy. New York, Columbia University Press, 1941.

Ravage, Mark-Eli. Iphigénie ou la vie de Marie-Louise. Paris, Michel, 1932.

Redlich, Joseph, Emperor Francis-Joseph of Austria. London, Macmillan and Co., 1929.

Reynieri, A.L. Da Montebello a Solferino Guerra per l'indipendenza italiana, aprile-luglio, 1859. Torino, Tipografia Arnaldi, 1859.

Ribeiro, Aileen, The Art of Dress Fashion in England and France 1750-1820, Yale University Press, 1995.

Robiquet, Jean. La vie quotidienne au temps de Napoléon. Paris, Librairie Hachette, 1944.

Rosen Charles. The Romantic Generation. London, HarperCollins, 1996.

Rousseau, Jean-Jacques. Emile, or On Education, trans. with an introd. by Allan Bloom. New York, Basic Books, 1979.

Rovigo, Duc de. Memoires pour servir à l'histoire de l'Empereur Napoléon. Paris, A. Bossange et Charles-Bechet, 1829.

Rumbold, Sir Horace. The Austrian Court in the Nineteenth Century. London, Methuen & Co., 1909.

Salata, F. Maria Luigia e I moti del trentuno: documenti inediti da archive austriaci. Parma, Officine Grafiche Fresching, 1932.

Sandrini, Francesca e Bianchi, Mariachiara. I gioielli di Maria Luigia d'Asburgo, Quaderno del Museo Glauco Lombardi n.11. Parma, MUP Editore, 2009.

Scaramella, Gino. Spirito Pubblico, Società Segrete e Polizia in Livorno. Livorno, Editore Livorno, 1901.

Schianchi Lucia Fornari. La Galleria Nazionale die Parma. Catalogo delle opera. Parma, Artegrafica Silva, 1999.

Schiel, Irmgard. Maria Luigia, una donna che seppe amare e che seppe governare. Milano, Longanesi,1983.

Servadio Gaia. Rossini. London, Constable 2003. The Real Traviata, the biography of Giuseppina Strepponi, wife of Giuseppe Verdi. London, Hodder & Stoughton, 1994.

Seward Desmond. Napoleon's Family. London, Weidenfeld and Nicolson, 1986.

Shepherd, William. Paris in eighteen hundred and two and eighteen hundred and fourteen. London, printed for Longman, Hurst, Rees, Orme and Brown, 1814.

Sked, Alan, The Decline and Fall of the Habsburg Empire 1815-1918, Longman, 2001.

Solmi, Angelo. Maria Luigia, duchessa di Parma. Milano, Rusconi libri, 1981.

Spaggiari, Pier Luigi. Il Ducato di Parma e l'Europa. Parma, Casa Editrice Luigi Battei, 1957; L`Agricoltura Negli Stati Parmensi, Banca Commerciale Italiana, 1966.

Spencer, E. Sketches of Germany and the Germans, with a glance at Poland, Hungary and Switzerland, in 1834, 1835, and 1836 by an Englishman resident in Germany. J. Griffin and Co. Portsmouth, 1886.

Spinosa, Antonio. Maria Luisa d'Austria, la donna che tradì Napoleone. Arnoldo Mondadori Editore, 2004.

De Staël, A.L.G. Oeuvres Complètes de Madame la Baronne de Staël-Holstein, 2 tomes. Firmin Diot Frères et Cie, 1836. An Appeal to the Nations of Europe against the Continental System: published at Stockholm, by authority of Bernadotte in March, 1813 by Madame de Stäel Holstein [or rather, August Wilhelm von Schlegel] [A translation of Schlegel's anonymously published work, "Sur le systeme continental et sur ses rapports avec la Suede"]. London, J. M. Richardson, 1813.

Stefani, Giuseppe. I prigionieri dello Spielberg sulla via dell'esilio. Udine, Del Bianco, 1963.

Stendhal, Correspondance inédite de Stendhal, Consul de France dans les Etats romains. Genève, Slatkine Moncalieri, Centro Interuniversitario di Ricerche sul "Viaggio in Italia", 1994.

Stirling Monica. A Pride of Lions, a portrait of Napoleon's mother. London, Collins 1961

De Stoeckl, Agnes. Four Years an Empress, Marie-Louise, Second Wife of Napoleon. London, John Murray, 1962.

Strakhovsky, Leonid E. Alexander I of Russia – The Man Who Defeated Napoleon. London, Williams & Norgate, 1949.

Surémain, Jean B.de. La Suède sous la République et le premier Empire,

Mémoires du lieutenant général de Surémain, 1794-1815, publiés par un de ses petits-neveux (G de Surémain), etc, Paris, 1902.

Sutherland, Christine. Marie-Walewska, Napoleon's Great Love. London, Clark, 1979.

Talleyrand, Charles Maurice. Corréspondance inédite du Prince de Talleyrand et du roi Louis XVIII pendant le Congrés de Vienne. Paris, E. Plon et Cie, 1881.

Taylor, A.J.P. The Italian Problem in European Diplomacy, 1847-1849. Manchester, Manchester University Press, 1934. The Habsburg Monarchy 1809-1918: A history of the Austrian Empire and Austria-Hungary. London, Hamish Hamilton, 1948. Europe: Grandeur and Decline. Penguin Books, 1969.

Thibaudeau, A.C. Mémoires de, 1799-1815. Paris, Plon, Nourrit et Cie, 1913.

Tommasini Giacomo. Istruzione popolare sul cholera-morbus. Composta a tenore del Decreto De La Tour du Pin, Marquise, Mémoires/Corréspondance (1815-1846), Journal d'une femme de cinquante ans. Paris, Mercure de France, 2002.

Sovrano 26 Maggio 1832 per le Commissioni Centrali di Sanità di Parma e di Piacenza. Firenze, Giornale di Commercio, 1835.

Trollope, Fanny. Paris and the Parisians (1835). Gloucester, Alan Sutton, 1985. Vienna and the Austrians. London, R. Bentley, 1838.

Tulard, Jean. Napoleon: The Myth of the Saviour. London, Weidenfeld & Nicolson, 1977.

Turnbull, Patrick. Napoleon's Second Empress. London, Michael Joseph Ltd, 1971.

Ullrichova, Maria. Clemens Metternich und Wilhelmine von Sagan. Ein Briefwechsel 1813-1815. Graz-Köln, Verlag Hermann Böhlaus Nacht, 1956.

Valenti, Patrizia. La condizione giuridica della donna nei lavori preparatorio nel codice parmense. Bologna, Università degli studi di Bologna, 1987-1988.

Valeri, A. Maria Luisa 1791-1847. Milano, Corticelli, 1934.

Valery M. Parme et Marie-Louise. Paris 1852.

SELECT BIBLIOGRAPHY

Viaene Antoine. Napoléon et Marie-Louise à Bruges, Mai 1810. Paris, Editions Universitaires, 1960.

Vivanti e Romano (coordinatori). Storia d'Italia. Dal primo Settecento all'Unità, 3 vol. Torino, Einaudi, 1973.

Wairy, Constant. Mémoires intimes de Napoléon Ier, par Constant son valet de chambre. Paris, Mercure de France, 2000.

Watson Peter, The German Genius: Europe's Third Renaissance, the Second Scientific Revolution and the Twentieth Century. London, Harper, 2012.

Webb Probyn, John. Italy 1816-1878. London, Cassell & Co, 1884

Weil, M.H. La Campagne de 1814 d'après les documents des Archives impériales et royales de la guerre a Vienne, la cavalerie des armées alliées pendant la campagne de 1814, Paris, 1891-96.Weill, Erwin. Vier Frauen und ein Kaiser. Berlin und Leipzig, Verlag Das Bergland-Buch, 1935.

Welschinger Henri. La Censure sous le Premier Empire. Paris, Charavay Freres 1882. Le Roi de Rome, 1811-1832. Paris, E. Plon, 1897. Le Pape et l'Empereur 1804-1815. Paris, Plon-Nourrit 1905.

De Wertheimer Edward. The Duke of Reichstadt: Napoleon II. London, John Lane, 1906.

Wheatcroft Andrew. The Habsburgs. Penguin Books, 1997.

Wicks, Margaret C.W. The Italian Exiles in London, 1816-1848, Manchester University Press, Manchester, 1937.

Wilcken, Patrick. Empire Adrift. London, Bloomsbury, 2004.

Wilson, Derek. Rothschild – A Story of Wealth and Power. London, André Deutsch Ltd, 1988.

Wittichen, Friedrich Carl und Salzer, Ernst, Briefe von und an Freidrich von Gentz, Dritter Band, Erster und Zweiter Teilen, Verlag von R. Oldenburg 1913.

Woolf, Stuart J., The Italian Risorgimento Vols 2, Longman, London, 1969.Zannoni, Mario, A tavola con Maria Luigia, il servizio di bocca della duchessa di Parma dal 1815-1847. Parma, Artegrafica Silva-Parma, 1991. Napoleone Bonaparte a Parma nel 1805, Parma, Monte Università Parma, 2006.

Zucchelli, Dante and Fedocci, Renzo. Il Palazzo Ducale Di Parma. Parma, Artegrafica Silva, 1985.
Zamoyski, Adam. Holy Madness, Romantics, Patriots and Revolutionaries 1776-1871, Penguin Books, 1999. Rites of peace, the fall of Napoleon and the Congress of Vienna. London, Harper Perennial, 2008.
Zaninelli, Sergio. Le ferrovie in Lombardia tra Ottocento e Novecento. Milano, Il polifilo, 1995.

ENDNOTES

Chapter One: The wedding of the century, April 1810

1. Cited by Pellegri, p125
2. These anecdotes are collated from the memoirs of Mme Durand and De Bausset, Prefect of the Palace, to whom Napoleon related the events in question.
3. Countess Lazansky to Marie-Louise, 20th April 1810, K&F
4. Memoires du Duc de Rovigo, t.IV p295-6
5. Marie-Louise to Emperor Francis, 29th March 1810, cited by Helfert p134

Chapter Two: The birth of an heir, March 1811

1. Diary excerpts are cited by Masson, Private Diaries of Marie-Louise
2. Emperor Francis to Marie-Louise, Baden, 26th June 1810, K&F
3. Maria-Ludovica to Marie-Louise, 28th March 1810, K&F
4. Cited by Masson, Private Diaries of Marie-Louise, p58
5. Emperor Francis to Marie-Louise, Laxenburg, 2nd August 1810, K&F
6. Cited by Masson, Private Diaries of Marie-Louise, p101

Chapter Three: The firm alliance, May 1812

1. These and various other anecdotes appear in Masson, l'Impératrice Marie-Louise, largely extracted from the memoirs of Mme Durand
2. Memoirs of Mme Durand, cited by Welschinger, King of Rome, p35
3. Marie-Louise to Mme Luçay, 29th May 1812, N/ML
4. Marie-Louise to Napoleon, 18th July 1812, N/ML

Chapter Four: Napoleon indomitable, December 1812

1. Napoleon to Marie-Louise, Reintenbach, 29th May 1812, N/ML
2. Napoleon to Marie-Louise, Posen, 1st June 1812, N/ML
3. Napoleon to Marie-Louise, Thorne, 3rd June 1812, N/ML
4. Napoleon to Marie-Louise, Marienburg, 12th June 1812, N/ML
5. Napoleon to Marie-Louise, Gunbunen, 20 June 1812, N/ML
6. Napoleon to Marie-Louise, Gumbinnen, 21 June 1812, and similar sentiments from Mainz, 21st April 1813, N/ML
7. Napoleon to Marie-Louise, Glouboukoé, 19 July 1812, N/ML
8. Napoleon to Marie-Louise, Moscow, 21st September 1812, N/ML
9. Napoleon to Marie-Louise, Moscow, 6 September 1812, N/ML
10. Napoleon to Marie-Louise, Moscow, 14th October 1812 N/ML
11. Napoleon to Marie-Louise, Moscow, 8th October 1812 N/ML
12. Napoleon to Marie-Louise, Moscow, 6th October 1812 N/ML
13. Napoleon to Marie-Louise, à demi chemin de Viasma à Dorogboug, 3rd November 1812, N/ML
14. Napoleon to Marie-Louise, Illia, 1st December 1812, N/ML

Chapter Five: Marie-Louise, Regent of France 1813

1. Emperor Francis to Marie-Louise, 24th January 1813, K&F
2. Napoleon to Marie-Louise, Mainz, 22nd April 1813, N/ML
3. Napoleon to Marie-Louise, Mainz, 24th April 1813, N/ML
4. Napoleon to Marie-Louise, Erfurt, 27th April 1813, N/ML
5. Napoleon to Marie-Louise, Lützen, 2nd May 1813, N/ML
6. Napoleon to Marie-Louise, Borna, 5th May 1813, N/ML
7. Marie-Louise to Emperor Francis, Paris, 10th May 1813, N/ML
8. Napoleon to Marie-Louise, Dresden, 9th May 1813, N/ML
9. Napoleon to Marie-Louise, Dresden, 16th May 1813, N/ML
10. Napoleon to Marie-Louise, 25th May 1813, N/ML
11. Napoleon to Marie-Louise, undated (sent between letters dated 31st May and 4th June), N/ML
12. Napoleon to Marie-Louise, Brunzeleau, 7th June 1813, N/ML
13. Napoleon to Marie-Louise, Dresden, 18th June 1813, N/ML
14. Napoleon to Marie-Louise, Dresden, 25th June 1813, N/ML

ENDNOTES

15 Napoleon to Marie-Louise, Dresden, 2nd July 1813, N/ML
16 Napoleon to Marie-Louise, Dresden, 7th July 1813, N/ML
17 Napoleon to Marie-Louise, Dresden, 16th July 1813, N/ML
18 Napoleon to Marie-Louise, Dresden, second letter dated 16th July 1813, N/ML
19 Emperor Francis to Marie-Louise, 28th July 1814 K&F
20 Napoleon to Marie-Louise, Dresden, 1st July 1813 N/ML
21 Emperor Francis to Marie-Louise, Brandeis 11th August 1813, K&F
22 Emperor Francis to Marie-Louise, 5th September 1813, K&F
23 Napoleon to Marie-Louise, Dresden, 14th August 1813, N/ML

Chapter Six: Invasion and flight, Spring 1814

1 Emperor Francis to Marie-Louise, 6th March 1814, K&F
2 Marie-Louise to Napoleon, 1st March 1814, Palmstierna
3 Marie-Louise to Napoleon, 3rd March 1814, K&F
4 Napoleon to Joseph, 16th March 1814, cited by Imbert de Saint-Amand, Marie-Louise and the Invasion of 1814, p113
5 Marie-Louise to Napoleon, Paris, 27th March 1814, Palmistierna
6 Marie-Louise to Napoleon, Paris, 29th March 1814, Palmistierna
7 Recollections of Ménéval and Mme Durand, reflected in letter from Marie-Louise to Napoleon, 29th March 1814, 10pm
8 Marie-Louise to Napoleon, Blois, 7th April 1814, Palmistierna
9 Baron de Bourgoing, Le Coeur de Marie-Louise, p17
10 Mémoires of de Bausset, tII derived from the Mémoires du colonel de Galbois
11 Napoleon to Marie-Louise, Fontainebleau, 8th April 1814
12 Napoleon to Marie-Louise, 8th April 1814, N/ML
13 cited by Imbert de Saint-Amand, Marie-Louise and the Invasion of 1814, p225
14 cited by Bourgoing, Le Coeur de Marie-Louise, p26
15 Emperor Francis to Marie-Louise, 7.4.1814 K&F
16 Marie-Louise to Napoleon, Orléans, 10th April 1814, Palmstierna
17 Marie-Louise to Napoleon, Orléans, 12th April 1814, M/L

Chapter Seven: The mountains of Savoy, Summer 1814

1 Marie-Louise to Napoleon, between Orléans and Rambouillet, 12th-13th April 1814, Palmstierna
2 Napoleon to Marie-Louise, Fontainebleau, 14th April 1814, N/ML
3 Acton, The Bourbons of Naples, p305
4 Acton, The Bourbons of Naples, p505
5 cited by Waltraud Maierhofer in Women Against Napoleon. Frankfurt/New York, Campus Verlag 2007 p58
6 Acton, The Bourbons of Naples, p305
7 Acton, The Bourbons of Naples, p306
8 Baron de Méneval, Marie-Louise et la Cour d'Autriche, p68
9 Schönbrunn, 5th June 1814, Palmstierna
10 Marie-Louise to Napoleon, 22nd June 1814, Palmstierna
11 Bourgoing citing an Austrian police report of 11th June 1814, p83
12 Marie-Louise to Napoleon, Schönbrunn, 5th June 1814, 5pm, Palmstierna
13 Marie-Louise to Napoleon, Schönbrunn, 22nd June 1814, Palmstierna
14 Emperor Francis to Marie-Louise, Paris, 9th September 1814, K&F
15 These and similar sentiments are contained in, among others, her letters of 21st July, 31st July, 3rd August and 10th August 1814

Chapter Eight: The untimely visit, September 1814

1 cited by Helfert p36
2 Marie-Louise to Victoria de Poutet, 8th August 1809, G
3 Emperor Francis to Empress Marie-Thérèse, 4th December 1805, Helfert
4 Maria Ludovica to Marie-Louise, 28th March 1810, K&F
5 This assertion is disputed by Mme Durand, who maintains that Napoleon never addressed the Duchess with the familiar "tu".
6 Masson, l'Impératrice Marie-Louise, p175
7 Marie-Louise to Méneval, Aix, 9th August 1814, Baron de Méneval, Marie-Louise et la Cour d'Autriche, p108
8 Marie-Louise to Catherine of Westphalia, 4th November 1814. Paris,

Au Siège, Revue des Deux Mondes, 15 May 1928, p386
9   Memoirs of De Bausset
10 cited by De Wertheimer, The Duke of Reichstadt, p9
11 Marie-Louise to Napoleon, 3rd January 1815, Palmistierna

Chapter Nine: Hopes pinned on Blücher and Wellington, June 1815

1   Maria Ludovica to Marie-Louise, undated, K&F
2   cited by Méneval, Vol III p500
3   Declaration dated 15th March 1815, cited by Méneval
4   Statement by the Great Powers, March 1815
5   Karl, brother of Emperor Francis, to Marie-Louise, 11th June 1815, K&F
6   Metternich to Marie-Louise, July 1815, VSA
7   cited by Cordingley, Billy Ruffian, p242
8   Leopoldine to Marie-Louise, 24th August 1815, K&F
9   Metternich to Marie-Louise, Paris, 18th July 1815, cited by Corti, Metternich und die Frauen, p522
10 Archduke Rainer Viceroy of Lombardy to Marie-Louise, 26th July 1815, K&F
11 Archduke Rainer to Marie-Louise, 26th July 1815, K&F
12 Emperor Franz to Marie-Louise, 11th August 1815, K&F
13 The Duchess of Montebello to Marie-Louise, 22nd July 1815, K&F
14 Metternich to Marie-Louise, 13th August 1815, cited by Welschinger, Le Roi de Rome, p192
15 Metternich to Marie-Louise, 1st August 1815, cited by de Bertier de Sauvigny
16 Emperor Francis to Marie-Louise, 30th September 1815, K&F

Chapter Ten: Parma, 1816

1   Emperor Francis to Marie-Louise, 6th August 1815, K&F
2   Cited by Paltrinieri, Napoleon's instructions to Junot, p118
3   Cited by Langsam, Francis the Good, p12
4   Emperor Francis to Marie-Louise, 15th February 1816, K&F
5   Marie-Louise to Emperor Francis, Parma, 21st April 1816, VSA

6   The Duke of Reichstadt, Vienna, March 1816, K&F
7   Marie-Louise to Emperor Francis, 5th January 1816, VSA
8   Dr. Frank to Marie-Louise, 31st January 1817, K&F
9   Metternich to Emperor Francis, 5th September 1817, VSA
10 Ludwig, brother of Franz I to Marie-Louise, 21st May 1816, K&F
11 Marie-Louise to Archduke Rainer, 28th July 1816, VSA
12 James Bielby to Marie-Louise, 23rd September 1816, K&F
13 Duke of Reichstadt to Marie-Louise, beginning December 1816, K&F
14 Leopoldine to Marie-Louise, 26th June 1816, K&F
15 Leopoldine to Marie-Louise, 28th November 1816, K&F
16 Marie-Louise to Emperor Francis, Colorno, 17th October 1816, VSA
17 Lady Priscilla Burghersh to Marie-Louise, 28.6.1818, K&F
18 Count Scarampi to Marie-Louise, 1816 undated, K&F
19 Karoline Auguste to Marie-Louise, 9th December 1819, K&F
20 Archduke Rainer to Marie-Louise, 8th June 1817, K&F
21 Leopoldine to Marie-Louise, 2nd April 1817 K&F
22 Archduke Rainer to Marie-Louise, 31st May 1817, K&F
23 Archduke Johann to Marie-Louise, 1st January 1817, K&F

Chapter Eleven: Absent motherhood, 1818

1   Marie-Louise to Emperor Francis, 24th November 1817, K&F
2   Marie-Louise to Emperor Francis, 28th October 1816, cited by Bourgoing, p526
3   Archduke Johann to Marie-Louise, 1st January 1817, K&F
4   Marie-Louise to Victoria de Crenneville, Sala, 13th October 1817, G
5   Victoria de Crenneville to Marie-Louise, 15th September 1817
6   Duke of Reichstadt to Marie-Louise, Autumn 18th September 1819, K&F
7   Duke of Reichstadt to Marie-Louise, amalgamation of letters 1824, K&F

Chapter Twelve: Napoleon's heart, 1821

1   Caroline Amelin de St. Marie to Marie-Louise, 16th July 1821, K&F
2   Marie-Louise to Emperor Francis, Sala, 30th August 1821, VSA

ENDNOTES

3   Leopoldine to Marie-Louise, 2nd July 1821, K&F
4   Marie-Thérèse to Marie-Louise, amalgamation of letters 6th August and 2nd September 1821, K&F

Chapter Thirteen: Resisting the witchhunt, 1822

1   Marie-Louise to Emperor Francis cited by Casa, p82
2   Emperor Francis to Marie-Louise, 23rd April 1825, K&F
3   Memorandum dated 7th March 1823, cited by Casa, p105
4   Casa, p162

Chapter Fourteen: Bereavement and revelation, 1829

1   Duke of Reichstadt to Marie-Louise, 22nd December 1827 K&F
2   Marie-Louise to the Duke of Reichstadt, Sala, 24th July 1821, cited by McNair Wilson, The King of Rome, p81
3   Count Dietrichstein to Marie-Louise, 1st August 1821, K&F
4   Marie-Louise to Count Dietrichstein, 10th August 1821, VSA
5   Countess Lazansky to Marie-Louise, 17th July 1821, K&F
6   Lady Priscilla Burghersh to Marie-Louise, 5th August 1821, K&F

Chapter Fifteen: The beings, 1829

1   Count Dietrichstein to Marie-Louise, 21st March 1829, K&F
2   Karoline-Auguste to Marie-Louise, 6th March 1829, K&F
3   Karoline-Auguste to Marie-Louise, 28th October 1828, K&F
4   Emperor Francis to Marie-Louise, cited by Bourgoing, p540-541
5   Karoline-Auguste to Marie-Louise, 17th April 1829, K&F
6   Emperor Francis to Marie-Louise, cited by Bourgoing, p540-541

Chapter Seventeen: Feeling widowhood

1   Marie-Louise to Albertina, 24th May 1824, GL
2   Marie-Louise to Albertina, 20th May 1826, GL
3   Marie-Louise to Albertina, 6th August 1828, GL
4   Marie-Louise to Albertina, 20th August 1845, GL
5   Marie-Louise to Albertina, 18th April 1824, GL

6   Metternich to Neipperg, 18th May 1827, cited by Corti, The Rise of the House of Rothschild
7   Mémoires de Vitrolles, p475
8   Leopoldine to Marie-Louise, 17th September 1826, K&F
9   Leopoldine to Marie-Louise, 8th November 1817, K&F
10 Leopoldine to Marie-Louise, 30th November 1817, K&F
11 Leopoldine to Marie-Louise, 26th September 1819, K&F
12 Leopoldine to Marie-Louise, 1st October, 1818, K&F
13 Leopoldine to Marie-Louise, 2nd January 1819, K&F
14 Leopoldine to Marie-Louise, 1st August 1822, K&F
15 Leopoldine to Marie-Louise, 7th March 1822, K&F
16 Leopoldine to Marie-Louise, 23rd June 1822, K&F
17 Leopoldine to Marie-Louise, 30th April 1817, K&F
18 Leopoldine to Marie-Louise, 16th March 1813, K&F
19 Leopoldine to Marie-Louise, 8th August 1826, cited by Prantner, p823

Chapter Eighteen: Repercussions of the July Revolution, 1830

1   The Duke of Reichstadt to Marie-Louise, 16th August 1825, K&F
2   Count Dietrichstein to Marie-Louise, 3rd August 1826, K&F
3   The Duke of Reichstadt to Marie-Louise, 18th April 1826, K&F
4   The Duke of Reichstadt to Marie-Louise, 14th October 1826, K&F
5   Duke of Reichstadt to Marie-Louise, 22nd December 1827, K&F
6   The Duke of Reichstadt to Marie-Louise, 25th March 1830, GL
7   The Duke of Reichstadt to Marie-Louise, 16th January 1825, GL
8   Victoria de Crenneville to Marie-Louise, 22nd May 1824, K&F
9   The Duke of Reichstadt to Marie-Louise, Schönbrunn, 6th August 1829 K&F
10 The Duke of Reichstadt to Marie-Louise, Schönbrunn, 20th September 1829, K&F
11 The Duke of Reichstadt to Marie-Louise, Vienna, 26th May 1830, K&F
12 Unknown writer to Marie-Louise, 29th May 1830, K&F
13 Maria Amalia to Marie-Louise, 9th July 1831, K&F

ENDNOTES

Chapter Nineteen: Challenge to sovereignty in the Central Italian States, 1831

1 Count Dietrichstein to Marie-Louise, 15th January 1831, K&F
2 Metternich to Marie-Louise, 27th February 1831, K&F
3 Count Dietrichstein to Marie-Louise, 20th February 1831, K&F
4 Sophie, mother of future emperor Franz-Josef, 6th April 1831, K&F.
5 Marie-Louise to Victoria de Crenneville, Piacenza, 11th April 1831, G
6 Count Dietrichstein to Marie-Louise, 2nd April 1831, K&F

Chapter Twenty: Impotent against Metternich's vengeance, 1831

1 The Duke of Reichstadt to Marie-Louise, 25th March 1830, GL
2 Duke of Reichstadt to Marie-Louise, 11th December 1830, K&F
3 Prokesch Tagebuch entry, 27th December 1830

Chapter Twenty-One The tragedy of competing loyalties, 1832

1 Marie-Louise to Count Dietrichstein, 5th May, 1832, K&F
2 Metternich to Marie-Louise, 5th May 1832, K&F
3 Count Dietrichstein to Marie-Louise, 23rd June 1831, K&F
4 Count Dietrichstein to Marie-Louise, 26th July 1831, K&F
5 Count Dietrichstein to Marie-Louise, 28th May, 1832, K&F
6 Count Dietrichstein to Marie-Louise, 30th May 1832, K&F
7 Dr. Malfatti to Marie-Louise, 3rd May 1832, K&F
8 Baron Mareschall to Metternich, Parma, 9th May 1832, K&F
9 Baron Mareschall to Marie-Louise, Parma, 7th May 1832, K&F
10 Baron Mareschall to Marie-Louise, Parma, 9th May, K&F
11 Marie-Louise to Albertina, Venice, 28th May 1832, GL
12 Marie-Louise to Albertina, Trieste, 4th June 1832, GL
13 Marie-Louise to Albertina, Trieste, 9th June 1832, GL
14 Victoria de Crenneville to Marie-Louise, 15th May 1832, K&F
15 Duke of Reichstadt to Marie-Louise, 22nd April 1830, K&F
16 Marie-Louise to Albertina, Vienna, 4th July, 1832, GL
17 Marie-Louise to Albeltina, Vienna, 11th July 1832, GL
18 Marie-Louise to Albertina, Vienna, 14th July 1832, GL
19 Marie-Louise to Albertina, Vienna, 21st July 1832, GL

Chapter Twenty-Two: Manuscripts and pariahs

1   Albertina to Marie-Louise, 1st July 1832, ASP
2   Albertina to Marie-Louise, 7th June 1832, ASP
3   Albertina to Marie-Louise, 25th June 1832, ASP
4   Albertina to Marie-Louise, 9th July 1832, ASP
5   Albertina to Marie-Louise, 13th July 1832, ASP
6   Albertina to Marie-Louise, 14th July 1832, ASP
7   Albertina to Marie-Louise, 30th July 1832, ASP
8   Gustav to Marie-Louise, 14th July 1832, K&F
9   Albertina to Marie-Louise, 30th July 1832, ASP
10 Marie-Louise to Letizia Bonaparte, Schönbrunn, 23rd July 1832
11 Méneval to Marie-Louise, 4th August 1832, K&F
12 Sophie Durand to Marie-Louise, 8th September 1832, K&F
13 Victoria de Crenneville to Marie-Louise, 27th August 1832, K&F
14 Foresti to Count Dietrichstein, 2nd August 1832, cited by Bourgoing, Papiers intimes et journal du Duc de Reichstadt p10
15 Marie-Louise to Count Dietrichstein, 15th September, 1832,
16 Count Dietrichstein, 9th September, 1832, K&F
17 Metternich to Marie-Louise, 24th December 1832, K&F
18 Metternich to Marie-Louise, 6th February 1833, K&F

Chapter Twenty-Three: Realising a daughter's happiness, 1833

1   Marie-Louise to Albertina, Milan, 15th May 1833, GL
2   Marie-Louise to Albertina, Piacenza, 1st March 1833, GL
3   Marie-Louise to Albertina, Piacenza, 2nd March 1833, GL
4   Marie-Louise to Albertina, June 1833, GL
5   Marie-Louise to Albertina, Sala, 29th October 1833, GL
6   Marie-Louise to Albertina, Baden, 18th July 1834, GL
7   Marie-Louise to Albertina, Baden, 6th August 1834, GL
8   Marie-Louise to Albertina, Piacenza, 9th July 1835, GL

Chapter Twenty-Four: The world destabilised at a change of emperors, 1835

1   Victoria de Crenneville to Marie-Louise, 12th March 1835, K&F

2   Marie-Louise to Albertina, Piacenza, 10th April 1835, GL
3   Metternich to Marie-Louise, 21st March 1835, K&F
4   Metternich to Marie-Louise, undated 1835, K&F
5   Marie-Louise to Albertina, 9th July 1834, GL
6   Marie-Louise to Albertina, Venice, 6th October 1838, GL

Chapter Twenty-Five: Cholera, 1836 and its aftermath

1   Marie-Louise to Albertina, Vienna, 13th July 1836, GL
2   Marie-Louise to Albertina, Vienna, 18th July 1836, GL
3   Marie-Louise to Albertina, amalgamation of letters 29th June and 13th July 1836, GL
4   Marie-Louise to Albertina, August 1836, GL
5   Marie-Louise to Albertina, August 1836, GL
6   Albertina to Marie-Louise, 21st August 1836, ASP
7   Marie-Louise to Albertina, Sala, 10th September 1836, GL
8   Emilie Victorine Baroness of Wolfsberg to Marie-Louise, 29th June 1833, K&F
9   Marie-Louise to Albertina, Parma, 18th April, 1835, GL
10 Marie-Louise to Albertina, Sala, February 1841, GL
11 Marie-Louise to Albertina, 17th February 1835, GL
12 Marie-Louise to Albertina, amalgamation of letters 8th September 1835 and 10th May 1842, GL
13 Marie-Louise to Albertina, Vienna, 18th June 1836, GL
14 Marie-Louise to Albertina, Piacenza, 1st May 1842, GL
15 Marie-Louise to Albertina, Piacenza, 3rd May 1842, GL
16 Marie-Louise to Albertina, Piacenza, 9th April 1834, GL
17 Marie-Louise to Albertina, amalgamation of letters 3rd and 10th May 1842, GL
18 Marie-Louise to Albertina, 23rd July 1842, GL
19 Marie-Louise to Albertina, Piacenza, 17th April 1834, GL
20 Marie-Louise to Albertina, Baden, 18th July 1834, GL
21 Marie-Louise to Albertina, Baden, 29th July 1834, GL
22 Marie-Louise to Albertina, Milan, 3rd May 1836, GL

Chapter Twenty-Six: Railways and derailment, 1838

1 Baron Mareschall to Marie-Louise, 9th November 1832, K&F
2 Baron Mareschall to Marie-Louise, 1st December 1832, K&F
3 Marie-Louise to Albertina, Piacenza, 19th April 1834, ASP
4 Marie-Louise to Albertina, Schönbrunn, 17th July 1838, GL
5 Marie-Louise to Albertina, Schönbrunn, 12th July 1846, GL
6 Marie-Clementine to Marie-Louise, 8th March 1838, K&F
7 Marie-Louise to Albertina, Vienna, 23rd July 1838, GL
8 Marie-Louise to Albertina, Wirninzel, 27th June 1834, GL
9 Marie-Louise to Albertina, Schönbrunn, 3rd July 1838, GL
10 Marie-Louise to Albertina, Schönbrunn, 3rd July 1838, GL
11 Marie-Louise to Albertina, Brandhof, 18th June 1838, GL
12 Marie-Louise to Albertina, Schönbrunn, 12th July 1846, GL
13 Marie-Clementine to Marie-Louise, 30th July, 1839, K&F
14 Marie-Louise to Albertina, Graz, 13th June 1845, GL
15 Marie-Louise to Albertina, Celje, 9th June 1846, GL

Chapter Twenty-Seven: Verdi and the power of opera, 1846

1 Marie-Louise to Albertina, Venice, 5th June 1846, GL

Chapter Twenty-Eight: Death of a duchess and expiry of the moratorium, 1847

1 Count Dietrichstein to Marie-Louise, 6th August 1831, K&F
2 Lady Priscilla Burghersh to Marie-Louise, 10th October 1833, K&F
3 Marie-Louise to Albertina, Schönbrunn, 22nd June 1844, GL
4 Marie-Louise to Albertina, Trieste, 7th June 1846, ASP

Afterword

1 Albertina to Luigi, Fontanellato, 13th April, 1860, ASP
2 Records of Archduke Rainer, the Court Library in Vienna, quoted by De Wertheimer, Duke of Reichstadt, p58

INDEX

Albert, Duke of Saxe-Teschen, Marie-Louise's uncle, 107
Albertina, see Montenuovo
Aldobrandini, Prince, 67, 75
Alexander I, Tsar of Russia, 32, 94, 103, 104, 137, 145, 162 163, 189, 194, 195, 204, 240
Amelin de St. Marie, Caroline, lady-in-waiting to Marie-Louise, 207
Antommarchi, Dr. François Carlo, 227
Auber, Daniel, composer, 295
Auzou, Pauline, artist, 10
d'Azeglio, Massimo (Massimo Taparelli, marquis d'Azeglio), Piedmontese statesman, 431
Balbo, Cesare, Piedmontese writer and statesman, 431
Bandiera, Admiral Francesco, 310
Bandiera, Emilio and Attilio, 428
Bausset, de, Baron Louis François Joseph, Prefect of the Palace, 108, 126, 132, 139, 152
Beauharnais, Eugène de, Viceroy of Italy, Napoleon's stepson by Josephine, 16, 140, 166, 215, 230, 280, 297
Beethoven, Ludwig von, composer, 154, 157, 233, 275
Bellini, Vincenzo, composer, 281, 295
Berchet, Ambrogio, Italian patriot, 217, 218, 223, 224
Bernadotte, Crown Prince of Sweden, 133

Berry, Duke of, nephew of Louis XVIII, 202, 212
Berthier, Marshal Louis Alexandre, Prince of Neuchâtel, 69, 158
Bessières, Marshal Jean Baptiste, Duke of Istria, 16, 55
Bielby, James, 186
Blessington, Lady (Countess), Marguerite Gardiner, 271, 449, 450
Blücher, General Genhard Leberecht von, 55
Bombelles, Charles René de, 397, 398, 423, 424, 432-435, 438, 439
Bosio, Baron François Joseph, French sculptor, 22
Boulay-de-la-Meurthe, Count Antoine, French politician and magistrate, 80, 81
Brignole, Countess de (change Mme to Countess), 98, 108, 129, 132, 139, 232
Burghersh, Lord John Fane, English Ambassador at Florence, composer and founder of the Royal Academy of Music, London, England, 145, 185, 396
Burghersh, Lady Priscilla, wife of Lord Burghersh, 185, 188, 202, 244, 396, 423, 424, 450
Caderini, Giuseppe, President of the Interior, Parma, 216, 223
Cadore, Duke of, see Champagny

489

Cambacérès, Archchancellor, Napoleonic Duke of Parma, 50, 52, 53, 61, 64, 80, 81, 82, 250, 251, 254

Canova, Antonio, Italian sculptor, 38, 417, 447

Cantelli, Count Girolamo, liberal Parman politician, 434

Caroline of Brunswick, Princess of Wales, 235

Caroline, Queen of Naples, Napoleon's sister, 6, 11, 12, 16, 22, 75

Caroline-Ferdinande, Marie-Louise's fifth sister, 107, 343

Caselli, Carlo Francesco, Bishop of Parma, 358, 359

Castlereagh, Robert Stewart, English Secretary of State for Foreign Affairs, 161, 162, 240, 245

Catherine, Queen of Westphalia, husband of Jérôme, 6, 16, 28, 43, 137, 244

Caulincourt, Armand Augustin Louis, Duke of Vicence, 91, 100

Champagny, Jean-Baptiste de Nompère de, Napoleon's Minister of Foreign Affairs, 52, 80, 81, 82

Charles II, see Charles-Louis

Charles III, Bourbon Duke of Parma, son of Charles II, 180

Charles X, King of France, 273, 292, 294

Charles Albert, King of Piedmont-Sardinia (1831-1849), cousin of Victor Emmanuel I, 296, 396, 432, 442

Charles Felix, King of Piedmont Sardinia (1821-1831), 246, 281

Charles-Louis, Duke of Lucca, who becomes Charles II of Parma, 195, 281, 377-378, 432, 439, 441, 444, 445

Chateaubriand, François-René de, author and diplomat, 245

Clary-de-Aldringen, Prince, 5, 6, 12, 24, 42

Cocchi, Francesco, University Professor and Councillor of State, Parma, 383

Collin, Matthäus von, tutor of the Duke of Reichstadt, 174, 176, 227,

Colloredo, Countess, Marie-Louise's childhood governess in Vienna, 45, 107, 108, 263

Confalonieri, Federico, Italian patriot, 212

Constitution of Cadiz 1812, 202, 204, 226

Cornacchia, Ferdinando, President of the Council of State, Parma, 302, 308, 309, 311

Correggio, Antonio Allegri da, foremost painter of the Parma school of the Italian Renaissance, 173, 179, 432

Corvisart, Dr. Jean Nicolas, Baron, Napoleon's personal physician, 22, 27, 44, 75, 90, 98, 100, 124, 129, 233

Crenneville, Victoria de, Marie-Louise's life-long friend and confident, 54, 107, 173, 184, 198, 199, 245, 263, 283, 287, 310, 311, 330, 338, 350, 369, 373

Czartoryksi, Adam Jerzy, Polish minister of Russia, 320

Dalberg, Duchess of, lady-in-waiting to Marie-Louise, 129

Dalla Rosa Prati, Marchese Guido, Parman politician, 444, 449

Denon, Vivant, Director-General of the Musée Napoléon, 45, 404

Dietrichstein, Count Moritz von, 175, 199, 200, 229, 242, 247, 248, 262, 284, 285, 289, 291, 297, 311, 316, 318, 321, 330-333, 338-339, 351-354, 378, 396, 405, 423

Dom Pedro, First Emperor of Brazil, 189, 190

Donizetti, Gaetano, composer, 296, 311, 365, 380, 430

Dubois, M. the midwife, 26, 27

INDEX

Duplan, M., Marie-Louise's hairdresser and manicurist, 37

Durand, Sophie Cohendet, wife of General Durand, 21, 30, 93, 95, 128, 350

Elisa, Princess, Napoleon's sister, married to Félix Bacciochi, 6, 11

Elisa, Princess, daughter of Hortense and Louis, 31

Esterhazy, Prince Mikios, 100

Ferdinand, Marie-Louise's brother and heir to the Austrian throne, 107, 368, 375, 376, 378, 441, 442

Ferdinand, Grand Duke of Würzburg, 11, 16, 37

Ferdinand, Marie-Louise's grandfather, King of the Two Sicilies, 203, 270

Ferdinand III, Grand Duke of Tuscany (1814-1824), 132, 185

Ferdinand VII, King of Spain, 136

Ferdinand, Bourbon Duke of Parma, 243, 263

Ferdinand, Archduke of Este, Marie-Louise's cousin, 440

Ferrari, Count Ottavio, Chief of Police in Parma, 312, 333, 399, 435

Fesch, Cardinal, Napoleon's uncle, 6, 7, 11, 99, 348

Floret, Austrian Chargé d'Affaires in Paris, 57, 58

Foresti, Captain Giovannbattista, 175, 176, 228, 351

Francesco IV, Duke of Modena-Este (1814-1846), Marie-Louise's cousin, 206, 217, 220, 222, 223, 281, 296, 298, 310, 312, 397

Francesco V, Duke of Modena-Este (1846-1859), son of Francesco IV, 442

Francis I, Emperor of Austria, 1, 14, 22, 32, 36, 38, 53, 57, 71, 72, 74, 78, 103, 104, 112, 116, 118, 120, 139, 142, 145, 148, 149, 159, 160, 166, 195, 198, 204, 207, 240, 246, 249, 250, 308, 312, 318, 322, 324, death of 368-378, 425, 454

Francis Charles, Marie-Louise's brother, 107, 377

Franz, see Reichstadt, Duke of

Franz-Josef, Emperor of Austria, 447

Frimont, (Austrian) General Johann Maria Philipp, 309, 310

Gentz, Friedrich von, secretary to Metternich and to the Vienna Congress, 137-139, 239, 240, 323, 349

Gioberti, Vincenzo, Piedmontese Presbyterian, patriot and philosopher, 430, 431, 445

Goethe, Johann Wolfgang von, German writer and poet, 38, 272

Hardenberg, Karl August, Prince von, of Prussia, 161

Hartmann-Klarstein, General, 332, 333, 334, 338, 351

Haydn, Franz Josef, composer, 120

Hitler, Adolf, 455

Hohenwart, Count, Archbishop of Vienna, 140, 142

Hortense, Queen of Holland, Napoleon's stepdaughter by Josephine, 6, 9, 26, 27, 31, 45, 48, 63, 86, 103, 140

Hudson, Sir James, England's ambassador to Piedmont-Sardinia, 446

Hurault de Sorbée, Captain, 133

Isabey, Jean-Baptiste, painter, 2, 22, 38, 68, 241

Jérôme Bonaparte, King of Westphalia, husband of Catherine, Napoleon's brother

Jesuits, 11, 21, 92, 93, 230, 244, 426, 427, 429, 436

Johann, Archduke, Marie-Louise's uncle, 150, 159, 192, 193, 204, 291

Joseph, King of Spain, Napoleon's brother

and husband of Julie, 11, 80, 86-88, 92, 93, 230

Joseph II, Holy Roman Emperor, Marie-Louise's great-uncle, 170, 175, 292, 370, 372

Josephine, Empress, Napoleon's first wife, 9, 12, 120, 140, 358, 392, 452, 455

Junot, Jean-Andoche, First Duke of Abrantès, 166, 167

Karl, Archduke, Marie-Louise's uncle, 19, 154

Karoline-Auguste, Empress of Austria, 188, 189, 248, 260, 268, 286, 373, 425

King of Rome, see Reichstadt, Duke of

Kotzebue, August von, 212

Koželuch, Leopold, composer, 121

Lacépède, Comte de, President of the French Senate, 80

Lafayette, Marie-Joseph Gilbert du Motier de, Marquis de, French promoter of American independence, 306

Lamprecht, Monsignor Marie-Antoine, 367, 439

Lannes, Marshal Jean, Duke of Montebello, 125-126

Lažansky, Countess Maria, 3, 33, 42, 229, 242, 328

Lecomte, Jules, French writer, 355

Lefèvres, Gérard and Robert, painters (brothers), 47

Leopold II, Holy Roman Emperor, 170, 185, 196, 372

Leopold II, Grand Duke of Tuscany (1824-1859), 284, 441

Leopold of Saxe-Coburg, King of Belgium, 309

Leopoldine (Marie-Leopoldine), Marie-Louise's third sister, First Empress of Brazil, 41, 107, 186-191, 193, 210, 269, 275-278, death of 279, 287

Letizia Ramolino Bonaparte, also known as Mme Mère, Napoleon's mother, 9, 11, 87, 99

Leroy, the Paris couturier, 12, 128, 156, 347-349

Linati, Count Claudio, painter and patriot, 216, 218

Linati, Count Filippo, President of the provisional government 1831, 312

Louis, Archduke, Marie-Louise's uncle, also referred to as Ludwig, 186, 378, 404

Louis XVI, King of France, husband of Marie-Antoinette, Marie-Louise's guillotined great-uncle, 89, 116, 230

Louis XVIII, restored King of France, surviving brother of Louis XVI, 116, 153, 158, 161, 233, 292

Louis, King of Holland, Napoleon's brother and Hortense's husband, 11, 186, 230

Louis-Napoleon, Napoleon's nephew through Louis and Hortense, later Emperor Napoleon III, 421, 446, 447

Louis-Philippe of Orléans, Citizen King of France, 294, 296, 319, 392, 422, 427

Louvre, Musée du, 20, 24, 437, 442

Luçay, Madame de, Lady of the Wardrobe to Marie-Louise, 25, 37, 39, 45, 85, 93, 129

Magawli-Cerati, Count Filippo Francesco, Parman minister, 171, 182

Malet, General Claude-François, 50, 51

Malfatti, Dr., 318, 321, 327, 329, 330-333, 339, 342, 349

Manzoni, Alessandro, author and patriot, 430

Marchand, Mme, mother of Napoleon's valet, Louis-Joseph Marchand, 175, 176

Mareschall, Baron Philipp Leopold, 313,

INDEX

329, 333-335, 342, 350, 351, 357, 397-399

Maria-Amalia, Queen of France, wife of King Louis-Philippe, 294

Marie-Anne, Archduchess, Marie-Louise's sixth sister, 107, 377

Marie-Antoinette, Austrian Archduchess and Queen of France, Marie-Louise's guillotined great-aunt, 1, 23, 82, 109, 143, 147, 230, 263, 439

Maria-Carolina, Queen of the Two Sicilies, Marie-Louise's grandmother and sister of Marie-Antoinette, 65, 108, 109, 110, 111, 158, 234

Marie-Clementine, Archduchess Marie-Louise's fourth sister, 107, 186, 406, 409

Marie-Louise, Archduchess of Austria, Empress of France, Duchess of Parma, Piacenza and Guastalla, weddings in France, 1,3 and 8; marriage by proxy in Austria, 3-4 and 19; in Dresden, 36-41; appointed Regent, 52, 73; emergency meeting of the Council of Ministers, 80-84; flight to the Loire, 85; at Rambouillet to see her father, 100, 102-105; departure for Vienna, 105-106; installed at Schönbrunn, 107, excursion to the Savoy Mountains with Méneval, 102; sojourn in Aix-en-Savoie, 114-115 123-4, 129-136, 230-233; arrival in Parma, 173; riots in Parma, 299-309; return to Parma after riots, 310; cholera, 381; death, 423.

Marie-Ludovica, Empress of Austria, known to her stepchildren as Maman Béatrice, 15, 36, 37, 38, 56, 57, 60, 106, 108, 116, 118, 119, 121, 122, 123, 141, 145, 147, 156, death of, 172

Maria-Luisa, Queen of Etruria, 191

Maria-Theresa, Empress, Marie-Louise's great grandmother, 143, 175, 250

Marie-Thérèse, Empress of Austria, Marie-Louise's mother, 372, 373

Marie-Thérèse [Capet], Duchess of Angoulême, only surviving child of King Louis XVI and Queen Marie-Antoinette, 143, 274

Marie-Thérèse, Queen of Saschen [Saxony], 62, 211, 287

Marie-Walewska, Countess, Napoleon's Polish mistress, 136, 234, 320

Marmont, Marshal Auguste de, 134, 318, 319

Martini, Giacomo, member of Marie-Louise's Parman Guard of Honour patriot, 216, 220, 222

Mazzini, Giuseppe, patriot and activist for the reunification of Italy, 415, 426, 428, 429, 431

Meli Lupi di Soragna, Prince Casimir, 303

Melegari, Francesco, Honorary Professor of Law at the University of Parma and member of the provisional government in 1831, 312

Melloni, Macedonio, Professor of physics at the University of Parma and member of the provisional government 1831, 297

Méneval, Baron Claude-François, Napoleon's private secretary, 35, 47, 50, 52, 95, 97, 104, 108, 111, 114, 115, 130, 132, 139, 145, 147, 151, 152, 153, 163, 174, 235, 236, 237, 241, 350

Mercadante, Saverio, composer, 296

Metternich, Prince Klemens Wenzel Lothar von, Foreign Minister and later Chancellor of Austria, 1, 2, 8, 11, 16, 44, 59, 73, 103, 105, 111, 130, 131, 138, 149, 152, 156, 161, 163, 182, 190, 191, 195, 207, 210, 212, 213, 217, 218, 222, 230, 233, 236, 238, 240, 242, 272,

493

278, 289, 290, 296, 297, 307, 313, 319,
323-325, 330, 334, 349, 351, 353, 354,
361, 374-378, 396, 397-403, 406, 410,
441

Mistrali, Vincenzo, Governor of Parma,
307, 309, 310, 311, 313, 356, 432

Moll, Baron Johann Bernard von, 341, 342

Montbel, Count Guillaume Isidore de,
biographer of the Duke of Reichstadt,
353, 354, 361

Montebello, Louise, Duchess of, widow of
Marshal Lannes, Duke of Montebello,
Marie-Louise's Lady of Honour, 19,
25-28, 46, 61, 64, 80, 67, 85, 90, 95, 98,
123-129, 140, 159, 184, 196, 231, 233,
235, 396

Montenuovo, Count Wilhelm Albert de,
249, 263-265, 267, 269, 270, 289, 290,
305, 329, 343, 347, 348, 351, 361-365,
377, 385, 394-396, 398, 399, 405, 408,
409, 422, 427, 431, 437, 438

Montenuovo, Countess Albertina Maria,
249, 263-271, 289, 290, 305, 336, 337,
339-345, 347, 348, 351, 352, 377, 382,
385, 386, 388-396, 397, 398-400, 402,
404, 407, 408, 422-424, 426, 430, 431,
436, 437, 446

Montesquiou-Fezensac, Louise de,
governess to the King of Rome, 43, 61,
67, 79, 85, 95, 105, 108, 130, 151, 153,
154, 174, 227, 237

Montesquiou, Anatole, son of Mme de
Montesquiou, 96

Montet, Baronne Alexandrine de, 156,
157, 243

Moreau de St Mèry, Médéric Louis Elie,
Napoleon's administrator in Parma,
170, 214

Mortier, Marshal Adolphe Edouard, 134

Mozart, Wolfgang Amadeus, 233, 252,
350, 417

Murat, Joachim, King of Naples, 11, 241

Napoleon I (Bonaparte), Emperor, first
meeting with Marie-Louise 3; playing
with his son, 34; leaving Dresden for
the Russian Campaign, 39;
instructions as regards his son, 81;
death of 206; attitude to women 251,
252; leaving to Elba, 91; escape from
Elba, 145; despatch to St Helena, 165;
death of, 202; return of remains to
France, 292; creation of the shrine,
446

Napoléon-François-Charles-Joseph, King
of Rome, Prince of Parma, see
Reichstadt, Duke of

Napoleon II, see Reichstadt, Duke of

Napoleon III, see Louis-Napoleon

Naudine Karolyi, 332

Neipperg, General Adam Albert von, 73,
123, 124, 132, 133, 138, 166, 173, 175,
182, 188, 194, 204, 208, 216, 217, 222,
230-233, 235-237, 240, 242, 244-250,
261, 264, 269-272, 274, 287, 307, 308,
355, 358, 359, 364, 387, 389, 410, 423,
449-451, 453

Neipperg, Alfred, eldest son of General
Neipperg, 264, 265, 329, 361, 394

Neipperg, Erwin, fourth son of General
Neipperg, 247, 361, 394, 395

Neipperg, Ferdinand, second son of
General Neipperg, 264, 361

Neipperg, Gustav, third son of General
Neipperg, 247, 282, 289, 290, 329, 346,
347, 361, 394, 395, 396

Nelson, Vice-Admiral Horatio, 109

Nesselrode, Count Karl of Russia, 161

Neuschel, Bishop Johann, Marie-Louise's
confessor, 307, 357, 358, 359, 360, 383,
424, 440

Pagannini, Nicolò, violin virtuoso and
composer, 411, 412

INDEX

Panizzi, Sir Antonio, Italian patriot and later Principal Librarian of the British Library, 219

Parmigianino, (Francesco Mazzola) Italian Mannerist painter, 179

Pasta, Giuditta, opera singer, 283

Pauline, Napoleon's sister, married to Camillo Borghese, 11, 16, 20

Paveri-Fontana, Marchese Giuseppe, Parman dignitary, 274, 444

Pellico, Silvio, Italian author and patriot, 212

Périgord, Countess, lady-in-waiting to Marie-Louise, 129

Popes: Pius VII (1800-1823), 119

Gregory XVI (1831-1846), 328, 422, 429

Pius IX (1846-1878), 429, 432, 433, 436, 441, 445

Potocka, (Polish) Countess Anne de, 4

Prince of Parma, see Duke of Reichstadt

Prokesch von Osten, Count Anton, Austrian orientalist and diplomat, 291-294, 323, 324 325, 331, 338, 341, 374

Prud'hon, Pierre Paul, French painter, 22, 38, 45, 319

Pury de Neuchâtel, Marianna de, nursemaid to Albertina and Wilhelm, 263, 265, 361, 366

Radetsky, Field-Marshal Joseph Wenzel von, 346, 384, 401, 442

Rainer, Archduke and Viceroy of Milan, Marie-Louise's uncle, 157, 159, 178, 184, 190, 191, 195, 453

Reichstadt, Duke of, birth of as King of Rome, 28, with Napoleon, 34, as toddler 43, 47, 61, 75, 79, 85, 105, 114, 160, 163, 174-179, 196-201, on death of Napoleon 208, 209, 227, 229, 230, 246, 247, 260, 261, 271, 272, 282, 284-294, 296, 315-322, 323, 324, 327, 328, deterioration and death of 327-342, 343-354, 455

Romilli, Monsignor, Archbishop of Milan, 436

Rossini, Gioacchino, composer, 193, 245, 287, 295, 296, 365, 413

Rostand, Edmond, playwright, 354

Rothschild (bankers), 306, 376, 387

Rothschild, Salomon, 271, 272, 307

Rousseau, Marie-Louise's cook, 355

Rousseau, Jean-Jacques, French philosopher, 345

Rudolph, Archduke, Marie-Louise's uncle, 107

Sagan, Dorothea von Biron, Princess of Courland, Duchess of, 238

Saint-Aignan, Baron de, 94

Sanvitale, Alberto, Marie-Louise's first grandson, 367, 382, 385, 390

Sanvitale, Jacopo, Professor of Eloquence at the University of Parma, poet and patriot, cousin of Luigi, 213, 214, 215, 216, 218, 220, 222, 304, 305, 356, 357, 430, 446, 454

Sanvitale, Luigi, Marie-Louise's courtier and son-in-law, and patriot, 213, 214, 274, 305, 355-357, 360, 362, 430, 431, 438, 444, 445, 446, 454

Sanvitale, Stefano, Grand Chamberlain and intimate councillor to Marie-Louise, 130, 182, 213, 214, 356, 385

Sanvitale, Stefano, Marie-Louise's second grandson, 386

Sartorio, Odoardo, Chief of Police Parma, 412

Savary, Napoleon's Chief of Police, 80, 93, 214

Scarampi, Countess Elisabetta, lady-in-waiting to Marie-Louise, 156, 182

Schwarzenberg, Prince, Austrian Ambassador, 11, 21

Schwarzenberg, Princess Marianne, the Austrian Ambassador's wife, 21

Schwarzenberg, (Austrian) General Karl Philipp and brother of Emperor Francis, 47, 50, 107

Schwarzenberg, Princess Pauline, 21, 22

Shakespeare, 390

Sidoli, Giuditta Bellerio, Italian patriot, 414–415

Soufflot, Mme and daughter Fanny, 174, 176

Sophie, Archduchess, wife of Marie-Louise's brother Franz-Karl and mother of the future Emperors Franz-Josef I of Austria and Maximilian I of Mexico, 307, 337, 339, 376, 404, 405

Staël(-Holstein), (Anne-Louise) Germaine de, political opponent of Napoleon and writer, 182, 183, 418

Staudenheim, Dr., 327, 332, 418, 419

Strauss, Johann, composer, 177

Strepponi, Giuseppina, opera singer and wife of Giuseppe Verdi, 417

Talleyrand(-Périgord), Charles-Maurice de, Napoleon's duplicitous minister, 80, 136, 233, 238

Teatro Regio, Marie-Louise's Ducal Theatre, 281, 355, 412, 415, 451

Tillot, Guillaume du, enlightened 18th century French reforming minister of Parma, 170, 179

Tommasini, Dr. Giacomo, 246, 297

Trauttmansdorff(-Weinsberg), Count Ferdinand, Austrian courtier, 106

Trollope, Fanny, mother of English author Anthony, 392, 421

Ugolotti, Josèphe, head of Marie-Louise's Parman National Guard, 305

Ypsilantis, Alexander, Greek national hero, 205

Varron, Michele, General under Napoleon rewarded by him with the gift of the Rocca di Sala, 243, 305

Verdi, Giuseppe, composer and Italian patriot, 414–418, 428, 430, 448

Victor Emmanuel I, King of Piedmont-Sardinia (1802-1821), 203

Victor Emmanuel II, King of Piedmont-Sardinia and later first King of a unified Italy, son of Charles Albert, 447

Vigée-le-Brun, Elisabeth, painter, 142

Vitrolles, Baron Eugène François de, 273, 274, 280, 281

Wagner, Richard, composer, 448, 449

Wellington, Arthur Wellesley, First Duke of, 150, 155, 162, 240, 241, 245

Werklein, Baron Colonel Joseph von, Marie-Louise's prime minister after Neipperg's death, 271, 281, 291, 300, 301, 302, 303, 308, 309, 334

Wilhelm, also referred to as Guglielmo, Gil and Gilles, see Montenuovo, Count Wilhelm Albert, de

William II, King of the Netherlands, 309

Zode, P.L., tutor to Albertina and Wilhelm, 355, 400

Zucchi, (Italian Napoleonic) General Carlo, Italian patriot, 298, 299, 304, 312